The **Television**

H A N D B O O K

The Television Handbook provides a critical introduction to both the theory and practice of the television industry. Patricia Holland considers the history and structure of UK television at a time of rapid change and explores the implications of the cable, satellite and digital revolution.

The Television Handbook offers practical advice on many aspects of programme making from commissioning through to the post production process. It discusses important genres and concepts such as narrative, documentary and news, and analyses the 'ordinary television' of sport and daytime programming. Specialist sections from James Curran, Tony Dowmunt and Robin Small consider *Newsnight* and television journalism, access programming and production management.

The Television Handbook bridges the gap between theory and practice and brings together a wide range of information on all aspects of television. It includes interviews with major television figures such as Stuart Cosgrove and Phil Redmond, with innovative producers and directors, and with many other practitioners, from trainees to commissioning editors.

Patricia Holland is a writer, lecturer and programme maker. She is a visiting lecturer at Goldsmiths' College, University of London.

Media Practice

edited by James Curran, Goldsmiths' College, University of London

···

The *Media Practice* handbooks are comprehensive resource books for students of media and journalism, and for anyone planning a career as a media professional. Each handbook combines a clear introduction to understanding how the media work with practical information about the structure, processes and skills involved in working in today's media industries, providing not only a guide on 'how to do it' but also a critical reflection on contemporary media practice.

···

Also in this series:

The Radio
H A N D B O O K

Peter Wilby and Andy Conroy

The Newspapers
H A N D B O O K

Richard Keeble

The Advertising
H A N D B O O K

Sean Brierley

The **Television**
H A N D B O O K

....

....

Patricia Holland

London *and* New York

First published 1997
by Routledge
11 New Fetter Lane, London EC4P 4EE
29 West 35th Street, New York, NY 10001

Typeset in Times by Florencetype, Stoodleigh, Devon
Printed and bound in Great Britain by
Biddles Bookbinder's, King's Lynn

British Library Cataloguing in Publication Data
A catalogue record for this book is available from the British Library.

Library of Congress Cataloging in Publication Data
A catalogue record for this book has been requested.

ISBN 0–415–12731–9 (hbk)
       0–415–12732–7 (pbk)

Contents

Illustrations

Acknowledgements

This book is the result of very many conversations, meetings, discussions and debates, both formal and informal. I'd especially like to thank all those who agreed to be interviewed and trusted me to transcribe their views accurately. Also my thanks go to Tony Dowmunt for his ideas about documentary and access television and Jim Hornsby for his comments on narrative television and both of them for their assistance while teaching at Goldsmiths' College. Also thanks to cinematographers Anne Cottringer and Nick Hale for making comments on the camera section; Diane Tammes, camera/director, for discussions on the role of women in television on pp. 75–6; Sue Inglish of ITN for reading through the news section; Maggie Ellis, producer, sound recordist and co-ordinator of the London Production Fund for conversation, advice and comments; David Martin of ft2; Tana Wollen for letting me read her unpublished paper on television in the 1990s; Garry Whannel for help with the section on sport; James Curran for essential editorial advice; Roger Graef for the information on p. 175; Dave Rushton for that on p. 256; Christine Pearce for that on p. 163. Also, Christine James of BFI Education; Bob Millington of John Moore's University, Liverpool; and my colleagues Joy Sisley of King Alfred's College, Winchester, Liz Wells of the London Institute and Vicki Wegg Prosser of Brunel University for many enthralling discussions. My special thanks go to several generations of postgraduate students at Goldsmiths' College for their enthusiasm, initiative and ideas that have always been fresh and interesting.

Part I: Introduction

1 On television practice and television studies

....

Television in a changing world

Television is many things. Raymond Williams called it a combination of technology and cultural form (Williams 1990). It is a transnational business and also a national institution. It is our most celebrated form of entertainment and our most important source of information. It is an outlet for creativity and a medium through which social concern or political views may be expressed. It is a substantial employer of accountants and office workers as well as skilled engineers, technicians, programme makers and performers. This book looks at the practicalities of television production from the point of view of someone new to this complex industry.

Television has been a central and much loved part of British culture. As a comfortable, home-based medium, a warm glow in the corner of the living room, it has provided a companionate voice and a circle of friends old and new – Bet Lynch of *Coronation Street*, reliable figures like Desmond Lynam with the sport and Trevor McDonald with the news, through to the anarchic disruptions of a Chris Evans or a Jennifer Saunders. The glamour of television is daily celebrated in the popular press. In its aim to offer a 'window on the world' (*Panorama*'s first description of itself), it has provided the major source from which most of us get to know and interpret domestic politics and world affairs. Those who work or aspire to work in the medium may aim to contribute to one of its many diverse areas.

Although those who produce television programmes tend to inhabit what Jeremy Tunstall described as a genre-specific world (Tunstall 1993: 2), each absorbed in their own very different fields, the special characteristic of television in the UK is that it has prevented those diverse areas from drifting apart, arguing that audiences do not always know in advance what it is they want to see, so they should be given something of everything. The very proliferation of our television system, allowing disparate expectations to rub against each other, gives it a richness that remains unique and valuable. Variety, diversity and unexpected juxtapositions are at the core of a television service which takes seriously the privilege of entry into people's homes. UK television has maintained a unique balance between its commitments to both entertainment and politics, both information and relaxation, by containing the drive to satisfy a substantial audience within a regulated public service system.

But television is not all about cosiness. The glow in the corner of the living room has also been seen as a dangerous opening, a wound, a gash through which alien and possibly unwanted material pours in. Like the much-reviled children's favourite *Mighty Morphin' Power Rangers*, it may transform its friendly local faces into terrifying fighting monsters. Television has come under biting attack from parts of the popular press, as a corrupter of childhood, a purveyor of sex and violence and a hotbed of biased, left-wing politics. As veteran politician and commentator Conor Cruise O'Brien wrote:

> The minds of most citizens may have been so boggled by televised varieties of instant gratification, including pornography, as to turn into mere sentient sponges, compulsively feeding on flickering images. And if so, how long is democracy likely to last?
>
> (O'Brien 1995)

The final years of the twentieth century are a challenging time in the history of broadcasting in the United Kingdom. The television landscape is changing possibly beyond recognition as the very ground on which it is built is heaving and resettling. The secure foundations of public service broadcasting based on four well-established and familiar channels, are giving way to an unfamiliar moonscape of multiple channels fuelled by unpredictable technologies from a science fiction world and multinational business interests. Weakening regulation is making access to the broadcast media a rich prize for the moguls and an outlet for entrepreneurs, advertisers, sponsors, celebrity agents, public relations companies and marketing people. Debates about the social value and function of television have become more intense under pressure from economic changes which give more power to profit-making interests. We now hear talk of 'product' where we once spoke of programmes, and of 'the market' where we once meant the audience.

Yet programming is evolving in more than one direction. The move towards the populist – from 'tabloid' current affairs to late-night grunge – reflects market ideologies and the pressures to increase audience size as well as appealing to a younger, more hedonistic audience. In a counter-vailing tendency many programmes have become more self-reflexive and more democratic, involving a wider range of viewers and contributors (*see* James Curran p. 193 and Tony Dowmunt p. 202 below). The scope of UK television from hugely popular drama series, through to investigatory documentaries, observational series, games shows, Hollywood movies and those hybrids which mix entertainment and information is, if anything, broader than ever.

At the same time, the notion of what a 'programme' is, is itself changing as an unprecedented number of new channels are being launched. The television set is no longer the centre around which the united family gathers, but a personalised accessory. With many sets now dispersed around the house, each is likely to be tuned to a different channel. The targeting of niche audiences is becoming a regular pattern as whole channels are given over to a particular type of programming – say cartoons or sport. Many cable channels, taking their cue from the United States, provide something that is closer to visual conversation than to programmed television.

The newest technologies of CD-ROM and the Internet operate at the borders of television and it is unclear whether they are part of a completely new medium or can be seen as part of the revolution within television itself (*see* Types of new technology p. 253 below). As time goes on, it will be the people now entering the media professions who will be instrumental in developing these new structures. New skills are needed, old skills are being revised. The need for a dialogue between those who think about television and those who make it has never been more acute.

Television training and tele-literacy

This is a handbook for the tele-literate and those who aim to be tele-literate. I use the term to combine a knowledge of the skills of television practice with a critical appraisal of the content of television and an enthusiasm for the medium in all its responsible and irresponsible proliferations – from *Eurotrash* to *Panorama*, from *Good Morning with Anne and Nick* to Dennis Potter's posthumous exuberance with *Karaoke* and *Cold Lazarus*. The book puts practical advice on 'how to do it' within the context of academic theory, current debates between television professionals, and issues that concern the public at large.

Television professionals and those who study the medium have brought different perspectives which at times have seemed totally at odds with each other. Many who work in the industry argue that media studies are irrelevant, since television theory has nothing to do with the real world of television production. Students spend their time deconstructing *Neighbours* rather than learning practical skills (Petre 1996). Media theory is abstract and sceptical, they say, attacking rather than helping practitioners. Although there is some justice in these criticisms, in many ways they miss the point. To make useful critical judgements, television studies can never simply take the perspective of the broadcasters. As two researchers into television talk shows wrote:

> Whatever the intentions of broadcasters in making these programmes, these do not determine the nature of the product. This must be revealed through textual analysis, and the programmes have many unintended consequences which only audience research can discover.
>
> (Livingstone and Lunt 1994: 2)

Television studies have their own history. On the one hand they have grown out of the empirical tradition of US communications studies, which began in the early years of the century, grounded in fears of media influence and media power (Curran *et al.* 1987). On the other they have drawn on what are now called 'screen studies', that highly theoretical body of writings that came to the fore in the 1960s and 1970s, drawing on a European tradition of semiotics, post-structuralism and psychoanalysis to form a heady and highly critical brew. A third input has come from British cultural studies, with its neo-Marxist critical approach, which sees television and news reporting as part of the lived texture of resistance, relaxation and ways of coping with the modern world (Fiske 1987; Allen 1987; Inglis 1990). But contemporary television theory has not always been cut off from a concern with practice. Another of its origins was in the campaigning groups of the 1970s, such as the women's groups and the regional and special interest workshops, who argued that theory and practice must evolve together and inform each other. If the lessons of critical theory are learned, they claimed, television practices must change and television programmes will be different too (Baehr and Dyer 1987: 117). When Channel Four was set up in 1982, many of these arguments were taken on board.

However, for many years, education and practical training had little to do with each other. Training had been largely on the job, oriented to technical expertise and with the prospect of a secure career ahead. But the structures of employment are changing. Television is now a casualised industry with less than half of its workers on contracts of a year or more (BFI 1996). A long period of apprenticeship is no longer appropriate. In response to student demand, the universities and colleges have stepped in to offer practical training alongside their more critical teaching. It is a development which has been greeted with alarm in the industry. The new-style courses are turning out unprecedented numbers of graduates at the very time when employment is in crisis and many experienced technicians are seeing their prospects disappear. What is more, this college-based 'training' is ambitiously close to a critical liberal tradition and produces students unwilling to confine themselves to the specific skills that employers need. The mutual suspicion between those concerned with theory and those concerned with practical work has been exacerbated by this state of affairs (*see* Who needs media studies?, p. 214 below).

Yet, as television itself is changing, the relationship between education and programme making is changing too. Links are being built between colleges and television companies. Phil Redmond, who originated *Brookside* and *Grange Hill*, writes of the initiatives between his company, Mersey Television, with John Moore's University, Liverpool (p. 222 below). Granada Television is amongst the companies with regular links to local colleges. The cynicism and anti-intellectualism within the television industry, which was part of a backlash against the high theory days of the 1980s, is giving way to a new reflexivity and media interest in its own practices and ways of doing things. The industry-financed organisation Skillset is evolving a more structured understanding of the skills that are needed in a rapidly changing medium (p. 217 below). At the same time a more diverse group of people is gaining access to television skills, often for uses other than employment in the television industry. Knowledge about television and access to television is much more widely dispersed in the population.

Thinking about television, creating tele-literacy, is an activity that is carried on in many forums, from the pub to the starchiest of academic journals, between tele-people and viewers, students, academics and journalists. People new to the industry and all who seek to be tele-literate are now able to follow and take part in a television debate which is more than just 'did you see?' The daily and weekly broadsheet press carries extensive comment on policy and personalities, on technology and legislation, on the deliberations of channel controllers, on scheduling, commissioning, and other matters that have aroused public concern. Unlike the celebrity pages of the popular press, which speak to their readers exclusively as non-participant viewers, the broadsheet media pages have in mind a readership of informed media practitioners as well as viewers who take the media seriously. The many forums in which television is debated are increasingly accessible to the general public. They include public meetings and seminars organised by educational institutions, informal groups, pressure groups and bodies like the British Film Institute; they include trade magazines, such as *Broadcast* and *Televisual*; they include the courses run by educational institutions from schools to evening institutes and universities; and on television itself there are programmes such as *Right to Reply*. Susan Williams (p. 218 below) writes of how she has been able to keep up with the television world in the gaps between working and training.

The distinction between education and training is still there, and the gap between studying television in a spirit of disinterested and critical enquiry and making television programmes remains an important distance which needs to be preserved. Independent intellectual values should not be abandoned in the face of an onslaught from those who feel that, in the new competitive atmosphere, only the most pragmatic of approaches will do. This book will not suggest that theory and practice should collapse into each other, but that they should inform each other. It will look at examples of good practice (*see* James Curran, p. 193 below) as well as showing how some theoretical perspectives have illuminated day-to-day production norms within some television genres. The practitioners who have contributed to the book, some as written contributions, some in the form of extended interviews, are all aware of the contribution that their education has made to their careers. They range from trainees on the industry-sponsored technical courses, to experienced producers and educators. They include policy makers and commissioning editors as well those who are making their way through the television jungle.

As a study aid, or for those who simply wish to read further on a particular topic, each chapter or section is followed by a list of key texts and other references. All of the television programmes mentioned in the text are listed in the Programme References section at the end of the book, where further details (e.g. year of screening, channel, etc.) are given.

The interviews are based on transcripts taken by P. Holland over 1995–6.

References

Allen, Robert C. (ed.) (1987) *Channels of Discourse*, Chapel Hill: University of Carolina Press

Baehr, H. and Dyer, G. (eds) (1987) *Boxed In: Women and Television*, London: Pandora RKP

British Film Institute (1996) *Television Industry Tracking Study*, interim report, London: BFI

Curran, J., Gurevitch, M. and Woollacott, J. (1987) 'The study of the media: theoretical approaches' in O. Boyd-Barrett and P. Braham, *Media, Knowledge and Power*, London: Croom Helm

Fiske, J. (1987) *Television Culture*, London: Routledge

Inglis, F. (1990) *Media Theory: An Introduction*, Oxford: Blackwell

Livingstone, S. and Lunt, P. (1994) *Talk on Television: Audience Participation and Public Debate*, London: Routledge

O'Brien, C. C. (1995), the *Independent*, 13 January, London

Petre, J. (1996) 'Students "misled" over jobs in the media', *Sunday Telegraph*, 4 February, London

Tunstall, J. (1993) *Television Producers*, London; Routledge

Williams, R. (ed.) (1990) *Television: Technology and Cultural Form*, London: Routledge

2 The landscape of television in the United Kingdom

··

The growth of public service broadcasting

Politics, technology and cultural history have intertwined to create the characteristic institutions of UK television. The BBC was set up in 1927 as a public corporation so that the expansion of radio broadcasting could be planned and avoid the competitive chaos of the airwaves that was taking place in the United States. Under its charismatic Director General, John Reith, the BBC negotiated for itself a position that was independent both of the government and of pressure from market forces. With an assured income from a levy on all who owned radio receivers, it was controlled by a board of governors who were not just political placemen. The Corporation was free to broadcast to the public as a whole, with a commitment to educate and inform as well as entertain enshrined in its Charter. Reith used that freedom to plan a range of programming that would, as he saw it, uplift the taste of the mass of the population and make available to them cultural experiences that they would otherwise have no opportunity to encounter. Those lofty, paternalistic aims were modified when the Second World War made BBC Radio essential listening for the nation as a whole and where the morale of the people, mobilised into a dedicated wartime workforce, was boosted by comedy, entertainment and popular music, as well as a news service committed to being truthful and reliable (Scannell and Cardiff 1991). The loyalty built up during that period was inherited by BBC Television and, it is arguable, continues to this day.

When the BBC Television service was re-established immediately after the Second World War, despite the heavy hand of paternalism, the Corporation maintained a commitment to diversity and universality in its appeal, and independence in its coverage of public affairs. When Richard Dimbleby's reverential tones enhanced the live pictures of the young Queen Elizabeth's coronation in 1953, television sets were purchased in unprecedented numbers. But it was the coming of the Independent Television network (ITV) in 1955 that confirmed the dominance of the medium over the nation's entertainment and cultural life. The mass audience was built on a fascination for royalty on the one hand, and on a delight in brash entertainment values on the other.

At first, this network of privately owned, regionally based companies aimed to be a competitive commercial enterprise, posing a radical challenge to the BBC's public monopoly. But the system soon settled down to what has been described as a 'comfortable duopoly'. The independent television companies were financially secure as they had a monopoly of broadcast advertising, and they were responsible to the Independent Television Authority (ITA), which ensured that they too followed a public service remit, placing their highly popular entertainment shows within a broad range of programming. The regulations became more stringent over the 1960s. For example, the network was required to schedule programmes that were less 'popular' but nevertheless recognised as important, such as news and current affairs, at peak viewing times. Education and children's programmes must also be part of the output and must be available at suitable times. Together the independent companies financed a separate company, Independent Television News (ITN), which was committed, like the BBC, to objective and impartial news reporting. ITV franchises only run for a limited period, so the companies have been constantly on their toes, ensuring that they comply with ITA requirements for fear of losing their licence to broadcast in the next round of applications.

Since the 1920s a string of government committees and enquiries have investigated broadcasting and made recommendations about its future. Following the strong educational and public service tone of the Pilkington Committee, the BBC gained its second channel in 1964. BBC2 was not expected to compete for the largest audiences, but was free to broadcast programmes that had greater cultural content and were more demanding on audience attention. The new channel pioneered colour television on its higher quality signal. As well as its London base the BBC also has regional offices, three in England – Midlands and East (Birmingham), South (Bristol) and North (Manchester) – and three 'national' regions in Scotland (Glasgow), Wales (Cardiff) and Northern Ireland (Belfast).

This history is a live one to many who work in television in the UK. With a 'Reithian' sense of public service, of a duty to appeal to the whole audience and a commitment to high quality, varied television is still at the basis of scheduling and programme making. Several of the producers who contribute to this book give their own versions of that commitment (*see* comments made by Tony Garnett p. 132, John Wyver p. 160, and Rupert Rumney p. 145 below). For many years the BBC retained its image as everyone's 'Auntie'.

It was the coming of Channel Four that brought a decisive change. However worthy, the BBC and ITV were highly exclusive institutions, both in terms of those who worked for them and those who were able to express their opinions through them. Regional accents were rarely heard; women and black people were seriously underrepresented. Jobs were hard to get. They were either craft based, controlled by unions who operated a rigid closed shop, or they were seen as gentlemanly occupations, part of the civil service, suitable for those highly educated in the liberal traditions of Oxford and Cambridge (many contributors mention this, *see* Beryl Richards p. 239 and Phil Redmond p. 223 below). Consequently, during the 1970s a vigorous campaigning movement of film and video makers arose outside the television institutions. Channel Four was set up in recognition of the limitations of the BBC and ITV. It was required to 'cater for tastes, interests and audiences not served by ITV (or other television channels) and to innovate in the form and content of programmes' (C4 1994–5). This was achieved through a new model of how a television station could be run. Channel Four was a 'publisher' rather than a producer. It commissioned its programmes from independent production companies. Channel Four is not privately owned, but is run by a public trust. Although it showed advertisements, it did not compete for advertising funding, but received an agreed amount from the Independent Television companies. In Wales, the Channel Four frequencies are used by the Welsh language channel, Sianel Pedwar Cymru (S4C).

This arrangement of four channels, competing in the friendliest of ways, but largely complementary, established what the ITV companies have described as a 'delicate television ecology' striking a balance between commercial forces and public commitments' (ITV 1995: 2). Together they subscribed to the principles of public service broadcasting as expressed by the various government committees up to the Annan Committee (1977), which had recommended the establishment of Channel Four. These have been codified as follows.

- Geographical universality. Broadcast programmes should be available to the whole population.

- Universality of appeal. Broadcast programmes should cater for all tastes and interests.

- There should be special provision for minorities, especially disadvantaged minorities.

- Broadcasters should recognise their special relationship to the sense of national identity and community.

- Broadcasting should be distanced from all vested interests, and in particular from those of the government of the day.

- Universality of payment. One main instrument of broadcasting should be directly funded by the corpus of users.

- Broadcasting should be structured so as to encourage competition in good programming rather than competition for numbers.

- The public guidelines for broadcasting should liberate rather than restrict broadcasters

(Broadcasting Research Unit 1985; Scannell 1990).

The non-commercial priorities of public service broadcasting became the centre of a heated political debate which intensified in the mid-1980s, when the free marketeering government of Margaret Thatcher set its sights on the broadcasting industry. Until then it had not been technically feasible to challenge the four channel arrangement, as there was limited 'space' on the broadcasting frequencies. However, by the mid-1980s there were satellites in place which could broadcast potentially hundreds of channels either directly to people's homes through their own private satellite dishes or via specially laid cables. A network of underground cables had the potential to carry so many channels that the number could become limitless. With the disappearance of the physical restrictions on the number of channels, what was at issue was whether the public service system, which depended on regulation as a defence against market forces, could survive. Media moguls, notably Rupert Murdoch, who owns 40 per cent of BSkyB, as well as many television stations, newspapers and other media enterprises around the globe, were at the forefront of a campaign to let market forces rip. He declared:

> This public service television system has had, in my view, debilitating effects on British society, by producing a television output which is so often obsessed with class, dominated by anti-commercial attitudes and with a tendency to hark back to the past.
>
> (Murdoch 1989)

His argument, and that of those who agreed with him, was that audiences should be free to choose from as many channels as possible, and that those channels that were not successful would fail because they were not wanted. The commercialisation of British television was under way.

The Broadcasting Act of 1990 for the first time required ITV franchises to be 'put up for sale' and awarded partly on financial grounds. The new ITV regional franchise holders have tended to move towards the 'publisher' model, as they are mandated to give 25 per cent of their production to independent producers. They remained hybrids, partly committed to commerical values, but still part of the public service broadcasting system. A new regulatory body, the Independent Television Commission (ITC), was set up to regulate with a 'lighter touch' than previously. Rather than getting together to barter over which programmes would be networked, as the old ITV companies used to do, the ITV Network Centre was established to commission programmes from the franchise holders on to the national ITV network. For the first time Channel Four was to sell its own advertising and ITV's monopoly on advertising sales was lost.

Channel Five is the newest terrestrial channel set up in 1997. It aims to be a popular channel whose biggest innovation is a form of scheduling known as 'stripping', offering the same strand of programming – sport, a soap opera, consumer programmes – at the same time every day, every week.

The BBC remains dependent on the licence fee, which is effectively a tax on all owners of a television set. The fee is set by the government and renewed by Act of Parliament. In 1996 the Corporation's right to be funded by a licence fee was renewed, but its situation remains insecure. It has responded to the new economic climate by setting up an internal market known as 'Producer Choice', which means that producers must also become managers, shopping around for the cheapest facilities, rather than accepting those provided by the Corporation itself (Tunstall 1993). The idea is to make it more 'efficient' and 'cost effective'. Many people have lost their jobs, others have become more cautious.

The harsh reality for new people coming into the industry is that the old certainties of job security and union protection have gone. Media watcher Peter Fiddick put it like this:

The net effect of the profound changes in television is that many people are working harder for less satisfaction, good people in every age range are scarcely working at all, career-structure has gone out of the window, even entrepreneurial enthusiasts are waking up to a crisis in training and a clutch of quite ordinary people are seriously rich.

(Fiddick 1994)

Are we seeing a radical change from working in television as a vocation, to nothing more than working in an industry? An underlying question is the relationship between television and its audience. A public service system addresses its audience as citizens, to be involved and informed, whereas a market system sees its audience as made up of consumers, to be satisfied by giving them the programmes they demand (*see* James Curran p. 194 below).

The biggest changes in the television landscape are coming from the newer broadcasters, the satellite and cable channels, which are radically transforming television as we have known it for the last half century. These are discussed in detail in Chapter 17, Changing technologies. However, the great popularity of programmes currently broadcast by the four established terrestrial channels and the commitment to quality and original programme production which their secure funding makes possible, suggest that their public commitments will remain. Different ways of paying for television

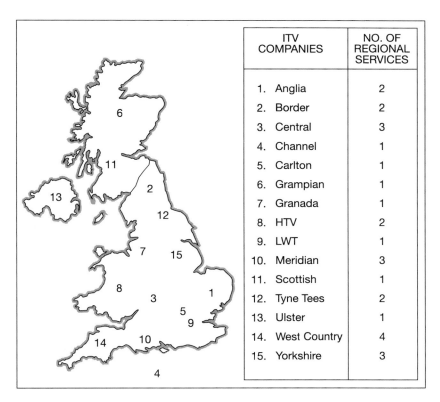

ITV COMPANIES	NO. OF REGIONAL SERVICES
1. Anglia	2
2. Border	2
3. Central	3
4. Channel	1
5. Carlton	1
6. Grampian	1
7. Granada	1
8. HTV	2
9. LWT	1
10. Meridian	3
11. Scottish	1
12. Tyne Tees	2
13. Ulster	1
14. West Country	4
15. Yorkshire	3

Figure 1 ITV companies and services
Source: ITV Companies 1996. Courtesy Spectrum Strategy Consultants

viewing, such as subscription channels and pay per view from satellite, are beginning to get under way, but as the landscape of television alters, the full implication of the changes cannot be predicted. The future is up for grabs.

Regulation

When it hits the headlines of the tabloid press, popular concern about television has taken two forms. The first is an outcry against unacceptable programmes – *Mighty Morphin' Power Rangers, The Word*, violent movies. These programmes corrupt our children and young people, it is said. They cause unstable individuals to go out and imitate their violent behaviour. They should be *banned*. The second is a tirade against nannying and censorship. This time the cry has been, 'Who are these self-appointed regulators and moral guardians who tell us what we are allowed to see?' Very often the same newspapers that call for banning will also be those railing against censorship (Barker and Petley, 1997).

The public service system depends on the broadcasting organisations conforming to certain statutory requirements, enshrined in the BBC's Charter and the various Broadcasting Acts. The advocates of a free market system, on the other hand, argue that the only regulation needed is audience response. What the audience does not like, it will turn off. If there is suffi- cient demand for pornography, then who are the nanny regulators to tell those customers that they cannot have pornography? However, there are very few supporters of a totally free market, since a large body of opinion recognises that without statutory protection important programmes whose audiences are large but not huge, such as current affairs and special interest programmes, may get marginalised, and certain types of audience, such as children or those seeking education, may not be served at all. At the same time, many who in the past have claimed that the broadcasters have the sole right to make decisions on what the public should see, are now paying more attention to audience response.

The right to broadcast on the airwaves is granted to the BBC, the ITV companies, and Channels Four and Five by various Acts of Parliament which lay down certain requirements. Their output is regulated in the BBC by the BBC Board of Governors, and in the independent companies by the Independent Television Commission, to ensure that they stay within the law and abide by their remit. The coming of more channels has led to a 'lighter touch' regulatory system, but economic deregulation has gone along with the establishment of bodies to respond to audience concerns, in particular worries about excessive sex and violence, bad language and mis- representation.

Independent Television Commission

The Independent Television Commission is in charge of allocating access to the airwaves for the ITV companies, and of monitoring the performance of ITV licensees, Channel Four and other UK based broadcasters, such as

BSkyB and cable companies. The commission produces a series of codes and guidelines with which broadcasters must comply. They cover:

- Advertising standards and practice, to ensure that advertisements are not misleading, offensive, or likely to encourage dangerous or anti-social attitudes or behaviour.

- Programme sponsorship, to protect editorial independence and prevent sponsor credits from intruding unacceptably on programmes (for a comment on how these regulations affect sports programming see Rupert Rumney p. 145 below).

- A *Programme Code*, which gives detailed advice on matters including taste, decency, the portrayal of violence, impartiality, intrusion into an individual's privacy, charitable appeals and religious programmes.

The code is reviewed and updated from time to time to reflect public tastes and attitudes.

Regulation by the ITC includes ensuring neutrality and objectivity on the part of television news, which, unlike a newspaper, may not have an editorial opinion. In the past, regulatory bodies have taken an active role, intervening when programming deals with contentious areas, such as reporting Northern Ireland, where the perception of what counts as 'balance' is in dispute.

It also protects those programmes that are part of the mandated schedule, including children's programmes, religion, news, current affairs and programmes with regional interest. It ensures that a diverse range of programmes will be broadcast, even at maximum audience viewing hours. As one previous channel controller put it sourly, this means 'broadcasting unpopular programmes at popular times'. Put more generously, it has ensured that factual and current affairs programmes have not been driven off the screens by Hollywood movies and what was once uncharitably described as 'wall to wall *Dallas*'. The ITC has power to order a company not to repeat a programme. It can fine a company, can shorten the length of a licence, and in extreme cases can revoke a licence. Since licences only run for relatively short periods of time (the current licences run for ten years), companies regularly have their eyes on renewal dates.

The ITC does not hesitate to be critical. In its first annual review after the 1993 franchises began, it described the first year's output of the new London weekday franchise holder, Carlton, as 'not distinctive or of noticeable high quality' (ITC 1994).

Details are available from ITC, 33 Foley Street, London W1P 7LB
Tel: 0171 255 3000 Fax: 0171 306 7800

BBC

The BBC regularly produces codes of practice and producers' guidelines which cover similar ground, including such issues as violence on the news or in fictional programmes, the limits on sponsorship and advertising, suitability of programmes for children, the use of bad language and so on. It has in recent years become far more responsive to audience comments and concerns, and has a Programme Complaints Unit to follow up specific complaints from members of the audience. All the broadcasting organisations observe a 9 pm 'watershed', after which children are considered to have gone to bed. It is intended to operate rather like a 'waterfall' in which the more violence and explicit sex a programme contains, the later in the evening it should be broadcast.

Details from BBC Programme Complaints Unit, Broadcasting House, London W1A 1AA

Broadcasting Standards Commission

In 1996 the Broadcasting Complaints Commission (BCC), which had dealt with complaints from the public since 1981, merged with the Broadcasting Standards Council (BSC), set up in 1990 to monitor standards of taste and decency on television. The Broadcasting Standards Commission (BSC) carries on the work of both bodies. Like the BCC it deals with complaints from individuals about unfair treatment in programmes and infringement of privacy. It also continues the BSC's remit to monitor issues of taste and decency, sex and violence, which clearly disturb many members of the audience. This includes producing a code of practice, following public consultation, and monitoring the incidence of violence and explicit sexual material in programmes, as well as bad language – which brings in by far the greatest number of audience complaints. Viewers' complaints and the BSC's responses to them are published in a monthly *Complaints Bulletin.* Research commissioned by the BSC has provided valuable data on audience responses to television, including responses to violence in factual and fictional programmes. It has surveyed the representation of women on television and has looked at who complains and why. Currently it is co-sponsoring a three-year long study on children's uses of television and the new media. The research has policy implications in areas which broadcasters themselves take very seriously.

Details from Broadcasting Standards Commission, 7 The Sanctuary, London SW1P 3JS

'Taste Police'

Some programme makers are concerned about the degree of interference with their autonomy from what Channel Four Chief Executive Michael Grade described as 'small groups of unaccountable, politically nominated worthies' whom he condemned as 'the taste police'. Regulators are predominantly male, white and middle class, he argued, and 'their views on "quality" must inevitably tend to represent those of their own milieu. *The Word* and *The Young Ones*, for example, hardly conform to conventional canons of taste, but choice and diversity would be poorer without such programmes.' Those who run investigative journalism programmes are also wary of complaints about misrepresentation, concerned that they will come from powerful individuals and from organised pressure groups, who want to protect themselves from justified media exposure.

CHANNEL	PRINCIPAL LICENCE CONDITIONS	
	PROGRAMMING	FINANCIAL
ITV	• Channel 3 companies must fulfil the proposals made in their applications • Programming of particular regional interest and of regional origin must be broadcast • Programmes as a whole must appeal to a wide variety of tastes and interests, including – arts, general factual, sport, drama plays, series and represented • Specific programme requirements include the following – News: 3 programmes each weekday, plus at weekends – Current Affairs: 1 hour and 30 minutes weekly – Children's: 10 hours weekly – Religion: 2 hours weekly – Central and North Scotland licensees: 1 hour weekly of Gaelic programming • At least 65% of programmes, to be original commissions • At least 25% of programmes must be independently produced • 50% of programmes to be subtitled by 1998	• Licence bid • Companies pay between 0–15% of Qualifying Revenue • If C4 fails to receive 14% of the advertising and sponsorship revenue generated by commercial terrestrial TV, and its reserve fund is exhausted, then ITV must make up the shortfall
Channel 4	• Should contain innovative and experimental material calculated to appeal to tastes and interests not generally catered for • Specific programme requirements – News: 4 hours of high quality news weekly – Current Affairs: 4 hours weekly – Education: 7 hours weekly – Schools: 330 hours yearly – Religion: 1 hour weekly	• If C4 receives more than 14% of the advertising and sponsorship revenue generated by commercial terrestrial TV, it must pay – 50% of the excess to ITV – 25% of the excess to a reserve fund

Figure 2 Licence conditions of ITV and Channel Four
Source: ITC 1996. Courtesy Spectrum Strategy Consultants

However, regulation is intended to be enabling as well as limiting. The ITC Licence Conditions protect quality and diversity in programming. Research funded by the BSC gives a real insight into the responses of audiences rather than being led by the occasional hysterical outbursts of the tabloid press.

Most broadcasting organisations and the trade unions, the National Union of Journalists (NUJ) and the Broadcasting, Entertainment, Cinematograph and Theatre Union (BECTU), also have equal opportunities policies and codes of practice, intended to ensure that stereotypes and insulting materials are not broadcast, and that there is no discrimination against people because of their gender, race, class, religion, sexual preference or disability.

Genres, schedules, ratings and the television flow

The flow

Raymond Williams described a 'planned flow' as 'perhaps the defining characteristic of broadcasting, simultaneously as a technology and as a cultural form' (Williams 1990). In the early days there were breaks between the programmes; during the 'Interlude' the screen was filled with restful images such as goldfish floating gently around in their bowl. In the hectic 1990s any moment of boredom which may cause the audience to switch channels in search of more exciting material is anxiously scrutinised by the schedulers. Producing a flow of programmes, carefully paced through the day, which will keep a reasonably sized audience tuned in to your channel, while bearing in mind what the other channels are showing, is an art in itself.

On ITV and Channel Four the movement of the programmes is punctuated by the advertisements. On the BBC the gaps between programmes can be the most innovative of spots – including witty 'stings' and station identifications, like the extraordinary 2s that metamorphose into squidgy toys or metallic objects to mark BBC2; trailers; short interventions such as *Sister Wendy*'s unpredictable comments on a well-known painting; and *Sarajevo: Street Under Siege* – a nightly three minutes from a single street in the devastated city, broadcast daily until the end of the siege in March 1994. The space between longer programmes has allowed opportunities for new directors, as with the BBC's *10x10* (*see* Jeremy Howe, p. 233 below), and contributions by the viewing public, as with *Video Nation*, in which viewers send in their own videotaped reflections on life in general and their own lives in particular.

What has distinguished television from other forms is not just its continuous flow, but the way in which that flow organises within the day a range of radically different genres. Viewers have the option of staying with the channel with which they feel most at ease, appreciating either the more popular touch of ITV or the more intellectual approach of BBC2, or may follow their favourite genre across different channels, whether it be sport, games shows or soaps. Either way they are likely to sample a variety of different inputs from the continuous flow on offer (Hargrave 1995).

Genres

Viewers may watch a range of programmes in different genres, but for the programme makers, especially producers, the division is much more rigid.

Jeremy Tunstall writes that 'producers are locked into a genre-specific world' (Tunstall 1993: 2). Programme genres are organisationally separate. Programme makers work in departments which also function as career ladders. Each genre has its own style, its own norms, its own grammar of programme making, its own history and culture. The skills and standards are often different. Those who work in any one of the fields may have little contact with the others.

Departments broadly divide into:

- *Drama*, including single dramas, series, serials and soap operas

- *Factual* including documentary, science, consumer programmes, business programmes, ethnographic films, crime investigations such as *Crimewatch UK*, or reconstructions such as *999*

- *Arts* covering theatre, music, dance, cinema, visual arts, photography, literature

- *News*, which may or may not be associated with current affairs, including series such as *Panorama* and *World in Action*, and documentary-style current affairs as in *Dispatches*, and special journalist-led series

- *Entertainment* including comedy, games shows, sitcoms, popular music, chat shows, variety shows and satire

- *Children's* including drama, information and entertainment

- *Religion* including issues of morality, faith and belief as well as acts of worship

- *Sport* including magazine and news programmes as well as coverage of sports events

- *Youth programmes*

- *Education* including programmes made for use by schools, and adult education such as the BBC's *Learning Zone* made together with the Open University

- *Daytime* programmes

In the BBC many of the regions originate their own programmes which may be marginal to some of these categories (Leanne Klein writes about working on *Small Objects of Desire* from BBC Bristol p. 171 below).

These institutional divisions change with time and with different tastes and needs. In the 1950s the BBC had a Women's Programmes Unit, which was abolished in the 1960s in favour of a Family Programmes Department which also included the Children's Department (Leman 1987). There are specialised units like the BBC's Community Programmes Unit, Disability Programmes Unit and Afro-Caribbean Unit.

Familiarity with a genre means building up a set of expectations about a programme's style and content, both on the part of the producers and their regular audience. This includes accepting the conventions – like the laughter from the unseen audience during a sitcom – and it also includes relishing a knowledge of the genre itself: as in the endless self-reference of the entertainment world in which soap opera actors appear on chat shows to discuss how their character is doing, comics do impersonations of other comics, and competing programmes trade sly digs with each other.

Across each of the departments established genres are recognised which are common not only to television but also to cinema, literature and other cultural forms. Dramas refer to different sets of conventions for different genres, say thrillers, psychological dramas, comedy dramas, police series and others. Each type builds up certain audience expectations which legitimise forms of presentation. Science fiction need not stick to the natural rules of the biological world, for example, whereas a courtroom drama would be ruined if strict logic were not followed in the sequence of cause and effect. The violence which is a regular part of a cartoon, as in the much-quoted example of *Tom and Jerry*, would be totally unacceptable in a realistic drama.

Programme genres are not necessarily confined to the departments that originate them. Drama-documentaries draw on traditions of both factual and fictional genres. New genres are constantly being invented, and sometimes they extend beyond the boundaries of their original department. The video diaries style is a recent success. Evolved by the BBC Community Programmes Unit as a way of giving greater access to the airwaves to more members of the public, it has developed into something that can now be recognised as a genre in itself.

Scheduling

Ever since Lew Grade established *Sunday Night at the London Palladium* as the weekly blockbuster for ABC television on the ITV network in 1955, it has been recognised that audiences will respond to a regular slot for their favourite programmes. Indeed, many people organise their day and their week around their television viewing. Schedulers are keen to maintain a predictable sense of structure for their channels. Steve Morrison, Managing Director of London Weekend Television, has written of the three essential ingredients for his schedule. They are the well-loved 'perennials' – 'the family friends we all come home to relax with, *Coronation Street*, *The Bill*, *Blind Date*, *Barrymore* and many more'; then there are 'events' – major dramas or blockbuster Hollywood movies that give the channel that 'must watch feel'; and finally there's the 'grit' – 'It's got to be about something . . . This is where factual drama and drama-documentaries score. They cause controversy.' He describes ITV's schedule as

> like the architecture of a house, the viewer can watch *This Morning* in the kitchen, *Coronation Street* with the family in the living room; later the kids go off to bed and Mum and Dad settle down to strong narrative drama at nine; *News at Ten* is there for the late working professional and the set's still on in the bedroom after 10.30 for the teenage kids.
>
> (Hargrave 1995: 120)

Until the mid-1980s the channels ambled along together more or less amiably, but as the competitive market culture caught hold, things changed. When he was Controller of Programmes at BBC1, Michael Grade acquired a reputation for 'aggressive scheduling', defined by Jeremy Bugler (at that time (1985) Editor of LWT's *London Programme*), as the 'law' which says 'the scheduler should pitch his most popular programmes against his opponent's weakest. He will then scoop the pool and possibly ruin his opponent's ratings for the rest of the evening' (*Guardian*, 15 August 1985). The question is whether schedulers should compete by putting like against like, which may protect less popular programmes, by ensuring that they are not marginalised by being transmitted against an audience pulling show, or whether they should give audiences the benefit of complementarity, allowing the viewer to follow their favourite genre across the channels (*see* Rupert Rumney, p. 145 below). BBC1 and 2, both run by the BBC and each with a different brief, can always offer a complementary schedule.

Since the coming of the remote control has given 'grazing' power to the audience, there has been a greater need for branding and channel identity – hence all those 2s and trails. There has been a move to programme 'zoning' with differing expectations for programmes at different times of the day and different days of the week. *Def II* in the early evening for young people and *Children's BBC* in the morning and late afternoon for children, can clump together dramas, news and entertainment items under their single logo. Programmes of a certain type are regularly grouped under a series title: Channel Four has *Dispatches* for current affairs, and *Cutting Edge* for observational documentaries. Individual programme titles appear under headings which have already marked out the kind of programme viewers can expect at that point in the schedule. The disadvantage, loudly voiced by some programme makers, is that programme editors come to expect a more standardised product. Themed seasons, such as Channel Four's *Bloody Bosnia*, which included many different types of programme about the war in ex-Yugoslavia, have been another way of gathering programmes together. The one-off programme made outside a strand is now a rare creature.

All the terrestrial channels offer a varied schedule, based on prestige and a view to public service as well as audience ratings. By contrast, satellite channels and cable channels either offer a single type of programme – say Hollywood movies or sports – or use the system know as 'stripping', which places the same type of programming at the same time every day.

Ratings

To maintain the ecology of terrestrial broadcasting, schedulers must design the flow of their channel so that the audience stays with it in sufficient numbers. BBC1 and ITV compete for the biggest audiences with soap operas *Coronation Street* and *EastEnders* leading the field. They can both draw between 16 to 18 million viewers for each episode.

Audience sizes are calculated by the broadcasting organisations themselves and by the Broadcasters' Audience Research Board (BARB), using a variety of overlapping methods, including monitoring the switching on of television sets and conducting polls amongst the public. Weekly figures are published in the *Radio Times* and in more detail in the trade magazine *Broadcast*. They are the subject of much discussion and press comment, which plays up the competition between channels, especially at times like Christmas. Programme makers have tended to value the Audience Appreciation Index (AI) equally highly. This is a survey of viewers' opinions on the programmes they have seen, and gives some sense of the audience's evaluation of their work.

Audience numbers matter to both ITV and the BBC. ITV must provide audiences for the advertisers on whom its income depends. Indeed, one cynical view of independent television programmes is that their most important function is to 'sell' viewers to advertisers. The better the audience, the more the advertiser will pay. Advertisers are not necessarily interested in the biggest audience, but in the audience that will contain most people likely to buy their product. Hence people with very low incomes, such as old age pensioners, are less interesting than ones with high incomes, or specific needs. Children, for example, will definitely pressure their parents to buy the correct brand of trainers or the most popular toy. At Christmas 1994 there were stories of parents coming to blows outside Toys'Я'Us when the chain ran out of Power Rangers dolls (Holland 1996). Niche programming, directed at a particular interest group, suits advertisers aiming at niche markets. The BBC must also keep its audience figures up, to justify charging its licence fee.

The average percentage of audience share divided between the four terrestrial channels is now being shaken up by the coming of cable and satellite. In Spring 1996 ITV was drawing 37.3% of all viewing, BBC1 33%, BBC2 10.6% and Channel Four 11.3% while cable and satellite channels shared the remaining 7.8%. It is predicted that the cable and satellite share will rise, while that of all the terrestrial channels will fall. The fear is that both advertisers and licence fee payers will be less willing to fund the terrestrial channels, and that both budgets and quality will fall. Even so, through the regulatory structure, there remains in the last years of the twentieth century a commitment to a huge range of programming on UK television, which recognises that a programme that addresses a small audience, or a poor audience, may well be of as much value as the blockbusters at the top of the charts.

References

Barker, M. and Petley, J. (1997) *Ill Effects*, London: Routledge

Bianculli, D. (1992) *Teleliteracy, Taking Television Seriously*, New York: Continuum

Broadcasting Research Unit (1985) *The Public Service Idea in British Broadcasting*, London: Broadcasting Research Unit

Channel Four (1994–5) *An Introduction and Guide for Producers*, London: Channel Four

Fiddick, P. (1994) *Guardian*, 20 June, London

Hargrave, A. M. (1995) *The Scheduling Game: Audience Attitudes to Broadcast Scheduling* (the Broadcasting Standards Council Annual Review 1995), London: John Libbey

ITC (1994) *ITC Performance Review 1993*, London: ITC

ITC (1996) *Factfile*, London: ITC

ITV (1995) *Television and the Role of ITV*, London: Spectrum Strategy Consultants

Leman, J. (1987) ' "Programmes for women" in 1950s British television' in H. Baehr and G. Dyer (eds), *Boxed In: Women and Television* London: Pandora RKP

Murdoch, R. (1989) *Freedom in Broadcasting*, London: News Corporation Ltd

Petley, J. (1995) 'Regulation overload', *The Television Book 1995*, London: Edinburgh International Television Festival

Scannell, P. (1990) 'Public service broadcasting: the history of a concept' in A. Goodwin and G. Whannel (eds), *Understanding Television*, London: Routledge

Scannell, P. and Cardiff, D. (1991) *Social History of Broadcasting 1922–1939: Serving the Nation*, Oxford: Blackwell

Key texts

Allen, Robert C. (ed.) (1987) *Channels of Discourse*, Chapel Hill: University of North Carolina Press

Allen, Robert C. (ed.) (1993) *Channels of Discourse Reassembled*, Chapel Hill: University of North Carolina Press

Baehr, H. and Dyer, G. (eds) (1987) *Boxed In: Women and Television*, London: Pandora RKP

Boyd-Barrett, O. and Braham, P. (1987) *Media, Knowledge and Power*, London: Croom Helm

British Broadcasting Corporation (1992) *Guide to the BBC*, London: BBC Information Services

Broadcasting Standards Council (1994) *Code of Practice*, 2nd edn, London: Broadcasting Standards Council

Corner, J. (1995) *Television Form and Public Address*, London: Edward Arnold

Curran, J. and Seaton, J. (1991) *Power without Responsibility: The Press and Broadcasting in Britain*, 4th edn, London: Routledge

Fiske, J. (1987) *Television Culture*, London: Routledge

Fiske, J. and Hartley, J. (1978) *Reading Television*, London: Methuen

Goodwin, A. and Whannel, G. (eds) (1990) *Understanding Television*, London: Routledge

Holland, P. (1996) 'I've just seen a hole in the reality barrier! Children, childishness and the media in the ruins of the twentieth century' in J. Pilcher and S. Wagg (eds) *Thatcher's Children? Politics, Childhood and Society in the 1980s and 1990s*, Brighton: Falmer

Inglis, F. (1990) *Media Theory: An Introduction*, Oxford: Blackwell

Tunstall, J. (1993) *Television Producers*, London: Routledge

Vahimagi, T. (1994) *British Television*, Oxford: Oxford University Press

Williams, R. (ed.) (1990) *Television: Technology and Cultural Form*, London: Routledge

Magazines, journals and organisations

BECTU
Broadcasting, Entertainment, Cinematograph and Theatre Union. The trade union representing employees in the film, television and theatre industries.
Head Office: 111 Wardour St, London W1A 4AY
Journal: *Stage, Screen and Radio*

British Universities Film and Video Council
55 Greek Street, London W1V 5LR
Journal: *Viewfinder*

Broadcast Magazine
Weekly trade magazine of the broadcasting industry.
33 Bowling Green Lane, London EC1

Free Press
Magazine of the Campaign for Press and Broadcasting Freedom which campaigns for a 'diverse, democratic and accountable media'.
8 Cynthia St, London N1 9JF

National Union of Journalists
  Acorn House, 314 Grays Inn Rd, London WC1X 8DP

Televisual
The business magazine for independent producers, facilities and the broadcast
  industry: monthly.
  St Giles's House, 50 Poland St, London W1V 4AX

Voice of the Listener and Viewer
  Campaigns for 'quality in broadcasting'.
  101 Kings Drive, Gravesend, Kent DA12 5BQ

Part II: The practitioner's perspective

3 Television from the practitioner's perspective

··

Working in television

Those who wish to work in television find themselves on uncertain ground. This handbook on television production comes at a time when the very idea of what television production *is*, is in a state of flux. On the one hand programme making continues within the specific rules and practices that are well established within each television genre. But on the other hand, these rules and practices are breaking down in unexpected ways. Television is no longer a set of rigid, recognisable structures. Part of the excitement about being new to television is the opportunity to contribute to the changing shape of the medium itself.

Working in television involves jobs which range from typist in the accounts department to presenter of *The Big Breakfast*; from carpenter in the scenery store to producer of the *Nine O'Clock News*; from skilled electrician to comedy writer; from camera assistant to commissioning editor (*see* Work areas in the television industry, p. 28 below). And the people who do those jobs are as diverse as the jobs themselves. They come from different backgrounds, require different types of training, have different professional and technical skills, use different jargons, and are accustomed to different working environments. Some of the jobs that are important to television – say public relations, finance or administration – are about working in the institution, others are about high-level technical and engineering knowledge which is way beyond the scope of this book.

However, the job of getting a programme on the air involves certain basic understandings and several major tasks. This section will outline some of the principles of production, directing, camerawork, lighting, sound recording and editing. These underlying principles apply both to those aiming for full-time employment in the industry and those who, in the new, casualised structure within which television operates, aim either to get a programme commissioned, or to make programmes independently of the television institutions. The rapidity of current technological changes means that techniques are more important than technologies, and understanding is more important than routine training – a view that is reinforced by Phil Redmond (p. 222 below).

Working in television can be very demanding. Long hours, stress, a highly competitive atmosphere, dealing with difficult colleagues and inflated egos; it's all par for the course. This book contains several first-hand accounts from practitioners on coping with the day-to-day problems which are inseparable from practical work. In a changing environment the next generation of programme makers will need to arrive in the medium with a critical understanding not only of the mechanics of television, but also of the context within which they are carried out.

Work areas in the television industry

The following list of work areas from the *Careers Information Pack* are reproduced courtesy of Skillset, the industry training organisation for the broadcasting, film and video industries.

Figure 3 The work areas

▶ ANIMATION:

Animation is a growing career area, involving the (increasingly high-tech) design, creation and operation of animated production and effects.

Essential skills: Understanding the technical and budgetary constraints of a conceptual design when translated into production. Analytical skills, time management, attention to detail and the ability to work well in a team. Many animators are freelance, and require personal and business management skills.

Useful background: Art school training – especially in drawing, experience of relevant software and a knowledge of the industry.

▶ ANNOUNCERS:

Announcers work to detailed and carefully timed scripts, communicating information to the viewer from a soundproof 'behind the screens' office. They sometimes write or adapt their own material.

Essential skills: Ability to work independently for long periods. Clear communication. Attention to detail. Calm and 'user friendly' manner.

Useful background: Any general working experience (especially drama or teaching). TV administration.

▶ ARCHIVISTS/ LIBRARIANS:

Archivists and librarians collect, collate, preserve and make available collections of recorded visual, sound, written and other materials for use by various productions.
Essential skills: Ability to assess the age, quality, authenticity of any material. Organised and methodical.

Useful background: Specialist training, plus relevant work experience outside the industry.

▶ ART AND DESIGN:

The Art and Design function is to create a visual effect to meet the needs of the production, creating manual or computer generated graphics.

Figure 3 The work areas (contd.)

Essential skills; the ability to interpret a brief and relistic ideas within tight budget and time communications . Excellent communication skills.

Useful background: Specialised art college training, and experience outside the industry in a commercial environment.

COSTUME/WARDROBE:

The wardrobe department interpret the production requirements in terms of costumes and accessories to ensure historical accuracy and an accurate portrayal of the style and ethos of the period.

Essential skills: The ability to design, make, adapt or hire costumes, communicate effectively with artists whilst dressing them and to service all costumes requirements, Planning and organisation and administrative skills. Working within budgets.

DIRECTION:

The Director is responsible for achieving the creative, visual and auditory effect of a production.

Essential skills: The ability to effectively co-ordinate the skills and personalities of performers, designers and technical specialists. Proven creativity in sound and image. Audience and financial awareness. High stress tolerance.

Useful background: High level academic ability. Practical television, film or theatre experiences. Work with a wide range of people.

ENGINEERING:

Engineers provide a design maintenance and installation service to the production site and equipment. Research specialists are usually employed by the equipment manufacturers or design consultancies.

Essential skills: Problem solving, quick neat working. Good interpersonal skills. High safety awareness.

Useful background: A qualification in Electronic, Electrical Sound or Mechanical Engineering. Work experience with equipment manufacturers.

FILM, VIDEO & AUDIO TAPE EDITING:

Raw tape or film is shaped to interpret the requirements of the director, either by physical cutting (film) or by selecting sequences and re-recording onto a master tape using sophisticated technology.

Essential skills: Creative visual thinking, self motivated, technical ability, manual dexterity, computer literacy and an interest in the work. Work to tight deadlines.

Useful background: Technical computer or scientific training, combined with a experience as a runner, or station assistant.

GRAPHIC DESIGN:

Graphic Designers, using film and the latest video and computer technology, produce opening titles, credits and programme information sequences that embrace a variety of visual styles. The designer also helps to brand the Channel through animated station idents and on-screen promotion of programmes.

Figure 3 The work areas (contd.)

Essential skills: The ability to think imaginatively and logically to combine image with sound. To keep pace with changing technology and co-ordinate a wide range of production resources. To work as a member of a team.

▶ **IT SPECIALIST:**

IT specialist support many aspects of broadcasting, film and video, either within the companies or as consultants, providing and maintaining relevant systems and software.

Essential skills: High level computer literacy A 'feel' for the industry. Good interpersonal skills. Quick working.

Useful background: Relevant degree. Work within a software house, management consultancy or manufacture.

▶ **JOURNALISTS:**

Generate and report on local, national or international stories and research relevant background information. Bi-media (radio and TV) contracts are increasing. Some journalists present their own work.

Essential skills: Flexibility of approach to reflect the needs of different audiences. Clear communication skills. Ability to work to deadlines. Calm. Tenacious.

Useful background: Training and experience in newspapers or periodical journalism.

▶ **LABORATORY:**

Lab technicians develop, grade and process film, duplicate and check video tapes ensuring high technical quality.

Essential skills: Technical ability, analytical skills. Quick and accurate. Good vision.

Useful background: Chemistry qualification (film). Still photography and home developing.

▶ **LIGHTING:**

Lighting specialists ensure that the stage or set is correctly lit to meet the needs of the production.

Essential skills: The ability to design lighting layouts, organise lighting effects and operate the lighting system to meet the requirements of the indoor or outdoor production. Computer literacy. Physical agility, good head for heights.

Useful background: Specialist college or industry based training. Theatre experience.

▶ **MAKE-UP AND HAIRDRESSING:**

Make-up and hairdressing professionals interpret the requirements of the production and research to ensure accurate representation of the historical or design concept. They maintain a continuity of approach throughout the production in studio or on location.

Essential skills: Ability to translate abstract ideas into practical applications quickly. Inventive and lateral thinking. Calm and reassuring communication skills.

Figure 3 The work areas (contd.)

Useful background: Relevant training and experience outside the industry. History and art qualifications.

▶ MANAGEMENT:

Direct and co-ordinate the different elements of the industry to ensure their efficient function – ranging from commissioning a production to negotiating international rights.

Essential skills: Specialist knowledge of chosen function area (e.g. Personnel, Finance). Ability to communicate with the creative team. Strong financial awareness. Planning and organisational skills.

Useful background: High level academic training, often supplemented by a professional qualification. Experience outside the industry.

▶ MARKETING AND SALES:

Marketing and sales staff work in an international marketplace to raise revenue for broadcasters or filmmakers. Airtime is sold, sponsorship and co-production rights negotiated and spin-off products developed, e.g. books, toys, videos.

Essential skills: Persuasiveness. Self motivated (especially to make money). Analytical, computer literate. Excellent communication skills on telephone and face to face.

Useful background: Professional sales or marketing experience outside the industry.

▶ PRODUCERS:

Producers perform a variety of management and operational roles to bring together the many elements of a production either in studio or on location. Often responsible both for the initial concept and raising the essential finance, they are the team leaders.

Essential skills: Creative thinking. Excellent communication. Planning, negotiating, motivating others. Financial awareness.

Useful background: Team leadership. Experience of finance, marketing or the law. Work as a researcher.

▶ PRODUCTION ASSISTANTS:

Production Assistants provide high quality administrative and secretarial support to the Producer and Director at every stage of production, co-ordinating all activities and preparing schedules and scripts.

Essential skills: Excellent secretarial and administrative skills. Effective communicator. Cheerful and unflappable. Problem solving. Good mental arithmetic.

Useful background: Relevant experience both inside and outside the industry.

▶ PRODUCTION MANAGEMENT:

Production managers organise all essential support facilities for the team – accommodation, catering, transport etc. S/he will also roster crews and arrange payments.

Essential skills: Good 'people' manager. Organised, sound admin and financial skills. Calm, problem solving. Practical.

Useful background: Crew member or floor manager. Stage management training.

Figure 3 The work areas (contd.)

▶ PRODUCTION OPERATIVES:

Perform the operational duties of the production such as vision mixing and autocue operations.

Essential skills: Technical ability. Attention to detail. Reliable, calm, quick reactions.

Useful background: Machine or computer operation. Often relevant secretarial, admin or 'running' experience.

▶ RECORDING STILL AND MOVING IMAGES [CAMERAWORK]:

Workers in this area operate and assist with still, film and video cameras to record images, as directed using different techniques.

Essential skills: Creative flair. General technical skills. Ability to accept direction. Good visual sense.

Useful background: Technical qualification and work experience. Amateur photography or fine art.

▶ RESEARCHER:

Supports the producer, helping to turn ideas into reality – providing and following up ideas, contacting and interviewing people, and acquiring relevant factual material. Writing briefings for presenters.

Essential skills: Very well organised. Able to take initiative and work unsupervised. Excellent interpersonal skills.

Useful background: High level academic qualifications (possibly in specialist areas of interest). Experience in newspaper or magazine journalism or TV administration.

▶ RUNNERS/GOFERS:

The traditional entry level job for the industry. Bright, highly motivated – often highly-qualified – people act as general assistants, taking messages, making deliveries, being indispensable and learning the basics of the commercial business.

Essential skills: Broadly based practical skills. Helpful 'good to have about' personality. A passion for every aspect of the industry. Sensitivity to the needs of colleagues, especially when under pressure.

Useful background: Formal or informal knowledge of the industry. Administrative experience. Teamwork.

▶ SET CRAFTS/PROPS:

People working in this area construct the scenery, sets and backdrops to meet the production brief reflecting both historical accuracy and required design and style. They also maintain sets during a production and operate any mechanical features as directed. Props (hired or made) are used to dress the set.

Essential skills: Specialised craft skills. Ingenuity. Safety conscious. Attention to detail. Quick working. Budget awareness.

Useful background: Training in industrial 3-D design, sculpture, architecture, or theatre design, in association with work experience.

Figure 3 The work areas (contd.)

▶ **SOUND:**

Sound craftspeople interpret requirements of a production in terms of sound collection. During post production they may be involved in recording, editing and dubbing using a range of sophisticated equipment.

Essential skills: General technical ability. Calm, quick to respond. Perfect hearing.

Useful background: Technical qualification and work experience. Amateur sound recording. Playing musical instruments.

▶ **SPECIAL EFFECTS:**

Special effects designers create and operate effects for a production, within technical limitations and budget and operate the necessary machines.

Essential skills: Creativity, lateral thinking. Technical and computer literacy. Communications of ideas. High safety awareness.

Useful background: Art or science qualification. Design experience.

▶ **STAGE/FLOOR MANAGEMENT:**

Co-ordinate and manage everything that happens on the studio location or rehearsal room 'floor', from cueing actors to organising props. When there is a studio audience, the Floor Manager will be in charge. There is close liaison with the Director.

Essential skills: Organised, practical, unflappable, with a broad range of TV skills and knowledge. Excellent communication skills and the ability to command instant respect.

Useful background: Experience in theatre, especially on tour, followed by several years as an assistant.

▶ **SUPPORT STAFF:**

Many people working in Film, Video, Television or Radio fulfil essential support roles, including administration, catering, driving, cleaning.

Essential skills: As appropriate for the individual job.

Useful background: Practical training and experience outside the industry.

▶ **TRANSMISSION:**

Technicians and engineers work to exhibit the production in a high quality form which can involve projecting images or operating transmission equipment linking electronic signals from the studios to a transmitter.

Essential skills: High level of technical ability. Self motivated. Attention to detail. Quick thinking and problem solving.

Useful background: Relevant qualification with practical experience of telecommunications or computers.

Figure 3 The work areas (contd.)

▶ **WRITERS:**
Writers work to produce or edit
scripts for a variety of radio. TV,
video or film productions

Essential skills: Creative flair.
Ability to realise other people's
ideas. Reliable. Work to tight
deadlines. Willingness to accept
criticism and implement changes.

Useful background: High level
academic training. Practical
experience in special interest areas.
Published work in other media.

Programme production types

We can make a broad distinction between three types of programme that are part of the daily television flow. These types are based on the practicalities of production, a different classification from the 'genres' discussed above.

- *Live programmes:* These may either be broadcast simultaneously with the action, or they may be 'as live', recorded, then broadcast without change sometimes only minutes later. These originate either from a studio or from an Outside Broadcast (OB) Unit. Typically they use multiple camera set ups, in which as many as five studio or OB cameras feed simultaneous signals into a control room, or gallery, where they are instantaneously edited to create the broadcast programme. Studio programmes include programmes either in front of a studio audience or using the audience as part of the show. These include talk shows like *Kilroy*, chat shows, most comedy programmes – including sitcoms where the audience's laughter is important, games shows, and late-night discussion programmes, such as *The Midnight Hour*. OBs include public events, such as the *State Opening of Parliament* and, most importantly, sport.

- *Filmed programmes:* In this case 'filmed' includes programmes made on film or videotape in all the different formats available, from Hi-8 to super 16mm (*see* Cameras, film stock and formats, p. 49 below). 'Filmed' programmes are shot on a single camera, either on location or in a studio. The accumulated rushes, or original filmed material, are then selected and reordered into the shape of the final film in an editing suite or cutting room. Programmes from major dramas to current affairs investigations are made in this way.

- *Segmented programmes:* These are programmes made up of short inserts, which may be live or pre-filmed. This type includes collaged or bricol-laged programmes such as magazine programmes, the daytime format

Figure 4 Studio control room re-equipped in 1994
Courtesy Granada Television

and news bulletins. It includes the cracks between the programmes which hold together the television flow – advertisements, trailers, station identifications such as the outrageous and unpredictable 2s of BBC2. In the old days these 'presentation' inserts had very low prestige, usually they were announcements voiced over grimy captions. Now they have become the height of trendy design. Items for segmented programmes may be made up of short sections, or, as with news bulletins, the items may be linked together by a live studio set up.

This section of the book will refer to all three types, but will offer more detail on the second group, the 'filmed' programmes. These are the ones which are most likely to originate with independent producers. They can be made with the least capital equipment and depend least on the resources and structures of the broadcasting institutions. Characteristics of 'filmed' programmes also apply to many of the short 'segments' supplied to segmented programmes.

Filmed programmes

Whether drama or documentary, current affairs or arts, 'filmed' programmes or segments have certain characteristics in common, which they share with classic cinema:

- *They are usually pre-planned.* In the case of a drama, that may mean that every word is scripted and the shooting is carefully storyboarded; in the case of a current affairs documentary it may mean that the research has revealed a line of investigation and decided which events should be filmed and which people should be interviewed. This is in contrast to the very loose organisation of the studio sofa show or the unpredictability of a news bulletin.

- *They begin with what is described as a 'pro-filmic event'.* This is the scene which the camera will film. This 'event' may be highly contrived by the programme makers, as it is for a costume drama, with sets, props and costumes all carefully designed and put in place. On the other hand, the filmmakers may aim to intervene as little as possible with events as they unfold, as with a fly-on-the-wall documentary which seeks to film real life as it happens. The different genres need different sorts of preparation and different kinds of expertise. For the documentary there will be researchers, advisors and experts; for the drama, set and costume designers, historical experts, casting experts, wig makers, etc. Work on the pro-filmic event prepares the *'mise-en-scène'* – the characteristic 'look' of the programme.

- *They are made up of discrete shots,* as the camera records the scene on film or on videotape. In contrast with studio programmes, the shots will almost never be taken in the sequence in which the audience finally sees the programme. The shots will be set up one by one, in such a way that they can later be put together to make filmic sense.

- *The shots are then edited,* combined first into sequences, then finally into the whole programme. The editing work is crucial to the construction of the programme.

- *The sound-track may be added separately,* offering the possibility of music, commentary or special sound effects, in addition to the natural sound recorded during the filming.

The planning and production of a programme may be extraordinarily complex, involving a wide range of expertise and specialist skills. However, the job of pre-production basically involves getting a programme financed, organised and up and running. During production there are three indispensable technical skills needed by the programme makers, directing, camera, and sound recording. Finally, in post-production the skills of editing picture and sound come into play. These are the skills we will concentrate on here.

Producing and pre-production

In his fascinating study of television producers, Jeremy Tunstall describes British television as a producer-led medium (Tunstall 1993). Within the broadcasting institutions it is they who have historically had the greatest control over the creative output, and it has been producers who have risen to become programme controllers and heads of channels. His book is an account of how producers in seven programme genres, including drama, sport, documentary and what he calls 'edinfotainment' – that characteristically British mixture of informational and educational programmes presented in an entertaining way – see their job. The very lack of a clear-cut definition makes it a demanding role,

> The producer's role encompasses elements not only of the civil servant but of a latter-day Renaissance man, capable of playing all parts. . . . He or she needs some basic grasp of television technology, of tape against film, of sound, lighting and sets; requires (usually extensive) specialist knowledge of the particular programme genre, such a drama or news; needs to be able to juggle ideas against finance; needs plenty of sheer energy; needs some performance skills – the ability to enthuse and activate others during a long working day; and needs diplomatic skills to smooth ruffled egos and to persuade others to do things at different times and for less money than they would prefer.
>
> (Tunstall 1993: 6)

Many innovations and initiatives that have contributed to the development of the television medium over its history have come from remarkable producers pursuing their own vision (*see* the accounts by producers Tony Garnett, p. 132, John Wyver, p. 160, Stuart Cosgrove, p. 211, and Phil Redmond, p. 223 below). But being an established producer in a television organisation or an independent company, with all the long-term responsibility that entails, is not necessarily the same thing as producing a single programme, which largely involves common sense, persistence and hard work.

The producer is the person who gets the whole thing under way and carries ultimate responsibility. Producers deal with logistics and money. Some independent producers may be risking their own money; others who are employed by a television company must argue for resources and justify their budgets within their respective organisations. It is usually the producer who selects the writer, director and the crew, although often the commission to make the programme may depend on the use of a particular director, actor or presenter who is part of the 'package'. Choosing whom to work with, ensuring harmonious working relationships, and making sure that the crew get on well together as a team can be more important in the production of everyday television than a burning talent.

Any programme is the result of team action, and the producer's input will vary with the circumstances. In a small production the director or the writer may also do the producing, or the team may work collaboratively. There are few rules on how to get a programme off the ground, but training in financial skills, budgeting and knowledge of the law as it relates to programme making are all beginning to make an appearance on television courses.

The producer supervises the whole production, but works closely with the production manager on the preliminary budgeting, on planning the schedule, and on the monitoring and control of the budget and other organisational matters. Below we look in detail at the production process as it moves through its three major stages from the point of the view of the production manager.

The production manager's job

Production management means logistics and organisation. The job involves dealing with the budget and schedule, and managing people and equipment.

The purpose is to ensure the smooth running of the production, and the aim is to organise all of its aspects. This requires excellent interpersonal skills as well as an overall knowledge of everybody else's job and of the production process. Administration skills, a methodical approach to paperwork, and the ability to juggle several problems at once are essential.

The task can vary from a full-scale fiction shoot on an overseas location which lasts for three weeks or more, to a camcorder video diary shot in a single day. The same basic principles apply, even though their application will be different depending on the type and size of the production.

The production manager's work is divided into three distinct stages: pre-production, the production period and post-production: from the setting up of the shoot, managing the shoot itself, right up to the tidying up afterwards.

In an ideal world, production management should be a planned activity in which every eventuality is anticipated and prepared for. That is fine as a theory. In practice, production for television always involves tight deadlines and budgets. This can create a tension between the artistic aspirations of the creative director and writer on the one hand, and the practical need to deliver a finished programme on time on the other. If things are to be kept on course, the production manager must be able to react fast to ever-changing needs.

The skills of planning can be learnt, but it would be foolish to pretend that this is all that you need to be a good production manager. There is no substitute for experience. Over time a production manager begins to anticipate potential crisis scenarios and learns how to react to them. It is important to prioritise and always to ensure that you keep one step ahead.

Pre-production

Together with the producer, a production schedule should be drawn up, planning the time to be spent in the various phases of production. At this stage the decision will be taken on whether to shoot on film or video or a combination of the two, as this will affect schedule and costs. In relation to the schedule, a detailed budget must be prepared, using the script to estimate every cost. Standard budget forms for independent producers are available (obtainable from PACT or Channel Four). These break down the different cost areas, from wages and hire of equipment through to location costs and such essential items as insurance, office overheads and production stills. You will need to work backwards from the first shooting date to construct a realistic timetable and budget, identifying all the elements that the production will need.

Together with the producer and director, the next tasks will include booking the crew, the artists and the necessary equipment, and finding the locations. It is the production manager's job to ensure that these tasks are done efficiently and according to the correct procedures. For example, the

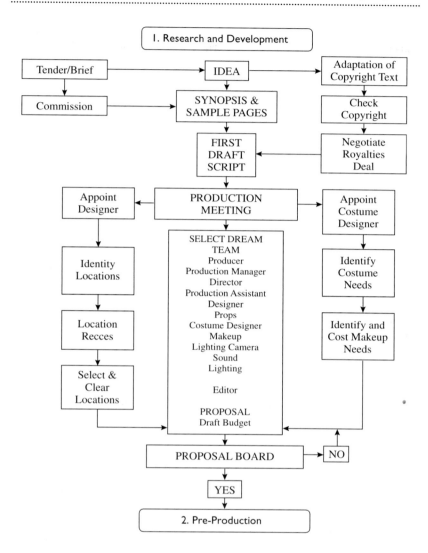

Figure 5 Production management: research and development
Courtesy Robin Small and Mike Healey

production manager should check the established agreements with the unions BECTU and Equity and the independent employers' association, PACT, for the rates agreed with artists and crew.

There should be a master book of contacts for artists and crew with addresses, phone numbers, and the contact number of their agent or representative if they have one. A separate emergency list should include NHS/NI numbers, and the phone numbers of their doctor and next of kin.

If filming overseas, passport numbers should be noted and medical cover arranged. Make sure any vaccination and visa requirements are met by checking with doctors and the embassy of the country in question. The Foreign and Commonwealth Office publishes a regular update advice list.

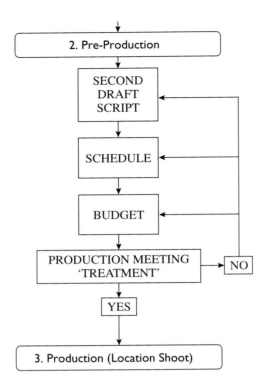

Figure 6 Production management: pre-production
Courtesy Robin Small and Mike Healey

The production manager should keep a contact list of suppliers with their phone numbers and postal addresses and a list of all equipment bought in or hired, including electrical machinery, ropes, chains, scaffolding, lighting and plant. Check that it is safe and has the appropriate test certificates. Make sure any operatives hold current qualifications.

As soon as the locations have been decided on, it is up to the production manager to make sure that permissions are in place and insurance is arranged. There should be a risk assessment for each location. If there are any special effects, proper experts such as stunt artists, pyrotechnic specialists and fight arrangers should be employed. Always make sure they have their own insurance and check their credentials before filming starts. Ensure that costume design and set construction are started early enough.

Travel and accommodation should be arranged well in advance, as should location support, including catering and first aid. Inform the relevant bodies, such as the police, of what you are doing and when.

This pre-production period should have its own detailed schedule. There should be enough in the original budget estimate to cover these pre-production costs, including insurance, contracts, office costs, transport, location finding, construction, equipment hire and research. Well organised pre-production will allow everyone to set out in an atmosphere of calm organisation before the storm of production gets under way.

The production period

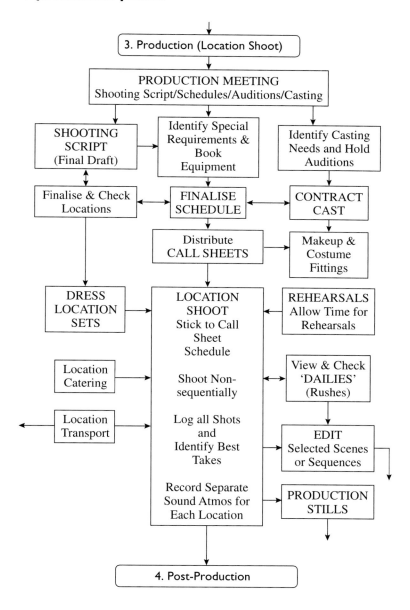

Figure 7 Production management: production (location shoot)
Courtesy Robin Small and Mike Healey

Logistics and cash flow are the main concerns during the production period. From film stock to costumes, it is up to the production manager to arrange that the production has what it needs when and where it is wanted.

Keeping the show on the road on a daily basis must be balanced with planning the following days' or weeks' activity. Keeping an eye fixed on long-term deadlines and overall costs, the production manager must ensure that daily needs are met with flexibility and speed. Pragmatism and patience are essential plus the ability to conjure a balanced weekly budget out of that changing animal experience called the shoot.

A good shoot runs on plenty of stock, food and petty cash plus a lot of goodwill backed up by quality information. Accommodation, catering, communication and transport should be in place and timed, so that the crew can get where they need to go, communicate vital information to each other, and be able to eat and rest with proper breaks. All crew and cast should have daily call lists showing what time they are needed and where. Close liaison with the director will ensure that the shoot goes smoothly.

Daily sheets which show expenditure on film stock, accommodation, food, telephone and petrol allow the production manager to compare actual with projected expenditure and so determine if the production is under or over budget on any given day or week. The producer should be given a regular update in order to make informed decisions about total costing and the artistic implications.

By this time the production manager should have booked the post-production facilities including editing, logging, sound dubbing, transfers and graphic facilities.

Post-production

Post-production is usually a race against time. The aim is to deliver the final programme, completed to the agreed brief, by the agreed date. Early production meetings with editors, graphics designers and musicians ensure that everybody knows each other and understands the deadlines involved.

Costing post-production will vary depending on the type of editing processes to be used (*see* Chapter 7, Editing). Shopping around for facilities helps. Remember that edit suites are two a penny but good editors are harder to find. So a good production manager will bid down on the mechanics but will not compromise on quality by settling for an operator who is second best.

Post-production involves three complementary processes. The edit must be kept on track, while putting together any sound and graphic effects that will need to be added. The production manager should work out when each of these needs to take place and should plan backwards from the deadlines for the fine cut and the on-line master.

This is the time to book the narrator if one is needed and to plan the music. Original composed music may turn out to be cheaper than using popular material. Check how long the composer, dubbing editor and graphic designer need, and check the compatibility between their systems and yours.

At this point the production manager should also be thinking about other important processes including:

- Making sure all the promotional activities are under way

- Paying off all outstanding bills and contributors

- Checking all contracts and dealing with any legal problems

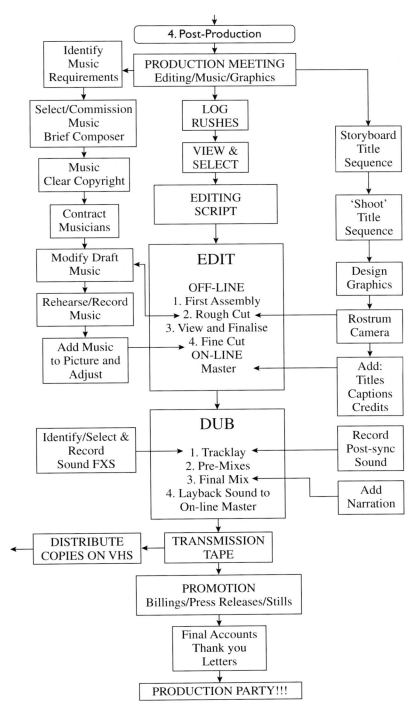

Figure 8 Production management: post-production
Courtesy Robin Small and Mike Healey

- Working out any foreign sales and checking the technical requirements for these

- Arranging for duplication of the programme if copies are needed

- Drawing up the final budget statement

- Winding down the production office

Publicity should include programme billing, stills, interviews, press previews, advance screenings, advertisments on radio, press and television and, if you still have the energy, getting the launch and final night party in place.

The clearance of legal problems and all copyright and contracts prevents any future claims or liability (Crone 1995):

- Did you remember to get signed waivers and consent forms from anybody who was interviewed?

- Was anything which was said libellous or was there any pop music playing in the background from which a future claim could arise?

- Do the people who may be doing interviews know of their commitments and are they available as part of their contract?

- Have you checked up on the residuals such as book rights and secondary video sales?

If the film is finally delivered on time and on budget, before you turn the light out, did you remember to bring a bottle opener, order the wine and a taxi home so that you can start all over again tomorrow – once the headache tablets you managed to forget finally take effect!

Robin Small is production manager at the University of Lincolnshire and Humberside.

References and key texts

British Film Commission (published annually) *The Check Book*, 70 Baker Street, London W1M 10J

Crone, T. (1995) *Law and the Media: An Everyday Guide for Professionals* 3rd edn, Oxford: Focal Press

Gates, R. (1995) *Production Management for Film and Video*, 2nd edn, Oxford: Focal Press

Health and Safety Executive, *Health & Safety Publications*, Broad Lane, Sheffield

Maier, R. C. (1994) *Location, Scouting and Management Handbook*, Oxford: Focal Press

Skillset (1995) *Outline of NVQ/SNVQ Standards*, London: Skillset

Tunstall, J. (1993) *Television Producers*, London: Routledge

4 Production techniques: the visual dimension

Director and crew

Directors need to know something of camera, sound and editing practices, although they need not be fully aware of the technicalities of each of these media, nor necessarily skilled in their use. The position of director has been glamorised, on the one hand by the mythology around larger-than-life Hollywood figures, and on the other by the '*auteur*' theories developed in France in the 1950s, which argued that a cinema film is a total work of art and it is the director who is the artist. This approach seriously underestimates the contribution made by the whole group of programme makers, from skilled technicians to performers and support staff, and is far from appropriate to the routine task of producing daily television. Even so, its attraction lingers – given the occasional boost by the emergence of such over-hyped figures as Quentin Tarantino. On British television, the list of people noted for their innovative contribution to the medium includes comedians, camerapeople, channel controllers, newscasters, scriptwriters, graphic designers, engineers, producers and many others, as well as directors. That said, the director retains a pivotal role in the making of major television programmes, notably in drama and documentaries.

There are many different types of director. The person who sits in the Outside Broadcast (OB) van and makes instantaneous decisions about controlling and editing between the five cameras covering a football match, has a very different job from the director who is the main figure in filming and editing a year-long observational series of, say, children in hospital. In documentaries and current affairs, some directors are more concerned with the journalistic than the televisual content of the programme. Many directors are unaware of what is involved in the technical jobs of camera and sound and may well leave such decisions to the technicians, who are very much part of the creative effort.

In the radical 1970s, some independent programme makers argued that democratic, non-hierarchic practices should involve every member of the group, sharing the skills, and preventing power differentials arising. In particular, it was argued that women had been deprived of the opportunity to learn the more technical skills, and this was partly because of the rigid divisions between jobs. Helen Baehr describes such an initiative in her account of the early days of Broadside Productions (Baehr and Dyer 1987). In the professional television world it could never quite work out like that. Nevertheless, in the new television era, 'multi-skilling' has become the jargon, this time deriving from a desire to cut costs rather than from a politics of production. A de-professionalisation of institutional practices has gone together with an increasing simplification of equipment. The days when the skills of camera or sound technicians were highly specialised and protected by their trade unions have gone.

Programmes differ enormously in their budgets, from the feature films designed for cinema release, costing a million pounds or more, which are commissioned by *Film on Four* and *Screen Two*, to a strand like *10x10* which gives budgets of around £20,000 to new directors (*see* Jeremy Howe, p. 233 below). Size of budgets and scale of production inevitably affects crewing and the relationships between those who bring their different skills to the job. At all levels it remains a director's task to know as much as possible about those skills. A shoot always works better if the director recognises the implications of what their crew is being asked to achieve, and understands something of the technical problems they are posing. A 'them and us' relationship between director and crew can develop all too easily when directors do not explain clearly what their intentions are. Sometimes, of course, this is because they themselves have not thought the problems through carefully enough.

In this chapter, we will deal first with cameras and the task of the lighting cameraperson and their assistants, then with the construction of the shots, which is largely the director's task. We will indicate some 'visual grammars', outlining the structures of the television flow and the conventions that underlie both narrative and non-narrative television, enabling a programme to move along smoothly. That does not mean that these rules are hard and fast. Conventions change over the years, and often become less rigid. For example, it is now quite normal to see the microphone in shot in certain types of programme. Sometimes completely new conventions develop, such as the loose camerawork expected in a video diary programme. Older conventions may be deliberately broken. In the mid-1980s the hyper-active youth programme *Network Seven* hunted down the rules in order to smash them with a spectacular flourish, only to find that they were reasserted when the audience was deemed to be 'tired' of a particularly flashy style. However, underlying most variations, there still remain certain competencies without which the basic structures of television simply would not work.

We will be considering the perspective of:

- *The cameraperson*, whose chief responsibility, together with their assistants, is to produce the images requested by the director. Their concern will be with the type of camera used, the lenses and the stock chosen, the control of the lighting, and the content and composition of the frames. In most cases the overall style and effect will be decided well before shooting begins.

  Note: Because of the sexism implied by the more familiar 'cameraman' and the ugliness of the more recent formulation 'cameraperson', the word 'cinematographer' has been coming into use. Although it sounds rather grand, like the maestro controlling the crew, this was the word used by some of the very first practitioners. In the 1890s the Lumière brothers employed operators who travelled round the world to film and to entertain with their wooden box, the 'Cinematographe' which combined camera, film processor and projector all in one.

- *The director*, whose job is to decide on the overall effect, and to attempt to achieve that effect. They must plan which shots will be taken, in which order, and what their content will be. Very often they will find themselves working within a programme style that is already well established, and many decisions will be predetermined by the genre and institutional placing of the programme. The speedy newsy style of, say, *The Cook Report* may look obvious and natural, but it is carefully constructed none the less, developed over the years by the makers of the series. The detailed period reconstruction of a drama series, from the early nineteenth century of *Pride and Prejudice* to the Second World War of *The Camomile Lawn*, contrasts with the up-to-date urgency of *Casualty*. All of them need specific decisions about camerawork and visual styles well before the filming begins.

  During the shoot, the authority lies with the director, who is responsible to the producer. Within the given limits, it is up to them to make things work, and that includes the smooth running of the production as well as the content of the final programme. A director who is open and clear about decisions as they are taken, enabling each member of the crew to do their job to the best of their ability, is, in the current structures of television, the most truly collaborative.

- *The cameraperson/director*. In this case, the person with the camera is also the person who decides which shots will be taken and in which order, as well as the aesthetic effect desired. When the cameraperson is also directing, such decisions may well be made on the hoof. Examples from three very different filmmakers are Charles Stewart's *Town Hall* – a highly dramatic year in the life of a local Labour council at a time of government pressure; *The Ark*, Molly Dineen's moving and sympathetic look at the life of London Zoo when it, too, was coming under financial difficulties; and Nick Broomfield's series of cheeky and intrusive portraits of the powerful, from the militaristic Afrikaner nationalist Eugene Terreblanche to Margaret Thatcher, in which Broomfield himself, with his apparently bumbling inability to engage with his subject, figures as a player in the drama.

- *The sound people* who are responsible for producing sound that is clear and enables the audience to understand dialogue, and who also contribute to the 'audio design' of the programme.

- *The editor*. The shots must be arranged in order and the sound added in the way the director wants, giving shape, rhythm and structure to the film. There is a great variety of editing styles, based on the infinite possibilities of combining sound and image, but the editor cannot achieve a desired effect if the shots are not there. Cameraperson and director must keep the editing process in mind while they are filming.

Teamwork is all-important. Directors must gain the trust of their crew, and very often crew members will be chosen for their flexibility and ability to fit in as much as for the quality of their work. Producers speak of the need to 'cast' their crew. A shoot can be disastrous if those who are working so closely together, often under conditions of considerable stress, do not get on. A great deal of nervous energy may be used up in trying to keep the peace. Not causing upsets or creating scenes, the ability to work long hours and cope with all eventualities, these are the tough demands which are made on television directors and crews.

The visual dimension

The love of the image

Since the American Thomas Edison first patented his motion-picture camera, the Kinetograph, in 1891, the desire to do something more with moving images has driven technological invention. From a simple wooden box, which had a handle to wind the roll of film and a device to hold each frame steady behind the lens for long enough to make an exposure, a huge range of cameras and other devices have been developed. When cameras became electrically driven there were no more problems with the variable speed caused by the turning handle. By the late 1920s cameras could produce an image in synchronisation with sound. Now, a century after the first moving pictures, there are cameras with movable lenses, cameras with long lenses, cameras with lenses that can magnify hugely, cameras with 'fast' lenses that can shoot in the near dark. There are massive 70mm cameras for wide-screen Hollywood spectaculars, and a wide range of video cameras, including hand-size camcorders for home movies. Wide-screen, high-definition television (HDTV) and various forms of digital imaging systems are the newest development. Film of different gauges, videotape and digital recording systems are all currently in use. Each technical development has brought new aesthetic experimentation which has from time to time hardened into 'rules' – only to be broken when the next development came along. As the second century of moving pictures gets under way, these different systems produce the startling variety of imagery which makes contemporary television so endlessly fascinating.

Some have argued that the conservatism of those who commission programmes has tended to lead to an over-cautiousness in the range of visual styles that we see on the small screen (*see* John Wyver, p. 160 below), but a glance at the television schedules will show that the pessimists under-estimate the great range that is on offer – provided you are prepared to hunt for it. It includes 8mm film home movies and vintage black and white television programmes. It ranges from the static beauty of the documentary series *Beyond the Clouds*, superbly shot on super-16 by wildlife cameraman turned director Phil Agland, to the wobbly amateurish quality of *The Big Trip*, a travel programme shot on High-8 camcorders; from the sophisticated animation of *Wallace and Gromit* and the high-tech whizz and glitter of *Gladiators*, to the spectacular and intimate nature photography of a wildlife series, expanding human vision with unprecedented images such as those from miniaturised cameras attached to migrating birds. We have had programmes that show the inside of the human body, and others that observe the world from outer space. Whatever else is said of Oliver Stone's *Natural Born Killers*, a cinema film unlikely to be shown on television because of the violence of its subject, at least it celebrated the quality of the image.

A love of the image is not new. In Moscow in 1929 Denis Kaufman, known as Dziga Vertov, a name he chose because it sounded like the incessant cranking of a camera turned by hand, made *Man with a Movie Camera*, the film in which the camera takes a bow. He was determined to use 'every cinematic technique, every cinematic invention, every device and method' for this documentary of urban life in the Soviet Union. Determined to exploit to the full the resources of the camera, pushing it beyond what the human eye could perceive, he wrote,

> I am the cinema-eye. I am a mechanical eye. I, a machine, can show you the world as only I can see it. From today I liberate myself forever from human immobility. *I am in perpetual motion*, I approach and move away from objects, I creep up to them, I climb on to them, I move alongside the muzzle of a running horse, I tear into the crowd at full speed, I run before the fleeing soldiers, I tip over on to my back, I ascend with aeroplanes, I fall and rise together with falling and rising bodies. . . . My way leads to the creation of a fresh perception of the world. And this is how I can decipher a world unknown to you.
>
> (Enzenberger 1972–3)

The modern reader will recognise many of the shots Vertov describes here. Some of them have become clichés in the intervening years, but the exuberance of this description reflects an enthusiasm for the surprise of seeing things in a new way, the sheer pleasure of the inventive image. Of course Vertov was criticised, notably by the greatest filmmaker of his generation, Sergei Eisenstein, who called some of his tricks 'unmotivated camera mischief' (Michelson 1984: xxi). That debate between the two virtuosos of early Soviet cinema stakes out positions that are still defended, and will underlie much of the information presented in this book as we consider different forms of technology and what it is possible to do with them. Are there rules appropriate to each genre, so that what you do with the camera must be 'motivated' by the structures of the genre? Or does anything go? Is 'camera mischief ' still OK?

All of the differences discussed below create *meaning* of some sort or another. Every difference, whether it be a difference of acting style, a difference of camera angle, a graininess in the image or a difference in sound quality, carries its own sets of implications, connotations and meanings. Part of the pleasure of both making and watching television is in the fluidity of these meanings (Fiske 1987: 65).

Cameras, film stock and formats

All cameras used in making television programmes have a lens to resolve the image. Some record that image on film of one sort or another, just as in the early days of cinema; others produce an electronic image which may be either recorded on videotape or transmitted live. The image may be resolved in either a digital or an analogue mode.

A camera for a television programme can range from a Hi-8 camcorder carried in a beach bag, to a bulky 35mm camera mounted on a crane that needs a crew of ten or more to control it. Each type of camera is linked to a sound recording system so that the picture and the sound may be synchronised (*see* Chapter 6, Sound, p. 77 below). Below we list some of the most common types of camera and their mode of recording, together with the types of film stock and tape formats they are designed to use.

Film formats

For all film formats, the perforated film stock passes behind the lens, where it is held momentarily in position to create a static frame. For British television this is at a rate of twenty-five frames per second. The image is recorded in the film emulsion in a photo-chemical process. Several different gauges, based on the width of the stock, are in use, as are both black and white and colour stocks. For most of them, a negative image is produced in the camera, which is then sent to specialised laboratories to be processed and printed (*see* Technologies and contexts, p. 93 below).

8mm. The old home movie format, common before domestic camcorders were marketed, used an 8mm colour film stock. Super-8 is a variant in which the frame size is bigger. The film may or may not have a magnetic stripe down the side to record sound simultaneously. Sometimes there is a microphone attached to the camera. The film is 'sent away' to industrial laboratories for processing.

Although 8mm is intended for amateur use, the results may be valued for their texture and their low definition, especially by those who are interested in avant-garde filmmaking, or who are seeking particular effects such as grain, wobbliness and crudity of colour. Perhaps some of the most frequently seen, and almost certainly the most intensely studied of 8mm footage, is that shot by home movieist Abraham Zapruder, showing the assassination of US President John F. Kennedy in Dallas in 1963.

16mm. The lightweight professional format. A 16mm Arriflex or Aaton camera was regularly used by documentary crews for observational filming before the use of videotape became common, and is still favoured by camerapeople who prefer the quality of film to that of tape. The introduction of cameras light enough to be carried on the shoulder in the early 1960s gave rise to a new and urgent documentary style developed by Robert Drew and Richard Leacock in the US, as 'direct cinema', and in a completely different way by Jean Rouch in France, as 'cinéma vérité' (*see* Current documentary genres, p. 154 below). Fast 16mm colour stocks have been developed and refined in the years since Drew and Leacock and their associates hassled the manufacturers to make their basic black and white more flexible. Now there is a very wide range of high-quality stocks in a variety of speeds and latitudes, their quality hardly distinguishable from the larger 35mm format.

Figure 9 Diane Tammes filming with a 16mm Aaton camera for *Just Like Coronation Street* for Channel Four
Courtesy Partners in Production

Super-16. A modified 16mm camera, with a lens that covers a larger area of the negative. This is achieved by eliminating the sprocket holes on one side of the film. It gives a 40 per cent increase over the normal 16mm format and hence a higher quality. It produces a letterbox-shaped image, which, on the standard television set, is shown with a black space above and below. Newer television sets are made in the wide-screen format.

35mm. Now used for quality dramas and features, where smooth movements and clean, steady camerawork are expected. In the early days of television even news and current affairs were shot on cumbersome 35mm cameras. More recent models are much lighter and easier to hand hold.

Electronic cameras and videotape

Cameras which record on videotape may be 'camcorders', which combine the camera and recorder functions, or the two functions may be separated with the signal conveyed by a cable. The 'front end' includes the camera lens, while the recorder holds the tape which records picture and sound. This may be on the far side of the room in which the filming is happening, or it may be some distance away in a studio gallery, where the quality is monitored by video and sound engineers. In contrast with film, electronic modifications are made in the generation of the signal before it gets recorded. In using film there is a choice of stock to obtain different effects, but when shooting on tape, the effects are electronically manipulated.

Sebastian Buccheri

Figure 10 Camerapeople Terry Flaxton and Nick Barrett filming with Hi-8 cameras, Maxine Blake holding the microphone boom. On location in Coventry with the production *Blazed*
Courtesy Young People Now and the National Youth Agency

Hi-8. The 8mm videotape camcorder was developed for home movies. This is easy to handle domestic technology. There are, however, different qualities of Hi-8, from the simplest mass market models to those intended for television use. The sound is recorded alongside the image on the same tape. Usually there is a microphone mounted on the camera, but this tends to be too far away from the subject to produce good quality sound. The latest versions have a facility to plug in a microphone which can then be moved around separately from the camera. The development of Hi-8 by the BBC Community Programme Unit for the use in the *Video Diaries* programmes in the early 1990s gave rise to a new genre and a completely new 'look' on television, in which the roughness of the image gives its own sense of spontaneity.

Miniaturised cameras. Concealed in the lapel or in a briefcase, these are used for hidden camera work, when the subject is unaware that filming is taking place. Stringent regulations control their use. An early example was BBC Bristol's *Black and White*, which revealed with dramatic effect the unspoken and often implicit colour prejudice surviving in 1980s Britain. *World in Action*'s series on homelessness, *No Fixed Abode*, opened many people's eyes to the experience of being on the street. Channel Four's *Undercover Britain*, is a series which depends on the use of hidden cameras (*see* Current documentary genres, p. 154 below).

Other tape formats. There is a variety of different tape formats below broadcast quality, which have tended to be developed and then become obsolete very quickly. They include VHS, like the tapes used in domestic video cassette recorders (VCRs), super-VHS, U-Matic, and High Band U-matic. Many of these are used for non-broadcast and sponsored videos, both because they are cheaper and because some companies and colleges have invested in cameras and other equipment and continue to use them.

Betacam. Usually referred to as Beta. This is the standard tape format. The SP version is broadcast quality. Cameras may be of the camcorder type, or the front end may be separate from the recorder, and indeed, may be linked to recorders of other formats, such as U-matic.

Studio camera. Transmits its signal live or to broadcast quality videotape within the studio complex. A big studio may be equipped with three to five cameras, each with its own operator.

Automatic studio cameras. These are computer controlled. Smaller studios, like those used for the news, usually operate with robotic cameras, remotely controlled, which means that the operator is separated from the camera. These camera can be pre-programmed through the studio gallery. They include sky cameras, mounted in the ceiling of the studio – like those used on *Gladiators*.

Outside Broadcast camera (OB). This is part of an Outside Broadcast complex, including mobile studios, editing and broadcasting facilities.

Digital recording

Traditional filming is in the analogue mode in which the image is reproduced on the film or tape as an undivided whole. This means that every time it is transferred from film to tape or from one tape to another, quality is lost. The digital mode breaks down the signal into discrete elements, rather like morse code breaks down letters into dots and dashes. This means that the image does not lose quality, however often it is taken to pieces, copied and then reconstituted.

Digitisation may be introduced at various points in the recording process. For example, either end of a camera may be digital, so that a digital front end may feed into an analogue recorder.

Choice of format

Choice of format is more often than not a pragmatic one, controlled by decisions already made by the programme series, or by the equipment available. Despite the easiness and availability of tape stocks, many programme makers continue to prefer film for its wider range and finer quality. If the decision is to shoot on film, there is a wide range of film stocks available.

Film stocks

Film stocks have two aspects, namely speed and latitude:

- The speed indicates their sensitivity to light. A faster film needs less light than a slower one, but it tends to have a 'grainier' effect.

- The latitude indicates the range of light conditions over which the stock can produce a usable image.

The choice of stock and the exposure given – i.e. the amount of light allowed in through the lens by controlling the aperture through the f-stop – work together to create the desired effect. A cameraperson may be looking for a harsh contrast, with deep blacks, or may want a softer effect, with detail in the shadow. These differences can be obtained with different stocks. The fact that some film stocks have a very wide latitude – as much as seven stops, does not mean that the cameraperson can afford not to be accurate on exposure (*see* Nick Hale, p. 73 below for more on choice of formats).

The formats are constantly developing. For example, a digital memory in an electronic camera can be set up to 'dial in' the characteristics of different film stocks. As usual, aesthetic choices and changing technology are working together.

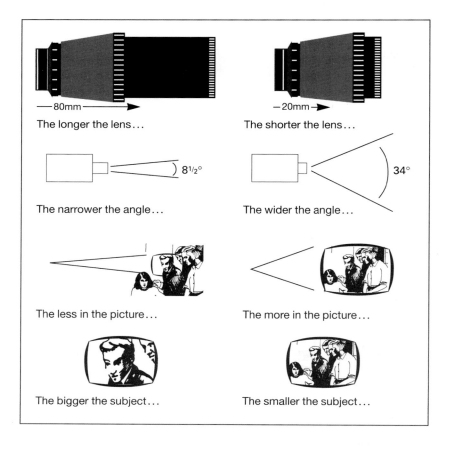

Figure 11 The relationship between focal length and horizontal angle of vision

Film stock manufacturers, Kodak, now speak of 'motion picture imaging' since, especially with the coming of digital technology and computer controls, video and film are becoming more closely interrelated.

Lenses

With all cameras, the use of different lenses produces different types of shot and different sets of relationships between background and foreground figures within the frame. Lenses on studio cameras are described in terms of the angle of vision; lenses on film cameras are described in terms of their focal length. The effect is the same:

- The longer the lens, the narrower the angle of vision – or 'angle of acceptance' – the less you will get in the picture, so the larger the individual subjects will be. A long lens is known as a telephoto.

- The shorter the lens, the wider the angle of vision, the more you will get in the picture, so the individual subjects will appear smaller. Short lenses are referred to as wide angle.

- A telephoto lens will give a crushed-up effect between a foreground figure and the background.

- A wide-angle lens will give a wide panorama behind exactly the same sized foreground figure. If you use a telephoto to produce a close-up head,

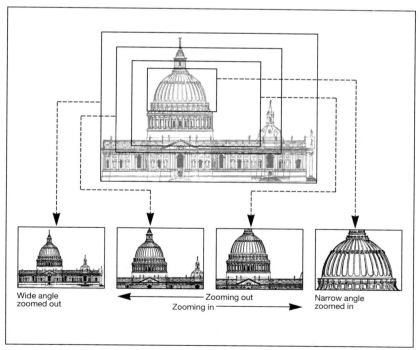

Wide angle
zoomed out

Zooming out

Zooming in

Narrow angle
zoomed in

Figure 12 Zooming in progressively fills the screen with a smaller section of the screen, narrowing the lens angle and increasing the focal length. Zooming out reveals more of the scene and widens the angle

the camera will need to be further away than if you use a wide angle. However, the face will appear differently for each of the two lenses. The wide angle will distort the image by spreading out the features. Horror movies and scary children's programmes use this distortion to great effect, which can be pushed even further by using the ultra wide-angle fisheye lens. Between these two extremes, the standard lens gives a relationship between foreground and background which is close to normal vision.

- A zoom lens is a single lens with variable focal lengths. The size of the figure in shot changes as the lens is zoomed in or out. A zoom lens tends to be described by the ratio between its longest and shortest focal length, e.g. a 'ten to one' has a zoom ratio of ten. Similarly a 'ten by twenty-five' is a zoom whose minimum focal length is 25mm and longest multiplies that by ten, i.e. 250mm.

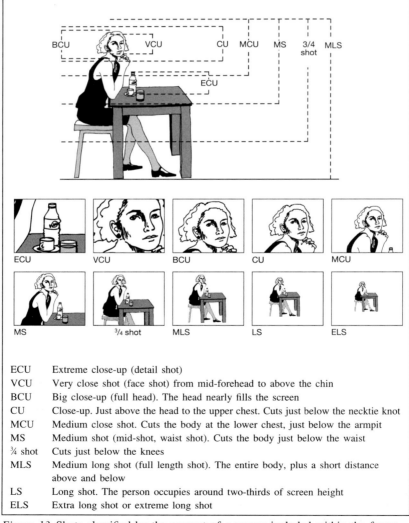

ECU	Extreme close-up (detail shot)
VCU	Very close shot (face shot) from mid-forehead to above the chin
BCU	Big close-up (full head). The head nearly fills the screen
CU	Close-up. Just above the head to the upper chest. Cuts just below the necktie knot
MCU	Medium close shot. Cuts the body at the lower chest, just below the armpit
MS	Medium shot (mid-shot, waist shot). Cuts the body just below the waist
¾ shot	Cuts just below the knees
MLS	Medium long shot (full length shot). The entire body, plus a short distance above and below
LS	Long shot. The person occupies around two-thirds of screen height
ELS	Extra long shot or extreme long shot

Figure 13 Shots classified by the amount of a person included within the frame

Types of shot

Shots classified by content

Shots may be described according to how they divide up their subjects, in other words by the amount of person included within the frame (*see* Figure 14).

When more than one person is included within the frame, they may be referred to as two shots, three shots and so on, up to 'crowd shots'.

A shot with a wide-angle lens which includes a broad view of the action is called a wide shot.

Certain aesthetic preferences have controlled what tends to be seen as an acceptable framing for routine use. Although such rules are often broken, the breaking of them usually serves to draw attention to the convention.

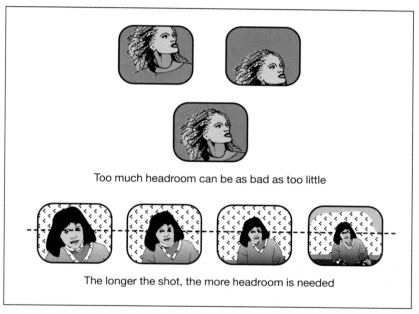

Too much headroom can be as bad as too little

The longer the shot, the more headroom is needed

Figure 14 Framing

Shots classified by camera angle

To achieve the desired angle within the frame, the camera must be placed at the appropriate level. Shots are described according to the possible positions of the camera in relation to normal eye level.

Viewpoints carry their own emotional impact and influence the way subjects are seen. If the camera is at at eye level, the gaze of the person within the frame meets that of the audience. Low-angle or high-angle shots

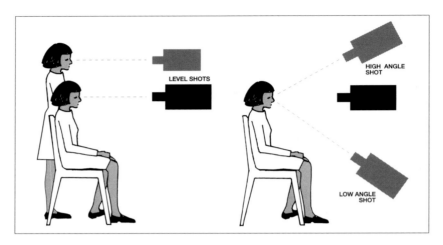

Figure 15 Camera angles

each create a specific effect. If the camera is low, looking up, the audience has the impression of a dominant character towering over them. In the Channel Four programme *Knee High*, the camera simulated the world view of a two-year-old, by remaining at the toddler's eye level, about 2 feet from the ground. For extreme low angles, such as those in *Citizen Kane* (1941) – a film which is in itself a university course for cinematographers – Orson Welles needed help from the set builders. For the notorious shots showing Kane looming over his wife against an expanse of ceiling, the stage itself was built up, allowing the camera to be positioned well below floor level (Kael 1971). If the camera is high, looking down, the character appears diminished within the frame. The angle increases a sense of their vulnerability.

Hollywood *film noir* of the 1930s and 1940s experimented with camera angles which derived from German expressionist cinema of the 1920s. In the Soviet Union, documentary filmmaker Dziga Vertov and others were experimenting with the medium of film itself. Their aim was to 'make the image strange'. One way of doing this was to show familiar things from unfamiliar angles. 'Always avoid the navel position', they declared. By contrast the British documentarist Edgar Anstey felt that the most straightforward way of shooting was the fairest to those he was showing. In his film *Housing Problems* (1935), he and Ruby Grierson pioneered the interview form. 'We always had the camera four feet off the ground (i.e. at eye level)', he wrote, 'because it was not our film.'

Shots classified by camera movement

Camera movements reframe a scene as it develops. This gives a very different effect from the movement of figures within a static frame. In a drama, one of the jobs of the director is to design the movement of the actors in interaction with the movement of the frame. Camera movements are described as 'motivated' when they follow an action or are prompted by an event within the scene – for example, a pan may follow a character as they cross the room; a tilt down may follow the direction of the character's gaze as they notice something on the floor; a track accompanies two characters as they walk together. A camera movement which follows no logic but its own is described as 'unmotivated'.

Static shots. A director may decide to keep the camera still and to move the characters within the frame. When the camera comes to rest after a series of moving shots, or when a film is composed without camera movement – Patrick Keiller's *London* (1994) and Chantal Akerman's *Jeanne Dielman, 23 Quai du Commerce, 1080 Bruxelles* (1975) are two very different examples – a lack of movement can have a striking effect.

Pans and tilts. When the camera head makes a pivoting movement from side to side, it is described as a pan; when it pivots up or down, it is a tilt.

Tracking. A movement which takes its name from the tracks, similar to railway tracks, laid on the ground to take the wheels of the dolly on which the camera is mounted. The use of tracks ensures a very smooth movement, but a 'tracking shot' may be any travelling shot in which the camera is moving along with the action.

Crabbing. A sideways movement.
These movements are achieved largely through different kinds of camera mountings. These include (starting with the largest):

A dolly or a crane. Mounting on a dolly will allow for controlled tracking; the addition of a crane means that rising and descending movements become possible, too. The opening shot of Orson Welles' *Touch of Evil* (1958) is a virtuoso use of a moving camera choreographed with developing action over two and a half minutes.

The bigger the mounting, the bigger the camera crew required to operate it. The crew will be under the control of a lighting cameraperson or cinematographer who is in charge of the overall look of the film. There will be a camera operator who, as the name suggests, actually works the camera; a focus puller, whose job is to follow focus on moving characters, by changing the focus setting of the lens as a shot develops; a clapper/loader, whose job is to mark the shots with a clapper board and also to reload the camera magazines with film; and at least one grip – the person who controls the dolly, moving it along so gently that no jolt or movement will be visible in the shot.

A tripod is part of the regular equipment of a cameraperson. A good tripod is stable with a fluid 'head' on to which the camera is mounted. This gives a steady, controllable frame, so that a great variety of movements may be made without unwanted jolts or judders. When there is only one assistant cameraperson, it is their job to move and place the tripod, as well as reload the camera, and when necessary, operate the clapperboard.

A hand-held camera usually means it is securely balanced on the shoulder of the cameraperson, although some cameras, such as a tiny Hi-8, are small

Figure 16 Steadicam: The Steadicam enables the camera operator to achieve rock-steady pictures even while moving or shooting from difficult positions

enough literally to be held in the hand. A hand-held – or rather shoulder-held – camera may be kept rigid, as if on a tripod, or may make a great variety of fluid and informal movements as the operator moves it around in imitation of the human eye. Sometimes derisively referred to as 'wobbly-scope', this is a modified version of the 'direct cinema' style evolved by Richard Leacock and the Maysles brothers in the United States in the 1960s. They aimed for a fluid set of movements, which need not be arbitrarily cut up in the editing room. In their film *Primary* (1960), John F. Kennedy's campaign for the Democratic nomination as President, a famous shot follows him into the convention hall, through the assembled delegates and up on to the platform in a single, mobile take (Winston 1995: 152).

Steadicam. This mounting straps the camera supports to the body of the operator, and incorporates a device which keeps the image steady. Phil Redmond was the first to introduce the use of steadicam into British television for video-tape shooting. When the quiet, suburban Brookside Close was converted into

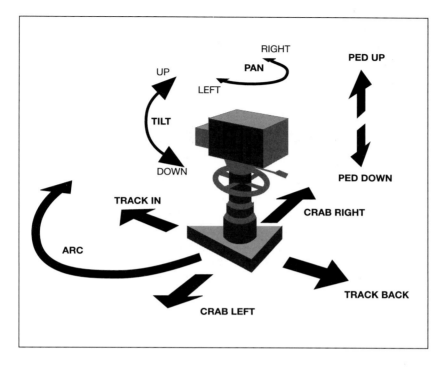

Figure 17 Studio pedestal movements

a set for a new soap opera in 1982, this was part of his strategy to create a naturalistic style, filmed within the four walls of real houses (*see* Phil Redmond, p. 223 and Beryl Richards, p. 239 below, on working on *Brookside*).

Other mountings. In the early days of cinema, cameras strapped to the front of trains gave exciting travelling views to the audiences at the variety shows where they formed part of the bill. Travelling shots may use any form of mounting, from aerial shots taken from a helicopter, to road shots from the window of a car, or simply a camera operator pushed in a wheel-chair to achieve greater steadiness of movement.

A studio pedestal. The standard studio mounting is a solid pedestal, trailed by substantial cables which carry the signal. Its various mountings ensure that it has great flexibility of movement.

On a rostrum. For animation shooting or for filming stills, a camera may be permanently mounted facing an illuminated desktop.

Shots classified by usage

From the point of view of the director and editor, shots have another set of classifications, which refers to their eventual use in the programme:

Master shot. A wide shot in which an entire sequence is played out. Close shots and other angles may be shot later and assembled into the master shot. This is an objective shot, taken from the point of view of an imaginary viewer outside the scene.

Point of view shot. A shot from the viewpoint of one of the actors in a scene. This is described as a subjective shot.

Over the shoulder shot. This may usefully link two or more participants in a conversation, as a partial view of the back of each person's head while the other is speaking reminds us of their presence.

Cutaway. A shot that is not directly connected to the content of a scene, but which may be inserted to speed up the editing or to cover a hiatus in the action. During a routine interview, shots of the interviewer or of the interviewee's hands, of objects around the room, or of objects to which the interviewee is referring may be used to edit an hour or so of material into a manageable 10 minutes or whatever length is required.

The director's concerns

Alan Wurtzel and John Rosenbaum use the concepts of 'video space' and 'audio space' to describe the imaginary worlds created for television viewers:

> The only measure of reality for the television viewer is what they see and hear through the television receiver. A 'real life' event that unfolds before the cameras does not exist for viewers until that reality is translated through the television realities and on to their sets.
>
> (Wurtzel and Rosenbaum 1994: 39)

Those video and audio spaces, the overall view which holds together the myriad of inputs that go to make up a television programme, are conjured up by the work of the director.

Programmes are usually made up of relatively self-contained sequences. A sequence will typically be shot in a single location, and will have some form of internal coherence. Bearing in mind that each shot is only a small segment of the sequence, thought must be given to how the shots will cut together in the editing room to create the whole.

As well as creating the emotional and aesthetic atmosphere of each sequence, the director has certain practical tasks:

Preparation and planning

The patterning of shots must be pre-prepared, and the shooting schedule planned and timed (*see* Robin Small on Production management, p. 38 above). In a drama, the sequence will be carefully prepared and sometimes storyboarded beforehand. A documentary is more likely to be more spontaneously shot and constructed at the editing stage. For the greatest efficiency, shots will inevitably be filmed in a different order from that in which they appear in the final sequence. Since every movement of the camera involves movement of the lights, microphones and other paraphernalia, and entails a huge disruption, it is more efficient to take all necessary shots from a single camera set up at one go. That may mean that if the beginning and end of a programme happen in the same location – beside a river, on top of a tower block – the beginning and end will both be shot at the same time.

The director must also fulfil the following functions:

- Ensure that enough shots are provided while a sequence is being filmed so that there is a degree of flexibility in the editing room. It is important to provide cutaways, wide shots and covering material. In a documentary situation where the crew have to keep up with fast-moving action, say in a hospital ward or a police station, the cameraperson must be briefed about what sort of cutaways are needed, as they, too, must be caught while the action is happening.

- Ensure continuity throughout the sequence (*see* Visual grammar, p. 64).

- Oversee the technical production of the scene. In an established organisation with regular procedures, say sports programmes or an ongoing soap opera, the picture and sound quality will also be monitored by a crew of specialised technicians. They will also check for technical problems, such as unwanted microphones in shot or lapses in continuity, but ultimately these are the director's responsibility.

- Make sure the crew are properly briefed so that they can make their own creative contribution.

- Control the number of takes of any given shot. Apart from some forms of news and observational documentary shooting, it is customary to repeat the action several times to ensure that the desired result is achieved. An actor may forget their lines; an aeroplane may pass overhead obliterating the sound; a microphone shadow may be seen in shot; or the director or cameraperson may simply think the whole thing could be done more effectively. Even in spontaneous interviews, where, for example, the interviewee feels they could express a particular idea better or temporarily runs out of ideas, the director will call 'cut' and another take will be set up.

Visual grammar

For a smooth flow which does not jolt the audience out of the illusion of continuity, certain conventions are followed. These are devices by which the actual space which exists between each shot is smoothed out in the finished film and in the audience's mind. It has often been stressed that such continuity is indeed an illusion.

The 180 degree rule

Crossing the imaginary 'line' which runs between the characters in a scene and the observing camera will involve a sense of discontinuity, as the person facing right will suddenly appear to be facing left, and hence away from

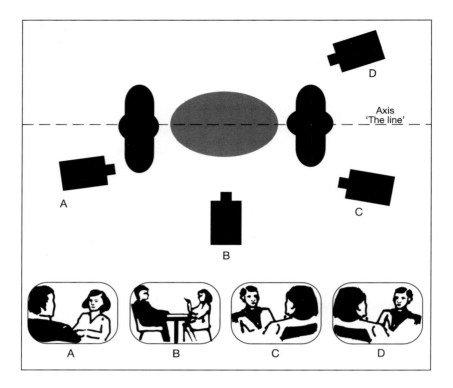

Figure 18 'Crossing the line': the three images from camera positions A, B and C all intercut because the characters maintain their screen directions. Position D, however, has 'crossed the line'. It reverses the characters' eyelines and so does not intercut with the other angles

their companion. In a football match, all the cameras must be on the same side of the pitch, or else there will be confusion about which team is running in which direction. If the 'line' is crossed, a cutaway will be necessary to bridge the gap, or a shot in which a camera movement allows the audience to observe the participants in the scene changing position in relation to each other. With hand-held, observational shooting, camera movements are often fluid and undefined. These conventions then come into play at the editing stage, when the editor selects which sections of the shots to cut together.

Similarly, if several shots show a character travelling, say walking along a street, they must consistently enter camera right and exit camera left, or else there will be the impression of reverse or random movement.

Shot, reverse-shot structure

This is a basic sequence in classical continuity narrative construction. For example, shots of two characters engaged in dialogue will favour first one and then the other. The camera will frame on one person facing right and on the other facing left. Edited together, this gives the illusion of two people facing each other, and enables cutting back and forth between the characters who appear to be interacting. The audience 'read' the alternation as a link between them, whether or not they were actually together when the shots were taken. For example, an interviewer's questions will often be filmed when the interviewee is no longer in the room. In this case it will be important to ensure that the eyelines of the two characters match. If their eyes do not appear to engage with each other, the effect is strange and disorienting. This is the sort of detail a good cameraperson will be able to recognise.

Continuity

To maintain continuity between shots the director must ensure that:

- Visual detail is consistent. For example, clothing should not be rearranged between shots – jackets should stay open or done up; hair should not suddenly change its style; spectacles should be consistently on or off; objects in the room should not change their position, and so on.

- Movement is continuous. A hand gesture begun in the long shot should be completed in the close-up; an entrance through a door should not show the door knob being turned in both the exterior and interior shots; if a character is running when they leave one shot, they should not be walking in the next – unless, of course, continuity is deliberately broken to achieve a special effect. A turn of the head, a gesture, the crossing of a car across the action temporarily blanking out the screen may all serve to carry over, to 'suture' in clinical terms, to stitch up the real gap between the two shots, and to make the audience perceive them as continuous.

There are forms of discontinuous editing, such as parallel editing, which must also be prepared at the shooting stage (*See* Styles of editing, p. 99 below).

The principle of motivation

A movement within a scene may prompt, or 'motivate', a camera movement or a cut. The camera may pan to follow the glance of a character, or the editor may cut to the object the character has noticed.

An intensification of emotion may motivate a cut to a closer shot, feeding the audience's desire to observe more closely. Classic examples are the *Man Alive* series, edited by Desmond Wilcox in the 1960s, and the *Face to Face* interviews, conducted by John Freeman in the 1960s and revived by Jeremy Isaacs in the 1990s.

The patterning of shots

Too many shots taken from a similar distance from the subject are tiring for the audience. Usually a wide shot will establish the scene, showing something of the setting and ambience, followed by closer shots, so that the characters' facial expressions become clearer and the viewer can follow their thoughts as well as their actions.

Two shots on the same person should involve a significant change of angle. A minimal change is read as a 'jump cut', an awkward twitch rather than a deliberate perceptual shift.

(*See* The processes of editing, p. 97 below, for a consideration of these principles from the point of view of the editor.)

References

Baehr, H. and Dyer, G. (eds) (1987) *Boxed In: Women and Television*, London: Pandora RKP

Enzenberger, M. (1972–3) 'Dziga Vertov', *Screen*, Vol. 13, No. 3, Winter

Fiske, J. (1987) *Television Culture*, London: Routledge

Kael, P. (1971) *The Citizen Kane Book*, London: Secker & Warburg

Michelson, A. (ed.) (1984) *Kino-eye: The Writings of Dziga Vertov*, London: Pluto Press

Winston, B. (1995) *Claiming the Real: The Documentary Film Revisited*, London: BFI

Wurtzel, A. and Rosenbaum, J. (1994) *Television Production*, 4th edn, New York: McGraw-Hill

5 Lighting and the cinematographer

··

Visions of light

The first and unavoidable principle of lighting is that there should be enough illumination for the image to register on the film or tape. Nowadays, film stocks are so sensitive that it is possible to find ways of shooting under a wide variety of circumstances without adding to the available light sources. Most lighting for television programmes that are shot on location, whether a street exterior or someone's home or workplace, will draw partially on the light that is available, whether from sunlight or from artificial sources. By contrast, a studio gives total lighting control. It has an array of light sources already in place, mounted in ceiling gantries and on movable stands.

Over the history of cinema and then of television, different lighting styles have been used for dramatic effect. In the early days of the century, the move to Hollywood was partly determined by the brilliance and clarity of the year-long Californian sunlight, but filming out of doors lost its popularity as techniques became more sophisticated and specialist studios gave greater control over the design of sets and lighting. The variations on studio lighting which developed are part of the artistry of the moving image, and they constitute a rich body of work to which the makers of television as well as cinema still refer. In Germany, the expressionist films of the 1920s used a dramatic chiaroscuro, with intense and exaggerated black and white, using deep shadows and clear highlights. The style was taken up by Hollywood, influenced by the influx of German émigrés fleeing from Nazism, and developed into the celebrated style known as *film noir*. It has been imitated on television many times. In one of the few detailed studies of television production, Manuel Alvorado and Edward Buscombe give an account of how Thames Television recreated the style for their detective series, *Hazell* (Alvorado and Buscombe 1978). Soap operas and sitcoms have inherited the brighter and more even lighting used in the domestic melodramas of 1950s Hollywood.

In the early days of television the black and white tube could only tolerate a narrow range of contrasts, so dramatic lighting effects were of necessity less common than in the cinema. The development of faster film stocks in the 1960s and 1970s meant that documentary filmmakers of that time were excited by the possibility of shooting with minimal lighting, aiming to interfere as little as possible with the activity they were filming. Drama directors like Ken Loach, with his celebrated *Cathy Come Home*, emulated the style, to the extent that they were lambasted by the popular press and some television executives for producing something which looked too real to be fiction (*see* the comments by Tony Garnett, producer of *Cathy Come Home*, p. 132 below).

With the coming of colour, the *effects* produced by lighting, as opposed to the mere illumination of the scene, became both more difficult to deal with and broader in scope. The sheer volume of visual information in any given shot was now huge, with the colour temperature – the warmth or coldness, redness or blueness – of the light adding a whole new range of possible variations.

By the 1980s, both drama and documentary producers were experimenting with a much wider range of visual styles. Television drama had become more cinematic, and documentary was developing a 'deco-doc' style, interested in visual effects and reconstructions as well as actuality filming. The American Errol Morris, whose *Interrotron Stories* were shown on BBC2 in 1995, specialises in carefully lit interviews and reconstructions, first explored in his classic *The Thin Blue Line*. The BBC series *The Underworld*, recalling the lives of the gangs who terrorised the London underworld in the post-war years, lit its subjects in a dramatic *film noir* style, using lighting in the manner of a drama, to enhance the emotional and aesthetic effect. This time the producers came under criticism for glamorising their subjects.

The overall effect of lighting within a scene depends on the direction of the light and on the degree of contrast between the bright and the dark areas. The cinematographer may work with the art director to consider the effect of colour within the scene as well. As with all technical areas, lighting ranges from the simple exercise of common sense though to the sophisticated knowledge and sensitivity brought by the experienced cinematographer.

When shooting with very small crews, the cameraperson, helped by their assistant, is responsible for moving and fixing the lights, as well as for deciding where they are to be placed. But on most productions it is the specialist lighting electricians ('sparks') who take responsibility for the practicalities of rigging, wiring and making sure that electrical power is available on location.

Lighting: basic principles

Reasons for artificial lighting

To provide visibility. Both film and electronic imaging are less sensitive to light and less flexible than the human eye, so, in the majority of set ups, extra light is needed. It is often necessary to lower the contrast between the highest and lowest illumination levels in the scene, in order to give the desired range of contrast in the image. Film tends to reproduce over a wider brightness range than electronic recording.

For routine interviews, or documentary filming where the crew want to remain as unobtrusive as possible, the aim may be to use the minimum lighting necessary. Michael Rabiger points out that 'the discomfort caused by injudicious lighting serves to inhibit the nervous' (Rabiger 1992: 119) and that the heat can be as uncomfortable as the unusually brilliant light. People should be given the chance to get accustomed to the lighting, especially in their own homes.

To enhance the scene. Given that extra lighting is necessary, it can then be manipulated for emotional or aesthetic effect.

To provide information. The quality of light tells us something about time of day: twilight is very different from a morning light; moonlight from sunlight. It can tell us about location – the flashing neon of a twentieth-century city, the whiteness of a snowbound landscape. Lighting contributes to the creation of the spaces within a scene: the shadow from a window where actually no window exists: 'sunlight' streaming in through a door which in reality has nothing behind it but a 2 kilowatt light. It contributes to the illusion of three-dimensionality in the flat picture.

As a functional light within the scene. A door opens letting light through; a torch illuminates a dark corridor; a lamp is switched on. In Alfred Hitchcock's *Rear Window* (1954), the introduction of Grace Kelly is contrived through an elegant use of the soft illumination from table lamps. She illuminates her own face as she brightens the room of invalid James Stewart, by switching on three lamps, one for each of her three names.

To create effects which may be non-naturalistic or impressionistic: to heighten the atmosphere of a scene or to mark changes in mood or mode. Changes in lighting effects, say in a games show, accompanying a rock group or in a late night entertainment, may be used purely for visual pleasure.

Light sources

Available light, from windows, artificial interior lighting, lamps, etc.

Key lights. Scenes which are brightly lit and colourful have a low contrast factor and are referred to as high key. They may exploit the use of colour – as with the bright reds and yellows of breakfast time programmes. The assumption is that 'they suggest youth, energy and happiness' (VideoTec n.d.: 6). Low-key images have a high contrast factor and create a sombre and more dramatic mood. Large areas of darkness revealing no detail are contrasted with strong highlights and splashes of light.

- *High key:* low contrast (bright, cheerful, energetic)
- *Low key:* high contrast (sombre, dramatic)

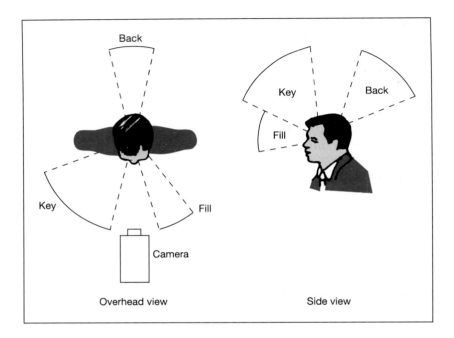

Figure 19 Three-point lighting

Three-point lighting. This basic lighting set up for a presenter, an interview or a simple set involves:

- *A key light* which provides the 'key' to the scene's appearance, defines the main shadows to be seen on the face. It is usually hard, providing clear, modelling shadows. A soft key gives a more glamorous, softer appearance. A shift in the position of the key may alter the lighting from naturalistic illumination to one with strange, unnaturalistic shadows.

- *A fill light* to reduce the harshness and contrast provided by the key. This will usually be a soft light, possibly softened even further by a diffusion filter. If lighting a single figure, it will usually be positioned below the eyeline. Some experienced women politicians have been known to insist on a low light for their interviews, so as to reduce the ageing effect of bags under the eyes. The low angle of the light can produce glints in the subjects' eyes which gives animation to their face. In a television studio, with lights suspended from a ceiling grid, a low position is not always possible, so a dark triangle may remain unlit beneath the chin.

- *A backlight.* A hard backlight can provide a highlight effect to the hair and shoulders, and separate the subject from the background. If it is diagonally opposite the key, it can give a balance to the shape of the face.

Bouncing light is light which is 'bounced' off a surface, either within the scene – say a light coloured wall – or outside it, where a sheet of white material could be held in the appropriate position. This gives an effect which is more diffused and general than direct lighting.

Note on continuity

Lights will inevitably be moved and lighting set ups adjusted between shots to provide the maximum effect. For example, as the camera moves in from a wide shot to a close shot, the light sources will also need to come closer, or else the face is likely to be underlit. Even so, an illusion of continuity must be maintained between the shots.

Light quality: intensity and colour

Hard and soft

Lighting is described as hard or soft depending on whether it gives shadows that are hard or soft edged.

- *Hard light:* the source is small in relation to subject, giving hard shadows
- *Soft light:* the source is large in relation to subject, giving soft shadows

Light spread: spot and flood

A spot is an intense, narrow angled beam of light. A flood or wide beam is a broader spread. Some lights are fitted with a Fresnel lens which enables a light to be adjusted between a wider or narrower beam. Side flaps, or barn doors, may be used to blank off part of the light and control its spread and direction.

Daylight and tungsten

There is a difference in colour bias between daylight and artificial (tungsten) light. If the two different sources are illuminating a single scene, coloured gelatine sheets on the windows and the light sources help match the blue of daylight with the redder quality of artificial lighting and bring the colour temperature into balance.

Colour conversion filters on the camera will affect the colour temperature of the whole scene. Electronic cameras have an adjustment which allows them to find an optimal colour rendition. Before shooting each scene the camera must be 'white balanced'. This means using a sheet of paper or some other white surface to 'tell' the camera what counts as white in these particular lighting conditions.

Gels, diffusers and reflectors

- *Gels:* Coloured gelatine sheets placed in front of the lights will create different intensities of reds, yellows and blues. Other colours and textures are available for effects.
- *Diffusers:* Flame-proof 'spun' fibreglass sheets fixed over the lamp, or some material such as tracing paper supported in a large frame, will diffuse the light, making it softer and reducing its intensity.
- *Reflectors* – including white umbrellas and huge circular white sheets – will add a filling of light, reflecting it gently back from its source.

Ginny Lindenbaum

Figure 20 Location filming in a young offenders' institution for the educational docudrama *Prison? Me? No Way!* Made by students and former students of the University of Humberside sponsored by HM Prison Service and Norwich Union General Insurance with assistance from Humberside and West Yorkshire Police Forces. Filming is on SVHS videotape and the room is lit with a redhead and a blonde.

Which lights?

The portable lights most frequently in use on location for programmes such as documentaries, interviews and short sequences are:

- *'External reflector'* or lensless spotlights, varying from 250 watt to 3 kilowatt. The most common are known as *Redheads* (800 watt) and *Blondes* (2,000 watt or 2kw). These are light and easily moved, mounted on stands or clipped on to a shelf or other object in the location.

- *HMI.* A single large intense light source, balanced for daylight, with a high light to heat ratio.

- *Sungun* around 250 watt, is a hand-held light which runs from belt batteries and can give an intense beam. Useful on location when other forms of lighting are impossible to set up.

Nick Hale: *cinematographer*

'A cameraperson is constantly working with innovation, although until it gets established an innovation can seem like a step backwards. John Schlesinger's remarkable black and white documentary *Terminus* (1961), about a day in the life of Waterloo station, used available light and a noisy 35mm camera which needed to be covered with a blimp for the conversation scenes. It was mostly made up of observational filming shot wild (i.e. without synchronised sound) and the sound-track was created in the cutting room. When colour was introduced, it was a great innovation, but the stock was so much slower at first, that we could not have made a film like *Terminus*.

When video came in, again it seemed like a backwards step, because the image had a much reduced dynamic range. The camera and the microphones all feed their signal into a recorder, so there was the additional problem of the linking cables. Video is now well established and more than half of what I shoot for television is on tape, but I still prefer film. It has a better image quality than the video formats available at the moment and the new, high-definition HDTV camera is still too cumbersome. Film gives more detail at both ends of the scale, in shade and in the highlights, and new emulsions are constantly being developed, balanced either for daylight or tungsten, which have very wide latitude. The choice of film stocks is huge, varying in speed, contrast and range.

You have to think harder when you're shooting on film because it costs more. When using tape, there is a temptation to shoot large quantities of material without pausing to consider what you're doing, such as long, rambling interviews which are hard to edit. Too much rushes material extends the editing process and increases the cost of post-production. Even so, there's a tendency just to keep on shooting, so the whole thing can become an exercise in getting through the schedule. On film it is different because you need to do much more research and pre-planning. The need to change the magazine when a roll of film is used up enforces a break which allows you to evaluate what is happening. For example, you can take time to consider whether the interviewee has said what you want them to say. Sometimes people decide to use tape because they haven't done enough decision-making beforehand.

The cameraperson must listen carefully to the brief from the director. It's not good enough to turn up on location and ask 'Where do you want the camera, guv?'. Of course, that may be the world weariness that comes from many years of routine work, and of having to cope with a series of new and inexperienced directors. But with modern techniques the crew needs to be briefed beforehand. As a cameraperson setting out to shoot a scene, I need to consider what sort of material I am expected to cover. To get the shots that are needed I need to know whether I am being asked to cover this scene as, for example, a news event. In that case I would record it from as many aspects as possible, knowing that I'm filming as if for posterity. On the other hand, I may be asked to express a particular point of view or look for a particular ingredient. The brief may be to film a demonstration with a view to observing how the police are dealing with it. In that case I would concentrate primarily on the police, rather than giving an even coverage.'

Nick Hale gives some examples from programmes he has worked on:

The Fishing Party A sequence of the family at Sunday lunch was shot with available light on 7292, the fastest 16mm colour stock available at the time. On film the highlights are not burnt out, as they would have been on video. Sometimes video cuts out altogether when it can't cope with the range of contrast in the scene, whereas film trails off gradually.

Making the Grade The schedule involved a considerable amount of movement between interior and exterior. Instead of changing stocks frequently, which would have meant loading each camera magazine with a different speed stock, I decided to use a fast stock in all the magazines and put a neutral density filter (ND) over the lens for the exteriors.

The School Kodak are producing new stocks all the time, and the new 7298 has a huge latitude. For this film I was able to do a single shot which started in the daylight and followed a character into a dimly lit corridor, where another character approached, in partial silhouette. In my view, scenes should not be over-lit. It's not necessary to reveal everything in full detail. It's wrong to think that it's not possible to shoot a scene if you can't get a light on the character's face. If the audience already knows what a character looks like, they are able to recognise their voice and shape so there's no reason why they should not be seen in silhouette.

Birds as Prey This one posed some challenging problems. These included an interior lit only by candles; birds filmed against a hot sky; and dawn shots where the sun rises in front of the camera. Inside the dimly lit hut I used three 12 volt lamps run off a car battery and a small 12 volt lamp which you can put on the top of the camera with a 5 watt or a 20 watt bulb to enhance but not destroy the candle-light. I don't like the powerful sungun that is so often brought out by camera crews in an emergency. I find that the light it gives is white and glaring, creating burnt out faces against a black background. I shot the candle-lit scene wide open between 1.3 and 2.8. The sequence was shot on prime lenses, without using the zoom.

Based on a talk given to the Sheffield Documentary Festival 1995. Nick Hale began as a film editor and has been responsible for shooting many television programmes.

A note on women as technicians

By the end of the 1970s there were hardly any women camerapeople, lighting engineers or sound recordists. Women have had a tough struggle in all areas of television, but these skilled technical grades have perhaps been those where their difficulty has been strongest. The tightness of entry into the industry, together with a macho conviction on the part of many men that technical work is a man's job, had effectively kept them out. When the current affairs programme *This Week* did a programme on abortion in 1975, it took weeks of letters and negotiations with the ACTT (since only members of the trade union could work on a television programme) to get permission to employ the experienced American Joan Churchill (Holland in preparation).

By the early 1980s, campaigns within the women's movement, within independent filmmaking and also within the ACTT, began to make a difference. The first woman cameraperson was employed at LWT in 1981 and the first woman on camera at ITN began work in 1985.

When the ACTT published its report on equal opportunities in 1975, the year of the Sex Discrimination Act, it showed on its cover a woman with a toddler on one hip and a camera on the other. Instead of recognising the intended message – that women have always been expected to carry heavy loads, provided they were associated with mothering and women's work – outraged male correspondents wrote that now we are expected to tolerate not only women on location but their children, too!

Women have needed to overcome the prejudice of crews who liked to be all boys together. They also had to show that being a good cameraperson did not depend on muscles and macho competitiveness. Men badly needed an education in equal opportunities. It was also important to provide training opportunities for young women whose schooling had tended to channel their interests away from the more technical side of things, and for whom entry into television was largely as secretaries and production assistants. By 1986 the situation had barely improved. ITCA figures showed 12 women camera operators out of 306, 8 female sound technicians out of 269, and 19 women engineers out of 1395 (Ross Muir 1988).

Although women are still very much in the minority, especially in jobs based on engineering, more women have, very gradually, moved into the technical grades. This has partly been the result of the expansion of education and training. The industry training scheme, ft2, recruits 50 per cent women (*see* Training and qualifications, p. 217 below). Most television organisations have equal opportunities programmes and equality officers and monitor their intake and promotion policies for discrimination against women as well as against ethnic minorities, people with disabilities and other disadvantaged groups. Many of the first generation of women camerapeople and sound recordists trained at the National Film School.

Today, the many respected women camerapeople working in television include director/camera Diane Tammes, who has produced prize-winning observational documentary series, including *Colluden*, which followed the work of an East London primary school at the time when the form of 'progressive' teaching it practised was coming under pressure from a traditionalist government. She pointed out that the battles are never completely won.

> Women producers support other women in many ways, but when it comes to the technical grades there is still an impression that a man will be more reliable. That's one reason why I went into production as well as shooting. Now, 80 per cent of the technicians I work with are women and I choose people who are good at their jobs. But even as you go through one door another door can close behind you, so it's important to look behind you as well as ahead to make sure that there are younger women coming up.
>
> (Tammes 1996, pers. comm.)

References

Alvorado, M. and Buscombe, E. (1978) *Hazell: The Making of a TV Series*, London: BFI

Gates, T. (1995) *How to Get into the Film and TV Business*, London: Alma House

Holland, P. (in preparation) *History of 'This Week'*

Rabiger, M. (1992) *Directing the Documentary*, 2nd edn, Stoneham MA: (USA) Focal Press

Ross Muir, A. (1987) *A Woman's Guide to Jobs in Film and TV*, London: Pandora

Ross Muir, Ann (1988) 'The status of women working in film and television' in L. Gamman and M. Marshment (eds) *The Female Gaze: Women as Viewers of Popular Culture*, London: The Women's Press

Skillset (1995) *Outline of NVQ/SNVQ Standards*, London: Skillset

Skillset (1996) *Careers Information Pack*, London: Skillset

VideoTec (n.d.) *Successful Lighting for Video: Study Guide*, London: Blueprint

6 Production techniques: sound

....

Television and the flow of sound

U nlike cinema, television began its life with the expectancy that its pictures would be accompanied by natural sound. We expect to see people speaking directly to us from the small screen, and we take it for granted that we will hear what they have to say. The powerful implications of this direct address were recognised by those who began television news in the post-war period. The earliest bulletins consisted of an anonymous voice accompanied by some rather uninspiring still images. Newsreaders were not permitted to be *seen* speaking to the cameras as it was thought that their facial expression might add a biased interpretation to the neutrality of the news. More recently, a similar fear of the visibly spoken word led to the surreal spectacle of Gerry Adams, the leader of Sinn Fein, the Northern Irish republican party, speaking always slightly out of sync to indicate that this was not his own voice we were hearing. For six years (1988–94) the government had imposed a broadcasting ban which forbad the direct broadcasting of Sinn Fein and other organisations associated with terrorism. The strongest effect of the ban was the mysterious dislocation of Gerry Adams' voice.

The flow of sound holds television programmes together, interweaving two major dimensions: the emotional appeal of music and the meanings carried by the human voice. Television is heir to radio, as much as cinema, theatre and music hall. The sense of many television programmes can be gathered by listening to the sound-track – while washing up or otherwise occupied – with only an occasional glance at the screen. Television is experienced as much as a form of 'company' (an extra voice in the corner of the room) as a visual medium that needs careful scrutiny. Whereas cinema is the object of the audience's 'gaze', television can be taken in by the occasional 'glance' (Ellis 1982: 164–5). The 'talking head' remains the basic building block of the television output. Major television genres, including news broadcasts, chat shows and programmes that range from David Attenborough's natural history travels to Jancis Robinson's wine course, are presenter-led, linked by a named and publicised individual, whose speech defines the programme and who addresses the audience intimately and directly. Other programmes, including current affairs such as *World in*

Action and many documentaries, are commentary-led. Such programmes are built up by a flow of speech, carrying a narrative or an argument. Below (p. 160) John Wyver speaks of his attempt to vary the conventional structure of the commentary for his series *State of the Art*.

The variety, flexibility, expressiveness and interest of the voice was developed by BBC radio over the 1930s. In the early days of the BBC, voices were formal, delivering 'standard', educated English with all the authority of a school teacherly medium. Indeed, 'BBC English' itself was recognised as the educated norm. But radio claimed to address the public at large, and some producers tried to broaden the range of voices that could be heard. Radio producer Olive Shapley has described her excitement when the mobile recording van was developed and, for the first time, microphones could be taken out into the streets to record ordinary people, talking in their own everyday style, introducing regional and working-class accents previously considered inappropriate for the airwaves (Shapley 1985).

As television established itself as the major public medium, the contest over which voices were suitable grew, if anything, more intense. For many years women's voices were thought to be too lightweight for the authority required from a newsreader (Holland 1987). Regional accents have only slowly crept into the 'serious' parts of national television. Dialects associated with working-class communities have tended to appear only in regionally based dramas such as *Boys from the Blackstuff*, *Making Out* or *Our Friends in the North*. When *Brookside* began it was criticised for its 'unremitting dialect' by the snobbish *Daily Telegraph*, which as recently as 1995 preferred the accents of BBC English to 'the strangled syllables of Liverpool or Rastafaria' (leader column 16 February 1995). It is still the respondents who speak with class or regional accents rather than the interviewers. Nevertheless the variety of voices on television has continued to increase and that increase has been linked both with changing expectations and with increasing flexibility in the technology that records the voices.

Sound of many sorts makes a crucial contribution to the mood, the emotional setting and the illusion of reality conveyed by a programme. Accompanying the flow of the human voice are the sound effects – the slamming door or the barking dog – either kept discreetly in the background or forming an important part of the action. Above all there is music, central to the broadcast experience. From the newest rock band to the most sophisticated classical or jazz performance, music is at the centre of the majority of entertainment programmes. It plays a part in almost every genre, setting a mood over opening titles, emphasising, intensifying emotion and moving a programme to its final climax. In a radical change from their austere beginnings, even the news headlines are now backed by music in some of the daily bulletins. Music forms a punctuation throughout the television day as well as offering its own particular pleasures.

Many different elements go to make up what Alan Wurtzel and John Rosenbaum (1994) describe as the 'audio space' that the makers of the television programme are creating to accompany the 'videospace' on the screen. Some are introduced at the filming stage, but many are added later at the editing and sound mixing stages.

The sound recordist's basic job is to get good quality sound, which matches from shot to shot. In general, the closer the microphone can get to the source of the sound, the richer and more flexible that sound will be. The choice of microphones and the decisions on where they should be placed are made for both aesthetic and acoustic reasons. Their positioning is always limited by the position of the camera and usually by the need to keep the microphone out of shot. However, as television conventions change and develop, so do the conventions concerning the use and visibility of microphones. In some genres it is perfectly acceptable to see a microphone in vision; in others the intrusion of even the shadow of a microphone boom will mean a call for another take. We expect a news reporter to be carrying a mike, and people stopped in the street, whether for random vox pop interviews (so called from the Latin *vox populi*, 'voice of the people'), or as celebrities pursued by the rat-pack, are not surprised if a microphone is thrust towards them. In audience talk programmes such as *Kilroy* or *100 Women* we occasionally see a microphone being swung around on the end of a boom, reaching towards the member of the audience as they begin to speak. These are programmes in which the presence of the audience watching at home is recognised by those on the screen, and it is accepted that these are knowledgeable viewers who understand the mechanics of the television medium.

Paradoxically, the more 'naturalistic' the genre, the more the techniques and tools of the television industry must be kept out of sight, and not interfere with the audience's perception of the programme. Television drama and many documentaries depend on the illusion that the action is taking place without the visible mediation of a television crew. Some dramas employ devices which ensure good quality sound by introducing a microphone into the narrative. CBS's *Northern Exposure*, for example, centres on a local radio station, K-Bear Radio. Chris, the announcer (played by John Corbett) speaks straight into a microphone which is part of the action. It allows him to provide narrative links and commentary on the story-line with a rich and intimate sound.

Sound engineers often complain that they are the last people to be considered in the design of a set or the planning of a shot. This is probably true, but the fact remains that sound is of crucial importance, whether we are considering the clarity essential for audience comprehension, or the overall package which makes the 'audio design' of a scene. Gerald Millerson lists possible problems with sound. It may be

> sibilant, muffled, distorted, of variable volume with random noise and distracting background sounds. [It] may not match the picture, voices may be inaudible or confusingly jumbled together. . . . Little wonder . . . that the professional audio man [*sic*] takes so much trouble to achieve the 'obvious'
>
> (Millerson 1990: 269)

Francis Ford Coppola's film *The Conversation* (1974) is a tribute to all sound engineers. It illustrates, within the context of a thriller, both the ways in which different sound elements in a single scene can be isolated and prioritised, and the way that a change in the interpretation of spoken words can effectively change the way an action is understood.

Types of television sound

Sound in relation to pictures

Synchronised (or sync) sound, recorded simultaneously with the pictures, is natural to television, which began as a live broadcast. Magnetic tape technology continues the capability to produce image and its accompanying sound simultaneously. Film, on the other hand, cannot but remember its early silent days. It produces only a visual image which has to be matched with its sound, recorded separately on magnetic tape. Over the years, various devices have evolved to keep the two 'in sync'. The famous clapper board, which has come to symbolise film itself, is used to begin each shot with a smart thwack, and provide an identifiable point so that the editor can match image and magnetic track at the head of each separate shot.

From the carefully controlled environment of the studio to the unpredictable circumstances of documentary location shooting, television sound can be classified by its relation to the image:

Synchronised 'natural' sound which is an intrinsic part of the content of the scene. Of central importance is dialogue and speech. The audience also expects to hear any sounds created by the visible action – footsteps, the movement of furniture, the opening and shutting of doors, cars passing in the background of a street interview and so on.

'Natural' sound which is *unwanted* for the meaning of the scene. One of the aims of sound recording is 'noise' reduction, i.e. the minimising of unwanted background sound, including noisy events that are invisible to the audience because they take place beyond the frame. In today's mechanised world it is virtually impossible to find a location free from unwanted sounds. There is invariably a pneumatic drill digging up the adjacent street, a barking dog or heavy traffic. Much valuable filming time has been wasted waiting for a noisy aeroplane to pass overhead or a truck to rumble beyond the range of the microphone.

Non-synchronised sound recorded on location. Additional sounds are usually recorded on location for use at the sound editing stage to enrich the final track. They include:

- *Buzz track*: A recording of the ambient noise, the background atmosphere, without speech or any other prominent sound. This provides a neutral background for the sound editor to bridge over any awkward gaps. 'Neutral' backgrounds differ to a remarkable extent from location to location, depending on weather conditions, traffic, central heating systems and a multitude of other factors.

- *Wild tracks*: Recordings of a wide range of interesting sounds made separately from the filming. They may include gentle noises, such as bird song and lapping water for a rural scene, or an urban cacophony – milk bottles clattering, traffic noise or babies crying. The aim is to get the best possible recording of each separate sound, so that they may be reassembled for best effect at the editing stage.

Non-synchronised sound recorded elsewhere. This may include:

- *Commentary or other 'voice-over' tracks*, recorded in a special commentary studio or in a suitably quiet place with minimal background noise.

- *Pre-recorded sound effects* of various types. These may be purchased from a sound library – which stores recordings of innumerable sounds, such as different makes of car revving up, changing gear, ticking over, etc.; crowds shouting or murmuring in many different languages; weather effects; animal noises; children playing. Despite the vast range of pre-recorded effects available, it is remarkably difficult to find exactly the one you want, hence the advisability of recording extra sound effects on location.

- *Specially recorded sound effects*: A cat miaows, a victim screams, a chair scrapes on the floor as someone stands up – all can be recorded quite independently, wherever the sound recordist can set up the suitable conditions. A wide range of effects gives the sound editor a great deal of freedom when composing the sound-track.

  Effects may be recorded in a special studio provided with equipment of various sorts, ranging from bells, hammers and creaking doors to different types of ground surfaces on which to make footsteps. Sand, gravel, parquet flooring, paving stones – to the practised ear they all sound different, to the non-practised ear something indefinable seems wrong if the sounds are incorrect. This is the specialised job of the footstep artist, who owns a variety of shoes and can tiptoe or stamp as required. Effects may also be created as 'spot effects' at the time of the dub, the final process when the different sounds are all brought together to make the final track.

- *Music*: This may be hired by the minute from a music library. It may be selected from well-known recordings and the copyright purchased for re-use. This is a complex and expensive process involving copyright clearance from many different individuals and companies, including composers, performers, the Performing Rights Society and the recording company, among others. The final option is music specially composed for the programme and recorded in a music recording studio.

The combination and orchestration of all these different types of sound is discussed under Sound editing (p. 103 below).

Sound quality

Perspective

The perspective of the sound must match that of the image, or credibility is threatened. An intimate, close-up voice coming from a distant figure in the frame may be used as a creative, non-naturalistic device, but on the whole the audience will expect to hear closer speakers sounding closer, and distant speakers sounding as if they are far away. Obtaining this effect is helped by the fact that, in a close-up shot, the sound recordist can position the microphone closer to a speaker and still remain outside the frame.

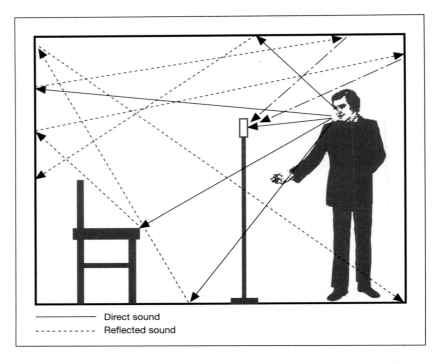

Figure 21 The acoustics of a room: As sound strikes it may be absorbed or reinforced by structural resonance. The reflected sound, now modified, adds to the original, augmenting or partially masking it

The acoustics of a room

Sound is not only direct, but multiply reflected from the surfaces of a room.

- *Reverberant rooms* have hard reflective surfaces. They tend to be 'live' and echoey, reflecting back wanted and unwanted sounds, such as footsteps, ventilation noise or scenery movement.

- *'Dead' rooms*, including television studios, have highly absorbent surfaces. Soft furnishings, carpets, curtains or special sound absorbing materials attached to the walls, muffle the sound.

Studios designed especially for sound recording will have a mixture of surfaces.

Sound presence

As a speaker moves closer, the sound of their voice changes in value and quality as well as in volume, becoming fuller and richer. This is described as sound presence. It is a function of the ratio between direct and indirect sound waves picked up by the microphone and depends on many factors, including the type of microphone used, the acoustics of the room or other location, and the volume of the sound source. Wurtzel and Rosenbaum give an American example of the effect of sound presence on audience perception, from NBC's *The Tonight Show*.

> From the show's beginning in 1954, its hosts – from Steve Allen and Jack Paar to Johnny Carson and Jay Leno – have used ribbon mikes placed on the desks in front of them. The guests have been covered by a boom microphone suspended overhead. The ribbon mike produces a richer, warmer, fuller sound than the boom mike. The result of the hosts using a ribbon microphone positioned nearby is that they have sounded 'closer' to the audience than the guests and seemed dominant among the performers on the show.
>
> (Wurtzel and Rosenbaum 1994: 47)

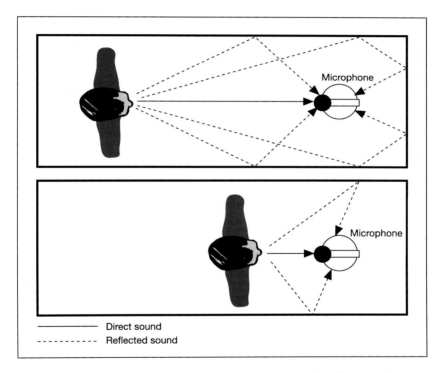

Figure 22 Sound presence increases as the subject-to-mike distance decreases because the microphone receives more direct sound waves and fewer reflected waves

Recording and 'audio-design'

There are three basic factors to be taken into account when setting out to record sound for a particular scene:

- The selection of the best microphone for the job
- The placement of the microphone
- Audio control

Microphone selection

In selecting a microphone, several aspects need to be taken into account. The aesthetic effect needs to be balanced against a consideration of the frequency response needed, the appropriate pick-up pattern, and whether the microphone is rugged enough to withstand the packing, unpacking and constant handling of some location shoots.

Examples include: the full frequency range of a condenser microphone is best for music; a highly directional mike may be chosen for an observational documentary in which the subjects are to be followed as they walk through a crowd; neck mikes (lavaliers) may be best for a discussion programme.

Microphones may be categorised in various ways. They have their own specifications (specs) which describe characteristics such as their frequency response and their pick-up pattern. We shall be concentrating on their use and referring to the technical factors only as they become relevant.

Some features of microphones which should be taken into account are listed below.

Physical features: shape, size, robustness, portability, etc.

Installation suitability: what mountings are available; can the microphone be concealed from vision? Radio microphones are useful because they have a miniature radio transmitter fitted into them, so they can be attached to characters or participants at some distance from the recorder.

Audio quality: the nature of the sound recorded, its fidelity and accuracy.

Sensitivity to a range of sound. This is a microphone's frequency response.

Directionality:

- *Omnidirectional microphones* are sensitive in all directions. They will pick up sounds equally from all sides, with a 360 degree sensitivity range. This can limit their usefulness, as they will pick up unwanted sounds from the direction of the film crew as well as from the subjects being filmed.

- *Unidirectional microphones* (with a cardioid, or a heart-shaped, pick-up pattern) are designed to suppress sounds which come from the non-sensitive parts of the mike. The use of a parabolic reflector, a metal or fibreglass dish about 3–4 feet in diameter with the microphone mounted at its centre, increases the directionality.

- *Highly directional microphones* (super-cardioid) are designed to pick up sound within a very narrow angle of acceptance. Mounted on a long tube, they are described as 'gun mikes' or 'rifle mikes' because of their appearance. They can be used at greater distances from the subject and may isolate the speech of an individual from that of the crowd. They are often used hand-held for observational or vérité filming, recording natural conversations in real situations and excluding many unwanted

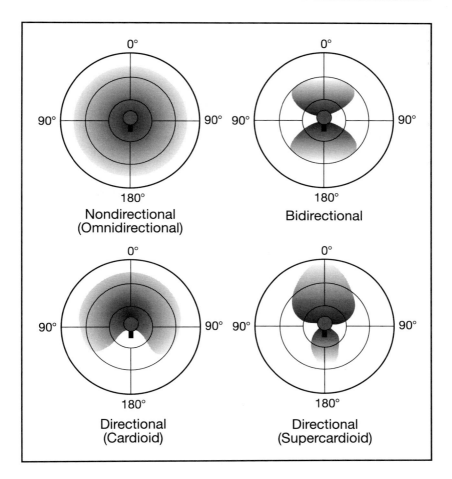

Figure 23 A polar diagram represents a microphone's pick-up pattern. The shaded sections show the area of audio sensitivity

sounds. The problem is that they must be pointed very precisely at the sound source or a weak or muffled sound will result.

Microphone placement

Some basic principles

- Place the microphone as close to the desired sound source as is practically possible so as not to pick up unwanted or reflected noise.

- Avoid feedback, that high-pitched screech that comes if a microphone faces the audio monitors, or speakers, in the studio.

- Avoid picking up unwanted ambient sound (even air conditioning may be able to be turned off).

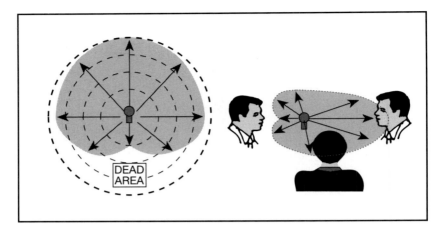

Figure 24 A cardioid pick-up pattern, which is a broad heart-shape, is insensitive on its rear side

● Avoid getting two nearby microphones picking up the same source. This leads to phasing, as they cancel each other out.

Microphones may either be visible in shot or invisible, kept beyond the edge of the frame.

In-shot, visible microphones

● *Miniature microphones:* These may be either 'lavalier' microphones suspended by a lanyard around the neck of the speaker or clip-on mikes attached to a lapel or tie. Their closeness to the speaker means that extraneous noise is excluded, but there is a danger of rustle from clothing or sudden movements. They will be attached to the recording machine by a long, concealed cable. Participants have to remember not to trip over it.

   Studio presenters also use an earpiece which allows contact with production staff in the gallery. While a presenter like Sheena McDonald is conducting her on-screen dialogue with the participants, she expects a second dialogue through her earpiece, as they offer advice on questions and give their prompts about how the interview might go.

   Miniature radio microphones have a small transmitter built in which sends a signal to a receiver and thence to the audio mixer. This gives greater flexibility of movement to the subjects but the sound is less predictable in quality. Also radio mikes do not allow for flexibility in sound perspective, as they always give a close-up sound.

● *Hand microphones*, designed to be held by the presenter or reporter, must be rugged, omnidirectional and have a mesh windshield to protect them from the sound of movement through the air and unexpected bumps and crashes. A hand microphone will either be cabled or will transmit a radio signal.

Figure 25 Sound recordist with a directional microphone covered with a wind gag, carrying a portable recorder. A director's training course at Granada Television
Courtesy Granada Television

- *In vision microphones* may be 'practical', playing a role within the scene, as in the radio station in *Northern Exposure.*

- *Stand microphones* are placed on a desk or table or in front of a performers such as stand-up comics or singers.

Out-of-shot, invisible microphones

Even when invisible to the camera, the microphone must be as close to the source as sound as possible. That may mean that it is concealed behind a vase of flowers or a piece of furniture or that it hovers just beyond the edge of frame. Invisible microphones may be:

- Hand-held by the sound recordist, as with the gun mike which is provided with a hand grip.

- Fixed around the set or location or invisibly attached to the speakers.

- Slung or suspended over the performance area.

- Held in position by the recordist or a 'boom swinger', usually the sound assistant, on a fishpole boom. This needs steady arms and strong muscles to keep the boom aloft while adjusting the microphone to follow the source of the sound. Nevertheless, the best effect is often achieved through skilled boom swinging.

Sebastian Buccheri

Figure 26 Sound recordist Ron Bailey on location with the Hi-8 production *Blazed* for Channel Four. Director Jonnie Turpie for APT/Maverick TV. The companies have been awarded a lottery grant to make similar, community-based dramas
Courtesy *Young People Now* and the National Youth Agency

- Mounted on a tripod or a 'lazy arm'. This may be on rollers so that it can be pushed around to follow the action.

- Mounted on a large boom fixed to a wheeled platform with a long, tele-scopic arm which may be extended and retracted. There is an elaborate system of belts and pulleys to control direction and position. The micro-phone is in a cradle at the end of the arm, and can be swivelled in multiple directions. This flexible but cumbersome studio device needs two people to operate it, and is becoming less common as a mixture of personal mikes, radio mikes and fishpoles are more often used.

Audio control

The sound engineer's job includes:

- Monitoring the sound levels, both electronically on the VU (Volume Unit) meter on the recording machine, and aurally through earphones which pick up the signal after it is recorded on the tape. The sound heard through the earphones will lag slighly behind the real-life sound. The levels should be adequate, even, and not distorting. The VU meter displays the intensity of the sound level measured in decibels and in percentage of modulation. One hundred per cent is the maximum the system can take: if the needle goes beyond that, it is 'overmodulating'. A signal that is too low or too high will result in a muddy or distorted recording.

- Ensuring that the desired sound, most usually the speaking voice, is sepa-rated from the background or ambient sound.

- Ensuring that the desired sound is free from interference or background 'noise'. It is up to the sound recordist to hear those things that the director, concentrating on the content of the scene, may overlook – the noisy traffic, the passing aeroplane which may obscure the dialogue, or the speech overlaps which make the scene difficult to edit. Sudden bangs, such as closing a desk lid in a classroom scene or the clash of knives and forks during a meal, can sound unnaturally loud and distracting in the context of a recorded scene.

- Providing suitable wild tracks and buzz tracks of the ambient sound.

- Contributing to the 'audio design' and the overall 'sound' of the scene.

In the studio

Usually in a separate control room away from the studio itself (the 'gallery'), the audio control engineer (sound mixer or sound supervisor) selects and blends the various programme sound sources through an audio control console (also known as the board or mixer panel). During the production, there will be talk-back between the director in the studio gallery, the crew working on the studio floor, and the control rooms where the picture and sound are monitored.

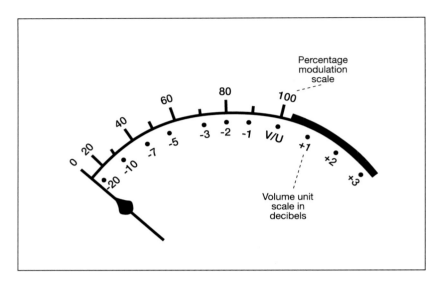

Figure 27 The volume unit meter which measures the audio power in the system

It is the audio control engineer's job to:
- Select and control outputs of various audio sources (microphones, discs, tapes, etc.)
- Keep the volume indicator within system limits by using the faders (also called amplifier gains) which increase or decrease the volume of each input
- Monitor the programme sound and communicate with the director when necessary
- Check audio quality
- Watch the picture monitors showing line and preview shots closely to check sound perspective, and to warn against microphones coming into shot and boom shadows.

References and Key Texts

Alkin, G. (1989) *Sound Techniques for Video and Television*, 2nd edn, Oxford: Focal Press

Corner, J. (1991) 'Documentary Voices' in J. Corner (ed.) *Popular Television in Britain: Studies in Cultural History*, London: BFI

Ellis, J. (1982) *Visible Fictions: Cinema, Television, Video*, London: Routledge & Keegan Paul

Holland, P. (1987) 'When a woman reads the news' in H. Baehr and G. Dyer (eds) *Boxed In: Women and Television*, London: Pandora RKP

Millerson, G. (1990) *The Technique of Television Production*, 12th edn, Oxford: Focal Press, pp. 274–6

Shapley, O. (1985) *Vox Pop*, 23 December, BBC Radio Four

Shapley, O. (1996) *Broadcasting Alive: An Autobiography of Olive Shapley*, London: Scarlet Press

Wurtzel, A. and Rosenbaum, J. (1994) *Television Production*, 4th edn, New York: McGraw-Hill

7 Post-production processes: editing

··

Sequence and structure

··

T he editing process is basic to the construction of every programme, from *Blind Date* to *Cutting Edge,* but is at its most powerful with those documentaries and dramas that are filmed shot by shot and then, at the editing stage, patiently built up into a coherent whole. This is the stage when the two-dimensional fragmented shots are reassembled into an illusion of three-dimensional space by bringing together different perspectives on the same scene, and by balancing the visual and the aural, the graphic and verbal. It is the editing which constructs the narrative or flow of every programme by creating sequences and linking those sequences into a structured shape. Editing decisions guide the audience through the movement of sound and images that make up an evening of television.

The aim is to create a rich but seamless flow, but every time there is a transition from one shot to another a decision must be made on whether the change will be smooth and imperceptible to the audience, or whether it will jolt them into attention. The Power Rangers are dramatically transformed into giant monsters; there is a surprise cut to Oprah Winfrey reacting to one of her guests; a commercial will produce an unexpected change of angle.

Editing conventions vary between genres, grouped loosely into those in which the logic of the programme is carried by action and dialogue, such as a drama or an observational documentary, and those in which it is carried by the flow of voice-over narrative, in which case there may be no connection between the images apart from the words to which they form an illustration. Each style carries conviction in its own way and has its own form of naturalism. However, televisual naturalism is a fragile construction, always in danger of being broken by unexpected juxtapositions and new ways of addressing the audience. The debate about editing between Vertov and Eisenstein in the Soviet Union of the 1920s (*see* The love of the image, p. 48 above) has its reverberations today.

Dziga Vertov argued that completely new meanings may be constructed through the rhythms of the editing and the juxtaposition of shots which are in themselves relatively meaningless. Filmmakers should manipulate their original material for their own creative ends; they should break rather than reinforce the audience's sense of reality. Sergei Eisenstein's response was that the flow of the shots must be determined by the demands of the narrative and its emotional effect on the audience (Schnitzer and Schnitzer 1973). In contemporary television, in which the spoken word has gained much greater importance, this narrative-based view has tended to win hands down, but supporters of a more deconstructive style continue to argue that other approaches are also needed and that more attention should be paid to the way in which the images work together (*see* Chapter 9, Narrative television; John Wyver also discusses some of these issues, p. 160 below). Although Eisenstein was in the narrative camp, he was ultimately less interested in smooth continuity than in impact. He wrote extensively about the many different forms of juxtaposition and sequence construction possible for maximum audience effect, proposing a 'montage of attractions', in which every shot would have its own special 'attraction', or intensity, which will either be contrasted with, or linked to, the next.

Whichever editing style is adopted, the decisions must be taken prior to the shooting, for the editor can only work with the material provided. The work of editing begins when the completed rushes, the material shot during the production period, are viewed and assessed for their own value. This should be done in what Michael Rabiger describes as 'a state of innocence' – by which he means putting aside any knowledge of the hard work that went into them, and of the effect that was hoped for, in order to see them as they are, as raw material for building the programme (Rabiger 1992: 202). The editor has a certain responsibility to the material, aiming to draw out its potential. For a drama the editing work can help both script and actors. Careful selection and juxtaposition of takes can enable a good performance to come through and can sometimes 'cut round' a poor one. A documentary rarely begins with a written script to follow and is more likely to be built into its final shape in the cutting room. This is the time when the all-important structure of the programme is worked out and built up, sequence by sequence, out of the original filmed material.

There is a genre of programmes which depends on archive research rather than location filming. Compilation programmes are created in the editing room. They include some that draw on archive material from the distant past, such as *People's Century*, and others that reassess more recent events, such as the Gulf War, supplementing archive shots with interviews with participants and commentators. Once more, it was one of that group of creative filmmakers working in Moscow in the 1920s who is credited with inventing the compilation form. At that time, as so often since, it was easier for women to become editors than camerapeople or directors. Esfir Shub, who with Elizaveta Svilova, the editor of *Man with a Movie Camera*, was one of the great editors of the time, put together *Fall of the Romanov Dynasty* from carefully researched and rescued archive film with an inventive irony that gave it a just reputation as the first compilation film in which a new narrative is constructed from old material (Cook 1985: 206).

The time and conditions available for editing vary enormously. At one end of the scale, a major documentary may have six to eight weeks to edit, during which time editor and director will usually work closely together. At the other, a topical current affairs programme may be put together at high speed, with the editor working throughout the night to meet the transmission deadline. In such cases there is little time for refinement or second thoughts. This is one reason why editing can be described as both a major art form and the most routine of technical tasks.

Types of transition

The cut is the simplest and by far the most frequently used transition, in which one shot is instantaneously replaced by the next.

The dissolve ('mix' or 'cross fade') involves the outgoing shot gradually disappearing while the incoming shot gradually appears.

The fade-out is the gradual darkening of the shot until the image disappears, leaving a black screen. This is a very slow transition, usually employed to mark the end of a sequence, and followed by a fade-in on the next shot. A fade-out indicating the end of the day may be followed by a fade-in suggesting the following morning.

The wipe is a device whereby the incoming shot and the outgoing shot are both at full intensity, but the incoming image chases the outgoing one off the screen. It may employ a variety of different shapes, from folding venetian blinds to star bursts. Very popular in black and white movies from the 1930s, the wipe made a come back on 1980s television, when computerised technology began to make visual effects of this sort much easier to achieve.

Other visual effects. Computer and digital technology have made a huge range of effects available, including superimpositions, the ability to run several shots in different parts of the screen, and the insertion of graphics and captions into live action. Channel Four's brief introduction to the history of the conflict in ex-Yugoslavia, *The Essential Guide*, commissioned for its *Bloody Bosnia* season, made full use of such effects to relate stark historical facts with visual panache.

Technologies and contexts

Although the effect may be similar, television editing can take place in four very different contexts:

- Real-time vision mixing
- Videotape editing
- Film editing
- Non-linear editing

Real-time vision mixing

This is used for a programme originating from a studio or from an Outside Broadcast. It may be done from a studio gallery provided with equipment for production switching, usually known as vision mixing. The director may cue the cuts from a pre-prepared script, or, especially in the case of discussions or chat shows, may make spontaneous, on the hoof, decisions.

Each source is fed into one of a bank of preview monitors which may carry irrelevant material, such as

> off shot cameras moving into position, film channels running up to their next cue, graphics being set up, lighting adjustments, VT shuttling through at speed. . . . With this background the director is busy concentrating on the sources of movement, guiding the production team, instructing, correcting selecting, co-ordinating their work . . . under such conditions it's little wonder 'editing' can degenerate into mechanical switching.
>
> (Millerson 1990: 153)

The director may operate the equipment him- or herself, or may call instructions to a specialist vision mixer. As the editing process is simultaneous with the action, a selection is made between the shots offered by the different cameras, but the order of the shots and the order of the whole programme can only be changed if the programme is pre-recorded.

Videotape editing

This includes the post-production editing that follows a studio programme, which is usually little more than inserting corrections and adding specially filmed sequences, through the whole range of videotape formats down to home editing on domestic equipment such as VHS or Hi-8. A programme shot on videotape is edited 'off-line' on a lower grade tape. The technicalities of off-line editing differ according to the sophistication of the equipment and the number of machines available as tape sources. Essentially it involves transferring, or dubbing, the selected shots from the rushes tapes on to a new tape in the desired order. No physical cutting is involved, but the task of assembling the programme is 'linear'. To make a change in the order or length of shots, the editor must start from the beginning each time. The 'off-line' assembly work, using non-broadcast quality tapes, is done by a VT editor.

The final editing takes place in an 'on-line' studio. Here the selected shots from the original tapes are edited on to broadcast quality tape. An EDL – edit decision list – indicates precisely which shots have been selected using the 'time code' numbers which identify each frame. At the on-line stage, sound and video effects are incorporated; titles and graphics are added by a specialist on-line editor.

Film editing

This is carried out in a cutting room, using specialised equipment, including a synchroniser and a Steenbeck motorised editing table. The selected shots are physically cut out of the rolls of film and are spliced together in the desired order. The actual film used in the cutting room is a relatively cheap 'work print' which serves as a model for the final print, and so can be handled without too much concern that it is collecting dirt or getting

Jason Wingrove

Figure 28 ft2 trainee Mark Neale working with a picture synchroniser at the National
Film School, Beaconsfield
© ft2

scratched. The job is carried out by a film editor together with an assistant
who looks after the unused film and must keep track of every spare frame
in case it is needed again. The flexibility given by actually handling the
film, and the fact that it can be easily assembled and re-assembled in any
order, gives greater possibilities than tape at the cutting stage. But if the
editor wants to incorporate electronic effects, the film must first be transferred to tape. Although the technical considerations are very different, many
of the aesthetic approaches and possibilities are similar to those of videotape editing and most editors can work in either mode. When using film, a
final print will be made from the original negative, exactly matched by
a specialised technician to the editor's cutting copy. The final print will be
'graded' at the processing laboratories, so that the shots are matched for
colour and quality.

Non-linear editing

Digital computer technology has brought us full circle, back to many of the
techniques more familiar from film than video editing. Rushes tapes are
scanned into a computer where the images are stored as digital code on a
hard disc. Each shot is logged, located by its time code numbers, so that
it can be played back instantly. The images and sound-tracks are displayed
on a large computer screen and the editor works with a keyboard and a
mouse. The computer can jump between any shot or part of a shot so that
sequences can be speedily constructed and reconstructed on the screen. The

Figure 29 Editing with Lightworks non-linear equipment
Courtesy Granada Television

manufacturers refer to the system as a 'media composer' as it brings together video, audio and graphics, rather in the manner of CD-ROM. Video effects are available, enabling one picture to burst through another or causing images to fold or swirl, and there are many other facilities. The sound-track can be edited on the same equipment, placing it in relation to the picture and manipulating several sound inputs at once. When the off-line edit is completed, an EDL is prepared which then goes to an on-line suite together with the original tapes.

Editors working with non-linear systems say that it gives greater freedom to experiment with different ways of cutting a sequence, as all the processes are speeded up.

New developments include the ability for cameras to record straight onto a computer memory which can then be brought directly into the editing room, avoiding the need to scan in the tapes, and an improvement in quality which means that broadcast quality results may be produced, doing away with the need for on-line editing.

The processes of editing

The best edited programmes are rarely simply strung together, one shot after the next – although shortness of time available, say for some news reports, does occasionally make this necessary. For most documentary and drama programmes, considerable time and thought will go into deciding the final shot order, cutting points and cutting rhythm as well as working with the sound-track. The programme may be structured and restructured several times before it is ready for the final broadcast quality print or tape to be made.

A broad overview of the processes which must be followed is presented below.

Dealing with the rushes

Viewing, listing and logging all the material to be used in the programme, including the specially shot rushes and any archive or other bought-in material. Each frame on videotape is provided with a time code number, and film has edge numbers along the side of the frames. These must be carefully noted in a log book so that every shot can be quickly retrieved when needed and nothing is lost.

Syncing rushes. If the editing is on film, the sound-track must be transferred to magnetic film and synchronised with the picture. This is known as 'syncing rushes' and is one of the first jobs of an assistant editor.

Compiling typescripts. If required, typed-up transcripts can be made of interviews and dialogue.

The editing process

Building up sequences, the units which carry the structure of each programme.

Making a first assembly, in which the whole film is loosely strung together to give some impression of a suggested overall shape.

Paper edit. Sometimes the editor or director may prefer to do a 'paper edit', in which the structuring work is done on paper. This is a useful way of trying out different segments from the transcripts of interviews, and is most effective if editing on video, which is less easy to reshuffle during the editing process.

Making a rough cut. This will be longer than the required programme length in order to give some flexibility when paring down to produce the fine cut. Television programmes have to fit their available slot exactly, so must be timed to the second.

Editing decisions

The selection of shots for inclusion in the final programme out of the mass of original material. People who do not understand the process, and even some who should know better, speak of a shot or sequence being cut 'out' of a television programme. Since shooting ratios vary from five to one (5 feet of film shot for every 1 foot used), which is extremely efficient, to fifteen to one or more, it would be more accurate to speak of cutting material 'in'. A drama, and many documentaries, will offer several 'takes' of the same shot. Often the director will have pre-selected which take is to be used; sometimes it is up to the editor to decide; or they may both work together. As documentary shooting is looser and less predictable, there are different types of choices to be made. Extracts from an interview, for example, must be carefully selected as they may form the spine of a programme and carry its argument. In the case of observational filming, the editor must select from a mass of unstructured material those sections that will create coherent sequences that appear to flow naturally.

The order of shots. The sequence in which the chosen shots will be arranged and how one will follow the other.

The speed and rhythm within each sequence and between the sequences. This involves decisions about the duration of each shot and the precise moment at which one shot will end and the next begin. There are occasions when quick cutting series of short shots may be more effective than one or two slow ones. The rhythm may be varied throughout the programme.

The overall structure of the programme. This is a continuous task when editing a documentary. Various devices may be used to hold the stucture together. Some possibilities are:

- A *time sequence*, following a single event throughout the day – a day in the life of a hospital ward, an unemployed youth, or a housing estate

- An *argument made by an interviewee*, around which sequences may be constructed, say a doctor putting a controversial case for a new cancer cure

- A *series of themes*. An oral history programme about the 1950s, for example, may cover first youth culture, then the coming of commerical television, then women's fashion and so on

- A *narrative structure developed around a moment of crisis* – a meeting of long lost relatives, a trial. This is the most usual structure for an observational documentary

- A *journalist's report carried by commentary*. This is the most usual way of linking a current affairs programme

Although such structuring devices may have been worked out before filming began, they are surprisingly often developed at the editing stage. The addition of a commentary or captions in the final stages of editing can strengthen the structure. (*See* Narrative television, p. 113 and Current documentary genres, p. 154 below, for more on narrative and structure.)

Final processes

- Preparing the sound-track and relating the sound to the visuals (*see* Sound editing, p. 103 below).

- Planning visual effects, graphics, captions and titles to be added at the on-line stage.

- Organising the final on-line edit in the case of tape, or the final print in the case of film, to produce the finished programme.

Styles of editing

Continuity editing

The work of editing controls the flow of a programme. Yet successful continuity editing erases the evidence of its own operations by maintaining an illusion of continuous movement between the shots within a sequence, and making the transition from one shot to the next as smooth as possible. It follows a series of conventions which achieve an illusion of reality. If the conventions are broken, the viewer will experience a jolt in perception and the illusion may be broken. Continuity is based on the cut, since the instantaneous transition from one shot to the next created by a cut draws minimal attention to itself, while devices such as fades, wipes and mixes break the flow and usually mark the end of a sequence (*see* Chapter 9, Narrative television, p. 113 below, for further discussion of the naturalist conventions implicit in maintaining continuity).

An impression of continuity depends partly on the imagination and expectations of the viewer. If the editing indicates a continuous action, that is what the viewer will tend to perceive, even if the original shots are actually completely discontinuous. For example, a man climbs the steps to the front door of a house and enters. We cut to an interior as he comes into the hall-way. These shots may be, and in most cases probably are, shots of two totally different houses, or of a location exterior and studio interior. Even so, the viewer 'reads' it as the same house and as a continuous action.

As well as temporal continuity, editing links action and reaction. The juxtaposition of two different shots leads the viewer to speculate on the relationship between the two. In the early 1920s the Russian filmmaker and teacher, Lev Kuleshov, conducted a series of editing experiments. The same shot of the actor, Mosjoukin, was juxtaposed, 'now with a plate of soup' now with a prison gate, now with images suggesting an erotic situation, (Kuleshov in Schnitzer and Schnitzer 1973: 70). The viewers commented on the subtlety of the acting, perceiving a change of expression when none existed in what became known as the 'Kuleshov effect'. The active work of the audience in interpreting a sequence of images can be played upon by the filmmaker's skill.

Whether it depends on dialogue or on commentary, the sound-track helps to carry the audience's attention across the cuts. In a drama the dialogue will dominate the audience's interest; in a commentary-led programme, the voice will provide the thread which the audience follows, so that the images are perceived as an illustration of the words. At its worst this can be seen as 'moving wallpaper', at its best the interrelation between words and image can be witty or illuminating.

Continuity conventions

The various devices that are used in composing the shots for a continuity sequence are described above (*see* The director's concerns, p. 63 above).

The following conventions need to be maintained during the editing process:

Avoid 'crossing the line' as it gives the illusion of a complete change of direction, thus:

- If editing together shots of two people walking in the same direction, or one person chasing another, the two should consistently move either from right to left or vice versa, unless a bridging shot or a cutaway breaks the sequencing.

- In a conversation, cutting between say a news presenter and their interviewee, if A is facing right, B must be facing left, or else they may appear to be looking in the same direction rather than facing each other.

- In a dialogue with both A and B in the same shot, a change of camera angle must maintain A on right of frame and B on left (or vice versa). If the director has inadvertently changed the position of the characters in this way, the editor must find a transition shot to enable the audience to readjust.

Maintain visual continuity in all details of a shot. Cutting away from a speaker wearing glasses, then back to the same speaker without glasses will feel discontinuous, unless there is a shot of the glasses being removed. The editor must search the frame for other such changes between shots, including jackets that had been done up suddenly becoming open, objects and people appearing or disappearing, vases of flowers apparently jumping around into different positions on a table.

Maintain the impression of continuous movement from shot to shot by cutting on movement. The movement or gesture which 'motivates' a cut 'sutures' over the gap between one shot and the next. Cutting on movement is normally planned when shooting a drama sequence. A movement which ends a wide shot, say when an actor sits in a chair, will be repeated in the close-up, giving the editor a variety of 'cutting points' to choose from during the movement. When editing vérité-style shooting, which does not have formal shots and does not provide the editor with pre-planned cutting points, the constant motion of the camera nevertheless gives plenty of moments where the transition can be seamlessly created.

Cutting between shots of a different size avoids confusion, when editing several shots of the same person together. A clear cut from medium shot to close-up, reads more naturally than one which goes from medium to only slightly closer; a cut from a right-hand profile to a left-hand one of the same person can be disorienting and not easily recognised.

Maintain consistency when cross cutting between shots of two different people. The size of their heads should be similar within the frame. Cutting between A in big close-up and B in medium shot would look very strange.

Other editing styles

Relational editing is the form of editing which builds up the rhythm of a programme through parallels and comparisons. For example, constructing an alternation between two or more different narratives for dramatic effect. In one episode of *Cracker* (28 Nov. 1995), two meals were intercut. The long-suffering wife of celebrated police psychologist Fitz (Robbie Coltrane) is having dinner with Fitz's rather less successful brother. The love/hate relationship that both the brother and wife have with the absent Fitz has drawn them together. The developing relationship between them is intercut with a developing relationship at a completely separate dinner where Janice, the murderous ex-psychology student, entices a potential victim. Once more the absent Fitz is the dynamic centre, since Janice's crimes have been committed as a direct provocation to him. The interrelation between the two meals is known to the audience but to none of the other characters. The complex dynamics of the intercut dinners makes each into a commentary on the other as well as drawing attention to Fitz as the pivot of the action.

Analytic editing is editing in which the sequence of images is constructed to follow an argument rather than a narrative. Sometimes the flow of the images matches the flow of a narrating voice on the sound-track, and makes no sense if seen alone. Sometimes the images create a visual dynamic of their own.

Montage editing. Although the word 'montage' can mean editing in general, it is most often used to describe a sequence which is built up through the juxtaposition and rhythm of images and sounds. This may be independent of narrative or argument, as in some avant-garde film and video making, or it may act to illuminate or enhance the narrative or argument.

References

Cook, P. (ed.) (1985) *The Cinema Book*, London: BFI

Corner, J. (1991) 'Documentary voices' in J. Corner (ed.) *Popular Television in Britain: Studies in Cultural History*, London: BFI

Rabiger, M. (1992) *Directing the Documentary*, 2nd edn, Stoneham, MA: Focal Press

Schnitzer, L. and Schnitzer, J. (eds) (1973) *The Cinema in Revolution: The Heroic Era of the Soviet Film*, London: Secker & Warburg

8 Post-production processes: sound and graphics

....

The aural dimension

A s we saw above, sound is both a separate dimension of the television experience and an inseparable part of its total communication (*see* Chapter 6, Production techniques: sound, p. 77 above).

The editing process adds to the image track a sound-track which is usually dominated by speech and dialogue. The editor's most important task when dealing with the sound is to ensure that the voices which carry the meaning of a programme are clear, audible and well placed. At the same time, the introduction of more layers of sound from different sources may create a rich and varied audio dimension. On feature films and large productions, a sound editor with his or her own assistants can concentrate on the sound-tracks alone, but on most television productions a single editor puts together both picture and sound. In the high-speed, near panic conditions that characterise much television work, sound editing may be reduced to some hasty 'track laying' a few hours before the dub, yet careful attention to sound can transform a programme. With digital equipment, sound editing has become much easier, since the sound-tracks are made 'visible' on the computer monitor. Their position can be altered and their volume-programmed at the touch of a mouse.

The power of sound is often overlooked in writing about television. The documentarists of the 1930s, working before location shooting with synchro-nised speech was possible, constructed richly textured sound-tracks, using music, poetry and voices. The innovative radio documentary developed by Archie Harding (Shapley 1985) and later Charles Parker, similarly combined the speech rhythms of everyday conversation with music and recitation. The great documentarist Denis Mitchell came out of the same tradition. His early television films, such as *Morning in the Streets*, contained sync dialogue, but were to a large extent made up of impressionistic silent shooting accompanied by a rich montage of voices, snatches of conversation, and regional inflections, which he captured with an unobtrusive tape recorder (Corner 1991). More recently, the tyranny of sync has made that sort of audio exploration less easy to conduct. *Blue* is an exception. Dying of AIDs, avant-garde filmmaker Derek Jarman was losing his sight. Commissioned by Channel Four, the image track for his last film was simply the intense and unvarying colour blue, but on the sound-track, a complex mixture of voices, music and commentary reflected on the tragedy of AIDS and Jarman's own mortality.

Non-naturalistic sound is a familiar feature of commercials and the linking material between programmes, the 'stings' and the sound effects that accompany programme logos and title sequences. The image of the broadcasting mast with its circulating waves which introduced the first television news came with its own jaunty tune. The famous *News at Ten* flourish, which ends with the 'bongs' of Big Ben, between which the headlines are read, is a relished landmark in British television.

Of all the sounds that enhance the television image, music is the most direct in its emotional effect. It is an essential part of most dramas and many documentaries, introducing and pacing a programme as well as intensifying the mood and adding its own ironic or foreboding comment. It introduces and closes most programmes, acts as a signature tune or familiar marker for well-known performers and series, and can transform a solemn moment into a light-hearted one and vice versa. In editing a programme, the selection and placing of the music are essential to the feeling of the programme as a whole.

Sound editing

At the sound editing and track-laying stages, different types of sound will be placed on separate tracks, so that they can be moved around in relation to the image and to each other. At the dubbing stage the separate tracks will be combined and balanced to produce a mixed final track.

If shooting is on film, the sound will have been recorded on a magnetic tape, transferred to whatever format is in use, usually 16mm magnetic stock, then synchronised with the picture, using the clapper boards as a reference point. If shooting is on video, the sound is recorded on separate tracks alongside the picture, and can either be manipulated during the editing process together with its picture, or be dubbed off on to another tape. If editing is on a digital editing machine, the different sources are digitised and fed into the computer, where they become available to the editor at the touch of a mouse (*see* Chapter 6, Production techniques: sound, p. 77 above for more on the recording of sound).

At the track-laying stage, where possible the different types of sound are isolated and placed on separate tracks. This means that they can be more freely manipulated at the dubbing stage. Different sound sources include:

- Synchronised sound (sync)

- Other voice sources

- Other sound effects

- Music

Synchronised sound (sync)

Most television programmes are shot with synchronised sound which comes to the editing room together with the picture, from the location or studio. If the programme is recorded and edited 'as live', the sound from the different microphone sources will have been balanced by a sound engineer as the recording goes along. If a programme is filmed with pre-planned shots, the editor's job is to ensure that when the shots are cut together, the synchronised sound flows evenly. This may involve removing the sound recorded on location (that scream may not be very convincing or a period piece may have been spoilt by traffic background) and replacing it with one created separately (a more bloodcurdling scream or a suitably period track of clopping horses and twittering birds).

Once the sync sound has been disengaged from its shot, it becomes possible to use it to complement as well as to accompany the action. We do not always want to look at the person who is talking, so sound over-laps may be used. In a conversation the sound of a character's voice may precede the cut to their face or it may continue during a shot of the person listening to them. The impression of flow is enhanced and a sense of inter-action between the characters is created.

Whether in an interview or scripted dialogue, strategically placed reaction shots of the listener add to our understanding of the scene. They also offer the opportunity for the editor to make a cut in the spoken track without breaking the flow of the sound.

Other voice sources

These will usually be separately recorded, sometimes before the editing begins, sometimes as part of the post-production process. They will be trans-ferred on to film, or on to a videotape for track laying.

The commentary or voice-over for documentary programmes must be 'laid' so that the spoken words are juxtaposed with the picture in an appro-priate way. There's no point in discussing the nesting habits of the blue tit if the image on the screen shows the blue tit in deep winter. Juxtapositions can be very precise. The exact moment at which a word emphasises a cut or a camera movement can create an impression which is sometimes witty and sometimes emphatic, in which words and image work together as a single, specifically televisual experience.

Other sound effects

These may have been specially recorded on location; or the editor may purchase them from a sound library; or they may be created live as a 'spot effect' at the dubbing stage. At the sound editing stage they are placed on the sound-track in the position where they will have greatest effect in relation to the picture.

Music

Specially composed music is usually written in relation to an edited sequence, timed to fit the action. It may be separately recorded then laid into position by the editor, or it may be recorded simultaneously with the projected film in a special studio. For a series, there may be music which is re-used in each episode.

Music may also be bought from a music library, at an agreed fee, or pre-recorded commercial music may be bought, at a fee negotiated with the Performing Rights Society, the publisher, the composer and the musicians (a complex but important process!). The music for a sequence may be chosen before the pictures are edited, and the editor may compose a visual sequence matching its moods and rhythms.

Dubbing

The final stage in the preparation of a programme's sound is when the prepared tracks are brought into a dubbing studio, where the dubbing mixer and their assistants combine and balance them according to the editor's pre-planned instructions.

For news programmes and some current affairs programmes that are very current – such as *The Big Story*, whose brief is to react to the events of the week – the track-laying and dubbing processes will happen in a tremendous rush, in the middle of the night or just before transmission. For dramas and documentaries with a more relaxed editing schedule, the dubbing may take several days. Editors who care about the sound-track are always fighting for more time to pay attention to the sound, since the pictures always come first and, as transmission day approaches, the processes become speeded up.

At the dub

- The tracks carrying the different types of sound – speech, music, effects and even background nothingness (a buzz track) – can be combined together.

- The tracks are matched with each other for volume and quality.

- The tracks are balanced against each other; for example, holding the music in the background when it is intended to back up the dialogue, then swelling it to a crescendo where needed; making sure that important speech is not drowned out by unimportant sounds.

- The sound may be 'treated' to give a special effect, such as adding echo, and 'spot' sound effects may be added.

The editor will have prepared a 'dubbing chart' to indicate to the dubbing mixer at what point the tracks occur. The chart will refer either to the footage counter on the film editing machine or the time code recorded on each frame of the videotape.

Titling, graphics and video effects

Visual fireworks

Computerised electronic systems have revolutionised television graphics and greatly expanded television's visual range. The title sequences that begin each programme and the list of credits that ends them, together with informational graphics such as maps, charts, graphs and tables, have changed from being simple cards placed in front of the camera, to complex, electronically produced, three-dimensional graphic events, spectacular or entertaining in their own right. They are an essential part of the language of contemporary programme making, in which 'explainer' graphics need to be as attractive as those presented for pleasurable effect. The necessary skills have changed from those of a graphic designer, based on drawing and design, to those of a 'graphics director', working with sophisticated, computer-aided animation machines.

The development of electronic effects technology in the mid-1980s led to a taste for high-tech gloss and sparkle as producers experimented with new techniques. Those were the days of *Max Headroom*, the computer-generated interviewer. Commercials and pop videos exploited the new technologies, and their influence made itself felt in the newly expanding area of youth programming, energetically promoted by Janet Street-Porter, first at Channel Four then at the BBC. Her *Network Seven* and *Def II* broke all the rules and pioneered a path towards the sparky and the outrageous. They exploited the new computer graphics for all they were worth, with multiple imagery and text all going at the same time, strange colours, floating figures and superimpositions, as if the high-tech electronic future that was predicted and dreaded had actually arrived.

Even interviews no longer needed to be presented as straightforward talking heads, as the image could be treated through electronic effects. The speaker could be superimposed on archive material; could be ironically lit to recall well-known filmic styles; could be enlivened with mottled backgrounds or glowing colours; or could be moved around the frame or combined with text or graphics in surreal fashion. Science documentaries and arts, history and current affairs programmes have all been keen to use such devices.

Graphics departments gained a new prestige. The transformation of titling from the dusty whitish captions of the 1950s and 1960s, placed on music stands in front of studio cameras and changed by hand, to the stylish polish of the 1980s was immense. The coming of Channel Four's multi-coloured logo based on children's bricks flying though three-dimensional space was seen as a design landmark. Channel identifications have become television gems in their own right, in particular BBC2's witty and predatory 2s which come alive, puff themselves up, transform themselves into unpredictable materials from the harshly metallic, to the furry or the squidgily plastic, and which plane their way round the floorboards with an alarming disregard for the normal realities of space and time.

By the mid-1990s styles had changed. The original exuberance has now given way to a desire to use graphics in a way that is more informative and less of an assault on the eye. The specialist graphics houses which offer the most sophisticated graphics equipment and operators remain highly expensive, but cheaper and more accessible technology is being developed. It is predicted that the technology used by television companies will be similar to that used in the home.

At the same time, low-tech graphics have never disappeared. The traditional ways of producing captions, illustrations and titles – on a rostrum camera or by photographing projected slides – still have a place, especially in low-cost programme making.

Uses of graphics

- *As titles for the beginning of programmes and as end credits.* If there is no special title sequence, the lettering may be superimposed on part of the scene. If the rolling credits at the end of a programme are to be superimposed, they should be printed in white on a long strip of black paper, which is then unrolled in front of a camera. In the early days of television when transmission was live, the roller caption was wound on by hand – not always smoothly. The superimposition is done at the on-line editing stage if working with tape, or at the laboratory stage if editing on film. Another possibility is to cut to a title or graphic on a blank or textured background, as in the silent movies.

- *As written information on the screen.* This includes the 'strap titles' at the bottom of the frame which name interviewees and participants, and the subtitles which translate foreign language programmes. The rule of thumb is to leave lettering on the screen long enough to be read aloud twice, so that even slow readers can assimilate it.

- *Statistical graphics such as graphs and bar charts.* They may be static or animated. Travel programmes often include maps, with an animated line tracing the traveller's route.

- *Pictorial graphics*, such as still photographs used as an illustration or a background. An effect of movement can be obtained by 'exploring' the picture with the camera, picking out details or panning across its surface.

- *Graphics as part of the scene.* We may see someone lecturing with a flip-chart, for more obviously didactic programmes such as those for the Open University; or a zoom in on the title of a book may turn out to reveal the title of a programme.

- *Animation* involves introducing movement into graphic elements, from the simple running graphs which illustrate the economic information on the news, to producing a fully animated, electronic graphic sequence, or a story film animated in one of many three-dimensional techniques. Innovative animation has had a resurgence in the 1990s, and ranges from the simple puppet and plasticine animations of children's programmes like *The Magic Roundabout* to the Oscar-winning *Wallace and Gromit*.

Figure 30 Granada's motion control rig in action, shooting the title sequence for *Stars in Their Eyes*
Courtesy Granada Television

Rostrum camera

A 'rostrum camera', either film or video, is set up facing an evenly lit surface on which drawings, still photographs or captions can be placed. It may run at various speeds, or may expose single frames one by one, so that a sequence of drawings may be filmed to acheive an animated effect.

When preparing material for the rostrum camera the following points should be kept in mind:

- Lettering should be clear and firm, delicate typefaces with thin lines tend to break up on the television screen.

- Work within 4:3 proportions for the standard television frame.

- Provide an adequate border for the 'cut-off' that occurs when the image reaches the television screen.

- Use matt materials to avoid reflections and glare.

- Avoid buckling and wrinkles and unwanted uneven surfaces.

- Keep information detail to the minumum for rapid assimilation.

References

Corner, J. (1991) 'Documentary voices' in J. Corner (ed.) *Popular Television in Britain*, London: BFI
Shapley, O. (1985) *Vox Pop*, 23 December, BBC Radio Four
Wilkie, B. (1995) *Special Effects in Television*, 3rd edn, Oxford: Focal Press

Key Texts

Alkin, G. (1989) *Sound Techniques for Video and Television*, 2nd edn, Oxford: Focal Press
Burrows, T., Gross, L. and Wood, D. (1995) *Television Production: Disciplines and Techniques*, 6th edn, Madison, Wis. and Dubuque, Iowa: W. C. Brown and Benchmark
Jarvis, P. (1993) *A Production Handbook*, Oxford: Focal Press
Millerson, G. (1990) *The Technique of Television Production*, 12th edn, Oxford: Focal Press
Patterson, M. (1993) *A Quick Crib to Video Documentary Making*, London: BBC Television Training
Rabiger, M. (1992) *Directing the Documentary*, 2nd edn, Stoneham MA: Focal Press
Selby, K. and Cowdery, R. (1995) *How to Study Television*, London: Macmillan
Vaughan, D. (1983) *A Portrait of an Invisible man: The Working Life of Stewart McAllister, Film Editor*, London: BFI
Wilkie, B. (1995) *Special Effects in Television*, 3rd edn, Oxford: Focal Press
Wurtzel, A. and Rosenbaum, J. (1994) *Television Production*, 4th edn, New York: McGraw-Hill

BKSTS (The British Kinematograph Sound and Television Society), also known as the Moving Image Society, publish useful wall charts showing film gauges and television formats. Available from BKSTS, 63–71 Victoria House, Vernon Place, London WC1B 4DA. Tel: 0171 242 8400. Fax: 0171 405 3560

Part III: Making programmes

9 Narrative television

....

Fictional narratives

....

I n a recent handbook it was stated with impressive typographical emphasis, 'There are two types of script. GREAT AND WONDERFUL OR CRAP. *There is no between.*' In his review of the book, David Aukin dismissed the search for a formula. Surveying the work of successful British cinema/ television filmmakers, with productions such as *Priest, Bhaji on the Beach* and *The Poisoner's Handbook*, he remarked,

> Probably the only thing any of these people have in common is that none of them approach filmmaking with a whiff of cynicism. Certainly they want their films to be successful and to be seen by as many people as possible, but their films work with people around the world precisely because they are *not* mass-produced, off-the-factory-line productions. That's the way forward for our filmmakers; that's the way to make a successful British film.
>
> (Aukin 1995: 35)

That was a heartening thought from the Head of Drama at Channel Four.

Fictional programmes on television range from feature films to soap opera, from innovative ten-minute shorts to popular comedy series that run over many years. Drama is a prestigious part of the television output, with its relatively high costs set against the relatively low proportion of screen time it occupies. Nevertheless all the major television organisations set much store by their drama output. Mainstream series with a genuinely popular touch, such as *Inspector Morse* and *The Darling Buds of May*, alternate with series that have pushed at the boundaries in many different dramatic genres, from the explorations of fantasy and hallucination in *The Singing Detective*, to the comic hyperrealism of *Boys from the Blackstuff*. 'You can forget the Old Vic,' said Tony Garnett, 'It is the National Theatre without a question' (Garnett 1970).

Strands such as *Film on Four* and *Screen Two*, which aim for cinema release, tend to be made by established companies using experienced direc-tors and crews, although the success of *Shallow Grave*, among others, has shown that new talent can find an outlet. Oddball strands with titillating titles like *Short and Curlies* and *Funky Black Shorts* offer opportunities for first-time directors and experimental styles. Although drama departments are still institutionally divided between series, serials and one-offs, each with their different approaches and rhythms of work, the distinctions are far more blurred than they ever were. The scope of drama on British television across the second half of the twentieth century has been huge.

One-off dramas

In his notorious address to the Edinburgh International Television Festival, 1993, television playwright Dennis Potter lamented the demise of the single play on television. In the early days of the medium, plays had been broadcast live. They were continuous and studio based, deriving more from the theatre than the cinema. Today one-offs tend to be large-scale co-productions intended for cinema release.

The idea of grouping single plays under a regular title and transmitting them at the same time every week was an innovation of the 1950s and 1960s, aiming to build up audience loyalty. Below, producer Tony Garnett (p. 132) writes of the early days of the BBC's celebrated *The Wednesday Play*. Sydney Newman, Head of BBC Drama, wrote in 1967 that new writers were 'encouraged to throw away the rule books of hitherto accepted drama conventions and encouraged to look at life with a new awareness'. Newman had come to the BBC after establishing the pioneering *Armchair Theatre* (referred to by its detractors as 'armpit theatre') at ABC Television in 1958. A specifically televisual form was evolved and two decades of truly remarkable single dramas followed, seen, above all, as the creative work of the new generation of writers. In the view of critic Sean Day-Lewis, the plays of the early 1970s 'continue to linger in the mind more than the imitation theatre that went before and the imitation cinema that has developed since' (Day-Lewis 1992).

Serials

Serials are dramas in which the plot develops over several episodes, sometimes three or four, sometimes as many as ten or twelve. They are written by a single writer and directed by a single director and in many ways are an expansion on the creative coherence of the single play. These are the novels of the air, and are often adapted from well-known novels: *The Camomile Lawn* and *A Sense of Guilt* are recent examples. Granada's serials such as *Brideshead Revisited* and *The Jewel in the Crown* are remembered as high points of television history, making the most of the scope that the serial form allows, with its large cast of characters, its opportunities for interesting locations – India, in the case of *The Jewel in the Crown* – and its slowly developing plots and subplots. Serials may be in many different genres, from science fiction to political thriller or comedy drama. 'Classics serials' are a subgenre, originally developed by the BBC from the straightforwardly produced *Pride and Prejudice* and *Barnaby Rudge* of the 1960s and 1970s, through to the high production values and hectic atmosphere of *Clarissa*, *Middlemarch*, and the *Pride and Prejudice* of the mid-1990s, exploiting Britishness with a clear eye on the overseas market. David

Edgar's stage-based *Nicholas Nickleby* was a remarkable exception to the resolute historical realism of these productions.

Drama series

These transmit approximately fifteen episodes per year and run on average from three to five years, thereby building on what John Fiske described as television's 'routine repetition' (Fiske 1987). They are more predictable for the schedulers than one-offs and also offer reassuring signposts to audiences, since the same characters and settings appear in every episode. The audience gets to know a group of individuals, but can watch a single self-contained episode without needing to follow a cliff-hanging plot line. Series are collaborative productions, using rotating teams of writers and directors who work within the basic formula. Such early successes as *Dixon of Dock Green* and *Emergency Ward 10* have been followed by many long-running serial dramas in which hospitals, police forces and law courts have figured large. From the gritty realism of the Liverpool-based *Z-Cars*, which first broke with PC Dixon's cosy image, through Thames Television's *The Sweeney* which came in for criticism for showing the brutality of plain clothes police, up to *The Bill*, the police have been an endless source of dramatic interest, including characterful women struggling in a man's world in series like *The Gentle Touch*. *Casualty*, the Bristol-based hospital series; *London's Burning*, the adventures in the lives of London fire-fighters, *Kavanagh QC*; *Rumpole of the Bailey* – these are just a few series in which long-running plot relationships between characters form a backdrop for each week's new drama. This is where writers, directors and actors have the opportunity to hone their skills over time, and where notions of 'quality' and 'popular' have come together. American series such as *Cagney and Lacey*, and several from the innovative producer Steven Bochco, including *Hill Street Blues*, *NYPD Blue* and *LA Law*, have proved an inspiration for British writers and producers.

Alongside this realist tradition, huge audiences have followed the more escapist genres. The historical romance *The Adventures of Robin Hood* was one of the earliest popular successes, and the surreal hokum of series such as *The Prisoner*, *The Avengers* and *Dr Who* have all built up loyal and sometimes devoted audiences.

Soaps

Then, of course, there are the well-loved soaps, whose audiences can hit the 20 million mark. Although when *Coronation Street* began in 1960, the *Daily Mirror* critic described it as 'doomed from the outset with its dreary signature tune and grim scene of a row of smoking chimneys' (Day-Lewis 1992: 10), by 1990 its thirtieth birthday was celebrated on television by ex-cabinet minister, Roy Hattersley. Soaps are never-ending serials, which continue on, just like life, their performers ageing with their characters. The priggish student Ken Barlow, who, in the first episode of *Coronation Street* berated his working-class parents for their lack of education and bad table manners, was still living in the Street thirty-five years and several marriages later, and the actor who plays him, William Roach, had mounted a libel

Figure 31 Behind the scenes at *Hollyoaks*, Channel Four's soap opera for a youth audience
Courtesy Channel Four/Mersey Television

case against those who considered him 'boring'. Each new British soap has been launched with its own special qualities and production values. *EastEnders* is busy and visually cluttered, with its market and pub scenes, its multiracial cast and its unhesitating use of contemporary social problems to fuel its plots. *Brookside* was conceived within an austere social realism, and keeps close to its roots in Merseyside.

The long-running development of character and the interweaving of multiple story lines which can never be resolved since the end is never in sight, are the defining characteristics of soap operas. As the characters develop, almost like friends and certainly like 'normal people', as one *EastEnders* viewer put it, all the participants see themselves with a special sort of responsibility to their audience. Sue Johnstone, Sheila Grant of *Brookside,* spoke of the incident in which Sheila was raped. 'It was more than just acting a role. I worked with rape crisis groups and responded to many letters' (*Soap Weekend*, C4 1995).

Soap opera is where many new directors and writers get their first opportunities. It is a demanding job, working under production-line conditions with very tight shooting schedules and deadlines. Teams of writers, directors and technicians overlap with each other. 'On any one day, I've calculated I've got 60 scripts in different stages of transition on my desk', one soap producer told Jeremy Tunstall (Tunstall 1993: 115) (*see* Phil Redmond, p. 223 and Beryl Richards, p. 239 below).

Sitcoms

Situation comedies, sitcoms, are located in the entertainment rather than the drama departments of the television organisations. Nevertheless they are fictional narrative series, in which an impossible and insoluble situation reveals each week new comic possibilities. Although the comedy may be resolved in each episode, the situation never is (Fiske 1987: 144). In the best of them, hilarity comes close to tragedy, as in *Steptoe and Son* with its poignant relationship between the not too bright but aspirant son, and the nagging, wickedly idiosyncratic but ultimately dependent father. Classic British sitcoms have pushed the unacceptable close to the bone, with the racist Alf Garnett in *Till Death Us Do Part* and the lovable hustler Del Boy in *Only Fools and Horses*. They have been able to relish social and psychological fissures, from *Dad's Army* through to *Absolutely Fabulous*, and to put their finger on the culture and politics of the moment, as with *Yes, Minister* and *Drop the Dead Donkey*. Writers like John Sullivan, and writing teams such as Ray Galton and Alan Simpson, and Lawrence Marks and Maurice Gran, have made a glorious contribution to British television.

Sitcoms are usually studio produced in front of a studio audience, whose laughter is heard, although they are not seen. They break the strict realism of straight drama which does not admit to the presence of an audience.

Narrative theory

Theorising narrative

Storytelling and narrative structure are at the heart of the television experience. As the French critic and theorist Roland Barthes wrote,

> The narratives of the world are numberless. . . . Able to be carried by articulated language, spoken or written, fixed or moving images, gestures, and the ordered mixture of all these substances. . . . Caring nothing for the division between good and bad literature, narrative is international, transhistorical, transcultural: it is simply there, like life itself.
>
> (Barthes 1977: 79)

In his survey of television theory, *Television Culture* (Fiske 1987), John Fiske began his chapter on 'Narrative' with the above quotation from Barthes, and a similar conviction of the all-pervasiveness of narrative has carried the day with many writers on television. All programmes depend on a relationship between the visual image and the flow through time, and the narrative structure is a powerful way of organising that flow. But perhaps nowhere has the gap between practitioners and theorists gaped so widely as over the tortuous complexities of some narrative theory as against the pragmatic common sense of many writers, directors and producers. Yet many of their concerns are similar. Narrative theory has a confirmatory, a critical and a utilitarian mode. It may be written as pure analysis, revealing the structural bones of a programme; as critique, in which narrative structures appear to be putting a strait-jacket on possible artistic freedoms;

or as instrumental advice for practitioners, based on the premise that if there is a clear-cut narrative structure, there will be clear-cut narrative techniques which can be studied and put into practice. We know that this *works*, goes the argument, and that's all we need to know. The charismatic writer and lecturer Robert Mackie has been a foremost exponent of such advice, as have various handbooks, notably those by veteran writer Syd Field. There *are* rules, they assert. These are immutable and they underlie all dramatic constructions. Despite the multitude of actual stories with which the world is filled, there are, underneath, very few narrative structures.

Ever since Aristotle's *Poetics*, written in the fifth century BC, theorists have been anxious to discover the 'rules' that reveal how fictions work, and practitioners have been more or less inclined to take such analysis as pragmatic advice. In the 1920s, a rigorous set of analyses was carried out by formalist critics and artists, working in Soviet Russia. They offered a method by which the different elements of narrative could be isolated and labelled, and the *structure* of an image or a literary or cinematic work revealed. Their work was revived in the 1960s by cultural critics, including Roland Barthes, notably in *S-Z*, his detailed analysis of a short story by Balzac (Barthes 1974). In the 1970s and 1980s the structuralist method was eagerly adopted first by cinema, then by television theorists. The bringing together of formalism with the complex and heady disciplines of semiotics, Marxism and psychoanalysis led to an extensive literature. In France, Christian Metz, and in Britain, Peter Wollen, Laura Mulvey and the writers around the journal *Screen*, explored the structure of the cinematic narrative and at the same time sought ways in which narrative might escape its formal shackles.

Analysis of the narrative form

Theories of narrative based on structure have proved more useful to practitioners than others, like that of David Bordwell based on audience cognition or that elaborated by Roger Silverstone based on narrative and myth. Structuralist theories look for those elements that *construct* a narrative, in order to put the finger on precisely what it is that turns a flow of images or words into a story. After all, even a five-year-old who demands 'tell me a story' knows what *counts* as a story and what does not.

Structuralist theories, both in their 1920s formulations and their 1960s and 1970s reformulations, have concerned themselves with definitions and distinctions. Below is an account of some of them. The terms and distinctions described here are those that are most helpful in understanding how narratives work. The books to which I refer give a more detailed teasing out of the various analyses, often introducing a much more complex set of subcategories and technical terms than I have chosen to use below. Some words are put in inverted commas because they are used here in a special sense.

Story and plot

The narrative has two modes, labelled by the linguist Tzevan Todorov, as 'story' (*fabula*) and 'plot' (*syuzhet*). The 'story' is what actually happens, the material of the tale, and the 'plot' is the way a narrative is realised. 'What actually happens' is always rich and diverse. In the writer's original concept, just like life, there will be a number of characters all engaged in different actions, possibly simultaneously in different places. There is no way of ordering such diversity into a time-based flow without using a range of plot devices. Narrative time, of necessity, is not the same as actual time. The 'story' has many dimensions, but the 'plot' must be linear. If I tell the 'story' of *The Singing Detective* to someone who missed it on transmission, my telling will be quite different from the way the series put its 'plot' together. In the case of Dennis Potter's celebrated serial dealing with sickness, murder and a fascination with the B-movie detective fiction, the realisation of the 'plot' is made up of a complex of flashbacks, fantasy sequences and musical interludes. To make sense of the 'story', the audience must be prepared to decode the 'plot'.

This distinction helps us see how the material a writer begins with may be organised in a multitude of different ways.

History and discourse

The story may be told as 'history' (*histoire*) or as 'discourse' (*discours*). 'History' is an apparently straightforward account of what happens with no indication of who is telling the story or to whom they are telling it. The normal conventions of television drama, as followed in *The Bill* (to take one example from thousands) insist that there is no recognition of a watching audience, nor is there any particular individual apparently 'telling' the story. It just unfolds, as if we were peeping in on 'life'. 'Discourse', on the other hand, is a way of creating narratives that involves an awareness of an audience and indicates the presence of a narrator. This may be explicit, as when Francis Urqhart, in *House of Cards*, winks at the camera/audience and lets them in on his dastardly plans for climbing the political ladder, or it may be revealed for the tele-literate members of the audience in hints and indications, such as authorial style. A Mike Leigh play has certain characteristics which are soon recognised by afficionados. In his filmed drama *Grown Ups* there is a scene between the wife and her slow-witted sister-in-law as they arrange various *objets d'art* in a new house. The scene is covered in one continuous panning shot. Although it is taken from an objective point of view, it seems to include the narrator's wry comment on the scene.

Dramatic convention, and perhaps more importantly the expectations of both audience and commissioning editors, rule that dramas should normally appear as 'history', and that 'discourse' may only become visible in certain, exceptional cases.

Open and closed narratives

A narrative may be 'open' or 'closed'. A 'closed' narrative is neatly rounded off, all the loose ends are tied up and the audience easily recognises that it has reached the end. Ending devices are many, ranging from the difficult reconciliation as at the end of *Priest*, to the death of the main protagonist, as in *The Final Cut*. 'Open' narratives may be less final, leaving problems unresolved or allowing audiences to draw their own conclusions. On television, the serial form means that there must be cliff-hangers at the end of each episode to persuade the audience to watch the next, whereas series must round off each episode, but must keep the main basis of the problem open. There's always another *Casualty* to be rushed into Holby General, always another villain to be arrested by *The Bill*. The best example of an 'open' narrative is the never-ending soap. Soap operas run multiple plots in parallel, and as long as the characters remain in the series, none of the plots is ever finally resolved. A character will continue to have effects on the others even after their death. The notorious murder of Trevor Jordache by his abused wife and daughter allowed the *Brookside* team to keep the question hanging in the air for two years of when his body will be discovered. As Fiske remarked, 'In soap opera narrative time is the metaphorical equivalent of real time, and audiences are constantly engaged in remembering the past, enjoying the present, and predicting the future' (Fiske 1987: 145)

Annette Kuhn has pointed to the more 'feminine' qualities of the open narrative, more suited to the rhythms of women's days, closer to the emotional texture of everyday experience (Kuhn 1987).

Narrator's image and viewer's image

The 'discourse' of a narrative tells us something about the 'narrator's image' and the 'viewer's image'. Not necessarily, you will notice, about the actual narrator/programme maker or any particular real viewer. Nevertheless, looking for discursive signs within a drama, we learn something about the narrator, about the fact that there *is* a narrator *there* who is communicating with us. This understanding underlies much critical writing which is devoted to teasing out the intentions and messages of a programme. As soon as we discover something about the narrator, we also discover something about the sort of viewer the narrator has in mind. *The Magic Roundabout* clearly 'expects' an audience made up of children, just as *Drop the Dead Donkey* 'expects' an audience who are up to date with the news items which the programme satirises. This question of who the audience is, how much they are expected to know, and what sort of demands are to be made on them is crucial to the pitching of much television drama. This is the viewer's image. '"I" and "you" the sender and receiver of the utterance, always appear together' (Chatman 1995: 482).

Real narrator and implied narrator

Thus there is always a real narrator – or more accurately in the case of television, narrators, the group of real individuals who actually made the programme – and there is also an implied narrator, the 'narrator's image'. There are real viewers, the actual people sitting in front of their television sets in their living rooms or wherever, and then there is an implied viewer, the 'viewer's image'. The implied narrator may bear a variety of different relationships to the characters:

- *In the view from behind*, the 'narrator' knows *more than* the characters, and can 'see through the wall of a house as well as through the hero's skull'.

- *In the view with*, the 'narrator' knows *as much as* a specific character. The audience follow the clues together with Miss Marple, instead of being shown who the murderer is before she finds out.

- *In the view from outside*, the 'narrator' knows *less than* any of the characters, and does not have access to anyone's consciousness. In this case, actions may appear mysterious and without explanation. (Todorov 1977: 29).

Of course, the real narrator knows everything, for it is, of course, the real narrator who invents and manipulates these fictional relationships for greatest effect, drawing on a variety of dramatic devices.

Showing and telling

The distinction between 'showing' (mimesis) and 'telling' (diagesis) points to the difference between the way a story may be conveyed in images, as in silent cinema, and the way a narrator tells the tale, most obviously in a novel written in the first person. Television, which combines words and images, uses elements of both modes, and the interrelation between the telling of a plot and the way it is shown – through the performance of the actors, the quality of the camerawork, the costumes and the multitude of other available elements – is basic to the creation of engaging and convincing television fiction. The visual, 'mimetic' qualities of a carefully recreated period serial, such as *Pride and Prejudice*, are strikingly different from those of a gritty contemporary hospital drama such as *Casualty*; *Neighbours* is very different from *EastEnders* in its visuals as well as other qualities. The telling of a narrative is linked to time, and movement through time, in a way that the showing or mimetic qualities are not.

Mimetic qualities are linked to forms of 'representation': the way people, or groups of people – say women, or people with disabilities – are shown, whether on television or in other media (Bordwell 1985: Chs 1 and 2).

Constructing narratives

Syd Field's paradigm

Syd Field, whose books are based on his Hollywood experience as scriptwriter, script reader and screenwriting teacher, offers concrete advice in a hard-boiled staccato prose. He makes clear his emphatic commitment to a basic underlying narrative structure, and offers a model, which he calls the paradigm of dramatic structure:

> What is a screenplay?
> A screenplay is a STORY TOLD WITH PICTURES.
> It is like a *noun* – about a peron or persons, in a place or places, doing his or her 'thing'. All screenplays execute this basic premise. A motion picture is a visual medium that dramatises a basic story line. And like all stories, there is a definite *beginning, middle* and *end*.
> (Field 1979: 7)

(It was Jean-Luc Godard who remarked that yes, his films did have a beginning, middle and end, but not necessarily in that order.)

Syd Field's paradigm is very precise and takes the form of a diagram:

Beginning	**Middle**	**End**
Act 1	Act 2	Act 3
set up	confrontation	resolution
pp. 1–30	pp. 30–90	pp. 90–120

	Plot point 1	Plot point 2
	pp. 25–27	pp. 85–90

In his spirit of bluff pragmatism, Field usefully asserts that the standard screenplay is 120 pages long, or two hours. 'It is measured at one page per minute. It does not matter whether your script is all dialogue, all action or both. The rule holds firm – one page of screenplay equals one minute of screen time' (pp. 7–8). (In fact the script for the 90 minute drama of marginal existence, drugs and comic survival, *Trainspotting* (1996) was 245 pages long, according to its screenwriter, John Hodge.) For Syd Field, 'the basis of all drama is conflict' and the movement through the plot, from the setting up of characters and situation through the confrontation to the final resolution, can be neatly measured out in minutes and pages.

> Don't take my word for it. Utilize it as a tool, question it, examine it, think about it . . . If you don't believe the paradigm, check it out. Prove me wrong. Go to a movie – go see several movies – see whether it fits the paradigm or not. . . . The *paradigm* works. It is the *foundation* of a good screenplay.
>
> (Field 1979: 10–11)

Formalist structure: actions

In more analytic language, Tzevan Todorov offers a model narrative structure which is remarkably similar. An equilibrium is disrupted, usually by a villain. The disruption is worked out and another equilibrium is established, similar to the first but never identical (Fiske 1987: 138).

Todorov describes the beginning of a narrative as expressing an enigma, a complex of circumstances just crying out to be unravelled. This is how Syd Field characterises the opening of a 'good screenplay':

> The style, the way the words are laid out on the page, the way the story is set up, the grasp of dramatic situation, the introduction of the main character, the basic premise or problem of the screenplay – it's all set up in the first few pages of the script, *Chinatown*, *Three Days of the Condor*, *All the President's Men* are perfect examples.
>
> (Field 1979: 3)

Formalist theories claim that however unlike each other different narratives may seem, they are constituted by a sequence of 'actions' (functions) which come out of the relationships between the characters. The arrangement of the 'functions' obeys a logic that employs certain recognised devices that underlie *all* narratives.

Vladimir Propp, who analysed 100 Russian fairy stories in 1928 found 32 narrative 'functions' common to them all. He divided them into 6 sections. David Bordwell described a similar 'canonical format' (Bordwell 1985: 35):

Propp: Preparation
Bordwell: Introduction of setting and characters

P: Complication
B: Explanation of the state of affairs

P: Transference
B: Complicating action

P: Struggle
B: Ensuing events

P: Return
B: Outcome

P: Recognition
B: Ending

The stage of 'complication' is an essential one to the maintenance of the narrative structure. This is where the device of 'retardation' comes into play. The Russian formalist critic Viktor Shklovsky spoke of a 'stairstep construction', with each step offering a hope which is then dashed. Alfred Hitchcock spoke of 'frustration'. In Hitchcock's films false trails are laid that retard the development of the plot. These are his famous 'McGuffins'. In *Rear Window* there are two: Is the dead Mrs Thorwald in the trunk? On investigation it's only her clothes. What is the connection between the little dog's interest in the flowers and its death? Lisa and Stella dig up the flowers but find nothing. Both these narrative threads run over a number of scenes before they are discarded.

> More often than we are usually aware, narratives invoke expectations only to defeat them. . . . Narrative art ruthlessly exploits the tentative, probabilistic nature of mental activity.
>
> (Bordwell 1985: 39)

The viewer makes hypotheses, builds up expectations, arrives at conclusions, while the narrator tempts and teases by laying false trails, dealing in exceptions and upsetting assumptions.

Formalist structure: characters

In formalist theory, characters, just like functions, are more important to the narrative because of the role they play, what they *do*, than what they *are.* The same role may be split between more than one character, and the same character may fulfil different roles.

Propp described eight character roles in seven spheres of action:

- *Villain:* involved in villainy, fighting and action

- *Donor* (provider): gives the magical agent or helper

- *Helper:* moves the hero, makes good a lack, rescues from pursuit, solves difficult tasks, transforms the hero.

- *The princess and her father:* These two character roles have a similar function. Both are played by a sought-after person, who assigns the hero difficult tasks, brands, exposes, recognises and punishes

- *The dispatcher:* sends the hero on a quest or mission

- *The hero* (seeker or victim): departs on a search, reacts to a donor, attempts difficult tasks, including marriage.

- *The false hero:* has unfounded claims to the hero's sphere of action.

Roger Silverstone (1981) has used a Proppian structure to analyse various television programmes. John Fiske applied the model to an episode of *The Bionic Woman* and found that it corresponded very closely. Speaking largely of American television, he wrote, 'the structure underlies the typical TV narrative with remarkable consistence' (Fiske 1987: 138).

Narrative realism and other realisms

Most narrative theories hinge on the creation of a coherent and convincing fictional world, sustained by certain codes of realism. As John Ellis writes, realism 'constitutes perhaps the basic demand that our society makes of its film and television representations, apart from a very few, limited exceptions'. It is a regime of 'unified portrayal: every criterion of realism aims at the same objective, to combine all the elements of the representation at any one point into a harmonious whole'. Forms of realism operate at many levels, not just sustained by some easy equivalence to the real world, but by 'a complex network of conventions of portrayal and conventions of audience expectation alike' (Ellis 1982: 9).

Codes of realism

- *A television drama should have a surface accuracy,* that is an accuracy of costume, setting and props. A police officer's uniform should be a *real* police officer's uniform or one level of credibility is lost. Critic Polly Toynbee complained of the blackly comic hospital series *Cardiac Arrest*, which makes no claims to realism of style, that 'it has some responsibility to the literal truth' (Toynbee 1995).

- *It should obey the laws of cause and effect* and explain itself adequately to its audience. At the mundane level of visible motivation, if a character is walking down the street with an open umbrella, it should be raining or the fact should be otherwise explained – perhaps the character suffers from Alzheimer's Disease or perhaps they think it's raining. The principle also applies to a more complex level of character motivation within the structure of the plot.

- *It should conform to expectations based on psychology and character,* so that the characters remain consistent even when 'weird' and 'unnatural' events take place. The search for the motive is the underlying thread for many a detective drama – the basic premise of *Cracker* hinges on this very point. The psychologist employed by the police has a special skill in explaining apparently motiveless actions and making sense of otherwise incomprehensible events.

- *The fictional world should be governed by spatial and temporal verisimilitude* (*see* Visual grammar, p. 64 and Continuity editing, p. 99 above).

- *A plot should not stray too far from what we expect to happen.* This means that it should obey the laws of physical and natural science, unless it is dealing in the supernatural, as with horror or science fiction. Even then it should be consistent. Expectations can also operate at the ideological level. John Ellis describes this as 'perhaps the most conservative' of realist requirements, because it 'represents the spectator's desire that a representation should conform to common sense and taken-for-granted notions of events' which may include questionable expectations about the relations between the sexes, for example, or stereotypical notions about racial characteristics (Ellis 1982: 7).

All of the above contribute to an internal coherence, which

> requires that the diagetic world appear self sufficient and unbroken. Everything that we need to know in order to understand it must be included, and everything that contradicts or disturbs the understanding must be excised. The diagetic world must not require the viewer to turn beyond it to find the means to understand it, but it must, like the real world, appear to make its own sense according to the 'laws of nature' not the conventions of culture.
>
> (Fiske 1987: 131)

Thus a main requirement of realism is that the conventions themselves should remain invisible.

Realism and genre

Each narrative genre has its own set of established conventions and audience expectations, which apply across narrative types. Detective programmes, hospital dramas, science fiction, political thrillers and costume dramas may be written as serials, or one-off plays or sitcoms. Soap operas tend to stick close to the genre of domestic melodrama, but can have their moments when they move into other areas such as crime or investigation.

Each genre brings its own sets of expectations and its own permitted deviations from naturalist representation. Generic realism means conforming to the conventions of the genre, rather than the realities of the world. A comedy writer can take liberties denied to someone working on a naturalist soap; a police series can condense much material concerned with police procedure because it is so familiar to the audience from other dramas in the same genre; a psychological drama can play tricks with external reality to convey the inner life of the characters. Although the conventions are not hard and fast – new genres arise and old ones change with the work of creative writers and directors – anyone writing a script will first be asked, what *kind* of a drama they are aiming for and where it will fit in. A genre like the docudrama, because it is treading a fine line between fiction and reality, is constantly redrawing its own boundaries (Neale 1995: 460).

At one extreme of the realist continuum are the conventions of the naturalist genre. They include an unemphatic acting style, the use of real locations, stories and characters drawn from ordinary life, and camerawork and editing that do not draw attention to themselves. On British television the naturalist style has a long and important history, from series like *Z-Cars* and *The Wednesday Play*, which pioneered a new level of biting social comment. Some argued that its naturalistic style tricked the viewers, by giving the impression that the heart-wrenching emotions of such dramas as *Cathy Come Home* or *Up the Junction* were indeed part of real life. Ken Loach, director of *Cathy Come Home*, explained, 'We wanted viewers to stop thinking of films as fiction, but to think of them as having a factual point' (Saynor 1993: 12). He speaks of 'that enervating atmosphere of show business that we hate' (Levin 1972). The work of directors like Mike Leigh, and writers such as Roddy Doyle, have re-interpreted naturalist conventions, each in their own way.

Critical narrative theories

In the 1970s, the rediscovery of formalist theories was part of an energetic, committed, exciting, if highly theoretical, development of critical work, which drew on Marxism and psychoanalysis as well as structuralism and semiotics. There was a sense that a new spirit was abroad, that forms of radicalism were possible which would draw together politics, the arts and popular culture. Abstract theory was carried along on a tide of enthusiasm created by the events of May 1968 in Paris and London, as well as the radical students' action in the US and the Prague Spring in Czechoslovakia. A demand for a politicised and committed practice energised writers, film-makers and critics alike. The new Marxism was strongly culturalist and an analysis based on the concept of ideology was central.

The rediscovery of formalist theories had led to an emphasis on the *constructed* nature of cultural forms and a recognition that they are put together according to well-worn formulae. It was a cause for outrage that, despite the effort that goes into their making, such forms were presented as if they were *natural*, setting out to conceal those all-important processes of construction.

The 'classic realist text', as Colin McCabe called the conventional narrative structure, is a prime example of such naturalisation (McCabe 1974). Every standard Hollywood film follows these basic 'realist' conventions. It has everything neatly sewn up. Every plot element falls into place in a way that is so convincing that the audience is swept along without question. A 'realist' narrative of this sort is constructed around a hierarchy of voices in which the voice of the real author is concealed, embedded within the text. The social and political assumptions on which the narrative is based also seem completely natural. The flow of the story is perceived as a 'metalanguage which tells the truth' and 'appears to emanate from no identifiable speaker' (Bordwell 1985: 18). Because the structure is so seamless and so convincing, it closes off the possibility of any alternative views or different perspectives.

The structure of filmic narrative is based on the cut, which stitches up (sutures over) the metaphorical wound, the gap which was actually there in the process of filming. From one shot to the next the lights must be changed, the camera moved, the set and actors' costumes checked for continuity and so on, but in the final film the action flows together seamlessly. The flow of a drama, even when it does not adopt a mimetic naturalist style, is a continuous illusion, rather like the realism of a dream.

Writers such as Laura Mulvey used psychoanalytic theory to demonstrate the dream-like nature of the cinematic experience (Mulvey 1989). Cinematic realism cannot reflect the real world, they argued. Its formal coherence and its ability to bypass reason and go straight for the dream world of the human unconscious, make it an *ideological* form. It is designed to lull the audience into assent, to pacify them by pulling the wool over their eyes, so that they are blind to social injustice and the harsh realities of everyday existence.

Karl Marx wrote that all ideas emanate from the ruling class and it is the ruling class who ultimately control the media which disseminate those ideas. The main interest of the ruling class is to stay in power and to keep everyone else in their place. Even so, ideas can be presented in a way that seems familiar and comforting to their mass audience. But that audience, because it is separated from power, is not seeing them as they really are, but rather, 'as in a camera obscura, upside down' (Heath 1981: 1). An ideological text conceals the underlying intentions and purposes of those who produce it, and if those who produce it are rarely part of the ruling class themselves, they are always in their pay. Louis Althusser gave a structuralist twist to his twentieth-century version of Marx's nineteenth-century critique. Althusser divided the far more complex society of the 1960s into separate 'levels' – ideological, political, legal and economic – of which, he argued, the economic level finally, 'in the last instance', determines the shape of the others. Ultimately, cultural forms follow economic requirements. But, at the same time, cultural products, like films and television programmes, could be seen as 'relatively autonomous' of their economic base. They could be challenged and radicalised in their own right without waiting for a transformation of society to generate cultural change.

Writers and filmmakers, notably Jean-Luc Godard in France, took up the challenge and went back to the ideas of documentarist Dziga Vertov and dramatist Bertolt Brecht to find ways of breaking the conventional narrative form. Both had rejected a naturalist style in favour of the formalist principles of attention to the text, making visible the means of production, and making reality *strange* rather than cosy and familiar. Tactics like actors stepping out of character to reflect on the action, of direct address to the audience and of the use of captions or photographic stills were designed to demystify by getting the audience to *think* rather than becoming caught up in the emotional flow of the story. Such techniques emphasised fragmentation and disharmony.

> Long live the consciousness of the pure who can see and hear! Down with the scented veil of kisses, murders, doves and conjuring tricks!' wrote Dziga Vertov in 1924.

(Schnitzer 1973: 83)

However, Godard's *British Sounds*, commissioned by London Weekend Television in 1969, was considered both too outrageous and too boring to be transmitted. What such a blanket condemnation of narrative realism did not take into account was the precise *nature* of the reality that was the subject matter of individual programmes. When Ken Loach made *Days of Hope* in 1975, tracing the progress of a group of left-wing activists from the First World War to the General Strike of 1926, Colin McCabe argued that it could not carry a radical message because of the realism of its style. Colin McArthur replied that what made this series radical was the shift to a working-class perspective that it carried. There were conditions, after all, in which realism could be radical (McArthur 1978).

During the 1980s and 1990s, a far wider range of dramatic forms have become familiar on television, not always inspired by the political motives of a Godard or a Loach. Writers like Dennis Potter have expanded the television language. The coming of computer technology has meant that the use of captions, graphics and non-naturalistic sequences may be seen as part of the dramatic repertoire. 1980s glitz and visions of a high-tech future gave series like *Capital City* and fantasies like *Max Headroom* the ability to express the spirit of the age. The movement out of the studio to a more cinematic style of production has also brought greater flexibility and range of styles.

Theories of postmodernity, which focus on fragmentation, disruption and a sense of the *unreality* of the everyday world, appear to represent contemporary consciousness more accurately than the concept of ideology, which depends on the ultimate truth or falsehood of a work. It came to seem natural for dramas to reflect on the nature of the medium they were using, and to acknowledge the presence of an author. John Hodge, writer of the screenplay *Trainspotting*, with its celebrated sequence of the addict swimming down the lavatory bowl in search of his lost drugs, expressed the view of many writers when he said, 'I am always looking for ways out of conventional realism' (National Film Theatre talk, March 1996).

The need to make dramas from a different perspective remains. British television has broadcast seasons of films from many different parts of the globe, including Africa, Japan, India and parts of the Arab world. They have produced narratives which follow different conventions which come out of different cultures. At the same time there remains a whole range of perspectives from the UK which are still underrepresented, including regional perspectives, those of black and other ethnic minorities, and, still, surprisingly, women (*see* Feminism and narration, p. 130 below).

Television narrative

Ideas developed in relation to cinema have been an important point of reference for television theories. But the intense, self-contained world of the cinema film is very different from the low-key, continuous flow of television. John Ellis has argued that the typical construction of the apparatus of television is its 'segmentation', the linking of short elements. Ellis suggests that the overall flow of television is thus based on *succession*, on one thing following another in a discontinuous way, rather than on *consequence*, one thing following another in a way that is structurally organised. Because of the constant interruptions to which it is subject, 'the self-sufficiency of the single diagetic world of the realist narrative can never be maintained on television' (Ellis 1982; Fiske 1987: 145).

Television itself, in the very continuity of its flow, deconstructs the narratives it contains. Films demand 'the gaze' whereas television is satisfied with 'the glance'. Its domestic location is very different from the dream-like intensity of the darkened cinema auditorium. The normal mode of watching, at home together with friends or family, means that viewing becomes part of a joint conversational experience, rather than one that is dominated by the flow of the programme. The viewer is not held static in their seats, but may turn their back on the set, go off to make a cup of tea or watch while doing domestic chores. The modes most suited to television, such as the long-running series or the soap opera, are the most open and least ideological of narrative forms, in their repetitive nature, their interweaving of many plots, and the knowledge that no possible final plot resolution is ever possible.

This openness to the future is unique to what John Fiske described as 'television's sense of time'.

> We know that there will always be more murders, more disasters, tomorrow, next week, next month . . . The future may not be part of the diagetic world of the narrative, but it is inscribed into the institution of television itself. The characters may not act as though they will be back with us next week, but we, the viewers, know they will. The sense of the future, of the existence of as yet unwritten events, is a specifically televisual characteristic, and one that works to resist narrative closure.
>
> (Fiske 1987: 145)

In a very useful book of American television theory, *Channels of Discourse*, Jane Feuer argues that television has, in fact, *three* 'diagetic worlds' (Feuer 1987). The first is that of the programmes themselves; the second is that of the advertisements and the promotional material that comes between the programmes; and the third is that of the 'viewing group', the bunch of programmes or bits of programmes put together by each viewer. Sandy Flitterman Lewis points to the the narrative interrelation of the different television elements, as programmes pick up and build on material from elsewhere in the television output, and themes echo back and forth between different types of programme. This intertextuality means that dramas pick up themes from the news, and that chat shows and celebrity interviews constantly reference and satirise other television shows, creating new narratives. For example, Lewis argues that advertisements may act as a 'closure' to the soaps, by providing a 'limited sense of achievement that is constantly deferred in the programme itself' (Flitterman Lewis 1983).

Feminism and narration

Feminist studies of narrative and attempts to create different, more woman-centred narratives all refer back to Laura Mulvey's classic article, 'Narrative cinema and visual pleasure' written in 1975 (Mulvey 1989). Mulvey's work has been part of that 1970s mood which drew together filmmaking, political campaigning and high theory in a powerful conjunction. It has been urgently necessary to understand why women have been so visible on the screen and yet at such a disadvantage behind the cameras. The aim was to transform both the organisation of the media and the content of programmes.

Mulvey argued that classic Hollywood cinema is constructed around the masculine gaze, and that the flow of the narrative has tended to place the male central character as its agent and the woman as the object of his fascination and curiosity. The hero relays the gaze of the audience, who, in their turn, treat the woman as a form of spectacle, a fetishised object. The requirements of the classic realist text, all too often driven by investigation and enquiry, reinforce this structure, which gives rise to considerable problems and confusions on the part of female spectators, who find that the plot expects them, too, to identify with the male hero.

Taking up the argument in her article 'Women's genres', Annette Kuhn contrasted the experience of cinema – in which there is a sense of powerlessness in front of the film, as you sit next to a stranger in a darkened theatre, looking up at a brilliantly illuminated screen – to the experience of television, seen in a domestic environment, watched or half-watched by a small group of family members or a single person. In that context, the much more low-key, open narratives of television both depend less on exploiting the spectacular image of a woman and are more woman-centred in their construction. Soap opera, in particular, deals with family relationships and everyday life in a way that is close to most women's experience (Kuhn 1987).

Laura Mulvey's conclusion at the end of 'Visual pleasure and narrative cinema' is that women's only escape from this dilemma is to abandon conventional narrative and to turn to avant-garde work; and her own filmmaking has been in this style. Many women film and video makers have followed this advice, and there is a large and interesting body of feminist deconstructive work. Over the years occasional space has been made for such non-narrative fictional forms on television, for example, Channel Four's *The Dazzling Image*.

Vigorous campaigning, together with Equal Opportunities legislation and changing social expectations has led to ever more women coming to work in television as writers, directors and producers. More women have been at the centre of dramas of all kinds, from psychological dramas to police series. Paula Milne's political thrillers, including *Die Kinder*, in which a mother becomes embroiled in a complex conspiracy following the abduction of her children, and *The Politician's Wife*, in which the compliant and plausible partner effectively turns the tables on her smug cabinet minister husband, have made women the investigators rather than the investigated. Other dramas, such as *Prime Suspect* and *The Manageress* have centred on women characters who inhabit positions of authority without denying their femininity. Effectively the change has led to a re-evaluation of masculinity as well as femininity and a greater willingness to explore emotion and vulnerability.

Tony Garnett: producer

When *Between the Lines* was building up audiences for the most morally complex police drama for decades and the flip but deadly serious *Cardiac Arrest* was about to hit the television screens, critic James Saynor called producer Tony Garnett 'Britain's most influential film facilitator over the last 30 years' (Saynor 1993).

Garnett began as an actor with an interest in politics and in the sort of television drama that makes demands on the intellect as well as the guts. He was part of that urgent search for realism which, in the 1960s, was forcing articulate, working-class characters on to the screen, authenticating their speech and experience and looking forward, in their name, to social transformation. He became script editor then producer on the pathbreaking *The Wednesday Play*. As he told an interviewer in 1970:

> Producer is the best job in the hierarchy. You are able to be effective if you are prepared to fight. If you haven't lost touch with the creative act it's a pivotal position, the natural thing to be. . . . It's marvellous to have the opportunity of reaching a big audience as long as you do it the difficult and not the easy way. . . . It is the National Theatre without a question. You can forget the Old Vic.
>
> (Garnett 1970)

He collaborated on some of the most celebrated of the *The Wednesday Plays*, and together with director Ken Loach, among others, created a loose, naturalistic vérité style, which used everyday speech and location filming with a deceptively documentary look. *Cathy Come Home*, *In Two Minds* and *The Big Flame* were plays whose aesthetic aroused as much controversy as their content.

Through his independent company, Kestrel Films, Garnett produced Ken Loach's first feature *Kes*, and his television serials from the mid-1970s had, if anything, a sharpened political bite. They included *Days of Hope* and *The Nation's Health*.

Away for ten years in Hollywood, on his return to British television as an independent producer he turned to long-running series, taking two basic television genres and injecting an ambivalence and bitterness which makes *Between the Lines* and *Cardiac Arrest* quintessentially of the 1990s. Below Tony Garnett comments on today's prospects, without pulling punches on his views of the future of television, and on the prospects for newcomers to the industry.

Tony Garnett

'In my opinion television should be a bloody great circus with lots of acts. Many years ago at the BBC when we were asking ourselves what our function and role should be, I argued that our job was to tell the truth. Not The Truth, because only God, if he or she exists, knows The Truth, but our job should be to tell *our* truth, to bear witness, whether through a situation comedy, a news programme or a drama. That's what the public has a right to expect of us. But my truth or anyone's truth is partial, in both senses of the word, so we need a whole range of truths on television all the time. That's why it is culturally and politically a disaster to have made the recent structural changes to British television that limit decisions about what gets broadcast.

When I started in the BBC Drama Department we had producer power. Producers decided what plays went on screen, who would be in them, and who was going to write and direct them. Now if I want to make a piece of drama for British television, if the Controller of BBC1 says no and the scheduler for the ITV Network Centre says no, it just doesn't get made. The system is now so funnelled that very few sensibilities control a wide range of programming.

I used to say that all drama is political, only some drama *knew* that it was. I have had a lot of fun trying to create good entertainment, but it's the political ones that are remembered because they created a controversy. In the 1960s there was a mood of optimism with the end of the Tory government and Wilson's victory, backed up by prosperity and full employment. It turned out to be a false dawn, but nevertheless there was optimism, especially for those of us, writers, directors and producers, who were in our twenties. We had a BBC with a very liberal Director General and board of governors. It's much more difficult now. There is a climate where, if there is any social agenda at all, if there's any feeling of politics in a proposal, those who pick the programmes tend to back away from it.

The kind of television drama that should still have a place, and I'd like to be a part of it, is the drama of social criticism, the drama of anger. I'd like to see a drama which, through the experience of the characters, invites the audience to imagine an alternative, politically, socially and in the way that institutions are run, as we did in *The Big Flame*.

I don't think the single play, which is the individual voice of a particular writer, should be killed. During one year in the middle of the sixties we put out thirty-four original, full-length single dramas, each between 75 minutes and 100 minutes long, in one season. This was *The Wednesday Play*. Our best audiences were up to 12 or 13 million, but we were prepared to put on difficult plays which would only get 3 to 4 million. We varied them: a thriller one week, a difficult David Mercer play the next and a comedy the week after. Many of the plays were by new writers. Dennis Potter and a whole generation started there. We were trying to make a date for people every Wednesday at 9.25 pm and a lot of people stayed with us. In recent years, the BBC haven't had the courage to put on a season of single plays big enough and long enough to build up audience loyalty.

However, although I'm a late convert to the idea, I do think the action now is in the long-running series. I turned to series partly because that is now the reality of the industry, but then I discovered I was really excited by the challenge of it. Series are enormously difficult to keep fresh. It's easy to be repetitive and formulaic and it's easy to turn them into a branch of manufacturing, but if you fight very hard against those things there are enormous benefits. The long-running series is the natural form of television, the equivalent of the nineteenth-century episodic novel. If you can get an audience wanting to share a particular milieu with the same characters week after week, then you can explore a world and a set of ideas and individuals at length, through time, which is a great opportunity.

The big change that transformed television was the movement to create what was described as independent production. I started what was arguably the first independent production company in the country, certainly the first in drama, when, at the end of the 1960s I got the contract to supply all of LWT's drama for the first two years of its life. So I looked at this movement in the seventies with a wry detachment, because it seemed to me then, and it seems to me now, that although there was some idealism behind it, it was based on an *illusion* of independence. I'm sure that the Conservatives then recognised that by creating a channel supplied by so-called independent companies, as Channel Four was set up to do, you would atomise the business, virtually destroy the trade union and turn all these lefties into businessmen and women who were worried about their little firms. And some of the best people in our business *danced* into the trap, thinking they would be successful. It was a *petit bourgeois* fantasy. I don't want to minimise the advantages in the way Channel Four is organised, but in celebrating those advantages, in my opinion people have not really added up the political costs.

Many people now work outside the institutions. Newcomers are no longer on the same corridor as very experienced people, getting their training and building up experience. Now it's a foot-in-the-door, hit-and-miss, get-your-training-wherever-you-can environment, which is pretty tough.

When I came back to television in this country at the end of the eighties, after being away for ten years, I was faced with a generation that seemed to me to be cowed. I was hoping that people much younger than me would be storming up to my office, telling me that what I had been doing was a load of crap, and saying that *this* is what ought to be made and *this* is how we want to make it. But that didn't happen. Instead a lot of people came to see me with the air of the child who wants to see in the teacher's face what the right answer is, so that they could please and be accepted. Maybe this is what the 1980s did to that generation. You could tell that all they wanted was a job or a commission. They didn't come in with a raging passion, political or otherwise, for a way of doing things that was different. That was seriously disappointing to me.

I've never believed the old romantic idea that talent will out. I think that's nonsense. Talent will either grow and prosper in a good environment, or it will wither on the vine in a bad environment. But from my point of view as a producer, we're always hungry for good writers and I spend a lot of my time trying to find talented people. They don't need to know how to write a screenplay. If someone can create a believable world and the characters come off the page, they can be taught the rest. Part of what I do now with a generation growing up is try to create a secure atmosphere for them. *I'll* fight the broadcasters if necessary and I'll try to create a secure environment where I can *love* good work out of people. And you can only get good work if they can put their fear to one side. Too many people now are saying, 'where is the market, let us try and satisfy it,' rather than saying, 'I'm going to burst if don't get this on the screen.'

As for directors, too many people want to do it and not many of them do it beyond the mediocre. The problem with the film schools is that new directors emerge with the technical stuff coming out of their ears, very interested in how the camera moves, but with virtually no interest in or experience with actors. They've all believed the French nonsense about the *auteur*, and actually believe they are the authors of the film. Orson Welles said you can learn all you ever need to know about directing a film in an afternoon, and he was right. I would prefer to give a chance to someone who had done some work with actors in the theatre and who can actually get a performance. In my view the film schools have got the wrong priorities and should link up with the theatre schools.

I've always been interested in the nature of performance. Most television drama is the exploration of the human face. In fact, most *television* is about exploring the human face, even the sport. In football it's the close-ups that you really want – that moment of agony or ecstasy. A lot of directing is about achieving that.

Public service broadcasting of one sort or another will probably survive, but the days of paternal protection are over. They were days of creative freedom but also of self-indulgence. It's tougher now, but the technology is forcing a challenging change. It's still the most exciting way to express yourself and to reach people. I therefore remain a 51/49 per cent optimist.'

References

Aukin, D. (1995) 'The sweet smell of success', *Sight and Sound*, May, London: BFI

Bordwell, D. (1985) 'Principles of narration' in O. Boyd-Barrett and C. Newbold (eds) *Approaches to Media: A Reader*, London: Arnold

Chatman, S. (1995) 'Story and discourse (introduction)' in O. Boyd-Barrett and C. Newbold, *Approaches to Media: A Reader*, London: Arnold

Day-Lewis, S. (1992) *TV Heaven*, London: Broadcasting Support Services

Flitterman Lewis, S. (1983) 'The real soap operas: TV commercials' in E. A. Kaplan (ed.) *Regarding Television*, Los Angeles: American Film Institute and University Publications of America

Garnett, T. (1970) in *Afterimage* vol. 1 no. 1, April, London

Heath, S. (1981) *Questions of Cinema*, London: Macmillan

Kuhn, A. (1987) 'Women's genres: melodrama, soap opera and theory' in C. Gledhill (ed.) *Home Is Where the Heart Is: Studies in Melodrama and the Women's Film*, London: BFI

Levin, G. R. (1972) *Documentary Explorations: 15 Interviews with Filmmakers*, New York: Doubleday

McArthur, C. (1978) *Television and History*, BFI Television Monograph 8, London: BFI

McCabe, C. (1974) 'Realism and the cinema: notes on some Brechtian theses', *Screen*, vol. 15, no. 2, London: SEFT

Neale, S. (1995) 'Questions of genre' in O. Boyd-Barrett and C. Newbold (eds) *Approaches to Media: A Reader*, London: Arnold

Propp, V. (1995) 'Morphology of the folktale' in O. Boyd-Barrett and C. Newbold (eds) *Approaches to Media: A Reader*, London: Arnold

Saynor, J. (1993) *Sight and Sound*, December, London: BFI

Schnitzer, L. and J. (eds) (1973) *Cinema in Revolution*, London: Secker & Warburg

Todorov, T. (1977) *The Poetics of Prose*, Oxford: Blackwell

Toynbee, P. (1995) '*Cardiac Arrest* is not a warts-and-all portrait of the NHS, it's a warts only picture', *Radio Times*, 22–28 April, London

Tunstall, J. (1993) *Television Producers*, London: Routledge

Key texts

Alvorado, M. and Buscombe, E. (1978) *Hazell: The Making of a TV Series*, London: BFI

Barthes, R. (1974) *S/Z* New York: Hill & Wang

Barthes, R. (1977) 'Introduction to the structural analysis of narratives' in *Image Music Text*, London: Fontana

Bordwell, D. (1985) *Narration in the Fiction Film*, London: Routledge

Boyd-Barrett, O. and Newbold, C. (1995) 'Section 9: Moving Image' in *Approaches to Media: A Reader*, London: Arnold

Brown, M. E. (ed.) (1990) *Television and Women's Culture: The Politics of the Popular*, London: Sage

Chatman, S. (1978) *Story and Discourse: Narrative Structure in Fiction and Film*, Ithaca, NY: Cornell University Press

Cook, P. (ed.) 'The history of narrative codes' in *The Cinema Book*, London: BFI

Ellis, J. (1982) *Visible Fictions: Cinema, Television, Video*, London: RKP

Feuer, J. (1987) 'Genre study and television' in R. Allen (ed.) *Channels of Discourse*, Chapel Hill: University of North Carolina Press

Field, S. (1979) *Screenplay: The Foundation of Screenwriting*, New York: Delacourt Press

Fiske, J. (1987) 'Chapter 8, Narrative' in *Television Culture* , London: Routledge

Geraghty, C. (1991) *Women and Soap Opera: A Study of Prime Time Soaps*, Cambridge, Mass: Polity Press

Kozloff, S. R. (1987) 'Narrative theory' in R. Allen (ed.) *Channels of Discourse*, Chapel Hill: University of North Carolina Press

Kuhn, A. (1987) 'Women's genres: melodrama, soap opera and theory' in C. Gledhill (ed.) *Home Is Where the Heart Is: Studies in Melodrama and the Women's Film*, London: BFI

Millington, B. and Nelson, R. (1986) *Boys from the Blackstuff: Making a Television Drama*, London: Comedia

Mulvey, L. (1989) *Visual and Other Pleasures*, London: Macmillan

Self, D. (1984) *Television Drama: An Introduction* , London: Macmillan

Silverstone, R. (1981) *The Message of Television: Myth and Narrative in Contemporary Culture* London: Heinemann

Smethurst, W. (1992) *How to Write for Television: A Complete Guide to Writing and Marketing TV Scripts*, Plymouth: How To Books

10 Everyday television

....

Ordinary television

In 1972 the government removed the limits they had imposed on the hours during which television could broadcast. Since then, the great bulk of the output has been not in the prestigious mid-evening slots, where the dramas, major documentaries, news analysis, arts programmes, comedies and big name entertainment are to be found, but scattered throughout the day and in the late, off-peak evening hours. This is where we find program*ming* as much as programmes. It includes what could be described as 'ordinary television' – celebrity chat shows, studio audience programmes, consumer programmes, music and jokes, rolling news, local news magazines, games shows, youth programming, sport and so on.

This type of programming aims for a flow of action on the screen which is light and entertaining, mildly informative and involves lots of chatter, lots of personalities, some music and plenty of laughs. Like a tabloid newspaper it makes a space for scandal, a space for celebrities and a space for social conscience. It is a type of output which is television's own, in which the small-scale, domestic medium with its incessant words and images seems more like another group of people in the corner of the room than any sort of demanding cultural experience.

Despite its low prestige, it has been in the flow of routine television that many innovations that are characteristically televisual have evolved: the low-key, continuous format, for example, with weak boundaries between programmes; the development of presenters as friends, with a relaxed and easy address directly to the audience; the phone-in exchange between presenter and viewers. This type of programming bursts into the peak hours with the big fund-raising spectaculars such as *Red Nose Day* and *Children in Need*, but many daytime programmes operate on a very low budget.

This is where we find the heartwarming, the distracting, the trivial and the worthy. It includes what Jeremy Tunstall calls 'the edinfotainment maelstrom', 'the large, mixed bag of programming that seeks to deliver education and information entertainingly' (Tunstall 1993: 80). Many of the shows are high quality in their own right and many have become hugely popular – The *Antiques Road Show* regularly makes the top 20 in the viewing figures and, together with *The National Lottery Live*, is the BBC's most popular factual programme. The best of them get promoted to peak-time viewing, programmes such as *That's Life*, *Songs of Praise*, *The Clothes Show* and Esther Rantzen's *Hearts of Gold*, in which viewers write in to nominate people who have performed heroic acts.

These are the programmes where 'ordinary people' are recruited in large numbers. They take part in talk shows, phone-ins, games shows, and become the studio audience for all of these. Sonia Livingstone and Peter Lunt argue that programmes like *Kilroy* and *The Time . . . The Place . . .* provide an important space for a genuinely engaged public debate on issues of social concern (Livingstone and Lunt 1994). At the other extreme, programmes like *Confessions* have been deplored as a space where participation has been turned into voyeuristic entertainment. Ordinary people's willingness to be made fools of, in such long-running programmes as *Blind Date* and *Beadle's About*, seem positively innocent as the trade in embarrassment is pushed to ever greater lengths. By the mid-1990s, early morning and late night television have become the time for challenging the boundaries of taste, a trend led by the independent company, Planet 24, who began and ended the day with *The Big Breakfast* and *The Word*, both aimed at a youthful audience. A new generation of much younger people has been recruited as reporters, presenters, directors and producers. In this new technology world, there developed a culture of disrespect for the old skills.

The new channels on satellite and cable have opened up this dubious territory between the publicly responsible and the publicly exploitative, since this style of programming lends itself most easily to their high output, low budget requirements. In the next section Helen Swords speaks of her experiences as she moved between daytime and satellite programming. Rarely written about by the critics, rarely aspired to by those wanting to work in the medium, this is an important face of television at the end of the twentieth century.

Helen Swords: *research and production in daytime television and satellite*

Daytime programming needs researchers and producers who can recruit the 'ordinary people' who appear on the shows. In her account of her career between 1986 and 1994, Helen Swords reflects on some of this routine television research. She began as an 'information worker' on a Social Action programme. The Independent Television companies are required to provide some sort of 'Community' or 'Social Action' content to their schedule which will take up issues around health, crime, disability and similar topics that directly involve their viewers. Thames Television's *Help* programme was one long-running example. The mid-1980s was also the time of the big charity spectaculars – of which *Live Aid* in 1985 made an unprecedented international appeal – linking entertainment with social conscience and charitable concern. Steering well clear of anything with a political edge, raising money and sometimes offering direct services to the public, like Esther Rantzen's *ChildLine*, this type of programming was breaking new ground. It was ground that critics found difficult to categorise and this made some feel distinctly uneasy. Was this a broadening of the public consciousness within the realm of popular entertainment or was it cynical exploitation? One debate in academic and journalistic forums centred on the ways in which the recipients of charity were represented in the programmes, more often than not shown as helpless victims (Benthall 1993). The criticisms were to have their effect, and the image of disaster victims and people with disabilities underwent an important shift as those who made such programmes began to aim for a collaborative rather than an exploitative approach.

Helen Swords

'In the mid-1980s the Manpower Services Commission made funding available to TVS – the ITV franchise holder for Southern England at that time – to take on unemployed graduates in their Community Action unit. This was the context in which I began my career.

Ironically, my placement was on a programme about unemployment. *Employment Action* was a weekly 5-minute slot in which jobseekers sent in their details and were hopefully matched up with employers. We set the service up, wrote fact sheets and made all the contacts, and all for the grand sum of £4,000 per annum.

TVS then offered me a contract on a low, but rather more reasonable wage, to work on *Telethon 88*, ITV's fund-raising effort. The event aimed to give a laugh to the participants and the audience, to involve lots of viewers in zany fund-raising activities and to serve a variety of good causes. Part of my job was to think up original ideas and to make sure they worked. As well as the usual pub runs and pram races, the ideas ranged from blobbing paint out of a low-flying plane, to outlining the ancient Cerne Abbas Giant, carved into a Dorset hillside, with a human chain of candle bearers. The other part of my job was administrative, running the project for TVS, representing the company on the committees that co-ordinated the *Telethon* across the ITV network, and assessing the claims from 2,000 charities. This was the power-dressing 1980s. At 25 I wore my shoulder pads and attended my meetings with the best of them.

I was allocated a personal secretary who was very experienced and I'm indebted to her to this day. She effectively taught me how to dictate letters. Apart from speeding up the process of replying to the literally hundreds of letters that arrived daily at the *Telethon* office, it helped me to write in a style that reflects the way people speak. I had been accustomed to academic writing, but soon realised that a light, chatty style is essential to much television scripting.

Looking back, I can now see why I was uneasy with the world of fund-raising and appeals. The relationship with those who were the recipients of charity was not entirely straightforward. This became clearer to me as I went on to London Weekend Television to work on their Social Appeals Programmes. By this time it was 1990 and some of the criticisms of charity television had made themselves felt. A much wider spectrum of people was now working for the various ITV Community Units – including some whose background was decidedly more working class and at least one producer who was a wheelchair user.

At LWT it was my job to make three-minute, sympathy-driven films in an advertising style about people whose problems seemed insurmountable. I had to talk at length to potential interviewees, to research background statistical and factual information and recce locations for filming. Scripts were written in advance of shooting in order to clarify the main points on which the appeal would hinge. They consisted of an 'ideal' text, including voice-over commentary and a paraphrase of the comments the producer expected to glean from the taped interviewees. On the left-hand side of the page would be a description of the ideal shots to complement the text. The items I wrote included a young man dying of AIDS, a carer whose wife had advanced Alzheimer's Disease, and a child with terminal leukemia. It was emotionally very demanding.

I was becoming interested in the politics of access to the airwaves. Daytime television gives many more opportunities for ordinary people to appear and speak their minds than the more high-powered evening programmes and I was torn between thinking that my space gave people in distressing situations the chance to address a wider audience and my concern about the terms under which they were doing it. In one case I was instructed to make the subjects seem especially helpless. A song I had chosen hinted at an ability to stand on your own feet, but that was not acceptable. When we did an appeal for homeless people in London, we chose teenagers because it was felt that it would be impossible to arouse public sympathy for those who were elderly or senile.

My next job was a brief but enjoyable interlude rummaging through the wardobes of famous people, researching for the independently produced, off-beat fashion magazine series, *Posh Frocks and New Trousers*. I also found guests for a USA/UK special of *The Time . . . Place . . .* talk show and did the odd stint finding participants for the TVS game show *Tell the Truth*. This meant tracking down someone with an unusual skill (say falcon training) and two other people with the ability to *pretend* they had that skill. The contestants had to guess which was the real falcon trainer.

I next applied for a job at a newly set up independent company, 24 Hour Productions (later Planet 24), who were about to launch the notorious *The Word* for Channel Four's Saturday night 'youth slot'. I was part of a three-person unit whose job was to find comedy and performance artists who were not members of Equity, the actors' union which regulates fees. This was partly because the producer wanted a rough, amateur feel, and partly because the budget necessitated that performers be paid at lower rates. It was a difficult task, as most artists who were any good *were* in Equity and not at all keen to perform for nothing. Planet 24 have become renowned for their ruthlessly stringent business practices. Their staff contracts are as severe as any in the trade, with no overtime pay and total 'buy-outs' of staff time and skills. The young team, average age 24 like the company name, set out to revolutionise youth television by introducing undiluted grunge and rap from the latest in American black and, increasingly, transvestite street culture. It was a mix designed to shock parents into locking up their daughters – and their sons. At 28 I was already several years older than most of the team, and the atmosphere of the programme didn't suit me.

I later came back to work for the company when it went on to produce *The Big Breakfast,* which launched Chris Evans and grabbed the early morning youth audience for Channel Four, but now I decided to apply for a more permanent post – this time with Middle Eastern Broadcasting Centre, a Saudi-run satellite company based in London. Their aim was to work with British technicians and production teams and they had advertised for producers with some knowledge of the Middle East and an experience of fashion and magazine shows. As a student I had taught English to Palestinians in the Israeli occupied territory on the West Bank of Jordan and my couple of months on *Posh Frocks* stood me in good stead. I got the job.

MBC broadcasts to the pan-Arab audience stretched from the Middle East across North Africa, to Arabic speakers in the UK and Europe. There is a news division which puts pan-Arab issues to the fore, and a features division which takes British entertainment television as its model. I developed a number of programme ideas, and became a producer on the weekly *Flying Carpet Travel Show* – half an hour of travel infotainment. No cocktails or bikinis could be shown, as both were unacceptable to a Muslim audience. I wrote and directed features including 'The Latest Travel Gadgets, Accessories and Baggage', 'A Luxury Windsailing Holiday on Lake Windermere' and 'The Dizzy Delights of Eurodisney'. I also negotiated the purchase of bulk travel footage mostly from American companies, where I could buy 15 minutes of travelogue for £250! I was first shocked and then dismayed as I realised what poor quality material some satellite stations were prepared to broadcast. It was my first sobering experience of really down-market standards.

Nevertheless, I was excited by the chance to follow a programme through all its stages, from the original idea, through scripting, filming and editing to the final package. I was able to experiment with graphics and studio technology. For my pilot for a 60-minute children's programme, I worked with the in-house graphics team to create a computer-animated robot, which became the 'mascot' for the show. I also gained the invaluable but nerve-wracking experience of directing the three camera studio recording. It was a bit like navigating at breakneck speed through a mass of fairground dodgem cars!

Although I felt I was at the cutting edge of the new television era, I was becoming concerned about being out of the mainstream of British television, so in 1993 I applied for a job back with Planet 24, who were now one year into *The Big Breakfast.* The company were happy to re-employ me as I had proved my ability to find 'ordinary people' and could be seen as the sympathetic and friendly face of television. My interest in all types and conditions of people for their *own* sakes (not just as camera fodder or as interesting material), which was partly provoked by my sociology degree, had remained with me. In my view my personal characteristics were as important in getting me my jobs as my more technical skills. My lack of conventional ambition to become a prestigious director was probably a positive advantage to the way I was perceived. The lack of female studio directors in ITV who could act as role models certainly tempered my ambitions.

As an assistant producer on *The Big Breakfast*, my job was to find families who were willing to become part of the programme. *The Big Breakfast* 'Family of the Week' live in a house rented especially for them. It is close to the 'Old Keeper's Lock', from which the programme is broadcast live from 7 until 9 on weekday mornings. During 'their' week the family take part in scheduled slots in the programme. One member might have a dream fulfilled – I remember how a mother cried for joy as she spoke to her heart-throb, the singer Michael Ball – and another might show us their special talents, say fresh fish culinary expertise. Other crueller antics went on, such as inviting the boy secretly craved by the teenage girl of the family on to the programme, getting the mother to take a mock driving test on camera, and there were other atrocities I would rather forget!

My week was crammed full. We would put out a call for families to apply during the programme, and it was my job to screen the applicants and decide whom to invite. My weekly schedule was as follows: *Sunday:* Travel to meet next week's family if they lived some distance away. I've been to Belfast, Leeds and Devon as well as to places nearer my London base. *Monday*: Shoot a video with them and try to get home that night. *Tuesday*: In the office. Log the video material and write a script. Compile four or five pages of notes on the individual family members, with suggestions for feature ideas based on their talents, interests and experiences. Circulate the notes to the other producers. Get home late. *Wednesday*: Supervise the edit of the 3-minute family video. Midday meeting with the other producers to arrange the on-screen activities for the family. Oversee the practical travel arrangements for the family coming to London. Check the 3-minute video and supervise any necessary alterations. Get home late. *Thursday*: Administration morning, checking expenses, replying to viewers' letters, arranging the social diary – the trips and outings for next week's family. Read through the mail bag, sort out replies and sift through potential future families. Leave the office at 6 pm. *Friday*: Research the next family. Speak to them on the telephone, give them my home number in case of urgent problems. Make next week's travel arrangements. Book and collect the High-8 video camera. Check all equipment is working for next week's shoot. Leave the office at 6 pm – with camera, tripod, extra batteries and small light kit. Carry that lot on the tube home (no taxi allowed). *Saturday:* Free!

Until now the directing and location work I had done had been with camera and sound technicians, referred to as ENG (Electronic News Gathering) crews. For *The Big Breakfast* I was handed a Hi-8 camera and told to get on with it. Or rather, I was given a quick 10-minute rundown on which button to push by the woman who had been doing the job before me. Since my first assignment was in Cornwall, I was decidedly nervous, for if things went wrong, there was simply no space in the schedule to go back to reshoot. And things did go wrong. A local power-cut brought total blackout. I had to think on my feet, improvise, and appear unflappable. My very first family was filmed with the aid of candles and matches.

I simply didn't have time to stay in touch with the families after their week in London, nor to follow up their experiences. In many cases I felt they went back to their 'ordinary' lives with some sadness – feeling as if they had to leave the party too soon. I also realised it was impossible to prepare them adequately for what was about to happen to them, and I began to worry about it. But there was a final irony. I soon discovered that most of the families owned their own camcorder or could beg or borrow one fairly easily. They would much rather make their *own* 3-minute profile. My role was gradually transformed to that of advisor, as the participants took over the technology.

People new to television, who go to work in the parts of the television world where I found myself, must realise that they will be working extremely long hours, under many different types of pressure. They will get overtired, have no time for any other life outside their job, and may be working with people with totally different views to themselves. This sort of work means you must be a *reactive* person, throwing yourself wholeheartedly into today's story, then being able to leave it totally behind ready for tomorrow's. You've got to be interested in gossip, in the mythologies built up by television, and not too concerned about their relation to the 'real' world. Within those limits you must find the space to be creative. Of course, it can be thrilling for a few brief moments to meet some of the stars. I have talked with Tony Curtis, Take That and Barbara Windsor (even though she walked out on me in the middle of a shoot. I've never quite forgiven her, but my producer was very understanding). Even so, the week-in week-out stressful nature of the business can take its toll.'

Television sport

For many viewers, especially men, sport is the most important ingredient of their television fare. As a mixture of pure spectacle, primitive rabble rousing and gladiatorial combat, television sport has, in recent years, built itself into a major viewing ritual. Sport has an input into all news bulletins and the specialist sports departments have long followed the sporting calendar, turning major national and international events – the World Cup, the Grand National, the Boat Race, Wimbledon – into highlights of the televisual year. Watching the big fight or an important match in the pub, or at home with friends, is one of the few remaining contexts where collective viewing remains an essential part of the experience.

Nevertheless sport tends to have low prestige amongst television production departments and is rarely critically discussed (Whannel 1992). This may partly be because, apart from the major events, much sports coverage is made up of low-key, continuous broadcasting. Sports programmes use to the full the unstructured organisation of time which the television medium allows, their loose format held together by a great deal of unscripted talk. They are often transmitted live, usually from Outside Broadcast (OB) units. These are mobile studios, based in a fleet of specially equipped vans, from which as many as nine cameras can be co-ordinated by directors and producers, video and sound engineers. The work involves long hours and much travelling.

Although conservative in their content and style, sports programmes have been at the forefront of the organisational upheavals that are shaking British television. Complex financial deals surround the broadcasting and international marketing of sporting events. The sponsorship of programmes by advertisers has followed on the sponsorship of the sports themselves. Although the UK regulations require a clear distinction between programmes and advertising, sports promoters have negotiated an ever-more prominent display of the sponsor's name and logo, painted on the grass, displayed on the signs posted up around the stadium or arena, on the score board and all over the clothing of the players. The cycle racing on Channel Four, sponsored by Kelloggs, was the first to use the company's logo as part of the programme title.

Relations between the broadcasting organisations and those who run those traditional British sports, such as football and rugby, which attract loyal and devoted crowds, have not always been easy. The Football Association have moved from their original suspicion of the competition which broadcasting matches on television would bring, to realising that they could sell the right to broadcast to the highest bidder. Since 1992 the satellite company BSkyB has been acquiring the rights to live sporting events, in particular Premier League Association Football. This means that the live match can only be seen on a subscription channel, leaving ITV and the BBC with edited highlights. The consequent uproar led to a clause in the 1996 Broadcasting Act ensuring that the licence-fee paying public has the right to see certain 'listed' sporting events at no extra cost.

As the broadcasting of sport gradually becomes as important as the event itself, there has been growing concern over the adaptation of the sports to suit the needs of television. Matches may now be scheduled at times convenient for the broadcasters. American Football is played in short segments, to allow for the frequent commercial breaks on American television. Colin McMillan, General Secretary of the Professional Boxers' Association, has pointed to a growing 'culture of brutality' in the ring as a consequence of television's appetite for 'sensation, blood and gore' (O'Hagen 1995).

Much sports coverage remains predictable and uncritical. However, from 1982, Channel Four and its independent supplier Cheerleader Productions have tried to get away from the 'men in blazers' image. They introduced a wider range of sports, more exciting presentation and more explanation. In recent years there have been documentaries about sport and sporting personalities, and more programmes that look critically at the social and cultural context of sport.

Most sports departments in television organisations remain small. Those who work in them have tended to get in through luck, persistence or contacts. Below sports producer Rupert Rumney, of the independent company Grand Slam, discusses his work.

Rupert Rumney: *sports producer*

' I 've been working in sports television for ten years now. I did a media studies degree at the Polytechnic of Central London (now the University of Westminster), where I was taught by many distinguished theorists, some of whom managed to discuss successfully how you traverse the boundary between the theoretical and the practical side of things, which was always a big problem at college. I liked a lot of sport, watched a lot of telly, and decided that sports was a good area to get into. I did have a vague crusading notion, because I couldn't believe how much sport I watched yet how little I learnt about it. I felt that there should be more to it than just pointing the camera. Of course there have been radical changes in sports coverage over the last ten or twelve years.

At that time there were only the BBC, ITV and one independent production company, Cheerleader Productions, who were doing American football for Channel Four. That was *the* state of the art sports programme, the first to use rock music, graphics and an expensive character generator, a Chyron. It produced big characters with drop shadows and the whole thing looked like an American programme rather than an English one. Reading through my *Broadcast* and other magazines, it seemed to me that these were the people who were attempting to do something different and that's one reason I wanted to go there.

I had a roundabout personal contact with someone who worked at Cheerleader, so basically I squeezed it. Whenever I was doing anything that I thought might be of interest to him I'd write him a postcard. I literally picked on this one person and made him somehow impressed, not necessarily by my talent, because that would have been impossible to prove, but certainly by my tenacity and my desire for the job. Finally he gave me a job labelling tapes.

Ten years ago the commercialisation of sport as we know it today was just beginning, so when I'd been at Cheerleader a month or two, I was given the job of putting together a short video for the England Rugby Football Union to show to potential sponsors. This was a post-production exercise, a day's editing which involved taking shots from a couple of rugby matches and bastardising an old promotional video. It was a stroke of luck, being in the right place at the right time. My favourite and special sport is rugby. I played it quite well and I loved it, so I understood what worked about it visually and emotionally. I was given an excellent editor. If it had been a junior editor, which it probably should have been, we wouldn't have got half of what we did out of the editing suite. But it ended up with the Marketing Manager of the RFU writing to my boss and saying thanks for this excellent video, and they had just signed up their biggest ever sponsorship deal. After that it was going to be hard to get rid of me.

From Day One until now, some ten years later, I haven't been frightened of being given new jobs, because I'm not frightened of asking someone if I don't know the answer. That would be my lesson number one. No one in a superior position minds being asked a question, because it means they are the ones who know. What they *will* mind is when you mess it up because you were afraid to ask.

The next step was to become an assistant producer. At Cheerleader we cut our teeth on Italian football, which at that time went out on Sky. The games were played on Sunday, and we would get a 90-minute tape around lunchtime on the Monday together with another tape of the goals from the rest of the division. We would edit the game down from 90 minutes to 35 minutes and turn it into a package in about 6 hours. From the Cheerleader offices in Brewer Street, we'd literally run to Wardour Street with the tape and hope we'd got it there in time for transmission.

That is the bread-and-butter task of most assistant producers on sports programmes: taking a game, shortening it, and packaging around it. That's where the skill of logging comes in. As you're watching the tape, you write down where it's possible to make the edits. For example, you can always edit off the slomo (slow motion sequence) because it is clear that it is not part of the live game. You can edit when the ball is not in shot or if there's a cutaway of the manager. Even though the television version is only 20 minutes long, you have to show the kick-off, half-time, the start of the second half and the final whistle. The final edited 'game' is a complete con. When you smooth out the sound with your audio faders, mixing gradually from an exciting bit to a quieter bit, partly you are concerned with comfort to the ear, but basically it's a con that we're trying to achieve. It's an approach that goes back 30 years to a generation of unsophisticated viewers, because it pretends to show a whole game. Things are changing, but slowly. Sometimes now they do a DVE (Digital Video Edit) move when they get to the end of the first half, then superimpose a caption saying 'second half'. They're getting there, but how long's it going to take?

More elaborate programmes like American football would involve a presenter in the studio and links with a guest. There would also be a feature about a player, a city or a ground, then the game, then post-match interviews, a highlights package of all the other games, and a music piece at the end. Very simple editorial stuff. Everything depends on the budget. If the budget said, 'here's money for shooting links', then we shot links. We had a comfortable niche market and were happy to deal with the work that was coming our way. But since Cheerleader's demise, four or five new companies have come into being. There are a lot of people vying to get in there now.

At about the beginning of 1988, Trillion, the facility house that owned Cheerleader, based at Canary Wharf, went bankrupt. Alan Pascoe, the Olympic hurdler, who had a sports sponsorship and marketing company, wanted to expand into production, so we were bought by Alan Pascoe Associates as a management buyout, and formed Grand Slam Sports.

Now our programmes include live snooker for the BBC and European football and boxing for ITV using Outside Broadcast units. In sports television, producers usually direct their own single camera stuff for features or interviews. There is a division of labour on a live event when the producer controls the programme and the director actually pushes the buttons and edits the game while it's in progress. Sports can be pretty wallpaperish. A lot of hard work goes into it, but you have no say over most of its content. You do a nice pacy first 5 minutes to hook the viewer, like the opening of a James Bond film, then you can be incredibly lazy. You can run your titles then go to Des Lynam and Alan Hansen in the studio and let them fill the next 5 minutes. Mostly it just happens. As far as game coverage goes, it's just a question of having enough cameras so that you don't miss a tackle or an elbow off the ball or something like that. Some people work 40 weeks of the year on a single programme. For example, working on football means working every weekend from the middle of August to the end of May. It makes you very good at it, but it's not something I'd like to do.

The really creative end of it is in post-production. That's where you are working with people's heart beats, with people's vision, with people's ears, with people's senses. You have to work out what it is about the sport that makes people watch. It's in post-production that I feel most powerful. I talk about getting goose bumps. I feel I'm at the cutting edge of broadcasting when I'm editing something that's goddam hot and goddam sexy and I know I'm going to get something going up the back of their necks.

In post-production you can colourise things and make fancy shapes on the screen. Some of those flashy things are very good, but in my opinion they can be overplayed. Electronically generated colours and flying things around is a pretty ugly way of doing things. Being more of a film fan, I'm a believer in what you create with the camera. It can be enhanced in post-production, but more subtly.

I think a lot has fed off the 1990 World Cup presentation. Not just classical music and sport, but placing sport within national and cultural surroundings. For the poster for *Italia 90* they took a graphic of the Colosseum and placed a football pitch inside it, saying 'This is a land of great culture and football is part of it' rather than just saying 'Here's the 1990 World Cup'. The Italians came up with *Nessun Dorma* as a theme for the tournament and the BBC 'backroom boys' constructed the visuals for the series titles. That part is simple. It all comes down to the music and you know what the images will be – the goals, the celebrations, the fans and the despair. That's what you're doing when you're logging. You're noting the great close-ups, the disappointments, Gascoigne crying. Then when you go back you put all these things together.

I've been lucky in that I get the funny bits and pieces. I've done commercials, I've done a pop promo video for the England Rugby team, and I've just made my first documentary for BBC Scotland on Gavin Hastings, ex-Captain of Scotland Rugby, who's quite a special, well-loved figure. Normally as an independent producer in sport you don't get to consider your audience or your place in the schedule, but with BBC Scotland we had long discussions about the kind of progamme we were trying to make, how the audience would receive it and how it fitted into their New Year's Eve celebrations.

There is part of me that says that sports television will make us all into morons. I have just been working for Star TV, Sky's sister company broadcasting across Asia, India and Pakistan. I'm not arguing that India should be a place that we go and visit where they bake their own bread and don't watch television, but I am concerned about the kind of television that Sky and Star produce. It is bright visually, but it has no subtlety and no intellectual content whatsoever. If you watch Sky or Star you will see the same thing over and over again. The same promo will get run five or six times during the 2 hours that you're watching a game. The nature of international broadcasting now is to throw out everything that makes something interesting and make it as bland as possible. Watch the sports programme that goes out on Channel Four in the mornings and listen to the script. They will never use a complicated word or a complicated construction of a sentence because it's going to be dubbed into forty languages. That cuts out all possibility of nuance or humour or subtlety in what you say. Everything has to be over-simplified.

It's slightly less dangerous for us, because in Britain we're a very sophisticated audience – and I mean everybody. We've grown up with the BBC and with Reithian concepts of broadcasting. We can recognise the dross and we know when we are being overcrammed with sweeties. We can change channels and watch a good movie, or a documentary or the news. All they've got is Star TV – broadcasting images that have no meaning and no relevance. India now has their own version of MTV, called VTV, a bunch of young girls dancing around and showing off their bodies. I fear for that kind of imagery, because it's so new and it still has that aura of desirability about it.

The old relationship between a channel paying a production company to produce programmes is now pretty much unheard of in sports television. The financing of programmes is very complicated and most of it hinges on sponsorship. You may be making a programme sponsored by a tobacco company, but the ITC regulations on sponsorship do not allow you to receive the money directly from them. It has to go through an agency, then through the governing body of the sport and then back to you, even though everyone knows the tobacco company are paying for the production. Sponsorship means that they will have exclusive perimeter advertising and the tournament is called by the sponsor's name. Sometimes potential sponsors, such as brewery firms, come straight to us looking for ideas and wanting to back a strand of programming. There are a lot of things going on, some of them underhand.

For example, the regulations say that you're not allowed to generate the sponsor's logo electronically. It can be seen in the stadium on the perimeter banners behind the players, but it cannot be introduced specially by the television company. But now, in cricket, they paint the logo on the ground using a form of distorted perspective so that when the camera is at the right angle it looks exactly like an electronically generated logo on the screen. It's so perfect that you can't believe it. Because it's painted on the ground it gets through the ITC regulations.

Now I'm moving towards the business side. Because of the expansion of sports television as a global industry, my firm has decided to set up a production office in Delhi. Our major competitors have been there for a couple of years. There are forty channels to fill and millions of middle-class Indians who want Nike trainers and the like. A production manager and I are going out there for a six-month trial period to see what we can get up and running.'

References and key texts

Benthall, J. (1993) *Disasters, Relief and the Media*, London: I.B. Tauris

Harrison, P. and Palmer, R. (1986) *News out of Africa: Biafra to Band Aid*, London: Hilary Shipman

Lewis, P. (1991) *A Right Royal Event: The Making of an Outside Broadcast*, London, BBCTV Training

Livingstone, S. and Lunt, P. (1994) *Talk on Television: Audience Participation and Public Debate*, London: Routledge

O'Hagen, S. (1995) 'Television threatens tyranny', the *Independent*, London, 20 December

Strinati, D. and Wagg, S. (1992) *Come on Down: Popular Media and Culture in Post War Britain*, London: Routledge

Tunstall, J. (1993) *Television Producers*, London: Routledge

Whannel, G. (1992) *Fields in Vision: Television Sport and Cultural Transformation*, London: Routledge

11 Documentary and factual television

Representing reality

Factual programmes tend to be seen as the more 'serious' aspect of television. They aim to lead rather than follow audience taste as they draw attention to social issues and expound on politics, the arts or science. For this reason they have been the subject of much heated debate and policy adjustment over the last few years.

British television was launched with a commitment to reliable and objective reporting within a visual culture which valued the documentary, the everyday and the presence of ordinary people on the screen. Factual television was forged out of such diverse sources as cinema newsreels, radio features, the photo-journalism of illustrated political magazines such as *Picture Post*, and sponsored instructional and educational films (Corner 1991). It inherited the trust and affection that BBC radio had built up during the Second World War, and the prestige and social democratic commitment of British documentary cinema.

When John Grierson launched the documentary film movement in Britain in the late 1920s, he described his approach as 'the creative treatment of actuality' (Sussex 1975). The documentary filmmakers of the 1930s and 1940s explored the real world in ways that ranged from the pragmatic to the poetic, but, since the 1950s, it has been on television that this vision has had its greatest flowering. Grierson's broad definition has come to embrace genres and styles as widely disparate as dramatised documentary, reporter-led current affairs, observational filmmaking, interview-based programmes, expositions of art and science, and experimental, avant-garde image making (*see* John Wyver, p. 160 below). Some of these styles emphasise the 'creativity' of Grierson's description, others the 'actuality'. The 'treatment' has varied over television's half century or so according to fashion, changing technology, the requirements of the programme strand, and the personal style of the programme maker. Nevertheless, all factual formats bear some relation to the 'historical world' to use Bill Nichols' emphasis. It was Nichols who defined documentary as '*representing* reality', since the act of representing covers a whole complex of relationships, including reporting, engaging in dialogue with, investigating, observing, interpreting and reflecting on. All factual forms stand in some sort of relation to the reality that is their subject matter and bear some sort of responsibility towards it (Nichols 1991: Rabinowitz 1994). Television in the UK has by and large taken that responsibility seriously.

The first Documentary Department at the BBC, run by eminent filmmaker Paul Rotha, was studio based. It *recreated* 'real life' in the way that many earlier acclaimed documentaries, such as *Drifters* and *Night Mail*, had done. But directors were keen to get out of the studio and on to the still bleak streets of urban post-war Britain. At Granada, where *Coronation Street* was launched with the documentary feel of kids playing skipping games on the cobbles, Denis Mitchell developed a personal style which was allied to innovative work in radio. His dense, interwoven sound-tracks, made up of snatches of conversation, local sound effects and overheard music, were laid over a visual montage of faces and glimpses of street scenes (Corner 1991).

There was very little sync shooting in programmes like Denis Mitchell's *Morning in the Streets*, but these were exceptions. The quintessential devices for factual television rapidly established themselves as the interview and the personality presenter. Talking heads dominate our television fare and the flow of narrative speech forms the thread which leads the audience through a programme. Many documentaries are led by a charismatic presenter. David Attenborough's knowledge of his subject and his engaging manner have made him the audience's guide through forty years of natural history and wildlife documentaries.

As interviewees, both ordinary people and knowledgeable people, people with a story to tell and people who have an achievement to celebrate, have made up the millions who have taken part in factual programmes. Series that pioneered interview styles included Desmond Wilcox's *Man Alive*, which probed into 'feelings and emotions, not facts and opinions' (*Can I ask you a personal question? – The 'Man Alive' story* 1993). The programme's technique of moving to a big close-up and keeping the camera rolling despite the obvious distress of the interviewee has been criticised as intrusive, but it made gripping television and paved the way for many successors.

By the 1970s, the observational style which eschewed both presenter and formal interviews was greatly expanded by series such as Roger Graef's *Space between Words* and Paul Watson's long-running fly on the wall series *The Family*, in which the transmission of the programmes fed back into the lives of the real family who were being observed so that their reactions were re-incorporated into the programme. By the 1990s a modified version of the observational style has settled into being a major television documentary form, used for strands such as *Forty Minutes* and *Cutting Edge*.

British television has contributed to the development of ethnographic film-making with strands such as *Disappearing World*, and has not hesitated to deal with the major events of the century. Central TV's commissioning of Latvian filmmaker Juris Podnieks to make *Hello Do You Hear Us?* on the collapse of the Soviet Union, was indeed inspired. The series of five hour-long documentaries, in monumental style, which covered the scope and tragic history of Eastern Europe, were crammed with energy and drew on the work of the great Soviet filmmakers themselves. But substantial documentary making need not sweep across a global canvas. Lewisham Town Hall in South London was the focus for Charles Stewart's meticulous observation of a local government at work in *Town Hall*. From the council leader ironing his shirts after a late-night meeting, to the council's agonising over cuts in expenditure while the local nursery school staged a sit-in in the town hall vestibule, it shed unprecedented light on the the workings of local government.

Following the Broadcasting Act in 1990, there was a fear that factual programmes would be chased off the television screens by the newly enfranchised television companies and their need to maximise audiences. In a celebrated speech, Paul Jackson of Carlton UK, the company that was awarded the franchise for London weekday broadcasting, announced that no programme with viewing figures of less than 6 million was worth broadcasting in the middle of the evening, and, what is more, it was not the business of television to get people out of jail. This was a dig at investigatory journalism, and in particular at *World in Action*, which, backed by Granada Television, had mounted a long-running campaign over the six Irishmen convicted of bombing two public houses in Birmingham on behalf of the IRA in 1974. Despite much concern about the weakness of the evidence against them, the 'Birmingham Six' had been imprisoned for life and served sixteen years before the persistence of campaigners secured their release. *World in Action* had made several investigatory programmes which re-examined the evidence and followed them up with a fast-moving drama documentary, *Who Bombed Birmingham?*, which dramatised their own investigations. Political broadcasting across the spectrum of genres had been made possible because of the long-term commitment of the journalists, programme makers and Granada Television.

Glenwyn Benson, then editor of the BBC's main current affairs programme *Panorama*, was reported as saying that programmes like hers had a different sort of responsibility to the audience from merely building up numbers, and it would not matter if only six people watched. This off-the-cuff remark itself brought an outcry from the popular press and those who felt that the BBC licence fee could only be justified by high audience figures.

As it turned out, during the 1990s, factual programming had an unexpected flowering, due to a number of factors. There has been a long history of programmes that have mixed serious reporting with lighter items and a more popular touch, beginning with *Tonight* in the early 1960s. Recently, a growing number of factual programmes have been looking to increase audience appeal. Current affairs programmes which had seen themselves as issue based, were being replaced by current affairs programmes that were people based and story based. They sought popular presenters such as Roger Cook, whose *Cook Report* had pioneered the doorstepping, up-front, challenging style, as he thrust his microphone at crooked businessmen, bugged secret meetings with drugs dealers, and continually risked being beaten up. There was less inhibition about going for the sensational and shocking image as 'reality television' was copied from the US, with such 'ambulance chasing' genres as *Blues and Twos*, which gets closer to the blood and horror of real traffic accidents than ever before. There has been less restraint and less respect for the subjects of reports. Other new genres have included reconstructions, such as *999* and *Crimewatch UK*, and the use of the hidden cameras in such series as *Undercover Britain*, which revealed the abuse of servants from the Philippines and the illegal selling of guns on Manchester streets, as well as other hidden crimes and inhumanities.

There has been a concern that factual television would collapse into 'tabloid television', and that much documentary would thrive on audience voyeurism. But alongside the growth of these more exploitative genres, both Channel Four and BBC2 have expanded their scheduling of documentary and other factual material with the use of 'seasons' to bring together groups of films on similar topics, such as Channel Four's *Soviet Spring* and *Bloody Bosnia* and the BBC's *African Summer*.

Much lighter programmes, which come within Jeremy Tunstall's category of 'edinfotainment', include series on travel, gardening, cooking and collecting antiques (Tunstall 1993). These and innumerable other day-to-day topics continue to make up the staple diet of factual programming.

On genres, styles and formats

Classification by production types and styles

Factual programmes may involve all three of the programme production types described above (*see* Programme production types, p. 34 above). They may be studio based, involving either journalist-led interviews, discussion amongst specialists or audience participation. They may be made partly, or entirely, outside the studio. They include a large proportion of interview-based programmes and presenter- or reporter-led programmes, and they also include factually based dramas and dramatic reconstructions.

Classification by content

The broadcasting organisations classify factual programmes partly by content and partly by style and approach. Documentary programming can be found in several different departments, including Arts, Documentaries and Current Affairs, each with its own specific brief and production practices. Within the departments, as the years have passed, ever more specialised strands have been developed. By the late 1990s there are series devoted to politics, social issues, arts, science, history, criminal investigations, educational issues, moral dilemmas, the press, business and finance, local issues, international affairs, consumer advice, the media, ethnographic programming, natural history, travel and more. Such classifications have their uses and their limits. Introducing a conference on documentary, the distinguished television journalist Jonathan Dimbleby argued that 'the attempt to separate social, political, economic and human is an artificial attempt. . . . Although it is useful for those making strands, it can also be a self-damaging prison' (Sheffield 1995).

Yet classifications are never hard and fast. New genres are constantly emerging and producers and commissioning editors are always interested in developing innovative ways of making programmes, provided they are not so strange as to alienate their projected audience (*see* John Wyver, p. 160 and Stuart Cosgrove, p. 211 below).

Some documentary series have run over decades, others may consist of six, or up to twenty-six programmes. Each series has its own series editor or executive producer and typically will employ different producer/directors for each of the individual programmes. Below we look at some major documentary genres.

Current documentary genres

Observational narrative

The style derives from the direct cinema techniques evolved in the US in the 1960s when producer Robert Drew launched his own form of immediate journalism. Working with Richard Leacock, D. A. Pennebaker and David and Albert Maysles, he used lightweight equipment and a very small crew who could be right where the action is (*see* Camera, p. 49 and Sound, p. 77). The dramatic excitement of those early films made the traditional ways of shooting seem stale and artificial. In 1960 *Primary* followed John F. Kennedy's campaign for the Democratic nomination as President. More than thirty years later, the same crew working in the same style made *The War Room*, which followed Bill Clinton's presidential campaign team.

Drew and Leacock have continued to argue for a rigorous set of rules, which include 'Never talk to the subject, never intervene, never ask someone to repeat an action, never add music or special effects.' As Paul Arthur points out, this deprives filmmakers of many of the resources of their craft. Very few filmmakers follow the full puritanical rigour of the original formula (Arthur 1993). The style has developed in its own way on UK television, influenced by the National Film School, under Colin Young, which has trained many prominent documentary makers including camera/directors such as Nick Broomfield, Diane Tammes and Molly Dineen.

The observational narrative is led by sync dialogue and avoids voiceover or commentary. As it looks for the narrative component of the documentary, programmes tend to centre on specific individuals, often at moments of crisis (*see* Alan Hayling, p. 230 below). This means that the filmmaker must gain a rapport with the people who are the subjects of the programme, so that filming can follow events as they unfold, anticipating the important moments and getting the camera operator into the scene when there's drama going on. The style combines the rigorous direct cinema approach with a looser, more pragmatic method. It may include interaction between the crew behind the camera and those in front, with interviews done during the action, so as to keep the movement going. It may mean repeating an action which would otherwise not be recorded on camera, say the tape ran out, or the light was too dim, or the dialogue was inaudible. It may include interviews shot separately from the action then edited in.

Paul Berriff, producer of *The Nick*, a record of five months in a Leeds police station, says, 'The more time you spend, the better the film is. Three or four weeks is not enough. For *The Nick* we had two cameras for 24 hours a day' (Sheffield 1995). In recent years, British institutions such as the Navy, a Welsh Guards company, the Royal Opera House, the London

Zoo, a Hackney housing estate, schools, hospital wards, police drugs squads and many others have moved across our screens in what must be the most documented society in the modern world. It has been noted that the 'fly on the wall' has found it easier to peer down on the poor and vulnerable than on the rich and powerful, but over the years Roger Graef has turned his cameras round and built up a body of work about key institutions which has brought the structures of power under filmic scrutiny, from British Steel and the EC, to families and schools. His series on the Thames Valley Police, made in 1982, gave an unprecedented insight into the workings of the police force and, more importantly, into their attitudes and assumptions. The programme *A Complaint of Rape* caused a public outcry and led to a re-evaluation within the police of their policies towards rape victims.

Current affairs

In 1958 Grace Wyndham Goldie, Head of 'Talks' (as the factual depart-ment at BBC Television was then called), re-launched a programme called *Panorama* as 'something quite new on television'. Together with the other long-running current affairs programmes, *This Week* and *World in Action*, it set a model of journalist-led programmes whose aim was to address the news and the political agenda in greater depth than the news bulletins allowed. They aimed to get behind the headlines, to *explain* what was going on and to provide a 'window on the world' (Goldie 1977). Since those early years, the quantity of television has expanded, political progamming has grown, and technology has made far-flung parts of the world more acces-sible. The broad canvas those pioneer programmes set out to cover is now divided amongst a wide range of more specialised programmes. *Assignment* deals with foreign affairs, *Public Eye* with domestic social issues, *Taking Liberties* with miscarriages of justice and so on. But these more recent programmes in the current affairs mode have inherited the stress on the investigatory and the political, seeking out scandal and atrocity and getting behind official smoke screens of misinformation. As part of television journalism they are subject to the guidelines laid down by the BBC and the ITV regulatory bodies on objectivity and balance and the commitment to 'fair and honest reporting' (*see* Television news: fact and neutrality, p. 179 below).

Throughout the 1970s and 1980s, overseas reporting covered political upheavals in Cambodia, Rhodesia, the Middle East and many other parts of the globe. It monitored apartheid South Africa – which led to frequent ban-nings of programme teams from entering that country. Programmes recorded the human cost of natural disasters in places including Ethiopia, Sudan and Bangladesh and followed the British at war – in Aden, the Falklands and the Gulf. Closer to home, where government sensibilities are more easily ruffled, investigatory programmes have needed to address the issues of balance more scrupulously, risking attack either for bias or for cowardice. If their position is overtly oppositional, the press and government have cried that television is peopled by left-wing activists; if their criticisms are too mild, academics and the left have complained that their very structure makes them unable to question the status quo. Throughout their history current affairs programmes have been at the centre of noisy and highly politicised disputes. When programmes have directly challenged government secrecy, particularly when they covered the situation in Northern Ireland, they have faced a tightening of regulation which on occasion has moved into overt censorship (Miller 1994). Nevertheless, most current affairs programme makers agree that the aim is to follow John Grierson's formula and to engage the citizen in national and international debate. This includes, in John Pilger's words, 'telling people things they don't want to know'.

Current affairs remains a journalist-led genre. It is journalists who, as researchers or reporters, seek out the stories and are as influential in structuring the programme as the director. Programmes are organised around a journalistic report, which may be arguing a case or proving a point. Reporters frequently appear in vision, but may write a voice-over script which is narrated by the 'voice of the programme', as with *World in Action* and *Dispatches*. Jonathan Dimbleby has argued that the skill of writing is less valued today. For him a well-written commentary uses language with precision, avoids cliché and redundant terms, illuminates the visual without repeating it, and values the meaning of silence. 'A well-crafted script can pierce the surface of the image, shaping it often with memorable effect. Striving for it really matters' (Sheffield 1995).

Despite the high seriousness of much of the output, the current affairs genre has, from its early days, included lighter items and a more personal touch. Many current affairs programme makers argue that their programmes are more powerful if, as well as addressing the *issues* in question, they *also* tell a story. There is usually an effort to personalise a report, finding participants with whom the viewers can identify. During the early 1990s there was some concern that such personalisation may have gone too far, to produce a form of 'tabloid' current affairs, which is more concerned with audience appeal than tough reporting and analysis. However, as the decade progressed, the scope of journalist-led programmes, reporting on both domestic social affairs and the proliferation of global upheavals, from Bosnia to Chechnya, has been of unprecedented depth and sensitivity.

Polemic and authorship

The broadcasting authorities emphasise the distinction between news, which carries the authority of the broadcaster, and so must be seen to be neutral and without editorial voice; current affairs, which carries the authority of the programme team, and so may express carefully balanced editorial opinion, supported by evidence; and authored documentaries, in which the individual reporter is named, and is able to express more extreme and idiosyncratic opinions of their own.

John Pilger is an outspoken journalist who expressly states that he does not set out to be objective but to argue a case. A powerful series drew attention to poverty in the increasing prosperity of the 1970s, and, with director David Munro he has made a series of documentaries for Central Television, spanning a period of ten years, in which he has sought to publicise the oppressive regime in East Timor, a cause which otherwise had not made the headlines.

During the 1970s, television was subject to much criticism for the consensual nature of its programming, reflecting mainstream political opinion and taking for granted a wide set of assumptions about society and its structures. The Annan Report in 1977 recommended that due impartiality 'should not preclude committed public affairs programmes from having a recognised place on the broadcasting outlets' (Annan 1977). One of Channel Four's early aims was to balance across their output, rather than within a programme, and to allow both overtly biased programmes and a wider range of viewpoints access to the screens. More recently, series such as *War Cries*, *Correspondent* and *Frontline* have made space for much more polemical reporting.

In documentary making which is not part of the journalist-led current affairs strands, the filmmaker has tended to be seen as the 'author' of the film. Some, like Nick Broomfield, have built their programmes around their own personality and production practices. Many documentary directors see their programmes as forms of self-expression rather than a routine contribution to the television output. The creative use of documentary material both broadens and enhances the scope of factual filmmaking, but, at the same time, can give rise to many questions about the relationship between the director, as author, and those people represented in the film (*see* Documentary dilemmas, p. 172 below).

Television and history

Powerful documentaries like Debbie Christie's *We Are All Neighbours* (for *Disappearing World*) and Clive Gordon's *The Unforgiving* (for *True Stories*), both made during the war in Bosnia, record history as it is happening with a closeness to the lives of those involved inconceivable before the expansion of television. Current affairs programmes like *This Week* have monitored historical processes, such as the troubles in Northern Ireland, as they have occurred, and have been able to revisit participants and reinterpret events with the hindsight given by time and subsequent developments. The journalist, Peter Taylor, has reported on the Northern Ireland issue, getting to know many of the participants and gaining an insight into all perspectives, since he found himself caught up in the events of Bloody Sunday as an inexperienced young reporter in 1972.

This half century of factual programme making concerning issues of political and social importance has created an extensive archive of visual history which television itself has recycled in a number of different ways. Various documentary styles have evolved their own ways of recalling and reinterpreting the past. They include programmes made from archive material from both film and television sources, notably the mammoth twenty-six episode *The World at War*. Many documentary makers recognise that film and television material is never a simple record of events, but has its own history which in turn affects how events are remembered. Ilan Ziv's *Tango of Slaves*, which deals with his father's experience of the Warsaw Ghetto, is a programme that explores the interweaving of document and memory.

Programmes that deal in oral history have become a specialised, interview-based genre, in which people retell stories from their past. Pioneered by Stephen Peet in *Yesterday's Witness*, which ran between 1969 and 1980, it was taken up by the Television History Workshop in the early 1980s. It has been a way of either exploring particular historical incidents through the memories of witnesses, or of building an image of a previous era by gathering together disparate memories around a specific topic – say starting school in the 1930s. The Bristol-based Testimony Films has made several moving series on such previously taboo topics as sexuality and criminality in the earlier part of the century, recalling the hidden pleasures and cruelties of an earlier era in an engrossing but completely unsensational style.

Channel Four's *Secret History* sets out to give a new insight into a piece of history that had been taken for granted but can now be re-thought in the light of new evidence. Investigative and revelatory, it concentrates on a particular incident, using many historical methods, including archive footage, witness testimony and journalistic research. In several of the programmes, those people whose version of events has until now been excluded, are able to retell their stories.

New genres and innovative styles

The development of technology, together with critiques of the more established forms, has opened the way for a range of new genres in the 1990s. The demand for a wider access to the airwaves, and the recognition that the television output has excluded significant groups of people, has resulted in a wider range of community-based programmes (*see* Tony Dowmunt, p. 202 below) and the founding of such units as the BBC's Disability Programme Unit which have aimed to evolve their own characteristic styles. The video diary style, in which programmes are made with domestic video equipment by members of the public rather than by television professionals, has introduced a new way of making programmes. Low-tech, with a less polished appearance, they seem to bring the audience even closer to the realities they show. Community-based dramas, such as *Wingnut and the Sprog*, have been filmed on Hi-8 and the style has crept into other forms of factual programming, notably travel programmes.

The use of covert filming with miniature cameras, as in Channel Four's *Undercover Britain* series, is another innovation that has changed the visual aesthetic, apparently guaranteeing authenticity with its blurry images, often taken from strange angles and with the subject partially concealed.

The breaking down of hard and fast boundaries between the different forms has led to a plethora of hybrid styles, ways of making programmes which take an unusual slant on things or make a cultural comment (*see* Stuart Cosgrove, p. 211 below). Reconstructions and re-enactments are as old as documentary itself, but have had a resurgence since programmes like *Who Bombed Birmingham?* and *Lockerbie* set out to be journalistic investigations as well as drama. *Crime Watch UK* and *999* are based on reconstructions of factual events. Current affairs programmes do not hesitate to use reconstruction, slow motion and music to heighten their effect. As well as the new low-tech imagery, such programmes have also made use of the whole range of glossy impressionistic lighting and video effects.

Many documentary makers and critics have made the point that an expansion of documentary genres should go beyond differences in subject matter and style, to reconsider the whole relationship between the filmmaker to their work (Winston 1995). Over the 1980s, Channel Four's Independent Film and Video Department had commissioned critical work by those who felt that the documentary distance between filmmaker and subject cannot be justified. For many women documentarists this remains an important part of their own approach (Baehr and Dyer 1987; Rabinowitz 1994). Black filmmakers, too, have argued that a conventional, observational style has been impossible for them to use since, working as an 'underground' as members of an unrepresented group, they have needed to take a personal responsibility for the content of their work, making authored, polemical films (ICA 1988).

Arts

Programmes that deal with the visual arts, classical music and literature have a history on British television which was defined by Huw Wheldon's *Monitor* launched by the BBC in 1958. Arts programming has been the arena in which the traditional definition of art as 'high art' has been both reinforced and challenged. Against the early recognition that television should have a space in which the 'great tradition' of European culture is explored and where the work of contemporary artists is critically considered, critics of the mainstream arts programmes have pointed to their neglect of popular culture and the newer arts, and to their wilful disregard of the way that 'art' shades into media, photography and other contemporary forms. Even so, it was on *Monitor* that Ken Russell made his first baroque and exuberant reconstructions of the biographies of artists and musicians and in *Pop Goes the Easel*, celebrated the world of advertising and brash commercialism that was the subject matter of 'pop' artists of the 1960s.

Although arts programmes have tended to be middle-brow, avoiding both the extremely popular and the very unpopular – both mass culture and difficult modernism – their broadening scope over the 1970s opened the way to the 1980s explosion of programmes about style, the media, advertising, and design: those spaces where the avant-garde meets street culture (*see* Stuart Cosgrove, p. 211 below).

In any programme about an artist or a work of art, there remains a commitment to give the television audience the chance to see – or hear – and appreciate the work, within a documentary that is enjoyable, possibly critical, and creative in its own right. The landmark series (*see* John Wyver, p. 160 below) have been those that defined the meaning of art for those societies that have produced it.

By the 1990s, the BBC's *Omnibus* and *Arena*, and LWT's *The South Bank Show* were jostling with such irreverent hybrids as *The Media Show*, *The Late Show* and *Without Walls*. *The Late Show* was able to address the intellectual avant-garde, with items on the likes of Roland Barthes and Michel Foucault, in juxtaposition with a discussion on the design of trainers and a review of a Constable exhibition. Below, John Wyver, television critic and arts producer, discusses his own work and arts programmes in general.

John Wyver: *producer*

' lluminations is an independent production company which I started in 1982, when Channel Four first went on air. As television editor of *Time Out* magazine, I had watched a lot of television over four or five years, and had been writing about the debates and campaigns that led to the formation of the channel. I had been disappointed by the narrow range of possibilitIes television seemed to embrace at the time, in its forms and in its subject concerns. With Channel Four there seemed to be a genuine possibility of opening up television and widening both the range of producers and the range of possibilities. The really radical idea at the heart of Channel Four was that it would not be a producer/broadcaster as the BBC and the ITV companies were, but rather it would be a publisher/broadcaster drawing from a very wide range of producers, independent of the large broadcasting organisations. I had not made any television before, but I went into partnership with an experienced producer and director, Geoff Dunlop, who had been working on *The South Bank Show*, making some of the the most distinctive and innovative arts programmes within that strand. We wanted to contribute to an opening up and opening out.

There is a danger of being nostalgic about that moment in the early 1980s, but it did change British television in an important way. Television is now far broader and more diverse. It engages with society and the world far more richly and interestingly than it did before the advent of Channel Four.

The two most important things that we did in the mid-1980s were a series of six films called *State of the Art*, television's first engagement with contemporary visual art, and a series on artists' film and video, *Ghosts in the Machine*. More recently, the late lamented *The Late Show* and other programmes have dealt with contemporary art all the time, so it's easy to forget that prior to *State of the Art*, written by the curator Sandy Nairne, genuinely contemporary art simply didn't feature on television (Nairne 1987). Showing the work of Joseph Beuys, Jorg Immendorff, Cindy Sherman or Barbara Kruger was really presenting those artists to a television audience for the first time. We were aware that we were contributing to a tradition in arts programming, in which the key points had been Kenneth Clark's *Civilization*, John Berger's *Ways of Seeing* and Robert Hughes' *Shock of the New*. These three defining series about art had all been presenter-led. They had been illustrated lectures, presenting differently slanted views of the history of art, but in quite conventional terms. We wanted to break with that completely. We tried to find a form that was both different from what had happened before and appropriate to our subjects. So *State of the Art* has no presenter and the narration is split across four voices. The artists are shown in terms of their ideas and not of their lifestyle. The framework is drawn from ideas of sexuality, politics or identity. The sound-track is built up of quotation rather than narrative and we developed a filmic style which has its own pure and rigorous look at the art work.

We thought we'd made something very radical and remarkable, and we were extremely surprised when most people hated it. It got a very negative press and many people in television thought it was a complete failure. I certainly learned how hard it is to try to push the possibilities of the form.

Ghosts in the Machine offered a showcase for artists who work with video and film, bringing much of that work on to television for the first time. We tried to find a way of presenting, in a quite minimal format, the work of international artists like Bill Viola and William Wegman. Both the series were about the contemporary; about finding different visual languages and different formal approaches; and about being aware of the medium. We did not assume that the medium was something transparent and straightforward in its operation, but recognised that the medium itself structures what one sees, even when it has the illusion of transparency.

Those concerns have marked a great deal of the work we have done, although we have moved towards being less radical. Programmes that have gained funding have been ones that are more conservative than those we were able to make in the early years of Channel Four. That isn't necessarily a bad thing. Our more recent programmes, like the profile of Kenneth Clark I made for the BBC, have connected more with audiences and, certainly within television, they have been regarded as far more successful. They deal with the visual arts, but in more conventional terms. In today's climate, it would be impossible now to make something as different as *State of the Art* on as big a scale.

Although that is a cause for regret, one has to recognise that being an independent producer here is so much better than working in any other country. It is much harder to get cultural documentaries funded and seen, both elsewhere in Europe and in the United States. That said, I still feel that the possibilities of film and video are very limited on British television. People still use the kind of conventional television languages that were evolved thirty or forty years ago – based on a 1930s Griersonian documentary tradition crossed with live electronic television languages from the 1950s. The attitudes that lie behind those forms – such as looking for direct access to the outside world and creating, as it were, a window on the world – still shape most of the programmes in most of the genres on television. There have been some extensions to those styles, but television remains largely closed to directors, producers or artists working with a quite different sense of the visual possibilities of the medium, whether from an experimental, avant-garde tradition, or whether they are some of the *auteur* directors working elsewhere in European television. There are people who are trying to create different visual languages and different approaches to the medium which British television by and large resists and is the poorer because of it.

Examples would include the film Werner Hertzog made about the oil fields in the aftermath of the Gulf War (*Lessons of Darkness*). It is almost wordless, made up of spectacular images, very impression-istic and powerful in its use of visuals, but with no narrative, no char-acters and no sense that you're getting a chunk of reality. It's a heightened, fantastical view of the world, a Dantesque vision of hell, quite different from the dominant documentary vision that most programmes adopt here. There's the vision of Bill Viola, the American artist working with video, particularly in an hour-long tape called *The Passing*. At one level this is about the death of his mother and the birth of his son, both very familiar experiences in everyone's life, but he uses video technology and black and white images in a startlingly different and highly personal way. And there's the documentary work of Stefaan Decostere in Belgium. He's a television director concerned with the history of art and contemporary culture, who has made a series of travelogues about tourism, museums and world's fairs looking at the transformation of nature into cultural forms over the twentieth century. They are done with an exploration of the possibilities of image and sound that is, once more, quite different from anything that we see here. Also there is the tradition of European documentary from older figures who began in the cinema, people like Jean-Luc Godard and Chris Marker, who have tried to develop a poetic or imaginative language of film which is more oblique in its way of communicating.

I'm not arguing that Godard or Marker should be making programmes for *Cutting Edge* or that programme makers should be pushed towards adopting the visions of a Godard – I wouldn't inflict that on anybody – but that people in television should be more aware than they are of alternatives to the dominant languges. I wish there was more recognition that sub-vérité filming about ambulances or vets is not the only way of representing the world. There are many more possibilities which would give us a fuller, more appropriate and better picture of the world and still engage a significant audience. I'm not talking about making work which only appeals to an esoteric handful of people. I want to see this sort of programme making reach out and speak, if not to a mass audience, then to a relatively broad one.'

John Wyver is a producer and founder of the television company Illuminations. Based on an interview given in August 1995.

Techniques

Research and selection of subject matter

Research is the motor of factual programme making. Original ideas do not spring up fully formed, but come out of a considerable amount of poking around – including telephoning contacts, going to see people, following up press items, attending meetings, observing activities and spending time in the reference library (*see* Leanne Klein, p. 169 below). Often a great deal of research has been done before a programme gets off the ground. Once the programme is under way, the research changes its nature and becomes directly geared to the business of getting it made. The precise details will vary with genres and individual cases, but certain priorities remain:

- To be sufficiently informed about the topic under consideration – whether it be the work of a certain artist, the habits of a certain insect or the daily practices of a local fire brigade.

- To decide on who will take part in the programme and which of their activities will be filmed; and to get their consent.

- To decide on where the locations will be and what other facilities are needed; also to make sure these are available.

The chief skill of the researcher is to find out how to find out. The BBC and most larger production companies employ specialist researchers. Some are experienced generalists who can move with ease from one topic to another, drawing on contacts and a knowledge of sources built up over a number of years. Others are themselves experts in a particular area, say in medicine, crime, finance, or the arts. BBC researcher Kathy Chater, in her useful guide to television research, makes some rather depressing but realistic comments about the researcher's job within a big organisation. If a programme is a success, she says, the producer and director will accept the accolades. If it is a failure, they will say 'the research wasn't very good' (Chater 1989: 13). Nevertheless, especially in smaller companies, research is very often a collaborative effort between writer, researcher, producer and director.

There is always a great deal of preparatory research to be done before production can begin. Depending on the type of programme this may include:

- Factual research

- People research

- Setting up shooting

- Archive research

Factual Research

This is concerned with verifiable information and with accuracy. A programme may be aiming to establish the generally accepted facts of a case or it may be setting out to argue for an alternative set of facts, not accepted by the consensus. Another possibility is that it is seeking to reveal hitherto unknown information, or to make public facts that have been concealed. The investigatory mode based on factual research has been the stock in trade of current affairs programmes from *Panorama* and *World in Action* to *The Cook Report*. These are prestigious programmes with substantial research budgets which, on occasion, have been able to sustain an investigation over a number of years. At the other end of the scale, it was the research done by independent filmmakers Christine Pearce and Tessa Shaw, working with a tiny budget, that led to *The Dirty War*, the first programme to argue that Gulf War syndrome existed. Their work instigated the investigation of the Select Committee on Defence. Whatever the subject matter and whatever the budget, in seeking out the facts of the case the researcher should compare several sources, treating any one of them with a healthy scepticism.

Factual research may involve consulting:

- Experts and others working in the area researched: nurses as well as doctors, class teachers as well as head teachers.

- Press cuttings libraries.

- Reference libraries (for an outraged reflection on the inevitable shortcomings of television research in relation to published academic research, see Bruce Cummings, historical advisor to the Thames Television series about the Korean War, *The Unknown War* (Cummings 1992)).

- The specialist press in the areas being studied: there are several directories which list titles.

- Government departments and press offices.

- Press and public relations offices of other relevant bodies. From commerical companies to pressure groups, many organisations have written information on their work and a system for responding to press enquiries.

- Research agencies. Sometimes a programme will finance some specialised research or conduct their own poll to balance against those in the newspapers, or to compare with official figures.

People research

This includes finding

- *Subjects who will take part in observational filming:* those individuals who will be the source of gripping 'stories' as members of the golf club, the hospital ward, the newspaper office, the police station and the innumerable other institutions that have opened their doors to the television cameras. The researcher must investigate, get to know those involved and persuade them to take part. Once an institution has been identified as potential programme material, those in authority must agree to let the cameras in. Anyone who will appear in the final programme must give their written consent, usually by signing a 'consent form'. When the Yorkshire Television news magazine *Calendar* itself became the topic of the series *Deadline*, it was remarked how certain indivduals who had not given their permission rapidly left the scene whenever the cameras arrived.

- *People who will be sources of knowledge.* It has been said that a researcher needs to be an 'expert at finding experts'. These will be people with standing in the field, with recognised knowledge in the topic of the programme, whom the researcher can consult to check out the accuracy and the relative importance of information they discover from other sources. The programme may pay a fee to an 'expert' advisor. 'Experts' may also be needed as interviewees, either to give weight to an argument or simply to offer authoritative factual information. It is important to remember that these are usually busy people with very full lives, and it is as well to make a first approach by letter rather than telephone.

- *Other participants in an interview-based programme.* These may include people prepared to speak of their personal experiences, people who will argue a point of view; people who were witnesses to an event; people speaking of their memories. Suitable people may be found through advertisements in the local papers or the specalist press, through support networks and pressure groups, or through professionals working with, say, single parents, or tenants in poor housing (*see* Helen Swords, p. 139 above).

  The researcher will have preliminary conversations with potential participants over the telephone, then, depending on the nature of the participation, will keep in touch with them in the run-up to the filming.

  For discussion programmes, such as *Question Time*, participants include not only panel members who have knowledge of the subject under discussion but also 'ordinary people' who want to express their views, usually as members of the audience. Shows, like the Scottish Television programme *100 Women* chaired by Sheena McDonald, for six weeks brought together 100 women who had some sort of interest in the topic under discusssion – from cosmetic surgery to adoption. 'Experts' and 'ordinary women' were recruited to sit together in the auditorium, ready to offer views from each of their different perspectives.

- *Specific individuals.* As the history of television itself becomes longer, many programmes have attempted to follow the fortunes of those who had appeared in earlier shows: How are they faring five years after their heart operation? Do they remember singing in that choir when they were a child? For such programmes researchers need to track down specific individuals. The revealing Granada programme, *Seven Up*, made in 1964 showed a sample of seven-year-olds from different class backgrounds. The audience was amazed by the differences in their manner and attitudes. Seven years later, in *Fourteen Up*, the group were traced and their differing fortunes recorded. By 1985 with *Twenty-Eight Up* the task included finding a young man who had become a recluse, living in a caravan in a remote part of Scotland.

- *Celebrities.* Normally celebrities will have agents who will negotiate their fee and the conditions under which they appear.

Setting up shooting

Working together with the production manager (*see* Robin Small, p. 38 above) and the rest of the production team, this includes:

- Finding suitable locations, getting permission to use them and deciding exactly where the filming will take place. A recce includes checking out such practicalities as available parking space, where to have lunch and how long the journey to and from will take. Other factors are the expense, the appearance, and its suitability for recording sound. An elegant garden will pose problems if it is next to a car breaker's yard.

- Arranging visas and permissions through embassies and High Commissions for overseas filming. Also checking out what vaccinations are needed and research into such things as local regulations on alcohol consumption and dress codes. It would be inappropriate to travel around the world assuming that Western European practices were universally acceptable.

Archive Research

This involves selecting and acquiring ready filmed material and photographic stills. It is most important for a programme based on a historical topic, but may also be needed for newsy references to recent events or for other ready-shot material to be incorporated into a programme. The job of selection involves getting to know the specialist film and photographic libraries that hold archive material and knowing how to consult librarians and search through the catalogues for the specific topic that is needed. Many photo libraries use CD-ROM to make searching easier. Most television companies make their libraries available for re-use. Acquiring the material involves negotiating permission to use the footage or the photograph in the context for which it is planned, and negotiating the fee. This is usually done through the library or agency, sometimes directly with the copyright owner.

Archive film may be on 16mm, 35mm or more unusual film formats, or it may be on one of the many video formats. It will be important to find out how the original material can be transferred on to the format of the current programme and the cost of the transfer.

There are useful lists of libraries and sources in:

Chater, K. (1989) *The Television Researcher's Guide*, BBC Television Training
Peak, S. (1995) *The Guardian Media Guide*, London: Fourth Estate
Researcher's Guide to British Film and Television Collections (1993), London: British Universities Film and Video Council
Researcher's Guide to British Newsreels, vols 1, 2 and 3 (1993) London: British Universities Film and Video Council
British Universities Film and Video Council also run courses on such things as copyright clearance, negotiation skills and archive sources for film researchers. Contact: 55 Greek Street, London W1V 5LR
Tel: 0171 734 3687
Viewfinder is the magazine of the BUFVC.

Interview techniques

Michael Rabiger describes the documentary technique when dealing with participants as 'a search for naturalness' (Rabiger 1992). With very few exceptions this is the case. Even stylistically formal documentaries, like Errol Morris's *Interrotron Stories*, or Channel Four's *The Essential Guide* to the history of Yugoslavia, create their effects by manipulating the final image. They may present their interviewees in shaped boxes or with the camera weaving around them, but the speakers themselves remain relaxed and convincing.

It is important to distinguish between the different reasons for conducting an interview. What is needed from the interviewees will be determined to a large extent by the genre of programme. For example, the specialised knowlege of the interviewee may be all-important in a science-based strand such as *Horizon*. In a travel programme, by contrast, the interviewees often need only to be entertaining. There are three aspects to be taken into account; the initial briefing of the interviewee, the manner of the interview itself, and the way in which what is said is incorporated into the programme.

Interviews may be designed to elicit different type of material, including:

- *Factual or expert information:* in which case there will be a need to assess the weight of information given, partly by judging the reputation and standing of the interviewee, partly by preliminary research into other sources

- *Expert opinion:* in which case there will be a need to draw out the opinion by putting alternative opinions to the interviewee, and bearing in mind the question of balance

- *Personal, non-expert opinion*

- *Witness accounts:* in which case it will be important to ensure that the interviewee is indeed a competent and genuine witness

- *Anecdote:* in which case the interviewee should be a good raconteur or have a good camera presence

- *Emotion.* For interviewees to express emotion during an interview designed for television is sometimes described as therapeutic. However, the interviewer should always be aware of the potential distress that may follow in the aftermath of such an interview

Interviewers may adopt various different strategies, partly depending on whether the interviewer is a personality in their own right, to be featured in the programme, or on whether their questions are merely prompts for the interviewee, to be edited out in the final programme. Strategies include:

- *Effectively eliciting information or opinion* In this case the interviewer will be as self-effacing as possible

- *Challenging the interviewee*, usually in a political interview. This involves putting contrary opinions with provocative emphasis. The abrasive manner of Jeremy Paxman on *Newsnight* has become notorious. BBC Director General John Birt himself criticised aggressive interviewers who are 'sneering, overbearing and disdainful' so that the 'policy difference behind the disputes go unexplored' (Brooks 1995). John Birt himself, as editor of *Weekend World* in the 1970s, became known for what he described as the 'mission to explain', the need for television to clarify complex political issues, sometimes in the face of politicians' desire to obfuscate. Nevertheless, even the toughest interviewer must give those challenged a space to reply to their critics

- *The conversational interview.* This often takes the form of an interviewer and interviewee chat, possibly on a sofa in a daytime television show, or strolling informally through a park

- *The intimate interview* in the manner of *Face to Face*, first evolved by John Freeman in the 1960s, then revived by Jeremy Isaacs. The interviewee, often a well-known personality, agrees to respond to extended probing, in which they reveal many personal details

- *The emotional interview.* This was the *Man Alive* approach, continued by programmes in which interviewees are selected because of the personal and emotional nature of the stories they have to tell. The interviewer's job is to encourage that story to come out, often merely through sympathetic nodding. 'If somebody was in a poor way and the tears were rising', said Angela Huth, reviewing her time as an interviewer on *Man Alive*, 'and you did a bit of nodding and didn't say anything, then they felt that they had to help *you* out, so they'd come out with much more of the ghastliness, whatever it was, the tragic story. We all got quite good at knowing how to deal with them when they began to glitter.' (*Can I ask you a personal question? – The 'Man Alive' story*, BBC2, 30 August 1993)

Practical points

There are some practical points that are useful for most types of interview:

- Consider if the interviewee is competent and will come across well.

- Decide if the interviewer's questions will be included in the programme or will be edited out. This will change the way in which the questions are asked. If the questions are to be edited out, all the information must be included in the answer.

- If dealing with an inexperienced interviewee, explain the procedures to them. For example, if it is important to play devil's advocate and challenge their view, the interviewee should understand that this is to clarify the issues for the audience, and they should not take it personally or get annoyed (unless, of course, this is the interviewer's intention!).

- Have a list of questions prepared before the interview. Make them precise and designed to elicit the type of answer needed. However, it is important to maintain eye contact with the interviewee, rather than be constantly consulting prepared notes.

- Decide on the best place for the interview. The interviewee is likely to be more relaxed in their own home amongst their own things.

  Questions may be:

- Requests for information

- Follow-up, or supplementary questions, and requests for examples

- Leading questions which expect particular answers

- The carefully judged moment when the interviewer says nothing, allowing the interviewee space to expand on their thoughts.

Michael Rabiger's *Directing the Documentary* includes a sample list of questions, used in his film, *Tolstoy Remembered by His Daughter* in the BBC's *Yesterday's Witness* series (Rabiger 1992: 341).

Jonathan Dimbleby, one of the most experienced television interviewers, has argued for the importance of the reporter-led programme with its ability to investigate and challenge through interviews. In his view, a documentary that eliminates the interviewer could be seen as a deceit on the public because it gives the illusion of direct communication between subject and audience. The subject may then be used as fodder to support the filmmaker's case. Dimbleby argues that subjects must be reflected fully in the final programme, especially when they are presented as if they are speaking for themselves (Sheffield 1995).

Leanne Klein: *documentary director*

'I took my first degree in psychology and soon realised I didn't want to be a psychologist. But one of the reasons I'm drawn to documentary is that I'm really intrigued by people and what motivates them, and, as it turns out, I've been able to make good use of what I'd learnt. At Cambridge I became the producer for *Trouble and Strife*, one of the the first women's theatre groups, but I was more excited by the Cambridge Video Co-op. At that time it owned one VHS camera, kept in the room of Adam Barker – now a successful television producer – which you could hire out for £1 at weekends. (I never did discover what happened to it the rest of the week.) With a couple of friends I went off and made short films that no one else understood and showed them at video and performance arts festivals.

I realised that this was what I wanted to do with my life, so I went on to do post-graduate work at Goldsmiths' College, where my tutor was Phillip Whitehead, whose wide experience of television ranged from editing *This Week* in the 1960s to producing prestigious documentary series dealing with political history, including *The Kennedys*, and *The Unknown War*. Although he was always extraordinarily busy, he made valuable judgements on my production *Eastern Promise*, which looked at the 'mail order' agencies that arrange marriages between young women from the Philippines desperate to get out of poverty, and hopeful British men, bemused by the myth of orientalism and sexy subservient women.

Television documentary seemed to pull together everything I'd wanted to do. Ideologically it was an instrument for change; it satisfied my creative feelings and the craft aspects appealed to me. I really liked the technical side, thinking about the quality of the picture, the lighting and the sound. I also enjoyed writing about the media as part of my college course, but when I began applying for jobs, I was told over and over again that that was not relevant. The best qualification for becoming a television director, they said, was to sweep the cutting-room floor and make the tea. My reaction was to say, 'If that's what's needed, that's what I'll do.' So my first job was as a runner for The Palace, a video post-production company in Soho. It was shift work with terrible pay – £100 per week. The most exciting thing about it was delivering tea to Peter Greenaway, who was working on *The TV Dante*, but I never got a chance to chat to him.

As I had made films at Goldsmiths' I kept my confidence and wasn't knocked back as so many people are at this stage in their career. All the time I was developing ideas and writing proposals, as I have done throughout my time working in television, often together with other women. None of my proposals was accepted at that time.

Next, I got a job from the Union's circulated list of vacancies and became assistant to an editor working on corporate videos above a strip club in Dean Street. Then I was offered something more substantial by Ivor Gaber, a news producer who was also head of department at Goldsmiths'. Together with two partners, Ivor had just set up Sevenday Productions to provide coverage of party political conferences for the newly launched Sky News. For six weeks before the conferences in a hot summer I worked alone in a Portakabin next to the Sky offices. At first I had no idea what I was doing. Every morning I had all the papers delivered and I used the *Financial Times* on-line search system to research the background to the big issues of the conferences. I produced packs for the producers about the participants and the agendas and added relevant press cuttings for each day's transmission. During transmission, which was live gavel to gavel coverage, I sat in the continuity box, whispering down the feedlines, identifying the speakers to the technicians who were generating the name captions. In the breaks it was my job to get the politicians off the floor – or wherever they were – to do interviews. It meant being in constant touch with the various press offices, and I certainly got an insight into behind the scenes politics. At the Young Conservatives ball, Margaret Thatcher was greeted with Nazi salutes and chants of 'Ten More Years'. Her private speeches to her supporters were even more extreme than her public pronouncements.

When the work of the House of Commons was broadcast for the first time, Sevenday together with Barraclough Carey formed CCTV (Commons Committee TV) to cover the various select and standing committees for use by all the UK broadcasters. The whole thing was arranged like a military operation and I realised that I didn't want a production manager's job. But I did begin to take parliamentary politics more seriously. I had long been involved in the women's movement and as a student had taken part in direct action – chaining myself to the railings when Harvey Proctor came to speak and that kind of thing.

Next I worked for Scarlet TV, which had been commissioned to do a special investigation into the politics of childcare for Channel Four and wanted to use the parliamentary committee format. Then I went to Wall to Wall, who were launching a new series of *The Media Show*. They were an unorthodox company, run in a non-hierarchical way. As a researcher you could inititiate ideas, set up the filming and conduct the interviews. Once more I found myself in touch with Peter Mandelson at Labour Party Headquarters for a programme behind the scenes at the Party Conference. And I found myself working with Adam Barker, the keeper of the VHS camera from my student days.

When Channel Four axed *The Media Show*, Wall to Wall wanted to keep their staff employed, and gave me three months to research a series that would show how human babies develop but to film it in a 'natural history' style. I drew on my psychology training and produced a massive document. This was in the autumn of 1991. Two years later I co-directed six 30-minute documentaries – *Baby It's You* evolved from that original research.

Back in 1991 I went as assistant producer to *Under the Sun*, the BBC's anthropological documentary strand, and ended up working for the ex-series editor of *The Media Show*. Working partly as a freelancer I have realised how dependent you are on patronage. To an extent directors and programme staff are at the mercy of the people above them. When an editorial post at the BBC changes, you'll find a whole different set of people are making films. I liked the approach of Bill Hillary, editor of *Under the Sun*. He felt that ethnographic filmmaking should be more urban and more Western and should get away from showing only the exotic and the primitive. Part of my job was over-seeing independent productions for the strand and setting up co-production funds. We were able to find money for a woman who had been trying to get a film about Cambodia off the ground for many years, and for a programme by an Indian woman director about casual salesmen. Although I wasn't particularly keen on the producing role, events like my executive trip to New York to meet HBO taught me a lot about the funding world.

Under the Sun was relocated to Bristol, and Bill Hillary got the job of commissioning editor for Youth Programmes at Channel Four. At the time Peter Salmon was Head of Television Features at BBC Bristol and had launched a set of innovative and unusual programmes. I got my first directing job on *Small Objects of Desire*, the sort of programme where you could try out all sorts of visual ideas. My first Object was *The Syringe*. I went on to direct regularly for BBC Bristol.

All this time, Wall to Wall were trying to get *Baby It's You* commissioned. The BBC wanted it done on tape, interleaved with interviews by experts. This was not the programme we wanted to make, and Wall to Wall stuck to their guns. The American cable company Discovery promised to fund half, then ITEL, the distribution, company put in some money in advance of sales, and Channel Four put up the rest. David Hickman and I collaborated on producing and directing the series following a cohort of families and children. We filmed about thirty babies in all. The series turned out to be a commercial success for Wall to Wall, with an accompanying book and sales across the world. In 1995 I was awarded an Emmy for Programme One, *In the Beginning*.

My most recent work is *The Human Jungle*, another psychological study – this time of human behaviour in the modern city. I was series producer as well as co-director and found that dealing with the different television cultures of our French and American co-producers made for some difficult compromises. We had a trainee on the series from Leeds University, who was a great asset to the production. She became involved in all the stages and I'm sure she learnt a lot. Although her placement was arranged by her course, I was shocked to hear that her grant had been stopped for the year. Fortunately Wall to Wall were prepared to pay her a minimal sum.

The style of filmmaking I'm interested in is telling stories in a visual way and expressing ideas. A lot of documentary just points the camera and waits for things to happen. That is a camera operator's art as much as anything, but a series like *Visions of Heaven and Hell*, which I co-directed in 1994, was a real director's challenge. We were making a partisan series about the way we are going, and we used the camera to make a comment in a more strikingly visual way. I'm interested in creative television.'

Documentary dilemmas

Programme makers, their subjects and their audience

Working on documentaries can be a demanding process and in the excitement it is all too easy to overlook the ethical dimension which comes into play when real people are represented on the screen. In factual filming, the production team drops in on people leading their everyday lives. They bring their lights, cameras, monitors, endless cables and lots of big silver boxes. They are constantly on the telephone and they create a great deal of bustle and activity. They stay for a few hours or a few weeks then move on to their next assignment, leaving their subjects behind to digest the experience and to wait to see how they will appear in the final cut. The consequences of being part of a television programme may reverberate well beyond transmission. Questions of documentary ethics hinge on this relationship between programme makers and their subjects.

Apart from the BBC's Community Programme Unit and similar initiatives – and then only partially – television programme makers never relinquish editorial control over their material, and documentary footage is never transmitted unedited. As a consequence, once they have given permission to be filmed, subjects are in the filmmaker's hands. As far as the programme maker is concerned, once the filming is over, the subjects are primarily raw material, images on the rushes, waiting to be edited into a moving or convincing programme. The issue, then, is how a responsibility towards those who appear in the programmes may be balanced against the other demands on their attention – their desire to make a successful programme; their legal obligations; their own sense of what is right; their responsibility towards their audience; and whether to entertain or inform them. Some areas of programme making are more likely than others to allow space to think such dilemmas through. The demands of the schedule, the momentum of established practices, and questions of audience appeal all too often take precedence (*see* Helen Swords, p. 139 above).

There are many different reasons for making a documentary programme. Depending on genre and approach, the relationship between programme makers and their subjects takes various different forms. They include what anthropologist Jay Ruby has categorised as 'speaking for, speaking about, speaking with, or speaking alongside' (Ruby 1992). Programme makers may be reporting on their subjects, investigating them or observing them (*speaking about them*); they may be engaging in dialogue with them or interpreting and reflecting on what they do and have to say (*speaking with them*); or they may be arguing their subjects' cause or representing their case (*speaking for them*). In rare cases they may be working together with their subjects (*speaking alongside them*).

Some programme makers have put the needs of their subjects first, and have chosen to use the documentary as a form of activism. They seek a style of filmmaking that will 'intervene in history', in Paula Rabinowitz's words, 'representing' in both senses of the term, those who would otherwise not be represented and seeing 'visualisation as a precursor to mobilisation' (Rabinowitz 1994: 14). An example is Channel Four's series on indigenous peoples, *The 'Savage' Strikes Back*. For Rabinowitz the project of a documentary is not completed on the screen but in the real world, amongst those who are watching and those subjects who see themselves represented in a new way. In this view, the three-way relationship between subjects, programme makers and audience becomes a dynamic one, a stimulus to thought and action. Although the activist documentary has had only a marginal place in television, an address to an audience as engaged actors rather than as individuals passively seeking entertainment or relaxation remains a major impetus behind factual programming. Such an approach is in a direct line from John Grierson's vision of the documentary as part of the social democratic project, providing insight for an informed citizenry.

Documentary ethics

In a discussion of the ethics of documentary, several interleaving factors come into play, all of which affect the tension felt by progamme makers, between responsibility to their subjects and to their audience. They include:

- Questions of authorship and editorial control
- Questions of the filmmaker's commitment to a point of view, whether it is a view held by the subjects of the film, or one in opposition to it
- Questions of objectivity and factual truth
- Questions of informed consent to be filmed and its limits
- The issue of voyeurism and intrusion, of the programme maker's right

to look and sometimes to expose

- The legitimacy of broadcasting distressing material both from the point of view of those who are shown, and those who will watch

- Issues of representation and stereotyping

- Questions of patronage and sponsorship which may affect the content of a film

These areas are subject to regulation by the BBC and IBA, who issue guidelines covering the ethics of featuring members of the public in programmes. Moreover there are channels of complaint for those who feel that either they have been misrepresented, or that broadcasters have over-stepped the boundaries of taste and decency, or that factual mistakes have been made (*see* Regulation, p. 14 above). Many of them are regularly taken up on television itself, in programmes such as Channel Four's *Right To Reply*, in which programme makers engage in discussion with members of the viewing public. But often the concerns seem more nebulous and not easily pinned down to specific examples. Below we consider some of the issues which seem endemic to different documentary genres.

Observational documentaries

Since observational filming depends for its audience appeal on moments of conflict and emotional exposure, it has been accused of giving rise to the double danger of voyeurism and misrepresentation. Even the experienced programme maker and television executive Jeremy Isaacs criticised the director's priorities when the BBC made an extended series about the Royal Opera House, Covent Garden while Isaacs was Managing Director (*The House*).

Observation is largely restricted to reflecting the surface of events. In its purest form it does not seek to interpret or to criticise. However, it is diffi-cult for programme makers to resist the temptation to introduce comment in the editing and presentation of a programme. 'It's not so much what you get in the shooting, it's what you do with it afterwards', said the distin-guished documentary maker Paul Watson, whose series *The Family* had caused such a stir in the 1970s (Sheffield 1995). Editing may be used to introduce powerful juxtapositions, as in Juris Podnieks' *Homeland*, in which the build-up to the Latvian declaration of independence in 1990 is urged on by the massed choirs of the great Baltic song festival which had been repressed for many years. The sound of the counting of the votes inter-weaves with the musical crescendo as shots of the singers are intercut with shots of the politicians and of the demonstrators and the army restraining them outside the government building. It is a superb piece of emotional filmic manipulation which loses none of the complex political implications of such a vote in a country where half the population are Russian settlers.

At a more mundane level, editing can make cheap points or trivial jokes through the selection of shots and ironic comparisons. A subject may be presented as an irascible character if only his moments of anger are chosen; a dog owner's facial expression may be intercut in comparison with that of his dog. The need to construct a coherent one-hour programme out of many hours of unstructured filming inevitably means that the final result will reflect the filmmaker's vision as much as the participants' experience.

Documentary programme makers must get close to their subjects, but at the same time keep a distance from them. Over more than twenty-five years, Roger Graef has filmed many British institutions in the observational style, including pioneering programmes on a Whitehall ministry and the British Communist Party. Even so, he says that no one automatically has the right to take someone else's picture. Intrusion is not justified by journalism and particularly not by a filmmaker's claim to artistic self-expression. His aim has been to give a view of hitherto protected institutions 'on terms that the people didn't feel they'd been raped by us'. Although he asks for access to everything that is relevant to his subject, the crew films only what has been agreed in advance. He ensures that those who appear in the film get to see it in good time to request changes. Changes are guaranteed on the grounds of personal or professional secrecy or inaccuracies, and the participants can make a case for changes on issues of balance or fairness. The point is that any debate engendered by the film should be about content not about accuracy.

Graef is clear about his obligation both to the audience and to the participants. 'Our goal is to show the process of decision making about things that matter to the public at large. . . . If you want to be a fly on the wall, the most important decision is *which* wall to squat on' (Sheffield 1990). For him the filming process is 'evidence gathering with minimum impact on that evidence' so that 'we leave it to viewers to make up their own minds. We're not trying to say something, but to find out something' (ibid; see also Rosenthal 1980).

Other forms of fly-on-the-wall filming have been less respectful of their subjects. The Australian Donaher family, filmed in the extended series *Sylvania Waters*, complained noisily that they had been set up and shown in an extremely bad light. They had given their permission without realising how their extroverted lifestyle would be seen by a general audience. In response to this sort of complaint, some filmmakers have replied that as the population grows more media-wise, subjects and programme makers may well be engaging in a competition to exploit. Many people want to appear on television because they relish the notoriety and the money it will bring. Such a claim has sometimes licensed deliberately voyeuristic programmes such as *Hollywood Men* and some of the franker programmes about sex and private lives that have come into vogue in the mid-1990s.

Brian Winston has argued that, however conscientious the programme makers there is a degree of voyeurism inherent in the medium itself (Winston 1995). Factual television always involves a degree of exposure as the audience, cosy in their familiar homes, observe the activities and listen to the personal accounts of people they do not know. Those on the television screen are always deprived of their living presence. They have become performers in someone else's art form. They are *being* presented, not presenting themselves. Winston argues that this exploitative relationship can only be broken by documentary styles that give some control to those who appear in them, and which draw attention to the distortions brought about by the act of filming itself.

Current affairs

While the observational documentary tends to seek out the quirky and the unique, the current affairs programme is making a case, and will tend to look for the representative and the general. A programme needs an *example* of a terminally ill cancer patient or of an Asian family being harassed by their neighbours. This is what Brian Winston described as documentary 'metonymy'. The single individual stands in for many others. Although they usually take the side of the powerless against the powerful or against the bureacratic jungle, in current affairs programmes people and issues are always held in balance, giving rise to a real danger that those who are shown will feel that their own situation has been misrepresented for the sake of arguing a case. Weekly programmes are most likely to pick people up, use them, then drop them just as quickly, while harassed researchers are on the phone to dozens of possible participants, making contacts that can never be adequately followed up. On the other hand, the very regularity of a weekly programme remains one of its strengths. Journalists and researchers are able to build up their contacts over the years, and are able to return to the same person or situation and monitor its progress. Properly done, the indivdual and the general can ultimately be seen as part of a pattern.

Interviews, the privacy of emotion and the question of consent

From the early days of *Man Alive*, when interviewers encouraged their subjects to give vent to their emotions in front of the camera, there have been debates about the legitimacy of such tactics. Today, some argue that there is an increasing popularity of extremes, and that 'reality television' and ambulance-chasing genres pay less respect to the privacy of grief or of pain.

The question of consent is one that is difficult to settle. It remains uncertain what counts as informed consent. Frederick Wiseman's powerfully distressing *Titicut Follies*, which revealed the horrors of an American mental institution in the 1960s, was not shown for many years, and then only after a complex court hearing which considered whether the highly disturbed inmates could be said to have given their consent (Winston 1995: 222). Unresolved questions include whether a child can give consent, and what does it mean to give consent at a moment of distress? Is it possible for a participant to anticipate the after-effects of having their most private moments broadcast to the nation at large? A survivor of the *Marchioness* disaster who took part in a documentary soon after the event said, 'A few months later I cringed. What I had said was too personal to broadcast to a breathless nation' (Fielding 1994).

The increased use of doorstepping and covert filming poses problems of consent of a different sort. These techniques remain important for the sort of investigatory journalism that is able to reveal some well-hidden corruption.

Poverty, the Third World and disaster reporting

The ways in which those people are represented who inhabit the poorer parts of the world has come under increasing criticism (Benthall 1993). Parts of Africa are only visited when there is a war, disaster or famine. One effect of overseas reporting has been to give an impression of continuous chaos. Jonathan Dimbleby, whose career began with the striking *This Week* documentary *The Unknown Famine*, which publicised the famine in the north of Ethiopia in 1972, not only to the Western world, but to Ethiopians themselves, looked back in 1995 and commented on

> the prism of my own prejudice, which I liked to believe was objectivity. . . . There is something faintly absurd about young men and women trailing around the globe in what we have now come to call 'disaster tourism'
> (Sheffield 1995).

The criticisms which built up over the 1970s included the image of many who have been categorised as 'victims' (*see* Helen Swords, p. 139 above) More recently, and especially since the coming of Channel Four, there have been changes in stress and balance across the television output, but the pressures of production and the accepted priorities of the news agenda mean that the danger of a collapse into stereotyping remains.

Guidelines produced by the BBC, ITC and BCC deal with many of these dilemmas, but the competing demands of subjects, audience and the programme makers' own ambitions mean that there are no simple rule-of-thumb solutions. The introduction of styles that themselves question the basis of representation, and the broadening of the range of those who have access to the making of programmes, have changed the situation in which there is always a rigid separation between programme maker and their subjects. But not all programmes can be made in a deconstructive style. Many of the ethical problems to which Brian Winston and others have drawn attention remain built into the documentary enterprise and need to be renegotiated every time a programme is made.

References

Annan, Lord (1977) *Report of the Committee on the Future of Broadcasting*, Cmnd 6753, London: HMSO

Arthur, P. (1993) 'Jargons of authenticity ' in M. Renov (ed.) *Theorising Documentary*, London: Routledge

Baehr, H. and Dyer, G. (eds) (1987) *Boxed In: Women and Television*, London: Pandora RKP

Benthall, J. (1993) *Disasters, Relief and the Media*, London: I.B. Tauris

Brooks, R. (1995) 'Birt out to tame his monster', *Guardian*, 17 July, London

Corner, J. (1991) 'Documentary voices' in J. Corner (ed.) *Popular Television in Britain*, London: BFI

Cummings, B. (1992) *War and Television*, London: Verso

Fielding, H. (1994) 'Can TV ruin your life?', *Independent on Sunday*, 17 July, London

Goldie, G. W. (1977) *Facing the Nation: Television and Politics 1937–1976*, London: Bodley Head

ICA (1988) *British Film, Black Cinema*, London: ICA

Miller, D. (1994) *Don't Mention the War: Northern Ireland, Propaganda and the Media*, London: Pluto Press

Nairne, S. (1987) *State of the Art: Ideas and Images in the 1980s*, London: Chatto & Windus

Rosenthal, A. (1980) *The Documentary Conscience*, Berkeley: University of California Press

Ruby, J. (1992) 'Speaking for, speaking about, speaking with or speaking alongside: an anthropological and documentary dilemma', *Journal of Film and Video*, vol. 44, pp. 1–2, Spring–Summer

Sheffield (1995) Conference papers presented at The Second Sheffield Documentary Festival; various speakers

Tunstall, J. (1993) *Television Producers*, London: Routledge

Key texts

British Broadcasting Corporation (1992) *Guide to the BBC*, London: BBC Information Services

British Universities Film and Video Council (1993) *Researcher's Guide to British Film and Television Collections*, London: BUFVC

Broadcasting Standards Council (1992) *A Code of Practice*, 2nd edn, London: Broadcasting Standards Council

Broadcasting Standards Council (1994) *Perspectives of Women in Television*, Research Working Paper IX, London: Broadcasting Standards Council

Chater, K. (1989) *The Television Researcher's Guide*, London: BBC Television Training

Corner, John (1996) *The Art of Record*, Manchester: Manchester University Press.

Independent Television Commission (1995) *Programme Code* London: ITC

McCracken, R. and Gilbart, M. (1995) *Buying and Clearing Rights: Print, Broadcast and Multimedia*, London: Blueprint

Nichols, B. (1991) *Representing Reality*, Bloomington, IND.: University of Indiana Press

Peak, S. (1995) *The Guardian Media Guide*, London: Fourth Estate

Rabiger, Michael (1992) *Directing the Documentary*, 2nd edn, Stoneham MA: Focal Press

Rabinowitz, P. (1994) *They Must Be Represented*, London: Verso

Renov, M. (ed.) (1993) *Theorising Documentary*, London: Routledge

Rosenthal, A. (ed.) (1988) *New Challenges for Documentary*, Berkeley: University of California Press

Silverstone, R. (1985) *Framing Science: The Making of a BBC Documentary*, London: BFI

Sussex, E. (1975) *The Rise and Fall of the British Documentary*, Berkeley: University of California Press

Viewfinder, The Magazine of the British Universities Film and Video Council published 3 times a year from BUFVC, 55 Greek St, London W1V 5LR

Walker, J. A. (1993) *Arts TV: A History of Arts Television in Britain*, London: John Libbey

Winston, B. (1995) *Claiming the Real: The Documentary Film Revisited*, London: BFI

12 News, politics and television as information

....

News in a democratic society

Television news: fact and neutrality

'Our job is to present fact and truth with clarity, dispassion and neutrality, however inconvenient or dismaying much of that information may be', wrote a distinguished editor of BBC Television News (Yorke 1987: ii). The production of news that strives for neutral factual information is possibly the most important arena in which television carries out its remit to inform as

Figure 32 Nigel Thomson on camera and Paul Davies reporting for ITN during the Gulf War, January 1991
Courtesy ITN

well as to entertain its various audiences. The BBC and Independent Television News (ITN), the company who provide news programmes for ITV and Channels Four and Five, are both legally required to deliver their news with 'due accuracy and impartiality'. They must seek a reliable and balanced coverage of political and other events and, unlike newspapers, they may not have an editorial opinion of their own. In the immediate post-war period, the BBC took this obligation so seriously that its news readers were not allowed to be seen in vision. It was thought that the raising of an eyebrow or an inappropriate smile might introduce bias and personal opinion.

Fuller, more developed news programmes, as opposed to brief bulletins, began with the launch of ITN's half hour *News at Ten* in July 1967. *Channel Four News*, which went on air in 1982, for the first time gave 50 minutes to in-depth news coverage. By the late-1990s news programmes, news updates and news analysis are spread throughout the day. By 1996 television was giving us six and a half hours of news and news analysis daily. The BBC's rolling *Breakfast News* is followed by their half-hour programmes at 1 pm, 6 pm and 9 pm. These are backed up by discussion programmes and in-depth reports, from *Breakfast News Extra* at 9 am to *Newsnight* at 10.30 pm as well as regional news, news magazines and *Newsround*, a news programme for children. ITV also has its *Lunchtime News* and its regional news programming. There are discussions between politicians and journalists, such as the BBC's *The Midnight Hour*; programmes in which the audience put questions to politicians and decision makers, such as *Question Time*; and audience-based discussion programmes, such as *The Time . . . The Place*. There has been a burgeoning of political programmes on Sunday mornings and lunchtimes – most of them centring on a well-known presenter, such as *Breakfast with Frost*, *Jonathan Dimbleby* and *On the Record*. Television has become a major forum for political information and public debate (*see* James Curran, p. 193 below).

Each of the news programmes has its distinctive characteristics: *Channel Four News* is concerned with analysis and stresses its overseas reporting; *News at Ten* is punchy and dynamic in its presentation; and, despite its recent redesigns, the BBC remains more traditionalist. All declare a shared commitment to professionalism and established news values, although the nature of those news values and styles of presentation has changed over the years and, some would argue, is currently in crisis (*see* Changing news, p. 188 below).

The distinction between 'fact' and 'opinion' has from the early years of television been reflected in the institutional separation between news and current affairs. ITN's major output is news, while *World in Action*, *Dispatches* and other current affairs programmes are produced by ITV companies or independent producers. At the BBC, the reorganisation brought about by Director General John Birt brought news and current affairs together for the first time from 1987. BBC journalists also began to work for both radio and television, pooling information through newsroom computer systems and the ever-evolving communications technologies.

News follows a segmented structure (*see* Programme production types, p. 34 above). Each item feeds into the linking thread co-ordinated by the presenters in the studio. Since each 'story' is, in fact, an encapsulated version of an ongoing, developing event, watching a news bulletin is rather like negotiating the tips of many icebergs. News fits into the broad scope of political programming, but works to its own rhythms. Some stories are developed over days or even weeks; many are covered during the day; an increasing number are carried live or near live. The studio presenters conduct live interviews with reporters, via ENG crews or satellite, as well as with politicians, witnesses and other commentators.

As in other areas of television, debates have centred on the tension between audience appeal and the duty to inform. Domestic reports on crime, accidents, political developments, parliamentary reports, economics, social affairs and the rest, many of which affect viewers directly, vie with over-seas stories which may be more globally important but feel less relevant. There is a need to balance the depressing and the light-hearted. Newsreader Martyn Lewis is on record with his comment that 'good news' tends to get overlooked. On the other hand, the BBC's John Simpson has argued that 'The "feel good factor" is a betrayal of serious news values' (*Huw Wheldon Lecture*, 23 September 1993).

Television news evolved in what Jeremy Tunstall describes as the 'heroic tradition', in which 'firemen' reporters and crews went rushing off to the world's trouble spots. 'I've worked as a field producer in about thirty-four countries' one senior news executive told him (Tunstall 1993: 50). Although news is now produced within large bureaucracies, journalists still speak of the excitement of being there as events unfold. Disasters and violence make good television.

Some think that television, with its desire for conflict and excitement, has itself come to affect the way domestic politics are conducted. BBC Director General, John Birt, commented that

> The balance is swinging towards disputation and away from reflection. . . . The media resound with acrimony, allegations of incompetence, demands for resignations. . . . It's hard to believe that political decisions made in such circumstances are always the right ones, made to last, in the public interest.
>
> (Speech made in Dublin, February 1995 cited in Brooks 1995)

Critiques of News

Television news, together with the daily and Sunday press, is engaged in laying down the parameters of the public debate. Its editors make hourly decisions on which topics should be reported and on the relative importance of those topics. The focus and priorities of a story are established and decisions are made on who will be interviewed and who will be placed in the spotlight. Of necessity, journalists and news editors take note of those characterised as the 'primary definers' of the public agenda: the politicians, judges, civil servants, businessmen and others in key positions of power in modern society. A major criticism has been that television news has failed to challenge those dominant definitions (Hall *et al.* 1978).

In the radical 1970s the Media Group at Glasgow University and the Centre for Contemporary Cultural Studies at Birmingham University launched a powerful attack on what they saw as the smug self-satisfaction of television news. It was criticised for its conservatism and its easy acceptance of the status quo. It was accused of bias against dissenting political views, working-class understandings and the perspective of women and minority groups.

The Glasgow University Media Group's *Bad News* (1976) took industrial relations as the defining expression of a class-divided society. They analysed the coverage of several disputes, including the 1975 Glasgow dustcart drivers strike, and demonstrated that reports focused on the disruption but ignored its root causes. They showed how reporting that appeared to be neutral concealed attitudes and opinions. While employers were interviewed in the studio, asked deferential questions and given an air of legitimacy, the strikers were either not interviewed at all, or were interviewed in the street, asked antagonistic questions and made to appear unreasonable. The use of language whose biases were almost instinctive – 'Trouble in Glasgow with striking dustmen . . .' (ibid.: 247) – shaded into misreporting. *Bad News* was followed by several detailed studies of political news and war reporting from the Glasgow Group. Although Martin Harrison pointed to the small size of the Glasgow sample as against the weight of the accusations (Harrison 1985), there was a general recognition that journalists and news producers, who were almost all men, almost all white and predominantly educated at elite universities, were likely to lack understanding of those outside their charmed circle.

Researchers at Birmingham drew on Marxist theories of hegemony, which explore the mixture of coercion and persuasion which those in power employ to ensure that their view carries the day. A series of studies drew attention to the ideological structures of news and current affairs. Writers such as Stuart Hall were concerned with the construction of meanings by television in dialogue with other cultural and social experiences, and with the way in which different social and ethnic groups were represented within the news media. *Policing the Crisis* (Hall *et al.* 1978) took the 'moral panic' over 'mugging' as its central theme to trace the media presentation of law and order and reveal the ways in which the black community came to be defined as delinquent. Once more it was the buried meanings and the taken for granted assumptions which were brought to the fore.

Analysis of the language and imagery of news broadcasts was part of the approach of both Birmingham and Glasgow. John Hartley's rigorous semiotic analysis underlined their importance. Journalistic 'common sense' – despite the reliance that journalists themselves put on it – needs to be subjected to what one news editor condemned as 'tortured, hair splitting semantics' (Hartley 1982: 107). John Fiske went on to argue that news creates its own narratives, with mythological heroes and villains. Long-running news 'stories' are like soap operas. They can drift away from the world on which they claim to report and build up a narrative in which those who are reported on do not recognise themselves (Fiske 1987: 293).

Critiques were often expressions of political dissatisfaction. The concept of neutrality was a sham, it was argued, in a society in which many were excluded from access to the airwaves. Some thought that news *should* be biased, but in favour of the powerless. Although they became the stock in trade of many media studies courses, not surprisingly such critical writings received a mixed reception from journalists working in television news.

Sometimes they were defensive, deriding obscure academic language and concepts. Even when sympathetic to the broad critique, they pointed out that studies that concentrated on the news output failed to take into account the hot-house pressures of the production of news, and the many different approaches of news journalists and producers who were by no means a homogeneous bunch (see Schlesinger 1978 for close observation of BBC news at work).

The critcisms which had the greatest reverberations within the television news community were those expressed by Peter Jay (now economics editor of BBC News) and John Birt (now Director General of the BBC) which became encapsulated as 'the bias against understanding'. Writing two extended articles in *The Times* in 1975, they criticised news broadcasting for offering only the immediacy of events. Without knowledge of the extensive background to each moment, the typical news snippet was largely incomprehensible. They argued for a 'mission to explain', to provide information that would make sense of the inevitably condensed short news item.

When *Channel Four News* was established, there was an attempt to move towards a broader basis for news production and a more comprehensive news agenda. It was to include longer, more in-depth pieces with time to analyse and explain. It was also to look beyond the narrow elite of programme makers and interviewees. Other programmes, such as BBC2's *Newsnight*, launched in 1980, also set out to interpret and explain (*see* James Curran, p. 193 below).

As news coverage expanded, the government became more open in expressing its views on news reporting. Chairman of the Conservative Party, Norman Tebbit, publicly criticised the reports sent by BBC Chief News Reporter Kate Adie from the Libyan capital Tripoli, when it was bombed by American planes in November 1986. Tebbit claimed that the reports were biased in favour of Libya, and 'riddled with innuendo, inaccuracy and imbalance'. Adie had reported on the victims of the bombing, amongst whom were members of the family of the dictatorial ruler, Colonel Gaddafi (*The Independent* 1986, p. 15). There was an increasing antagonism between the Thatcher government and news and current affairs departments, in particular the BBC, which the Conservative government saw as a hotbed of lefties.

Government censorship becomes an important issue at times of war. Reporting the Falklands War at the beginning of the 1980s was restricted by the great distances and fact that only limited satellite communication was available. Reporting the Gulf War, ten years later, was controlled in a far more sinister way. An overwhelming quantity of news information was put out by the British and US Army publicity machines, giving an impression of great openness, while independent reporters were discouraged from leaving the protection of the allied forces.

While overseas reporting has expanded across the globe, political journalism remains disproportionately London based, where journalists are likely to share the culture of Westminster and Whitehall. However, political parties are increasingly unwilling to allow the journalists to set the agenda. With the development of ever-more sophisticated public relations operations, they have become expert at honing their own media presentation. The new accessibility of the airwaves to MPs means there is constant pressure on journalists from media advisors and 'spin doctors', many of them ex-journalists themselves, who scour the output for 'bias' against their party. They use their knowedge of what 'works' on television to ensure the representation of their party's personalities and image rather than their views (Jones 1995). The grooming of Margaret Thatcher in the early 1980s including the changing of her voice from its shrill accusatory tones to a new and ingratiating warmth, had set a precedent (Atkinson 1984: 113).

The television journalist's job is changing in many ways. As the 1990s progressed, a decade of turmoil in Somalia, Bosnia, Rwanda and Chechnya became also the 'decade of the dish'. In August 1995 the BBC was deploying four regular journalists in former Yugoslavia, each sending back prepared reports in the 'longest-running satellite newsgathering operation in the field that anyone has ever done' (*Radio Times* 1995) The extreme danger of such work had been underlined by the number of journalists killed in this unpredictable war, including the BBC's John Schofield. Yet, paradoxically, instant satellite technology has meant that reporters have less time to go out and research a story. Frequent updates are expected, which must be assembled then delivered in very short packages of a few minutes' duration at the most. As journalist Sheena McDonald commented,

> Getting the story right from the perspective of a battlefield or an unfolding crisis demands immense skills, with generalisation and equivocation common tools of the trade. Every error subsequently revealed undermines the authority of the indivdual and the entire trade.
>
> (McDonald 1995)

Polly Toynbee, in a thoughtful article in the *Radio Times*, compared the glamour and status that has accrued to some prize-winning foreign correspondents with her own work as a social affairs journalist. 'Everyday reporting from hospitals, social security offices or government departments just doesn't carry the same zip and zing as standing in a flakjacket in a battle field' (Toynbee 1995). However, she concluded that 'good journalism does matter. In a business where the pressure grows daily to be the first, loudest and brashest, it is worth celebrating some of the more thoughtful voices who are, after all, the front-line eyewitnesses of history' (ibid.).

Producing the news

The structure of news production

The following outline is based on the production of ITN's *Channel Four News* which broadcasts a 50-minute programme on weekdays at 7 pm. The BBC, which broadcasts several programmes throughout the day, follows a similar pattern but is constantly updating its reports.

News sources

News programmes look to a variety of different sources for the information that will become a news story. They include:

Figure 33 Recording the Kobe earthquake for ITN/Channel Four News, January 1995
Courtesy ITN

- News agencies, such as the Press Association and international news agencies, as well as local news agencies who collect and redistribute basic news items

- Stringers, or freelance journalists based around the world, who may be paid a small retainer

- The programme's own correspondents based in major British cities and overseas

- Other news media, the press, radio, other television broadcasts. Investigations done by an extended current affairs programme may give rise to a news item

- Public relations sources

Reporting

News broadcasts aim to cover all aspects of a story. For example, a famine in Africa will include reports from the area, the politicians' response and coverage of what the aid agencies are doing.

Cameraperson, reporter and producer produce the report working as a team. When they are overseas they may have a tape editor with them and will send back a completed package, edited and with commentary in place. Administrative assistants do the work essential to the smooth running of such an organisation, booking plane tickets, sorting out visas and similar tasks.

Editorial discussion

Programme editors meet throughout the day to discuss stories as they develop. They decide on the running order, the order in which items will appear on the screen, and how much time should be given to each story. On *Channel Four News* these meetings are open with reporters, presenters and other staff encouraged to attend.

Preparation

During the day news editors provide the back-up to the main stories. Tape editors and producers prepare the 'news belt' of short items and less important stories. Library researchers collect extra footage, including historical footage and material from earlier developments in the story. The videotape editor then works with a reporter who writes the commentary. Sub-editors check and compile the final programme.

Transmission

The programme editor and the studio director co-ordinate from the control room. They may alter the order, or shorten and lengthen items as the news changes during the broadcast. They communicate with studio crew and the presenters through their earpieces. The presenters are also journalists who take part in discussions throughout the day. They write the links between the items and prepare and conduct live interviews during the broadcast.

News technologies

- *Fax*
- *Telephone*
- *Video lines*: Both BBC and ITN have a network of special high-speed video lines
- *Courier*: Big organisations fly parcels all over the world, or bike them through the city
- *ENG*: Electronic News Gathering was introduced in the late 1970s. It is a system which involves filming with an electronic camera. The material may then either be sent back to base by courier, transmitted back to base directly or from an intermediate microwave point, or broadcast live and recorded at the same time
- *Satellite*: Both ITN and the BBC have their own satellite dishes around the world. Portable satellite transmitters which include a satellite dish and a large trunk full of electronic equipment can be relatively easily transported, making instantaneous transmission possible from, say, the middle of the Saudi desert. News from Sarajevo has been more consis-

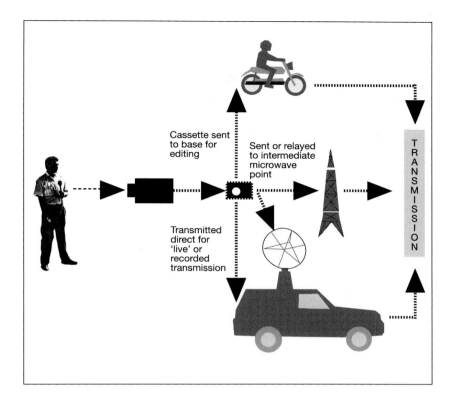

Figure 34 Electronic News Gathering (ENG)

tent than from, say Rwanda, because Sarajevo˜already had satellite transmission facilities in place following the 1984 Winter Olympics

- *Digital Newsroom Systems*: The newest technologies use a disk-based camera instead of videotape and a fully computerised system in the newsroom. The aim is for all incoming material to be transferred to a central video server to which everyone is connected. Potentially,

  'each journalist will have a multimedia PC and will call up the video footage from the server to his or her desktop. The journalist will then cut and paste the footage as one would with a word processing document' (McKay 1995)

- As in so many other areas of television, this move to converging technologies and multi-skilling will have unpredictable knock-on effects on the overall process of news production.

Figure 35 ITN control room 1995
Courtesy ITN

Changing news

Many of the 1970s criticisms have, in the 1980 and 1990s, been recast by those interested in letting market forces rip. Ex-*Sun* editor and head of Live TV Kelvin MacKenzie argues:

> With more channels there will be more television and more points of view. ... We can then ... stop panicking about controlling its content so closely. My own guess is that 20 years from now people will look back at the impartiality requirements on broadcasting as quaint pieces of history.
>
> (Brown 1996)

The news will be replaced with just news, operating in a transnational marketplace rather than a nationally based, regulated public service system. The rigidity of a news agenda defined by experts and professionals has been breaking down, but, by the end of the century, the arrival of a large number

Figure 36 Satellite dishes on the roof of ITN's headquarters in London, 1995
Courtesy ITN

of new channels and the consequent competition for audiences have become associated with radical changes within the concept of news itself.

Four major changes are currently in train: the coming of internationally based, 24-hour continuous news from satellite channels; the audience-driven 'tabloidisation' of news; the move to cheaper, less professional news production and 'job compression'; and the growth of a public relations industry which provides its own highly partial interpretation of newsworthy events. In this latter-day communications Babel, journalists are by no means the only purveyors of information.

Competition now comes from 24-hour channels devoted to news alone which cross national boundaries. They include the the Atlanta-based Cable News Network (CNN), which came to prominence in the Gulf War of 1991. Instead of packaged reports, CNN broadcast continuous live coverage from the war zone. For the audience it was as close as they could get to experiencing war for themselves. British-based *Sky News* is a continuous news channel broadcast by Rupert Murdoch's BSkyB, and the BBC itself is entering the fray with its satellite international news and information channel, *BBC World*, broadcasting across Asia, Africa, the Middle East, Europe, New Zealand and Canada.

British news broadcasters have also been taking note of American moves to make news more marketable. In the United States, news programmes have been revamped in response to detailed audience research which asked what sort of topics grab the audience's attention, what bores them, and what makes them linger as they surf through the sixty odd channels on offer. The aim has been to attract larger audiences by injecting entertainment values into news values. It emerged that audiences were interested in local rather than overseas or even national stories; that they had a short attention span and they wanted to relate to the anchor people as friends and celebrities (*Naked News*, Channel Four, 13 April 1995). The resulting changes became known as 'new news', 'action news' or, in a more pejorative tone, 'tabloid news'.

'We introduced a dynamism, a certain character', said consultant Frank Magid. He advised news programmes to introduce 'action' in the first 12 seconds of a broadcast, 'If it bleeds it leads'. 'Action' includes anything from a car accident to an armed hold-up caught on camera. Some American stations employ a full-time cameraperson in a helicopter to capture a 'breaking story' from the air – a fugitive on the run or the celebrated car chase that followed O. J. Simpson's attempted escape from the police.

Other advice was that the items should be short, locally based and introduced by carefully selected personalities rather than experienced journalists. News should be packaged in bright studio sets, delivered in tones carefully coached to be filled with excitement and energy. Reporters and presenters should be younger, newsreaders should be attractive and usually arranged in couples – a man and a woman, sitting close together, frequently looking at each other and smiling a lot. News was to be trailed in the manner of a drama. Although this market-driven news is found mainly on the local news channels in the US, the style is challenging the big networked bulletins of CBS and NBC.

Following the trend, in 1992 ITN's *News at Ten*, the British news programme with the highest audience appeal, called in an American consultancy to restructure their bulletins. The set became brighter, the items shorter and more personal. Audience research revealed that Trevor McDonald was the newscaster who inspired the 'greatest confidence' in the audience. Hence Trevor became the *News at Ten* anchor.

ITV regional news magazine programmes are also becoming much less formal and more geared to audience appeal in their choice of items, while the new cable channels are looking for ways to present news which will be original, attractive and unashamedly tabloid. They include Kelvin MacKenzie's 'news bunny' on Live TV, a furry toy who sits behind the newsreader and gives a 'paws up' or 'paws down' for a story.

On Channel One, the London-based 24-hour cable channel, news is produced by VJs: new-style journalists who go out with a video camera instead of a notebook. These 'video journalists' are often young and are 'people who aren't steeped in the traditional ways of making television, so they can go ahead and do it' said Director of Programmes Nick Pollard (Conference at the National Film Theatre, 1995). The thirty video journalists

employed by the station work 10- or 12-hour shifts, carrying their heavy
Betacam cameras, a tripod, tapes and a lighting kit as they cover home
news, features, sport, entertainment and politics.

Finally, there is the growth of well-financed public relations machines
which spread slanted information or disinformation. *Observer* journalist
John Sweeney fronted a BBC2 series, *The Spin*, which looked at some of
these pressures. 'It's hard for ordinary people to understand just how much
journalists are spoon-fed information', he wrote, describing the cars and
helicopters laid on for him when he was writing about British Gas. 'After
such treatment it took some considerable effort to bite the hand that had
fed me all this information' (Sweeney 1995). With decreasing news budgets,
there is an increasing chance that video material produced by campaigns
and pressure groups will be broadcast without attribution, appearing to be
the type of objective report to which British audiences have become accustomed. There was much concern in news organisations about the videos
provided by Greenpeace in their campaign against the demolition of the
Brent Spa oil platform, and animal rights campaigners know that horrific
videos can grab the airwaves at the expense of a considered investigation
of the issues involved (Culf 1995). The double danger is that, on the one
hand, without a proper journalistic assessment to put material into context,
the public may uncritically believe what they see, and on the other, that
there will be a blanket cynicism on the part of viewers who cease to believe
in the possibility of journalistic independence and objectivity.

At a time of dramatic change, as new technologies are transforming
working practices, those who are beginning their careers in the news media
will be those who are also forging the news values of the future.

References

Atkinson, M. (1984) *Our Masters' Voices: The Language and Body Language of
   Politics*, London: Methuen
Brooks, R. (1995) 'Birt out to tame his monster', *Guardian*, 17 July, London
Brown, M. (1996) 'Bunny, I shrunk the news', *Guardian*, 4 March, London
Culf, A. (1995) 'Greenpeace used us, broadcasters admit', *Guardian*, 28 August,
   London
Fiske, J. (1987) *Television Culture*, London: Routledge
The *Independent* (1986) 'BBC bias or Tory bluster?', 6 November, London
McDonald, S. (1995) 'World inaction' in supplement 'Whose news: democracy and
   the media' *New Statesman and Society*, 24 March, London
McKay, N. (1995) 'A revolution in the television newsrooms', *Independent*, 9
   October, London
Radio Times (1995) 'How does BBC News cover the biggest war in Europe since
   1945?", 26 August–1 September, London
Sweeney, J. (1995) 'Get out of my light', *Guardian*, September, London
Toynbee, P. (1995) 'Everyday reporting . . .' *Radio Times*, 4–10 November
Tunstall, J. (1993) *Television Producers*, London: Routledge

Key texts

Franklin, B. (1994) *Packaging Politics: Political Communications in Britain's Media Democracy*, London: Edward Arnold

Galtung, J. and Ruge, M. (1973) 'Structuring and selecting news' in S. Cohen and J. Young (eds) *The Manufacture of News: Deviance, Social Problems and the Mass Media*, London: Constable

Glasgow University Media Group (1976) *Bad News*, London: Routledge & Kegan Paul

Hall, S., Critcher, C., Jefferson, T. and Roberts, B. (1978) *Policing the Crisis: Mugging, The State and Law and Order*, London: Macmillan

Harrison, M. (1985) *TV News: Whose Bias?*, London: Policy Journals

Hartley, J. (1982) *Understanding News*, London: Methuen

Jones, N. (1995) *Soundbites and Spin Doctors*, London: Cassell

Negrine, R. (1994) *Politics and the Mass Media in Britain* London: Routledge

Schlesinger, P. (1978) *Putting 'Reality' Together: BBC News*, London: Constable

Yorke, I. (1987) *The Technique of Television News*, 2nd edn, London: Focal Press

Yorke, I. (1990) *Basic TV Reporting*, London: Focal Press

13 Television and the public sphere

TELEVISION JOURNALISM: *theory and practice*

The case of Newsnight

James Curran

Television has eclipsed parliament as the central forum of national debate. It is now the principal channel of communication in the public space between the state and the home, the main means by which citizens engage in a collective conversation that influences public opinion and the direction of society.[1]

In principle, this collective conversation should take the form of a free and open dialogue that encompasses a wide spectrum of opinion and social interest.[2] In practice, it tends to take a restricted form in which the great and the good, the accredited and the 'authoritative', do most of the talking, and set the terms of public debate.

In part this merely reflects elite preponderance in society. But it is also an unintended consequence of the way in which the media respond to the pressures of limited time and resources (Gans 1980; Sigal 1987; Tuchman 1978). News organisations tend to rely on a limited number of well-placed sources which are adept at servicing them, since this is a cheap and efficient way of reporting the news. This reliance is built into the organisation of news gathering in the form of regular 'news beats', which give to power-holders an inside track and influence what news is reported. The problems this poses are compounded further by passive news conventions and formats that reduce the truth-seeking autonomy of journalists. While these conventions are sometimes justified in terms of access and objectivity, their real purpose, it is argued, is to make news reporting easy, avoid accusations of partiality, and reconcile different political tendencies within the same mass audience. Whatever view one takes, their effect is generally to transfer a considerable degree of editorial control over the definition of news to competing elites.

This pattern of the elite shaping of news reporting and analysis has been observed in relation to print as well as broadcast media, public as well as private media, and news media in conservative as well as social democratic liberal democracies (Ericson, Baranek and Chan 1987; Hall *et al.* 1978; Hallin 1994; Herman and Chomsky 1988; Tiffin 1989). It is a problem that the continental European tradition of public service broadcasting has sought to tackle – with varying degrees of success – principally by incorporating representative groups into the management of broadcasting (Avery 1993; Blumler 1992).[3] This approach is regarded as anathema in the British tradition, which is wedded to a 'civil service', depoliticised conception of public service broadcasting, and does not regard social access as being a problem in need of a solution. Within this tradition, access has been conceived primarily in terms of the reception of broadcast signals in inaccessible areas, rather than in terms of the social distribution of opportunities to communicate. Diversity has been understood in terms of catering for different programme tastes rather than reflecting ideological differences in society. Enabling different social groups with divergent socio-economic interests, experiences and understandings to engage in a shared and reciprocal dialogue has not been an official objective of the British broadcasting system, as laid down in law (HMSO 1990), specified in the BBC's Constitution (BBC 1992a) or enunciated by the last major public enquiry into broadcasting (Home Office 1986).[4]

However, it is central to a bootleg tradition in British broadcasting with a long and distinguished tradition of programme making. This alternative tradition gave rise in the 1930s to pioneer radio talk programmes in which the unemployed spoke for the first time directly to the nation about their predicament, causing a political storm which changed the climate of political opinion (Scannell and Cardiff 1991). Giving voice to the voiceless was the inspiration behind the celebrated television play, *Cathy Come Home*, which changed the politics of housing in the 1960s and 1970s (Barendt 1981). It has been the driving force behind a rich and protean tradition of social realist drama in British television in the 1980s and 1990s (Nelson 1995). The advent of Channel Four, union workshop agreements, access programmes, phone-in talk shows, new forms of studio audience participation, community radio and the rise of the independent production sector – although containing contradictory aspects – can also be seen as being part of a generalised movement committed to extending social access to broadcasting.[5]

This movement is now lapping at the edges of mainstream journalism. It is causing the customary way of doing things to be questioned and revised, even in that citadel of convention, BBC2's *Newsnight*.

Questioning Convention

Newsnight is the television equivalent of the op-ed pages of the broadsheet press: feature comment by, and for, members of the political class. It is well crafted, intelligent and entirely predictable; its compass bearings being largely set by Westminster, Whitehall and its immediate hinterland. Yet, even in this bastion of traditional journalism, there are stirrings of change. *Newsnight* has made some modest but effective experiments during the 1990s, although none of these is entirely new.

One raft of experiments was inspired by a conscious desire to extend *Newsnight*'s repertory of sources and participants. 'Involve a wider range of experts and members of the public. Reflect the country, get away from white men in suits, get away from the M25', commanded one internal memorandum in 1995.[6] This led occasionally to members of the public being interviewed in a form that enabled them to speak in a general and authoritative manner rather than speaking (as in the case of witnesses to an accident) specifically about their personal experience. For example, in an inquest into the social significance of the killing of two-year-old James Bulger by two ten-year-olds, Olenka Frenkiel interviewed shoppers in their roles as moralists and as 'specialists' with a wide knowledge of children, as a counterpoint to a more conventional studio discussion between a bishop, a government minister and a leading psychotherapist (*Newsnight*, 11 November 1993). A second experiment involved elevating members of the public beyond the status of studio audience members to full accreditation as studio panel guests. Thus, a teenage drug user and a mother of a jailed drug addict debated drug control on an equal footing with a government minister and a teachers' leader in a particularly revealing discussion (*Newsnight*, 16 November 1995). A third break with convention involved bypassing spokespersons to interview the people they represented. This often gave rise to interviews which had an emotional force and authenticity generally lacking in the impersonal fluency of professional advocacy, and lifted conventional programmes out of their rut.

For example, a *Newsnight* item (21 August 1995) about people jailed for debt had interviews with predictable people (a magistrate, an enforcement officer and a reforming lawyer) and made predictable points: the law was being applied inconsistently and more indigent people were going to jail during the recession. What transformed the programme item, and made it both memorable and disturbing, were three interviews with debtors. One was interviewed as a deviant, pressed to justify her fecklessness within a law-and-order framework. Two others were interviewed as victims, in the tradition of *Little Dorrit*. There was a certain amount of stage setting in the programme. The daughter of the debtor interviewed as deviant was shot standing in front of the kitchen sink, a cigarette hanging out of her mouth. The debtors interviewed as victims were introduced in heartwarming shots with their families. One featured a mother, Julie Strickland, coming out of prison and being reunited with her children. Prison had been 'hell', she said, with the voice-over adding that she had been locked up next to a multiple murderer for non-payment of a television licence fine. Another mother of a small child, Jane Count, jailed for non-payment of £22, spoke of the humiliation of her prison strip search. The emotional charge of this interview came from its halting inarticulacy contrasted with that of the Chairwoman of the Magistrates Association speaking in a book-lined room, with smiling charm and boundless confidence – and total inhumanity – about why it was right to jail mothers at great expense for non-payment of very small sums of money.

Another way in which *Newsnight* reworked convention was to set up a debate within the ranks of the right or left rather than beween them. This tactic usefully extended the narrow arc of opinion usually represented on television. It also enabled the viewer to peer behind the controlled choreography of party politics, with its careful stage managing of political difference, to see something of the real strategic debates taking place within the political process. At best, as in a passionate and wonderfully eloquent discussion between Conservative party politicians and activists on the occasion of John Redwood's bid for the leadership, it offered a valuable insight into the choices facing not only the Conservative Party but also the nation (*Newsnight*, 30 June 1995).

However, the single, most important contribution *Newsnight* made to political dialogue was to step occasionally outside the conventional news frame. 'Broaden our political coverage away from Westminster. . . . Offer ideas and treatments on stories off the main news agenda' was how one office memo put it.[7] Sometimes this entailed reporting and discussing a story, such as a scientific breakthrough, that had received little attention. Alternatively, it involved questioning explicitly a dominant way of seeing things. The most effective way in which this questioning was accomplished was by inserting a mini-documentary into the programme's news magazine format. This created a space in which established terms of reference could be challenged, and an alternative framework of analysis could be advanced.

This will be illustrated by two *Newsnight* mini-documentaries: the first transmitted in 1991, which exemplifies a traditional style of concerned journalism; the second screened in 1994, which reveals a more contemporary style. The first of these took the form of a horizontal dialogue between elites; the second a bottom-up, vertical communication from a subordinate group.

Horizontal communication

On 8 October 1991, *Newsnight* covered the opening day of the Conservative Party Conference at Blackpool with an end item that questioned explicitly the ruling party's understanding of contemporary Britain. Its tone was set by the studio presenter, Peter Snow, who contrasted 'the debate about theory' at Blackpool with 'the reality of life on a Lancashire housing estate'. Excerpts from Conservative Party Chairman Chris Patten's opening speech, in which he celebrated 'more choice' in 'opportunity Britain' were followed by shots of a festival service taking place in Roman Road County School, Blackburn. The roving camera came to a halt at the festival offerings of flowers and fruit whose meagreness the voice-over commentary signified as an image of communal poverty. While the Roman Road estate did not look run down, explained the reporter James Cox, four out of five people were out of work, 90 per cent of the children left school at 16, and it contained a higher proportion of single parents than any other estate in Lancashire.

The remaining film profile of the estate conveyed an impression of demoralisation and despair. The local vicar, in the first of three excerpts of a 'keynote' interview, said that high expectations had given way to vandalism and violence, and then to resigned apathy. People got up late, he added subsequently, because they felt they had nothing to get up for. A local resident spoke of her 'suicidal depression', while her son talked of people 'going under' as local employment declined. A short clip showed the police intervening in a 'common' domestic dispute. The head teacher described how demoralised mothers sent sick children to school just to get them off their hands, and went on to say that parents' struggle to pay the bills generally eclipsed their interest in their children's education. The only discordant note in this image of blight was a short soundbite from the prospective parliamentary Conservative candidate for Blackburn, who talked of the government offering 'a ladder of hope' to people on the estate. This was tacitly repudiated by the testimony of everyone else who was interviewed. This film was then followed by more clips from the Conservative Party Conference and its fringe. The reporter, James Cox, wrapped up by saying that the message from Blackpool was 'likely to go unheard on the Roman Road estate'. The power of individual choice celebrated at the conference meant little to 'those who have fallen through the rungs of the Thatcherite ladder' because generally they lack 'the will and the means' to exercise that power.

The programme switched back to a studio discussion between two Conservative politicians, Rhodes Boyson and Edwina Currie, and left-wing 'agony aunt', Claire Rayner, all three of whom had grown up in poor areas. They broadly accepted the underlying validity of the mini-documentary, and constantly referred to it in an emotionally charged debate. The Conservative politicians sought to close the gap between rhetoric and reality in different ways: in the case of Rhodes Boyson by calling for a programme of moral reconstruction, and in Edwina Currie's case by advocating changes in education policy that would make people 'employable' and free mothers to go out to work. Claire Rayner extolled the multiple benefits of generating new jobs without indicating how this might be achieved.

The moral agitation of this debate was a tribute to the force of this documentary. However, the documentary's most glaring defect was that it provided a view of a depressed housing estate almost entirely through the eyes of local community leaders. There was only one interview with ordinary residents. This lasted 38 seconds in a filmed documentary of almost 8 minutes, and added nothing to what was said by other interviewees – apart from authenticity.

This 'from high to low' perspective was carried over into the studio discussion. Whether it was Edwina Currie regretting the lack of enterprise of Roman Road residents despite the money spent on them, Rhodes Boyson attacking the quality of their whingeing local leadership, or Claire Rayner discussing how their 'parenting skills' might be improved, we were exposed to a view from the executive lounge. The fact that all three studio speakers had lived in poor areas in their childhood did not alter this. Indeed, the programme functioned as a closed channel of communication between elites. In effect, it enabled an exchange of understandings of the underclass between senior members of the ruling party and leftish members of the liberal professions (a priest, a head teacher, a top journalist and, implicitly, *Newsnight*'s James Cox). Its mode of address also hailed the viewer as part of the 'us' who must decide what to do about 'them' – the sort of people who land up on a sink housing estate in Blackburn.

Vertical communication

Three years later *Newsnight* (6 January 1994) did something rather similar – and very much better. Once again it contrasted an official Conservative view of the world with life as it was experienced by a working-class community beset by high unemployment. However, this time round disadvantaged members of society spoke directly about their social experience, and were not mute objects of elite concern. The end product was very much more enlightening.

The lead item was the government's turmoil over its 'back to basics' campaign. Tim Yeo, a married government minister, had resigned after it had been revealed that he was fathering a child by a woman other than his wife. 'Back to basics', explained the Prime Minister, was about public policy rather than personal morality. This was contradicted by a succession of clips of ministers saying that it was about both, mostly from the 1993 Conservative Party Conference. The hapless Employment Minister, David Hunt, was forced to explain away this inconsistency in an interview with Jeremy Paxman that turned into the equivalent of a democratic blood sport.

This was then followed by a mini-documentary introduced by Paxman as revealing social relations 'light years away from the "back to basics" ideal home'. The documentary showed that many of the new jobs in the Welsh valleys were part-time, low-paid and filled by women. One in three men was out of work, their brawn no longer needed following the collapse of the steel and mining industries. In a series of revealing interviews the *Newsnight* reporter, Olenka Frenkiel, showed how different men adjusted to irrelevance. One sequence switched from a mechanical robot working in a factory to men working out in a gym, building their bodies into 'temples of masculinity'. 'If I didn't have this', said one unemployed man in the weights room, 'I would have nothing'. Another man, out of work, a former miner with a bristling moustache, was featured at home, clinging to the traditional male role. 'I do everything', he said, which turned out to mean that he took charge of paying the bills while his wife went out to work and also did most of the housework. A third man, a crushed eighteen-year-old with a wispy moustache, was introduced as eking out a meagre existence from his £26 social security. His girlfriend was having a child by him, but did not want to be lumbered with him. 'She doesn't want me there . . . it makes me a bit sad.'

The second key theme of the documentary was that the matriarchal system of single mothers was creating an island of stability in a devastated environment. A sequence of interviews revealed self-sufficient, resourceful women choosing to bring up their children alone because their menfolk were out of work, had nothing to offer or were otherwise unsatisfactory. 'You're better off financially [without the husband]', explained one woman because she could control how welfare payments were spent. 'Women wear the trousers in this house', commented another with a smile. But there was sympathy nevertheless among some of these women for the predicament of their men, denied the choice available to their fathers of going down the pit and earning a good living. The film ended with a poignant sequence featuring fourteen-year-old boys with low educational achievements, most of whom said they would have liked to have been miners. They were too young to be realistic about their future yet, concluded the reporter Olenka Frenkiel, already 'it was perhaps too late [for them] to take control of their lives'.

The power of the documentary derived partly from the way in which Frenkiel managed to get people to talk about their innermost feelings. What had been an intellectual abstraction in the previous documentary – a community blighted by unemployment – came alive in the form of individuals struggling, adapting, behaving badly or well, hanging on as best they could. Whereas the earlier film had provoked from studio guests responses ranging from pity to impatience, this one elicited a feeling of identification and empathy, and perhaps with it, greater understanding. The feckless and inadequate single parents of 'back to basics' ideology featured very differently in this documentary as the new pillars of a community in crisis. The connection between unemployment and crime, merely asserted in the previous *Newsnight* documentary, was given here an explanatory context: some young men shifting between mother, sister and girlfriend, their masculinity undermined by being out of work, were seeking to keep their end up through cash from petty crime. Above all, the programme enabled people to describe a reality at odds with that perceived by government ministers. It was a powerful example of bottom-up communication: of people speaking for themselves rather than being spoken for or at.[8]

This second documentary was also aesthetically far superior to its precursor. The 1991 documentary was essentially an essay in talking heads. Its relatively few images were generally superfluous or prosaic – such as interviewees walking through the door or children playing in the street – and were included merely as visual relief to the spoken word. By contrast, the 1994 documentary advanced its argument in arresting pictures as well as words. The opening sequence, for example, set the scene of a disappearing world: an elderly male choir singing of manly pride (Hammerstein's 'Stout Hearted Men'); a black and white clip of miners; a socialist realist sculpture of a massive working man with a dependent woman. This was followed by images of change: children streaming across a theme park which had once had busy pit-heads, and a small, disconsolate group of people at one end of a large hall trying to save the last mine in the region. Images of the past and present were then interwoven in fast cuts to convey a sense of flux and turmoil. This set the scene for the documentary's ambivalent narrative: a flawed past succeeded by a flawed present in which men are being emasculated by unemployment but in which women are making significant gains.

However, the comparison is not necessarily only to the advantage of the 1994 programme. Part of the impact of the first programme derived from the confrontation it set up between Conservative ideology and lived experience. The contrast between official thinking and ordinary experience was also highlighted in the second programme by two signposting cues which suggested in effect that an inherited ideology of family values and social scapegoating no longer correspond to a changed social reality. However, the dialogue between government and governed was made much less explicit in the second programme, and the connection between the two programmes – improvised at speed rather than planned – could have been missed.[9]

A direct comparison is also a little unfair because the second documentary was 6 minutes longer, and showed signs of having more resources devoted to it. Even so, these resources were not lavish: two weeks researching by the reporter and the producer, four days shooting, and two days editing.[10] The producer was Jessica Cecil and, like the reporter, Olenka Frenkiel, is aged under 35. Together they turned a piece of routine journalism into revelatory art. A simple idea, triggered by news reports that

girls were doing better than boys at school, was translated into an unfor-
gettable 14-minute film about the inner life of a traditional community.

James Curran is Professor of Communications, Goldsmiths' College, University of
London and author or editor of many books on the politics and sociology of the
media.

Notes

1 For a discussion of the role of the media in the 'public sphere', triggered by the
work of the German philospher, Jürgen Habermas, see Dahlgren (1995), Garnham
(1992) and Curran (1993).
2 A summary of the radical justification for this approach is provided by Curran
(1996) and of the traditional liberal justification, by Kelley and Donway (1990).
3 The nature and extent of elite domination is the subject of a heated debate. Those
seeing elite domination as being relatively uniform include Hall *et al.* (1978) and
Herman and Chomsky (1988); those emphasising elite dissension include
Schlesinger and Tumber (1994) and Hallin (1994); while those questioning the
extent of elite control include Miller (1993) and Murphy (1991).
4 But it does find anodyne expression in a key BBC policy document (BBC 1992b).
5 For futher discussion of this, see Tony Dowmunt p. 202 and, for a recent useful
appraisal of participatory programme formats, see Livingstone and Lunt (1994).
6 *Newsnight Objectives* 1995/6, internal BBC office memo, 1995.
7 As above
8 Ordinary people were being represented, however, through the mediation of a
journalist. This programme was in fact a relatively closed rather than open text
in which the comments of the interviewees were often interpreted explicitly by
the reporter.
9 The ease with which this implicit dialogue could be missed was perhaps indi-
cated by the fact that the producer of the second item had, almost two years
later, no recall of the first item on the government's 'back to basics' campaign
but a detailed recall of the second item. The link between the two was forged
at short notice and was not pre-planned.
10 Interview with Jessica Cecil, November 1995.

References

Avery, R. (ed.) (1993) *Public Service Broadcasting in a Multichannel Environment*,
White Plains, NY: Longman
Barendt, G. (ed.) (1981) *Television Drama*, Cambridge: Cambridge University Press
Blumler, J. (ed.) (1992) *Television and the Public Interest*, London: Sage
British Broadcasting Corporation (1992a) *Guide to the BBC*, London: BBC
Information Services
British Broadcasting Corporation (1992b) *Extending Choice*, London: BBC Corporate
Affairs
Curran, J. (1996) 'Mass media and democracy revisited' in J. Curran and M.
Gurevitch (eds) *Media and Society*, 2nd edn, London: Arnold
Curran, J. (1993) 'Rethinking the media as a public sphere' in P. Dahlgren and C.
Sparks (eds) *Communication and Citizenship*, London: Routledge
Dahlgren, P. (1995) *Television and the Public Sphere*, London: Sage
Ericson, R., Baranek, P. and Chan, J. (1987) *Visualising Deviance*, London: Open
University Press

Gans, H. (1980) *Deciding What's News*, London: Constable

Garnham, N. (1992) 'Media and the public sphere' in C. Calhoun (ed.) *Habermas and the Public Sphere*, Cambridge, Mass.: MIT Press

Hall, S., Critcher, C., Jefferson, T. and Roberts, B. (1978) *Policing the Crisis*, London: Macmillan

Hallin, D. (1994) *We Keep America on Top of the World*, London: Routledge

Herman, E. and Chomsky, N. (1988) *The Manufacture of Consent*, New York: Pantheon

HMSO (1990) *Broadcasting Act*, London: HMSO

Home Office (1986) *Report of the Committee on Financing the BBC*, Cmnd 9824, London: HMSO

Kelley, D. and Donway, R. (1990) 'Liberalism and free speech' in J. Lichtenberg (ed.) *Mass Media and Democracy*, New York: Cambridge University Press

Livingstone, S. and Lunt, P. (1994) *Talk on Television*, London: Routledge

Miller, D. (1993) 'Official sources and "primary definition": the case of Northern Ireland', *Media, Culture and Society*, vol. 15, no. 3

Murphy, D. (1991) *The Stalker Affair and the Press*, London: Unwin Hyman

Nelson, R. (1995) *TV Drama: Postmodernity and Critical Aesthetics*, University of Warwick, PhD Thesis

Scannell, P. and Cardiff, D. (1991) *Social History of Broadcasting 1922–1939: Serving the Nation*, Oxford: Blackwell

Schlesinger, P. and Tumber, H. (1994) *Reporting Crime*, Oxford: Clarendon

Sigal, L. (1987) 'Sources make the news' in R. Manoff and M. Schudson (eds) *Reading the News*. New York: Pantheon.

Tiffin, R. (1989) *News and Power*, Sydney: Allen and Unwin

Tuchman, G. (1978) *Making the News*, New York: Free Press

ACCESS: *television at the margins*

Tony Dowmunt

As has been seen earlier in this book, television has developed all over the world either commercially – shaped by major economic interests operating in the marketplace – or under the umbrella of the state. Underlying these two models is a basic similarity: they both assume a centralised distribution system of programming to a mass audience. In the United Kingdom, until the early 1980s, an enormous amount of cultural power was concentrated in the hands of the BBC and ITV (the 'duopoly' as they were known). Making and distributing television programmes was the prerogative of a small number of professionals employed by these two organisations.

The late 1960s had seen the growth of 'grass-roots' activism in many areas of social life, which for the most part focused on demands for more local, popular, or democratic institutions. These social upheavals found expression in television in movements of opposition against the duopoly. Within television this centred around 'access' programming, and outside the established broadcasters, around various forms of 'access workshops' and community channels on cable television.

Access programming

In the late 1960s the BBC2 'cultural' show, *Late Night Line Up,* sent a crew and a presenter, Tony Bilbow, down to the local Guinness factory to interview the workers about how they felt about the BBC's autumn schedules. The interviewees rebelled. They refused to be manipulated by the programme's agenda and vigorously attacked television in general for the way it misrepresented (particularly working-class) people. *Late Night Line Up*, to their credit, ran the whole interview unedited. Later, producers from the programme, influenced by new ideas about access from the United States, addressed the wider issues that the interview brought up by setting up the Community Programme Unit. Their remit was (and still is) to provide a platform on national television for voices and viewpoints normally unheard or misrepresented in the mainstream. Despite numerous disputes with the BBC management, the Unit has survived, producing a variety of programmes over the years, from the early *Open Door* (now *Open Space)* to more recent experiments with Hi-8, such as *Video Diaries* and *Video Nation.*

Some of the ITV stations followed the BBC's example and produced mostly regional access programming, but their commitment to the genre has been significantly weaker and less well resourced over the years. The coming of Channel Four, however, in the early 1980s broke the hold of the 'duopoly' over the structures of television. As well as providing access to television to a new range of independent producers (who in many cases, it must be said, were old 'duopoly' professionals gone freelance), the Channel did open up television to a significantly wider constituency of voices. Programmes by and for women, black and Asian people, and gays and lesbians, among others, appeared for the first time, and there has been a succession of 'access' slots from *People to People* to *Takeover TV*, which has to some extent fulfilled the Channel's remit to represent minority viewpoints and has allowed people who were not television professionals a voice on television.

The workshop movement

Arguably the most adventurous of Channel Four's experiments in access was its support for the 'workshops'. Since the late 1960s, all over the UK small groups and collectives of film and video makers had formed, some with the aim of working closely with a neighbourhood or community, others seeking to represent a 'community of interest', a cultural or political cause – all of them a reaction to the political and aesthetic blandness of mainstream television. The Independent Film and Video Department of Channel Four under Alan Fountain worked with these groups and the trade union, the ACTT (now BECTU) to create an industrial agreement whereby the Channel could provide long-term support for the groups in exchange for 'first option' to broadcast what they produced. This infrastructural funding was highly unusual and innovative in an industry which, before and since, has restricted its commissioning procedures to funding programme production only. The flexibility it provided enabled many new voices to be heard and new people to enter the television industry, in particular from the regions and from 'ethnic minorities'.

Among the workshop movement's most significant achievements were the volume and quality of video material coming out of the mining communities during the 1984 strike. At a time when national coverage of the dispute both focused narrowly on issues of violence on the picket-line, and was broadly in support of the government and the National Coal Board, the workshops helped to produce counter-propaganda on police violence and the case of the besieged communities. Some of the material found its way on to Channel Four, all of it circulated in mining areas and amongst solidarity campaigns on tens of thousands of video copies.

Channel Four was unable to sustain its infrastructural funding. It had been conceived from the beginning as a partnership with local government and public arts funding, and the ravages of Thatcherism had all but destroyed these other sources by the end of the 1980s. However, this has not meant the end of work shop style activity. In fact, with the increasing availability of camcorders, it could be argued that the prospects for this form of grassroots access have never been stronger. The 1990s equivalent of the miners' video campaign is the camcorder activism currently flourishing in the direct action campaigns on issues such as opposition to road building or support of animal rights. The regular video magazine *Undercurrents* collects much of this material together, giving a positive and vibrant picture of oppositional politics in the UK all but invisible on mainstream television.

Community cable television

For activists disillusioned with the inaccessibility of broadcast television, cable has long seemed a viable, locally based medium for community expression. In the US, where, for geographical reasons, cable has been widely taken up as a means of distributing television signals, a large number of towns and cities have developed lively community channels, and there is a well-organised national lobby to protect their interests against the purely commercial motivations of cable companies within which they operate. In the UK, the community use of cable has developed much more slowly and sporadically. Five experimental channels were licensed in the 1970s, and for a while, the Post Office ran a scheme in Milton Keynes. Despite some success in involving local people in production and in building audiences, none of these channels has survived. For the most part they were killed off by the indifference of their host companies.

In the 1980s and 1990s the development of community channels has remained a low priority for the majority of the cable companies poised to exploit the telecommunications potential of fibre-optic and digital technologies. The received wisdom in the industry is that audiences are still so low that reruns of successful terrestrial shows are a better bet in ratings terms than community experiments. There are exceptions. Clyde Cable in Glasgow had a lively community channel for a while in the early 1990s; Leicester's Cable 7 is doing so now. But for the most part the access potential of local cable in the UK remains under-explored and looks set to remain so. Only eleven out of the existing eighty-three franchises are operating local access services (White 1995), and there is no obligation under the 1990 Broadcasting Act for any new franchise to offer such a service.

Internationally

The centralising and commercial forces that work against access in the UK are just as evident the world over – as are the local acts of resistance to them. Wherever people find themselves excluded or misrepresented on television, they tend to find ways of representing themselves – using any modern technology they can gain access to:

- *The Democracy Movement in Taiwan* made camcorder recordings of the brutal police and army reactions to their demonstrations in Bangkok in 1992. They edited them together with BBC World Service footage, recorded off Star satellite, and sold the results on video cassettes on the streets – thereby subverting the blanket of censorship imposed by Thai Television (Philip Wood interviewed in *Tactical TV*, APT Film and Television for Channel Four, May 1993).

- *MED TV is a Kurdish satellite station*, beaming a range of programmes (including news of human rights abuses) into Kurdistan over the heads of the Turkish and Iraqi authorities. Turkish security forces are reportedly smashing satellite dishes, but dishes are now small enough to be virtually undetectable (Boseley 1995: 9).

- *In Johannesburg the Centre for Democratic Communication* runs an access centre and aims to train black, working class youth in television production. They have acquired a digital editing system through sponsorship and see their activity as part of 'our struggle to change our national broadcasting' (Cullis 1995: 10).

- *In the US, Deep Dish* use footage gathered from Community Cable stations and independent filmmakers to make radical series for showing on community channels, and sometimes more widely. Subjects covered include the Gulf War, the Los Angeles riots following the Rodney King verdict, and the lack of health care. They describe themselves as 'hitch-hikers on the edge of the eight lane information super-highway' because they hire satellite time to distribute their programmes all over the States. They alert the community channels who download the material at the notified times (Martin Lucas from Deep Dish, interviewed in *Tactical TV*, APT Film and Television for Channel Four, May 1993).

Notwithstanding these radical experiments, and many more like them across the globe, there is no sign that the centralising, homogenising forces at work in global television are abating. The cosy duopoly in the UK is being transformed by world market forces. Transnational media empires, such as that run by Rupert Murdoch, continue to expand. In the UK, camcorders are as likely to be used as a weapon in the television industry's cost-cutting war, as they are for innovation or genuine access. It is cheaper to shoot with one person and a Hi-8 camera, than a full Beta crew. This shows more commitment to the bottom line than it does to the project of democratising television. In addition, although it is obviously true that camcorder technology makes it easier for a wider range of people to access the means of production, the means of distribution – terrestrial broadcasting, cable and satellite – is firmly and increasingly the property of the transnational empires, and consequently even more remote from any form of democratic accountability.

Even so, there are those who assert (often, unsurprisingly, spokespeople for the 'empires') that the struggle for 'access' is over, that the technologies are by themselves opening up the media, widening access and choice. Their argument is that the information 'superhighway' will soon enable anyone who so wishes, to communicate with the world via digital technology. However, all the evidence of previous 'communications revolutions' is that the dominant social and economic forces which surround these revolutions co-opt and mould them for their own ends – even though different and more radical possibilities are always there and sometimes partially realised at the same time. The camcorder is simultaneously a harmless home-movie toy and a potent tool for democratic television. The information 'superhighway' is primarily an international conduit for financial and business data, but it has also enabled the growth of the Internet, with all its radical, anti-hierarchical potential.

At the moment technological utopianism is nowhere more evident – and with substantial reason – than in debates about the Net. There are innumerable instances where oppositional or minority voices are communicating where in the past they would have remained unheard. The Zapatista movement in Mexico is a recent example of a revolutionary group that has utilised the Net to get its message out to the world. But, with increasing commercialisation (possibly by the injection of advertising), the hierarchy of money is likely to reassert itself and consign radical movements to the status of 'hitch-hikers', here as elsewhere. In the light of this, George Stoney, a veteran of the movement for public access on cable in the US, has pointed out that public access activists have amassed a body of practical experience that could be an invaluable guide to those now about to determine whether the new communications medium supports democratic principles or the crushing dominance of media conglomerates.

(Stoney 1994: 36)

As with cable or any other communications technology, the open accessibility and democratic potential of the Internet will have to be fought for. It does not arrive as a given with the technology itself.

It may be that the crucial struggles over 'access' as we enter the next millennium will centre on the means of distribution at an increasingly international level, as it is here that the concentration of corporate power is at its most dense and impenetrable. There are many signs that this is already occurring – at international conferences, in growing networks, and the recent initiative from the Third World Network in Malaysia and the Centre for Communications and Human Rights in Amsterdam for a global 'People's Communications Charter'. There are also more immediately practical initiatives occurring at different levels. For example, Small World, who were involved with the production of *Undercurrents*, are collaborating with Associação de Vídeo Popular to set up an exchange of video material between Brazil and the UK 'to help strengthen the social movements in both countries by increasing and improving the flow of information' (*Videazimut CLIPS* 1994: 11). There are also (at least) two current attempts to make non-commercial interventions in the international satellite distribution of television:

- **WETV** is a 'Global Access Television Network', started by a Canadian development agency and supported by private sector investors, NGOs and broadcasters in both North and South. Its aim is to create a new television channel which will provide access to diverse voices throughout the world while raising awareness of issues of sustainable development and the environment (*Videazimut CLIPS* 1995: 6).

- **Mondial** is a new satellite service, initially to be based in Europe, which will show material from all over the world from producers 'whose work is shut out of the main television channels'. It is a conscious attempt to create an alternative to 'market-led global culture' and to use satellite distribution to foster 'much greater communication between countries and cultures and the expression of a dazzling range of voices' (Fountain 1995: 17).

For media students and people interested in pursuing a career in television the marginal 'access' sector poses something of a problem. There are few established points of entry and no easily recognised paths to follow to get work within it – apart from established areas like the BBC's Community Programme Unit. Most of the groups, projects and organisations in the sector were started by activists and enthusiasts (at the beginning at least) on a voluntary, unpaid or poorly paid basis. A number of projects in the UK were able to survive, grow and employ new workers because of financial support from various governmental arts-funding sources, as well as Channel

Four, in the 1970s and early 1980s. But, as we have seen, the practical and ideological victories of Thatcherism have all but dried up these sources. Public subsidy is unlikely for the foreseeable future as the main way of supporting marginal television activity, despite the funding released by the National Lottery. However, as always, the contradictions in the system will continue to throw up exciting opportunities, which people who have a mixture of political commitment, enthusiasm and entrepreneurial skill will be able to exploit and enjoy.

Tony Dowmunt is an independent producer with APT Film and Television, and MA Course Tutor in Documentary at Goldsmiths' College, University of London. He is the editor of *Channels of Resistance: Global Television and Local Empowerment*, London: BFI and Channel Four 1993.

References

Boseley, S. (1995) 'Kurds' London TV station makes Turkey seethe', *Guardian* 25 May, London

Cullis, S. (1995) quoted in *Zebra News*, April, no. 1, Copenhagen

Fountain, A. (1995) 'What choice do we have?' *20:20*, no. 1 Spring, Brighton: Bash Street Publishers

Stoney, G. (1994) 'Public access and the superhighway', *Dox*, no. 4, Hertogenbosch, Netherlands

Videazimut CLIPS (1994) 'News' *Videazimut CLIPS*, no, 6, September, Montreal

Videazimut CLIPS (1995) 'Reinventing television: it's all in the organisation', *Videazimut CLIPS*, no, 8, June, Montreal

White, J. (1995) *Survey of Local Channels on UK Cable 1984–1985*, Edinburgh: Institute of Local Television

Part IV: Education, training and television programmes

14 'A training in ideas?'

Stuart Cosgrove: *Controller of Arts and Entertainment, Channel Four television*

When Stuart Cosgrove became commissioning editor for Independent Film and Video at Channel Four in 1994, it was of a piece with a career that included writing on music and popular culture; presenting programmes such as *The Late Show* and Radio Scotland's comedy football programme *On The Ball*; and running his own Glasgow-based independent production company, Big Star in a Wee Picture. In March 1996 he took over as Controller of Channel Four's Arts and Entertainment. Below he talks about his beginnings in media studies, about commissioning new programme makers and about his views on Channel Four and its direction for the future.

Stuart Cosgrove

'Some television people who have grown up through conventional production companies have a contempt for ideas, but I think it's mean spirited to say that a training in ideas is not a training. When people say 'these media studies students don't know anything', they usually mean some technical skill. But we actually hire the technical skills when we need them. The idea that gets you the commission is brought about either by conceptual thought or by an engagement with popular ideologies. I began in academia and I'm often amazed at the number of people from the courses I taught who are now working around Channel Four, or as producers or whatever.

I'm interested in popular, radical culture. My PhD was called '*The Living Newspaper' history, ideology and form*, and it traced agitational theatre from revolutionary Russia, through the US anti-fascism of the 1930s to literacy campaigns in Central and Latin America.

As an independent producer – and this still ties in with media and cultural studies – we did a thing called *The Trainer Wars*. It was the first hip-hop business programme, commissioned by the commissioning editor for Business. We took a popular consumer object, the trainer, and looked at the war between Nike and Reebok. In telling that story we showed how a First World product, in the forefront of style and gang warfare, had Third World implications. We made what I'd like to think was a conceptual television essay.

I think my own background is a really invigorating jigsaw because I draw experiences from such a wide range of previous careers. I've got direct understanding of the loneliness of the independent producer, which is why, as a commissioning editor, I've been much more promiscuous about sending out tender documents and getting people to apply for particular areas of programming. I think ideas come from that kind of democracy of letting people know what it is that you're trying to achieve and what it is you want.

When I was commissioning Independent Film and Video I had to make quite brutal choices about what we could afford to fund. I tended to focus on the contemporaneity of culture, which doesn't mean I don't care about history – in fact it's one of the first loves of my life – but I decided to take the direction of contemporary commitment. At the heart of *The Red Light Zone* was one of the debates that has divided feminism in the 1990s. I wanted that division to be on the screen, with all the disagreements, all the scatology and all the rest of it for the audience. I wanted the shrapnel of contemporary politics rather than believing that I already knew the answer, for good and for bad. For marks on my school jotter I think I got 8 out of 10.

The single thing I'm most proud of is that we commissioned more new, first-time directors than at any time in the department's history bar none – even when the workshops were at their height. I'm proud of the volume of people who have come through this office – that's my direct connection back to being a teacher. I'm also proud of programmes like *The Dying Rooms*, which had an international impact. I'm hugely proud of what we did with the 'zoning' because in lots of ways it redefined how Channel Four thinks about some of its scheduling. The late-night zones proved there are still sizeable audiences around after 11 pm, particularly for more gritty material that's challenging and culturally charged.

We also did a thing called *The Shooting Gallery*, a showcase for short films, most of which we either bought completed or commissioned through schemes like the BFI. It was for young filmmakers making calling-card films: first films that they hope will open the door to making features or whatever. By pulling them together and launching them and giving them an identity, we could get someting like 800,000 people watching at midnight for films that had been made by college students. For lots of reasons that kind of thing excites me. When you look at the viewing figures and you think the second run of the US sitcom we bought six years ago is getting 700,000 and the new short film is getting 800,000, I know which one I'd go with. In that way you can have the sense of maintaining your relationship to the authenticity of Channel Four's remit. I'm utterly and totally committed to what Channel Four is. I'm not sure that the decisions I took in 1995

were the decisions I would have taken in 1975, but I feel I've reviv-
ified the Independent Film and Video department at least in terms of
what can be achieved in television of the 1990s.

Now my task is to take the Arts and Entertainment department and
manage it through what will be a vital period for it, a period of growth.
It's such a sprawling and diverse remit, including acquired and
purchased programmes, all the purchased feature films, all the major
American series, sport, children's, animation, arts and music and the
big entertainments, both sitcoms and stand-up comedy. I think that
the variety of my background has stood me in really good stead. I've
written books on football; I've got a PhD in Drama; I've done popular
programming; I've been an independent producer; and I'm not fazed
by debates about arts policy.

An argument that goes right back to the 1950s is the tension between
American popular entertainment as being a kind of cultural imperi-
alism and a sense of a robust, working-class authentic popular culture
from Britain. These have always be seen as rivals. I take a strategic
postion between them. I think that a lot of what we now consider as
major significant landmarks in popular entertainment in Britain – soaps,
Coronation Street, *Brookside* – are inconceivable without the existence
of their rubbishy American predecessors. I've commissioned a series
in Independent Film and Video called *More American Trash*. The
presenter lectures Britons about being so worried about America. If
we could find rivals to *Roseanne*, *Cybill*, and *Ellen* I'd die a happy
man.

At the heart of all this there has to be a sense of danger, a sense
of the innovative, a sense of the troublesome. I think that you've got
to allow originality to flourish wherever it is. That's where Channel
Four should be. I like the big publicity spats around *Dyke TV* or *The
Girlie Show*. If we're not in that territory, stoking and fuelling those
kind of debates, then we're not doing our job. This may be media
studies speak, but I think that when you reflect back on a programme
six months or a year later, you end up realising that the programme
became something more than the 24 minutes of screen-time. It actually became part of a popular discourse. Whatever you think of *The
Girlie Show*, it has generated widespread popular and media discussion about the image of young girls in the 1990s, the new ladette thing.
I love that argument. I don't want our programmes to creep on to air
and be all polite and to be the pick of the day in the *Guardian* and
to go gently into that good night. I want them to be in there and get
that kind of attention.

There are certain things in your life that you feel close to, and
Channel Four is one of the things for me. Scotland is the other.'

15 Education, training and getting into the industry

··

Who needs media studies?

Both the television industry and the British education system are changing rapidly as we reach the close of the twentieth century. The old, well-tried boundaries between industry-based 'training' and college-based 'education' are breaking down. This new fluidity, like so many other changes, is partly due to the increasing cheapness and accessibility of television and video technology, and partly to a fragmentation of both institutions. A more market-based system means that neither television nor education enjoys the security it did in the past, but at the same time they are both far more open to a wider spectrum of the population.

Up to the 1970s the film and television industry seemed completely impenetrable to outsiders. The old style of recruiting was though contacts; technicians' jobs often ran in families; and it was almost always a question of who you knew. The BBC ran a fast-track training scheme for its high-flyers, young graduates, almost all Oxbridge and almost exclusively male, many of whom became future Controllers of Programmes and Directors General. The BBC was for many years the only organisation to undertake any formal training for programme directors or the technical grades. Other 'training' tended to be on the job, through forms of apprenticeship and patronage. New entrants began as runners or tea makers and were expected to learn through observation and by picking up the crumbs of information dropped by the experts. Sometimes they worked their way up the ladder with no formal instruction at all. Simply by being around programme making, it was thought, the ethos would seep in. Tony Garnett (see p. 131 above) speaks of the advantages of this practice, and Leanne Klein shows how its mythology survives: 'The best qualification for becoming a television director, they said, was to sweep the cutting-room floor and make the tea. . . . My reaction at that time was to say, "if that's what's needed, that's what I'll do"', she writes (see p. 169 above).

As the independent sector grew in the 1970s and 1980s, many workshops set up their own forms of small-scale training. Women's groups, in particular, felt there should be training especially for them, where technologically confident men would not dominate. Organisations such as the London-based

Women's Audio Visual Education Scheme (WAVES), which aims to provide 'jargon-free information, training and advice for women at all stages in their careers in a challenging, dynamic, focused and supportive environment', have continued this tradition. With the coming of Channel Four in 1982, independent production proliferated and the initiative for industry-funded training shifted from the broadcasters to the independent sector. Commercial organisations that offered training were set up and a wide choice of courses, ranging from local-authority-subsidised evening classes to prestigious events run by well-known figures, sprang up around the country.

As these changes were happening in the industry, more and more educational institutions – usually the local polytechnics, which in the early 1990s were transformed into the newest group of universities – set up practical courses aiming at the creative production of film and video. These were usually separate from the burgeoning critical disciplines of media studies and cultural studies. The evolution of these two strands has led to much debate over the relative merits of 'education' which encourages a critical stance, and 'training' which simply prepares students for employment, and how the two counterbalance each other (*see* Television training and tele-literacy, p. 5 above). Practical courses have ranged from those specifically oriented to the production of experimental and avant-garde work within a fine art tradition, and those with their eyes firmly fixed on broadcast and commercial outlets. Within the same educational institution, those who teach practice and those who teach the more academic subjects could be, and still often are, either ignorant about each other's activities or openly at loggerheads.

With the expansion of higher education, ever more entrants to the television industry have been graduates, but media studies has not always been looked on with favour. Employers have tended to echo Gill Monk, head of personnel at Channel Four, when she said, 'we want discipline and intellect. You are as likely to get a job with a science degree as with one in media studies' (Ward 1996).

As courses have attempted to introduce more practical work, the industry has remained sceptical. First, it is said, colleges remain more interested in theory and criticism than in training; second, most colleges are unable to undertake the necessary training anyway; and last, but not least, the hoped-for jobs simply do not exist. 'Students "misled" over jobs in the media' ran a headline in the *Sunday Telegraph* (Petre 1996), arguing that students are lured on to courses in the hope of jobs, and then fobbed off with 'deconstructing soap operas such as *Neighbours*'. It sometimes appears that the trends are all tugging in different directions, and that education and television are mutually undermining each other.

The reality is more complex than these fears suggest. On the one hand, the broad sweep of media studies has invaded television itself, bringing both a breath of scepticism and a broader understanding of the medium. Despite the cynicism, many of the theoretical approaches first developed amongst activists and academics – on the position of women and ethnic minorities, for example; on critiques of news; and on the way the image itself can carry implicit messages – have been taken on board by the television institutions. Both Michael Jackson, Controller of BBC2, and Stuart Cosgrove, Controller of Arts and Entertainment at Channel Four (*see* p. 211

above), began their careers with media studies, and both have built on that foundation. Moving in the other direction, many journalists, producers and others have taken time off to research into television in an academic context. Media studies courses are now frequently headed by television professionals, and many practitioners move back and forth between teaching and their television careers. The gap between practical 'training' and critical 'education' is lessening.

This weakening of the boundaries has other implications. Colleges and sometimes individual students can build up a range of contacts amongst local television stations and funding bodies. Some of the links may be formal, like that between John Moore's University, Liverpool, and Mersey Television (*see* Phil Redmond, p. 222 below); others may be made on an *ad hoc* basis. For example, a college may take a commission to make public service or corporate videos, which they may partly fund themselves, or which may be wholly paid for by their sponsors. Courses are frequently approached with requests for students to do local research for independent companies. Commissioning editors regularly visit students' graduation shows, and strands for first-time directors, like BBC2's *10x10* and Channel Four's *Short and Curlies* look to college courses for some of their material (*see* Jeremy Howe, p. 233 below). Many students find themselves working on broadcast or non-broadcast professional material; others find that, through their tutors, they get an opening into a job that may lead to the career they are seeking. At the very least, valuable contacts may be made through college, and students are able to produce a showreel of their own work which will be useful in their hunt for jobs. Our case studies illustrate how some of these links have worked (*see* Beryl Richards, p. 239 below; Susan Williams, p. 218 below; and Leanne Klein, p. 169 above).

In all these examples, their college courses have been more than just instruments, more than just training in conventional styles, even though this is what some employers – and students – appear to demand. At their best they are an energetic and ever-renewing source of innovation. College-based work has been able to extend the television form in ways that are not possible for audience-conscious broadcast outlets. Without their original college base, the establishment of such groups as Sankofa, the independent workshop of black filmmakers, would not have been possible; nor would the practice of an exceptional filmmaker like Derek Jarman have evolved without his links to art education. British director, Peter Watkins, teaching in Sweden, worked over a number of years with a group of students to produce an extraordinary life of Strindberg, which otherwise would not have been made. However philistine it declares itself, the industry takes note of such developments.

However, the influx of eager new recruits, sometimes prepared to work for nothing just to get the experience, continues to cause concern in the industry. Both the more cut-throat employers and those who are just getting by on shoestring budgets can all too easily exploit this hopeful enthusiasm: leading established technicians and directors to predict that their rates will be undercut by low-paid and ill-trained young people. There are moves to produce a code for employers which would encourage them to pay trainees by making provision for them in programme budgets. However, television is no longer an industry whose form is secure and fixed. Many of the new

Figure 37 Students from the University of Humberside shooting their graduation film on young footballers training for the West Hull junior team. Filming is on SVHS videotape

entrants of the 1990s are finding themselves working in the newer sectors and will themselves be influencing the form that twenty-first century television will take.

Training and qualifications

Skillset and ft2

Those who have come into the industry as freelancers have long felt the need for practical, technical training and for regular retraining to keep up with changing technologies and equipment. The Association of Cinematograph and Television Technicians (ACTT), the trade union that represented those who worked in the television industry – now part of the Broadcast Entertainment Cinema Theatre Union (BECTU) – responded to its members' needs and initiated schemes for freelancers back in the 1980s. Building on those beginnings, Skillset was launched in 1992 as the Industry Training Organisation (ITO) for the broadcasting, film and video industries. Managed and funded by representatives of the independent producers, the advertisers, the broadcasters and the trade unions, Skillset has become a key organisation in the identification of training needs and training provision. In its first few years it has undertaken valuable research into work trends which indicate what the needs are for training and retraining; it has sought funds in order to subsidise courses and make training more accessible; it has promoted training initiatives and, most importantly, it has begun to develop codified skills and standards for the various grades within the industry. The first set of NVQs and SVQs (National and Scottish Vocational Qualifications) were launched in 1995 (*see* Qualifications, p. 221 below).

The idea was to bring some sort of informed order to a chaotic situation and effectively to make links between the industry and the training providers. Together with the BFI, Skillset produces a database of college courses and of short courses. Although they do not themselves conduct training, they facilitate it through a fund, consisting of money raised from various broadcasters and other bodies which supports schemes for new entrants and courses for retraining and skills updating. Bodies as diverse as WAVES (the training organisation for women), colleges, universities and television companies have received support from the freelance training fund.

The fund also supports Film and Television Freelance Training, known as ft2: an industry-based, apprenticeship-style training which covers technical grades, including assistant camera, sound, editing, art department, production assistant, grips and make-up. This is one course where students are actually paid a minimal wage, and 80 per cent of their training on the two-year course is as supernumeraries in a wide range of production companies. Trainees are reminded that the path is not necessarily easy:

> You should have drive, personality and ability to learn new skills and get on with everyone in a situation which can be stressful and tiring. Production attachments usually involve very long days, usually six days a week. However, it is only by doing the time that you will become a competent and professional technical assistant who will work in the industry.
>
> (ft2 1996)

The scheme has succeeded in broadening the basis of recruitment. As Tudor Gates, Vice-President of BECTU put it, 'we were prepared to take anyone off the street whom we felt would make a good junior technician. No educational qualifications were required, just talent, enthusiasm and commitment.' He reasserts the aim to 'break the mould of an exclusively white, male orientated industry'. The scheme tends to achieve groups of trainees who are approximately 50 per cent male and female and around one-third from ethnic minorities. 'As a result black faces are now seen on film crews, and more women' (Gates 1995: 52).

Below, Susan Williams, who graduated from ft2 in 1995, describes her experiences.

Susan Williams: *AFM and ft2 trainee*

'I used to watch television a lot and I always knew what was on, but didn't know you could actually study it until I went to Salford College of Technology – as it was then – for a B-Tech National Diploma in Visual and Communication Studies. Now there are dozens of courses that offer practice as well as theory, but when I started looking around there were only about five or six. I went on to do my degree in media production at Newcastle which offered 70 per cent practice. We did photography, film, video, animation and production research, a term on each. I found it all really useful. I learned about framing and lighting from photography, but it was television I was interested in. My favourites were the sitcoms – *Rising Damp*, *The Liver Birds* – and soap operas, but I had always been slightly worried that there were no black people in them. We learn that you watch soap operas to see people like yourself – but I didn't see people like myself. That's why I wrote my college dissertation about Afro-Caribbean and Afro-American sitcoms. From *Amos and Andy* to *The Cosby Show* in America, and from *Fosters* to *Desmonds* in Britain. I didn't want to say that television had been 'racist' in any straightforward way, but I was trying to understand it as part of its times.

At Newcastle we studied cinema – genre, 1950s melodrama and how film reflected society. It was all valuable stuff. The college was very helpful with its contacts when we made our own films. They arranged with a 16mm lab to give us cheap rates and sell us short ends. I only spent £400 on my film, some people spent thousands. You had to find your own money, and many people took out bank loans.

But if you think you'll go into the big world and continue the sort of thing you've been doing at college, then you're wrong. Students leave thinking 'I'm going to be a director'. No! You're going to be a production runner! When people say to me 'Do you want to direct?' I say, never. I want to work in television and learn a skill. I got my first view of a professional set on a one-week placement on *Coronation Street*, just shadowing the floor manager. I realised you should never leave college without experience of a professional production – student productions are quite different.

I'm still in touch with the Newcastle group. On the whole we've done quite well. Some people have become production managers; there's a production co-ordinator in an animation company; someone is working on a script and someone else is regularly employed as a camera assistant and clapper/loader. But it has taken a few years since we graduated in 1992.

I left college with a smaller overdraft than many of my contemporaries – the grant can barely pay for your accommodation these days. Even so I needed a job – so I did an NVQ in business studies. I learned fairly obvious things like typing, using the telephone properly, taking messages, filing – but I needed them. If you want to work in television it's important to recognise that you must have another skill, because television is all short contracts and you'll have to do something else in between. I kept on reading the *Guardian*, *Broadcast* and *The Stage* to keep in touch and find out what was in production. I was sending off for everything, but I knew I needed training. I could *tell* you how to set up a shot, how to light it, but I couldn't *do* it. I saw the ad for ft2 in the *Guardian*.

We started with a six-week course at the Short Course Unit at the National Film School. There were the twelve of us and we had such a good time. We learnt the newest technology, editing on Avid and other things you would need on your placement, such as how to load a magazine, how to do some research. ft2 wanted us to try all departments and not to decide too early. I really was unsure, and that's why I had so many placements, sixteen in all. For the first year I trained in most departments and had a go at everything. I worked on low-budget films, television drama and sitcoms including *Chef* and Dennis Potter's *Karaoke*. I shadowed the sound recordist on two documentaries about opera. By the second year I had settled into assistant director and assistant floor manager. My last placement was on *Agony* and the company have asked me to stay on to work on *Pork Pie*.

On ft2 you're *paid* for shadowing someone, but I met people doing the same thing as I was, working as production runners and assistants, for nothing at all. Companies can use you like cheap labour. Some trainees will do whatever they're told without questioning it, but I felt you had to draw the line. Once I was asked to stop traffic in a dark country lane with no reflective clothing, and I said I wouldn't.

The ft2 scheme gave me a lot more confidence. The essential thing was finding out that these jobs exist. They're the ones you don't learn about in college. Then you must find your own personal strengths. A friend of mine went into editing. She's perfect for it, because she's quiet with a lot of concentration. But as an AFM you're with people all the time, you're busy all day, and if you have five minutes to spare there's always someone to talk to. Also it gives you a new set of contacts. You should always be keeping in touch with everyone, including people from college, and building up your own network of contacts. They can help you and you can help them.

In the summer of 1995 I went to the Edinburgh International Television Festival on a scheme known as 'TV 25', for twenty-five young people who had just started working in television. Once more I had answered an ad in the *Guardian*. We had Masterclasses from top television professionals and 'power breakfasts' when we could chat to people like Stuart Cosgrove and Janet Street-Porter. That Edinburgh group still meet together, and we still get influential people to talk to us. We grab them by the scruff of the neck – producers, writers, executives, including Will Wyatt, Chief Executive of BBC Broadcast.

What I must now decide is what to do next, because people only know me as an AFM. I'd like to try script reading, because I love popular television and I think I know what works. I want to get into decision making. Also, as I come from the North, I think it's a shame that I've had to come to London to find work.

I think more black people should be in television – not just where they are visible, but where the power is, where the decisions are made in development and producing.'

Film and Television Training (ft2) is at:
Fourth Floor, Warwick House, 9 Warwick Street, London W1R 5RA
Tel: 0171 734 5141 Fax: 0171 287 9899

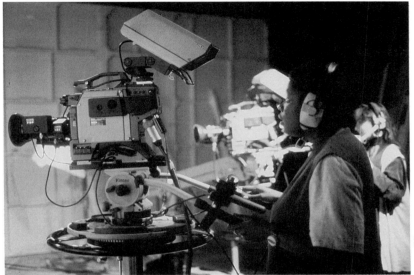

Jason Wingrove

Figure 38 Susan Williams with a studio camera at the National Film School in Beaconsfield

Qualifications

One of Skillset's main tasks has been to produce written standards for those skills necessary for the broadcasting, film and video industries, using the format adopted for the National Vocational Qualifications (NVQ) scheme. It aims to replace what had been rather *ad hoc*, casually acquired – and sometimes rather secretly guarded – skills with a set of codified, recognised qualifications 'developed by the industry and designed to meet the needs of employment' which will be 'based on someone's ability to do the chosen job in a real or realistic situation' (Skillset 1996). NVQs are awarded by Skillset together with the Open University in a comprehensive range of grades. Since 1994 twenty-seven NVQs have been launched, including camera, lighting, sound, production, journalism, makeup/hair and post-production. The advantage of a qualification in a casualised workforce is that it assures a new employer of a recognised degree of acquaintance with the equipment and terminology, even before they meet the applicant. At the same time, it is a way of maintaining quality and standards.

Each codified 'standard' is made up of several units, which are themselves composed of two elements: performance criteria and 'range statements', which are the contexts in which an individual would be expected to be able to achieve the standard. This means that performance as a whole can be assessed, rather than narrow tasks undertaken in isolation from their broader context. To obtain the qualification, an individual must obtain a certain number of units within a given group, which are assessed by experienced industry practitioners through approved assessment centres set up by employers or education providers. The initiative offers a form of objective assessment, which nevertheless takes place in a real working environment with all the real constraints of time and other production pressures.

The aim is to include every occupation in the broadcast, film and video industries, setting out 'common functions not just for the present, but which identify the needs of the future'. Skillset are aware of the 'tough, competitive world with no space for people who are not prepared to provide absolute commitment' (Skillset 1996). So, as well as the skills specific to such areas as camerawork or art direction, the NVQs identify a mix of 'transferable skills', which include 'creative skills, communication skills, problem solving abilities, team skills, a flexible approach to life, tenacity, and personal marketing ability'. Core units which are common to different sections and job grades cover such areas as health and safety and 'positive working relationships'. Their materials stress the need to be 'customer focused' and concerned with 'personal marketing'. This may sit uneasily with the more humanist approaches of media studies departments, but their underlying rigour makes the materials both comprehensible and accessible. Some colleges are now considering awarding NVQs in the various practice areas in addition to their academic qualifications.

Below Phil Redmond, Chairman of Mersey Television, describes his initiatives which combine practical training with academic education.

Information on Skillset, including copies of research reports, a *Careers Information Pack* and details of the NVQ Standards are obtainable from:
Skillset, 124 Horseferry Rd, London SW1P 2TX
Tel: 0171 306 8585 Fax: 0171 306 8372

Phil Redmond: Mersey Television

As the successful writer of the popular children's serial based in a comprehensive school, *Grange Hill*, Phil Redmond founded the independent company Mersey Television to retain creative control over his own work. The company launched *Brookside* for Channel Four when the channel began broadcasting in 1982. Redmond wanted to create a series that would be closer to real life than the existing soaps, *Coronation Street* and *Crossroads*, and would pose new challenges 'not just to content but to television production techniques' (Redmond 1987). Mersey Television bought up a real close of private houses (and one bungalow) in a 'desire to move from the often stifling atmosphere of drama in a TV studio' so that the actors could slam the doors and the walls wouldn't wobble, and the houses would feel like lived-in homes. *Brookside*, despite its realism and unflinching recognition of the seamier side of personal life, was launched in the enterprise 1980s, a time of working-class aspiration and home ownership. More recently, Phil Redmond's young people's soap, *Hollyoaks*, has abandoned realism for the glitz and intensity of youth culture in the 1990s. Redmond has maintained a consistent interest in training and education. He holds an honorary professorship at John Moore's University, where he is collaborating in the establishment of a new degree in media professional studies.

Phil Redmond

'**W**hen I studied sociology at university, I was struck by the way middle-class, cloistered academics tried to look at what the working classes were doing out on the streets. Then later on when *Grange Hill* became successful and a few of my other things began to take off, I found *myself* being studied. People would write to me and say, 'Why did you do this, was it because it was an allegory of this or an allegory of that?' They would pick on a certain scene and I'd think back and realise that we did it that way because it was raining and we'd had to switch locations or something like that.

When I started out on my television career I was conscious that people from my type of background – I was a typical working-class writer from a council estate who went to a comprehensive school – would break into the industry by writing about gritty social issues. Entry into television was still very skewed towards Oxbridge. I kept bumping into what I'd class as intellectual cabbages, very bright people who'd been around academia so long that they'd lost touch with common sense. So one of the things I think a television production course should have, is a common sense module. We have finance modules and law modules but a common sense module is what's really needed. It's all very well to be taught to analyse and ask questions, but in certain situations you need a gut reaction. So one element in my interest in training is to ask how people from my kind of background get into the business.

Because *Grange Hill* was set in a school, there was an interest in using the scripts as discussion texts in schools, or as texts on examination papers. I began to think that we should be a bit more open and let more people talk about how I work and how we produce. So I started a thing called 'script to screen' where we would go along en masse – myself, the writers, the production team, the actors and the technicians – and we would demonstrate to people how we put *Brookside* from script on to screen. The writers would talk about how the ideas get from storylines to script; production management and producers would talk about the logistics of putting it together; the actors would rehearse and we'd shoot a scene in front of the audience. Finally we'd take it into editing. It's a fun day, and at the end of it you come away with some kind of inkling about the way it's all put together.

The production process has to be done at speed because we're in the entertainment business. Those two words "entertainment" and "business" have got to be remembered. We want to entertain, but it *is* a business. The great films that people study, like *Brief Encounter* and *Casablanca*, all went through on tight budgets. It's not the system that's important, it's the people. It's a question of harnessing the energy and the creative talent.

We first started work with John Moore's University developing short courses which range from scriptwriting, to directing, and even operating steadicam and things like that. Now we have launched a new degree, Media Professional Studies. We are trying to turn out people who are media literate but also immediately employable. My ultimate aim is to get people to leave university with a degree and an NVQ in their chosen discipline. When they leave, employers will know that they've got someone who's employable, so they don't have to start from scratch. We will still allow the intellectual time for students to discover themselves and to do research, but we'll bolt on practical modules at Mersey Television. They'll do it under the guidance of their tutors at university, but also under the production disciplines with us. So we would all know that at certain stages in the year, we would have a team of students available, on placement with the various disciplines.

Then there's our involvement with Shout FM, the university radio station. We agreed to underwrite the project and help with advice, but they had to sell the advertising. That's the sort of thing I like doing with the university. There were a hundred students involved with that, and they got more media experience over the three short licence periods than any number of people standing up in front of them telling them "this is how I do it".

And we do a project with children called *Meadowcroft*. Every two or three years we go to different local authorities and sit down with local kids to write an episode of this fictional soap opera, *Meadowcroft*. Our crews go along to guide them, but within 15 to 20 minutes the kids are operating the gear themselves. They get the experience of recording and editing it themselves and we get a tape which we use as background material. If somebody on *Brookside* is watching something on the television, that's what they're watching. Because they know it's going on Brookie, the kids take it very seriously. It's just planting a few acorns out there.

Right now we're standing under a technological waterfall. We're being deluged with new technology. As soon as we buy something, we can guarantee it will be topped by something else. But the basic grammar is still the same. You still have to have your wide shots and your close-ups. You have to be covered, you can't have overlaps on the sound and all that kind of thing. My view is that students should learn on something like Hi-8, in order to understand the grammar. Keyboard skills are important, too. If they've got those they're literate. It's not up to them to worry about whether it's on D3 or D5 or digital Beta. We've got very expensive people who look after that sort of stuff. What matters if you're making a programme is whether you've got a strong story. Whether it's a fiction or a fact it's got to have a beginning, middle and an end and it's got to be very clear.

Soap opera is a difficult form. It's a complex operation because it's going all the time. If you're making a 90-minute film, you have a year to set it up and you might have twelve weeks to shoot it. We shoot three episodes in seven days. On *Brookside* you need to have a working knowledge of something like a hundred episodes; on *Hollyoaks* you need a knowledge of something like fifty episodes. We're shooting out of order and we're shooting very fast. The logistical problems are immense and the operation is labour-intensive. There are a lot more floor assistants, design assistants and so on, than with other kinds of drama. With 90 minutes you can shoot in story order, but if you're shooting a serial you're constantly doubling back. You have to do a rough cut of one episode at the same time as shooting the next. Budgets are tighter, so you have to be more inventive in the way you solve problems. You can't just build a new set and you can't recast. You have to tell a story more economically and faster.

The job ratio in the industry is enormous. I think it's still one person in front of the camera to twenty-five behind. Of course, in some areas of television crews are getting smaller, but with this waterfall of technology and the shift in the distribution mechanism, I think the job ratio will become 1 to 50 or 1 to 250, because the more channels you have, the more packaging you have. I know that people say the new channels will just be filled up with repeats, but somebody's got to find them, somebody's got to select them, somebody's got to negotiate, somebody's got to do the promos, somebody's got to make the promotional trail, somebody's got to get the machines together, somebody's got to transmit, somebody's got to maintain them, somebody's got to sell the advertising space, somebody's got to do the marketing, somebody's got to do the bookkeeping, and it goes on like that. So for the next few years new entrants are going to find more opportunities to get into television than ever before. I keep saying to them, don't get seduced by the old dinosaurs, don't listen to them. ITV and BBC are the hardest nuts to crack. But there's a hell of a lot of new outfits out there. It's people like the Learning Channel, Live TV, all the local cable stations, data-tech services and all that stuff. Get in, get some experience. If you've got someone who says, 'I was the guy who used to package 500 classified adverts in four hours every Friday morning', I'd think 'That's good, this guy's got a talent, he's got something we can use.' The majority of new entrants are still in their early twenties. Ten years on, things are going to be a hell of a lot different from now and it will be a great time for them.

To get anywhere they've got to start. You know that old Chinese proverb, 'A journey of a thousand miles begins with the first step.' At some stage on that journey, you'll realise that you're either going to make it or you're not. But unless you take that first step, you'll never do it.'

Phil Redmond is Chairman of Mersey Television, Executive Producer of *Brookside* and *Hollyoaks*, and trustee and Honorary Professor of Media Studies at John Moore's University, Liverpool.

Courses and where to look them up

Training and education on offer ranges from vocational courses to degree courses and open learning materials, including broadcasts on BBC2's night-time education slot, *The Learning Zone*. Different types of courses include:

- University based degree courses. Each of these has its own particular slant and balances theory and practice in its own way

- Other college-based courses, leading to A-levels, GNVQs or some of the older qualifications which are now being phased out. (These are listed in: *Media Courses, UK: A Comprehensive Directory of College-Based Provision* from the British Film Insitute (see below))

- Short courses run by evening institutes

- Short courses run by commercial organisations

- Workshop and local authority based short courses, often funded by regional arts boards

- Community based courses. These are listed in *A Listing of Short Courses in Film, Television and Radio* from British Film Institute Education Department, 21 Stephen Street, London W1P 2LN. Tel: 0171 255 1444

- Professional training within the industry, including specially targeted training, for example for people with disabilities, and regionally based training

- Seminars, workshops and trade organisation courses and conferences, run by such organisations as the Royal Television Society (RTS) and the Producers Alliance for Cinema and Television (PACT). (Contacts are listed in Skillset, *Careers Information Pack* from Skillset, 124 Horseferry Rd, London SW1P 2TX. Tel: 0171 306 8585)

- Courses at the National Film and Television School, including the National Short Course Training Programme for established freelancers. (Information from NFTS, Beaconsfield Film Studios, Station Rd, Beaconsfield, Bucks, HP9 1LG. Tel: 01494 677903.)

Throughout the year conferences, summer schools and other initiatives will be found advertised in the *Guardian* media pages and publications for the broadcast industry listed below. At the Edinburgh International Television Festival, top policy makers rub shoulders with new entrants on the 'TV25' scheme (*see* Susan Williams, p. 218 above) and the 150 seventeen- to twenty-one-year-olds who gather for the 'Television and Young People' (TVYP) event.

TVYP, 24 Neal St, London WC2H 9PS
Tel: 0171 379 4519 Fax: 0171 836 0702

References

ft2 (1996) *Applicant Information*, London: ft2

Petre, J. (1996) 'Students "misled" over jobs in the media', *The Sunday Telegraph*, 4 February, London

Redmond, P. (1987) *Brookside: The Official Companion*, London: C4

Ward, L. (1996) 'Lured by media hype', *Times Educational Supplement*, 2 February, London

Key texts

Angell, R. (1991) *How To Make It into Film and Television*, Plymouth: How To Books

BFI (published annually) *Film and Television Handbook*, London: BFI

Burder, J. (1994) *Getting Into Film and Television*, London: Saltcoat

Gates, T. (1995) *How to Get into the Film and TV Business*, London: Alma House

Langham, J. (1996) *Lights, Camera, Action: Careers in Film, Television and Video*, London: BFI

Orton, L. (published annually) *Media Courses, UK: A Comprehensive Directory of College Based Provision*, London: BFI

Orton, L. (published annually) *A Listing of Short Courses in Film, Television and Radio*, London: BFI

Ross Muir, A. (1987) *A Woman's Guide to Jobs in Film and TV*, London: Pandora

Skillset materials:

Careers Information Pack (1996) offers an introduction to the Broadcast, Film and Video Industry, with information on potential employers, on training schemes, on opportunities for employment, and an invaluable section on 'finding out more'.

Skillset Briefing Magazine published three times a year

Skillset Research Reports

NVQ/SVQ Skillset Publications which outline the requirements for standards and qualifications in the various grades

16 The commissioning process

Turning an idea into a commission

Many of those who study television do so because they want to make their own programmes and use the medium as a form of self-expression. They would like to create material of their own devising, under their own control, and produce programmes that can express their creativity, argue for a cause they care about, or achieve an aesthetic effect. A glance at the realities of the television world shows that the chances of becoming a full-time producer or director with a free hand are miniscule, but even so, many aspirants remain driven by something beyond the desire merely to do a job.

One way of getting to make one's own programme, or at least having a creative input into a programme of one's own devising, is to gain a commission as part of an independent production company. When Channel Four was established in 1982, it was the first broadcaster to rely almost entirely on programmes from the independent sector. The Channel's determined effort to widen the base of those with access to programme making included targeting specific groups. It had a commissioning editor for Independent Film and Video with a brief to make spaces for those whose approach was different from that of the hidebound professionals, and a commissioning editor for Multicultural Programmes to ensure that there were programmes made from a non-white perspective. Not surprisingly there followed a positive blossoming of small production companies which ranged from Broadsides, an all-woman collective commissioned to make current affairs from a woman's point of view (Baehr and Spindler-Brown 1987), to the community workshops described by Tony Dowmunt above (p. 202). Changes in the Channel since those early days have given rise to much debate. Inevitably its policies have evolved, but its commissioning editors continue to declare their commitment to its remit to cater for tastes and interests not served by the other television channels and to innovate in the form and content of programmes (*see* Alan Hayling, p. 230 below). Its arrival marked a decisive change in the range of people who have been able to make television programmes and it gave a start to many who were outside the charmed circle of broadcast professionals.

Since those exciting and eclectic days of the early 1980s, the industry as a whole has become more reliant on independent production. Both the BBC and the ITV companies are required to commission 25 per cent of their programmes from independent producers and several of the new ITV franchise holders are 'publishers' rather than producing companies. These changes have meant that the bigger independent companies have moved closer to the mainstream and are now an important part of the map of contemporary television. The moves to decentralisation mean that the opportunity is there for new programme makers to get their work commissioned, either through a company set up by themselves or with an independent company known to and trusted by the broadcaster.

This means that creativity has been forced to find sometimes uneasy bedfellows in accounting, law and business practices. To get a programme commissioned you must demonstrate not only that the idea you have is a good and viable one, but that you are competent to produce it, which is why many television courses now include units on financial control and the paraphernalia of running a company. Effective budgeting and working to deadlines are necessary components of the practice of programme making.

Cable and satellite are opening up relatively unexplored new fields, but only a small proportion of their output is originally produced. They have accelerated the push to television on the cheap, which often does not involve making conventional programmes at all. Instead they emit flows of transmitted time – chat shows, extended sports coverage, re-runs or strings of cheaply purchased stock footage (*see* Helen Swords, p. 139 above). Getting programmes commissioned under these circumstances is very different from working through from an idea to a completed programme which can stand by itself. Independent programme makers may well find that where they do find space on cable or satellite channels, they are asked for the use of their material for no fee or for a very low one, simply in exchange for the satisfaction of having it transmitted. The few community-based cable channels remain the exceptions.

On all the mainstream channels, programmes are commissioned within strands established as part of an overall scheduling strategy (*see* Scheduling p. 20 above). Both Channel Four and the BBC produce bulletins and hold regular information sessions to keep independent producers up to date with their plans, usually through the independent producers' organisation, PACT. Other ways of keeping in touch with commissioning editors is through such events as the Edinburgh International Television Festival, which holds controller workshops where delegates can quizz the channel bosses, and *Broadcast* magazine and other trade papers, which have regular interviews with commissioners and controllers. These are also ways of keeping track of the all-important changes of personnel, which in their turn mean changes in policy and sheduling strategy. A change in the editor of a strand very often means a whole new set of production companies are commissioned (*see* Leanne Klein, p. 169 above). Some sections of the industry are now taking the educational sector more seriously, and links with educational institutions are increasing (*see* Phil Redmond, p. 222 above, and Jeremy Howe, p. 233 below), but commissioning remains, inevitably, largely an informal process.

Someone who wants to get a programme made and who is not part of a production company usually has a better chance if the idea comes with a particular point of appeal, for example, bringing exclusive access to an institution or the involvement of a well-known personality. Applicants may write directly to a commissioning editor in a broadcasting organisation, or they may approach an independent production company, who, if they like the idea, may offer a short-term contract for research or scripting, or may agree to act as producers. There is also the option of going to one of the many funds, local arts organisations or other schemes which offer support for broadcast and non-broadcast work (Funds and opportunities, p. 236 below).

Targetting the broadcasters

Channel Four

Channel Four is made up of three programming divisions: Drama has two commissioning editors with three assistants; Factual Programming, and Arts and Entertainment both have a controller above the commissioners.

The Channel produces a *Guide for Producers*, which is essential to help fit potential ideas to the available slots. Each department produces a written account of its opinions and intentions, describing its strands and the special seasons into which programmes may be grouped.

In 1996 there were sixteen commissioning editors with nineteen deputies, the youngest aged 25. Alan Hayling, who began as an independent filmmaker, is one of the two deputy commissioning editors in the Documentary Department, responsible to commissioning editor, Peter Moore.

Alan Hayling

'Commissioning editors at Channel Four need programme ideas for the pre-planned strands, so as Peter's deputy I tend to be looking for that special thing that will fit the brief exactly. It may occasionally be possible for an idea which does not fit a strand to be slotted into another commissioning editor's output. For example, it might be suitable for a special evening like the *Pot Night* Channel Four broadcast about marijuana, or one of the late night 'zones'. One-off programmes are very rare.

We can get as many as a thousand proposals for a series of six programmes such as *Short Stories*. All proposals are read, but inevitably most are turned down. Really I should be called a 'non-commissioning editor'. With so many proposals to go through it's understandable that applicants may occasionally receive a slightly tetchy reply, but in my experience Channel Four commissioning editors take seriously their obligation to give a thought-out reason for rejections. They know that each proposal has taken a considerable amount of time and original research. We do read every single piece of paper that comes through. It's the idea that counts, not the packaging or the fancy typeface.

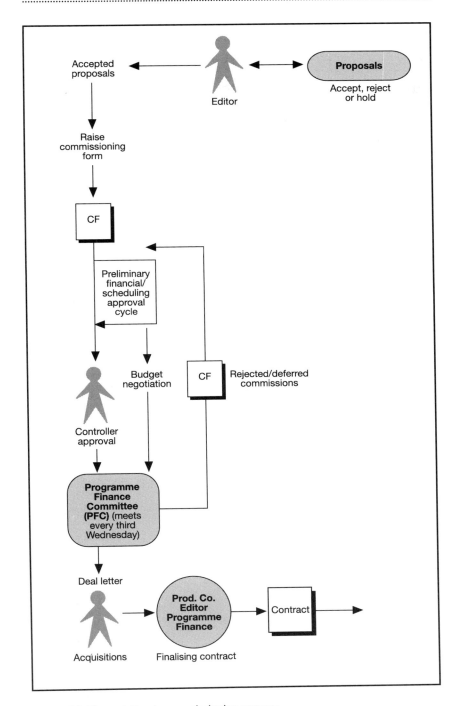

Figure 39 Channel Four's commissioning process
Courtesy Channel Four Television

It is true, however, that some of the more established documentary companies are much better at targeting their proposals at particular strands. Experience has given them a clear idea of what is in the commissioning editor's mind and what is suitable for the different strands. It has become a bit of a vicious circle. If they get more commissions, they spend more time with us and get to know our judgements better. They watch a lot of our output and target their ideas accordingly. If an untried person approaches us with a proposal we like, we may advise them to take the idea to one or two of these companies.

At Channel Four a very high value is placed on the autonomy of the commissioning editors and their deputies. We can exercise our own subjective judgement about the ideas that come to us and over how the programme should be made.

In the last five years, commissioning editors have involved themselves more closely in controlling the content and quality of programmes while they are being made. In this respect they have become more like executive producers. This has meant that the overall quality of programmes has gone up, but the other side of the coin is that the quirky, against-the-odds, high points of the Channel's output are less frequent. In making decisions, commissioning editors are always balancing two things. The first is Channel Four's remit to provide programmes of interest to minority audiences, distinct and different from the other channels. The second is that we are a commercial channel. We live by selling our own advertising space, so some of our strands have to achieve reasonable levels of popularity with audiences. Since Peter Moore has taken over, the Documentary Department has become very successful in showing that documentary can produce serious social programmes and still achieve high audiences.

Part of our job is to check that programmes do not break the law, nor the ITC code. We must ensure that a programme does not use excessive bad language before the 9 pm watershed nor excessive violence at any time.

Among the strands I have been responsible for are:

Short Stories Half hour programmes from up and coming directors. *Short Stories* runs two series a year in the 'narrative observational' style, which, in my opinion, is one of the most difficult to make. It should not be issue-led. We are looking for strong characters and a strong narrative. It has to matter. It has to have layers of meaning. It has to say something.

Secret History This series offers a new insight into a piece of history that had been taken for granted and can now be rethought in the light of new evidence. It should be investigative, revelatory, and concentrate on a particular incident.

Undercover Britain A series which uses covert filming. This form of investigation has revealed various scandals including the dire circumstances of servants brought from overseas and the scams worked by taxi touts. The ITC lays down a strict code which regulates filming with concealed cameras.

The department also commissions occasional series such as *The Nick* and *Beirut to Bosnia.*'

Channel Four Television *Writing Proposals to Channel Four* from Channel Four, 124 Horseferry Rd, London SW1P 2TX. Regularly updated. Tel: 0171 396 4444

BBC Bristol

The BBC is still the main employer, trainer and craft provider for the television industry. It is a mobile place, which still has the policy of the six-month attatchment, which allows employees to move between departments. However, the BBC is very hierarchically organised. Unlike Channel Four, it does not include independent producers in discussions on policy and ideas, but it is commissioning more independent programmes, both out of London and it regional bases. BBC Bristol has long housed a fascinating range of programming both from its prestigious Natural History Unit which produces David Attenborough's series such as *Life on Earth*, and the Television Features Department which has produced innovative, oddball series, such as *Small Objects of Desire* (*see* Leanne Klein, p. 169 above), and some of the BBC's most popular programmes such as *999* and *The Antiques Road Show*.

10x10 is a scheme based in Bristol which offers an opportunity for aspiring directors to make 10-minute films to be broadcast on BBC2. It has links with film schools and various arts funding bodies and it gives opportunities to people already working in television who want to break into directing. Jeremy Howe is the series producer.

Jeremy Howe

' *10x10* was invented in 1988 as one of the short items which fill the odd 10-minute gaps between programmes. Actually they are 9 mins 15 secs long, as the BBC asks for all programmes to be 45 seconds shorter than their allotted slot. Directors must be people who have not had a network television directing credit before. The first series was made up of quirky documentaries, which dealt with some odd aspect of society. Now, in an unusual commissioning mixture, they cover both documentary and fiction. It provides a rare opportunity for first-time directors to do fiction on television.

In my opinion a lot of commissioning editors are not interested in *your* view, they're interested in the view of the Editor of the strand.

I'm looking for directors with a style and with something to say, directors with a voice. I commission a huge variety of films that are distinctive and personal and I need a balance across the series. There's no point in me doing something that would suit any of the other strands. The rest of television wants something that's the same. I want something that's different. I'm turned off by the clichés – a script which begins with someone on the telephone or someone putting on lipstick in front of a mirror. There's no formula in *10x10* to lock into.

10x10 is often made in conjunction with film schools and art schools. *Vino Expresso* was made by two students who were second-generation Italian, and went on to make feature films including *Blue Juice*. Sometimes they are made in co-production with the Arts Council and local arts funding bodies. That link meant that we got significantly different films, in an avant-garde style, such as Deborah Collard's *Back to Eden*. South East Arts co-funded *Sixth Continent*, a contemplation of Romney Marsh by the filmmaker Tom Connolly. It was an expensive production which included aerial shots, slow motion, and a whole range of devices. Only the most experienced directors normally get that kind of freedom.

Sometimes programmes are bought in, sometimes they are commissioned from experienced television professionals who have no directing credit. John Strickland, a long-standing editor, made a *10x10*, and went on to win an Emmy for *Prime Suspect*. *Bill Posters is Innocent*, about those huge posters pasted up on the far side of the underground tracks, was a documentary by Stuart Greig who had been a dubbing mixer for many years. He's now a BBC Scotland producer, responsible for the BBC1 series, *The Gamekeeper*.

I tend to get around 600 applicants from very discreet advertising. That's sixty applications for every one chosen. Two-thirds of the proposals are fiction, even though the chances of getting a break as a director in fiction are minimal. You have to have God on your side and some other referees. A higher percentage of first-time directors get into the industry via non-fiction.

You send in your script or submission, together with a CV and a show reel and I select ten for each series. I then oversee the production rather than produce the film. I'm very stringent on script development. In my view, if you get the script wrong, you get the film wrong. Budgets tend to be from £10,000 to £25,000 – compare that with *Casualty*'s half million per hour – but I also raise co-production money. Directors aren't paid, so you've really got to want to make the film. However, out of the seventy films commissioned, thirty-six filmmakers now have regular work as directors. Others are cinematographers, producers or work elsewhere in the industry. My ideal commission would be Peter Chelsom who walked into Channel Four, never having directed before, and persuaded Karin Bamborough that he could direct *Treacle*, in my view one of the best of British shorts. He then directed *Hear My Song* and now the Hollywood movie *Funny Bones*.

Short and Curlies, Channel Four's strand for new directors (now replaced by *Brief Encounters*), used big professional crews, but I think that's difficult for new directors to cope with. I get them to crew at their own level, then I supervise the post-production. The BBC buys the right to broadcast, but the director owns the film. *10x10* have had a great success at film festivals.

Examples of *10x10*s:

Love, Love, Love was bought from Nick Quinn, made while he was at film school in France. It has a great economy of style, with an arresting opening and no dialogue. It's a film about love, marriage and separation. One and a half minutes into the film we have already seen the couple meet, marry and separate. The director uses clichés but plays with them. He follows the rule of thumb which says you should come into a scene as late as possible and leave it as soon as possible. The story is told through images, using oblique reference and metaphor. The couple feeding each other yoghurt instead of having sex leads to the gag when he feeds himself yoghurt. Television is often not particularly visual and one virtue of *10x10* is its visual character.

The Secret was commissioned from Clare Kilner, a first-year student at the Royal College of Art. It is the story of Arthur who suffers from obsessive-compulsive disorder. I was persuaded by the personal quality of her earlier films, impressed by the intensity of her interest, and convinced by her tutor at the RCA, herself a good documentary filmmaker. There is always a difficulty in persuading people to take part in a documentary. Clare Kilner had the ability to get Arthur to agree, and to treat his problem sensitively. She interviewed him and constructed a script out of his recorded voice. He never appears in the film, the part is played by an actor. A Helpline set up at the end of the programme received hundreds of calls. *The Secret* has just won the Royal Television Society Award for best student film.'

Pitching an idea

Researching a programme idea and writing a proposal can be a committed and time-consuming business, which is usually unpaid. Some independent companies employ researchers whose job it is to prepare programme proposals (Leanne Klein writes of her time as a researcher, p. 169 above), but even inside the BBC the leisurely evolution of ideas between those working on a particular strand has been replaced by a careful costing of time. For a researcher in the Arts Department every hour worked must now be allocated to a specific broadcast programme, so that the chance to explore the hunches that may not come to anything is becoming more rare. Those who are not employed by an organisation, but are simply dedicated to a particular project or determined to get a commission, must accept that their research effort is time spent that may not bring any reward.

Commissioning editors encourage applicants to be persistent. Such a large number of proposals are of necessity turned down that a rejection does not mean the idea was in itself a bad one. Even the bigger independent companies are prepared for a high proportion of refusals. They may well put in twenty proposals for every one accepted. Applicants must be able to bear rejection even if it is sometimes unkind.

A proposal usually takes the form of a document submitted to the commissioning editor. There are no rules, but common sense will tell that there should be a clear outline of the proposed programme, detailing its subject matter, its scope, its content, and the style in which it will be produced. It will be important to indicate whether the plan is to shoot on location, or in the studio; whether it will be observational shooting or will involve actors; whether the aim is for high-gloss, wide-screen format or a low-tech video diary style and so on. The proposal should say who the participants will be and show that they have agreed to take part. It should note whether there are directors, camerapeople or other key personnel attached. Applicants should target carefully and produce documents that are clearly written, well presented, informative and feasible.

At one meeting with independent filmmakers, a Channel Four commissioning editor showed proposal documents for three programmes she had commissioned. One was scribbled on a single sheet of paper, one was a thick and overflowing wodge of detailed research, the third was a neat package with a picture on the cover and the content clearly summarised under informative headings. However tolerant the commissioning editors, it's wise for new tenderers to go for this third type. Nevertheless, all commissioning editors agree with Alan Hayling that it is always the *idea* which is most important.

Funds and opportunities

Independent programme makers need to become adept at tracking down sources of funding. Obtaining even a small grant can mean that a piece of work can get made, even when not commissioned by a broadcasting organisation. Many television slots will buy in ready-made films, often from first-time directors, as Jeremy Howe describes above (p. 233).

Subsidies, and co-production funding are available from a variety of sources. The British Film Institute's Production Board, together with television companies, finances full-scale feature films, has a scheme for short films by new directors and a flexible 'Production Projects' fund, often used for co-productions. The BFI also part-funds the Regional Arts Boards and the London Film and Video Development Agency. Funds range from full-scale production finance to grants of a few hundred pounds. Some funders work together with colleges and educational institutions.

The BFI and local arts bodies aim to strengthen film and video culture by funding programmes that would otherwise not get made – partly because they don't fall into the categories expected by television. The Regional Production Boards seek to promote film and video making in their locality, for example, the Cambridge-based Eastern Arts Board has a film and video production scheme and works together with Anglia Television on a series for new directors, *First Take*. The London Film and Video Development Agency (LFVDA) looks for work that is 'new and innovative with activities and operations that interrogate and challenge established and traditional forms and practices'. This includes funding avant-garde or arts practices; giving opportunities to new film and video makers, and to those who are marginalised within the conventional media, such as women and people from ethnic minorities. Bodies like the LFVDA are careful not to set themselves up in oppostion to the mainstream media but aim to interact with and complement them. Such agencies also support training courses and festivals, can give capital grants to companies starting up, and grants for production or post-production costs. The associated London Production Fund administers a budget to support innovative film and video productions in London.

Other funds include the First Film Foundation, which is a charity set up to work with first-time filmmakers especially through script development; regional funds such as the Glasgow Film Fund; and the Merseyside Film Production Fund. The Arts Council also runs several schemes, usually in conjunction with broadcasters. Finally, there is a range of funds which come out of the European Union's various media initiatives.

Once their film is made, an independent programme maker needs to think about distribution and exhibition. Specialist distributors include The London Film Makers' Co-op and London Electronic Arts, as well as Cinenova, who distribute films by women. There are many film festivals around the UK that are looking for new and innovative work – in London, Birmingham, Edinburgh, Leeds and Brighton, to mention only a few. Sometimes there are specialised awards, such as the Cinewomen award, given for an experimental film made by a woman, which is awarded at the annual festival of Women's Cinema at Cinema City in Norwich. A network of film festivals also stretches across Europe.

Finally, there are the special opportunities for new programme makers made available by the television organisations themselves. Opportunities for first-time directors include the BBC's *10x10* (*see* pp. 233–5 above); Channel Four's occasional series such as *Short and Curlies* and *The Shooting Gallery*, and a number of special initiatives for new writers, documentary directors and others by Carlton UK and other ITV companies.

Addresses and useful publications

Carlton UK *Opportunities* from Carlton UK TV, PO Box 101, London WC2N 4AW

Chandler, C. (1996) *Low Budget Funding Guide*, London: BFI from: British Film Institute Funding Unit, 21 Stephen Street, London W1P 2LN

Channel Four Television, *An Introduction and Guide for Producers* (regularly updated) from: Channel Four, 124 Horseferry Rd, London SW1P 2TX, tel: 0171 396 4444

Channel Four Television, *Writing Proposals to Channel Four: A Guide for Beginners* (regularly updated) from: Channel Four, 124 Horseferry Rd, London SW1P 2TX, tel: 0171 396 4444

Channel Four (1995) *Short, Sharp Shots*, from: Channel Four, The Shooting Gallery, PO Box 4000, London W5 2GH

London Film and Video News (quarterly), from: London Film and Video Development Agency, 114 Whitfield Street, London W1P 5RW

Skillset *Careers Information Pack*, from: Skillset, 124 Horseferry Rd, London SW1P 2TX

Skillset Open Learning Materials, *Managing Your Business*, from: Plymbridge Distributors Ltd, Estove Rd, Plymouth PL6 7PZ
Cost for individuals purchasing for their own use £79.95

Televisual The business magazine for independent producers, facilities and the broadcast industry. Monthly. St Giles's House, 50 Poland St, London W1V 4AX

WAVES (Women's Audio Visual Education Scheme) The Wheel, 4 Wild Court, London WC2B 4AU, tel: 0171 430 1076

Beryl Richards: *writer and director*

Beryl Richards says that an interest in politics has driven her career as it moved from training in news reporting, through running a small company making non-broadcast videos for trade unions, local government and charities, to freelance writing and drama directing for the BBC and independent companies. During her career she has taken up numerous training initiatives, as well as making use of a whole range of other training schemes, small business support schemes and other grants and funds, as well as going back to college to do an MA.

In the 1980s, new forms of finance had become available outside the main television institutions. The arrival of relatively cheap video technology meant that the publicity video was part of a burgeoning public relations armoury. People aiming to work in television could, for the first time, cut their teeth on non-broadcast publicity work, whether for charities and non-profit organisations, for educational use, or for commerical firms. It also gave the opportunity for oppositional and campaigning groups to use video to get their message across or to experiment with a medium much cheaper and more accessible than film (*see* Tony Dowmunt, p. 202 above).

One exciting characteristic of non-broadcast work is that it does not have to conform to television genres. As long as a video makes the point that its sponsors want, its form is up for grabs. It may be a drama or contain dramatic sequences; it may use techniques from animation to musical interludes; it may stick to a strict, documentary form. The new face of this sector is on multimedia and CD-ROM. Working at a lower cost with less at stake, filmmakers have more space for experiment and more opportunity to become involved with every stage of the process, from the original idea through the scripting, the filming and the final edit. This was the sector where Beryl Richards developed her skills.

Beryl Richards

'While I was studying at the Polytechnic of Central London (since renamed the University of Westminster) I managed to get what was described as an 'internship' in a local news station in upstate New York, WSKG Binghampton. Being an intern meant working for nothing and turning my hand to everything from researching local news to working studio cameras or going out with reel to reel black and white portapak video gear. I was only 18 at the time but I was clear about what I wanted to do and put a lot of effort into getting the post. I wrote about 300 letters to television stations across the States and did my best to approach them in a way they would find acceptable. For example, no one then in Britain had CVs, but they did in the States, so I prepared myself a CV. I was determined to do everything right. Even so, I got into a bit of a muddle over New York. Binghampton upstate was a bit different from New York City, which I had hoped for.

The following summer I landed a four-month position as a researcher in San Francisco. The centre of the gay scene, it was in uproar following the assassination of the mayor, Harvey Milk, who had challenged conservative opinion by his commitment to gay issues. KQED was the seventh largest station on the Public Broadcasting System network – radical, exciting and wonderfully vibrant. My research encompassed the spectrum of local news items, from how to meet straight men in a launderette to sado-masochism.

My final project, when I got back to PCL, was a short drama, *The Hunt*, which I wrote and produced in collaboration with other final-year students. It dealt with a shop steward who was quoted out of context and thrust into the limelight on the national news during an ambulance drivers' dispute.

After graduating I stayed unemployed for almost two years. Surprisingly my US experience didn't help much. When I applied to the BBC, they did not believe that I could have gained the experience I had, and in any case weren't interested in the American system. I took some fill-in jobs at LBC – clipping newspapers for the newsdesk at the time of the Falklands War, then working as an assistant producer on phone-ins.

I kept up my involvement in video by working with other ex-PCL students and lecturers, who, like me, were keen to develop video for political uses. We contacted several trade unions and got a commission to make a publicity video for Southwark Council. Then, through a friend, I met George Smith who ran a small advertising agency, Smith Bundy. An ex-Lambeth councillor, George had kept his Labour Party commitment and contacts and now wanted to expand into video. He saw the script of my final project and the Southwark council video and invited me to run his new company. The idea was that his advertising company would guarantee a bank overdraft, and help get commissions from trade unions, local government and charities through their contacts and knowledge of direct mail and marketing. It was a remarkable offer for someone who was only 22 and not long out of college, but even so I was wary. In my idealism I was repelled by anything that smacked of advertising. I suggested bringing in collaborators, but that only complicated things. George and his other partners put their trust in me, and I ended up running the company and making well over 100 broadcast and non-broadcast programmes over the next eight years. I paid back the start-up loan within the first year.

I brought in a colleague from PCL, Sue Gibson, as a co-producer, and at first used facilities on the alternative video circuit because that's what I knew. I directed the vast majority, say seventy out of the hundred of the videos we made. I remember with affection a programme for the Children's Society on Chatsworth Summer Camp, and *Good Morning Britain* for NUPE about their low-paid council workers. Some of the shots in that film which followed binmen, home helps and cleaners were deliberate echoes of the documentaries from the 1930s I had studied on my BA course. When we made our campaigning film against the privatisation of British Telecom, it was fascinating to have free access to their archive of classic pre-war GPO documentaries. I poured a lot of myself into those first productions – I learnt later to be more cautious.

We went on to make a 40-minute drama for Shelter, written by David Stafford and produced by Gill Brown, and *Shut Up Kevin*, an up-market corporate production, shot on 35mm for the Bradford and Bingley Building Society. We won various awards, including International Monitor Award for a commercial for the Greater London Council encouraging claimants to take up their benefits. Both of those were shot by Wolfgang Suschitzky, the celebrated cinematographer and stills photographer, then in his seventies. Wolfgang had set up the first film Co-op in Britain and had worked for the National Coal Board, which produced regular cinema shorts in the documentary tradition. Our broadcast productions included a Channel Four *Dispatches* on the modernisation of NATO's nuclear weapons, and a *Media Show* item on political advertising in the US. For that I drew on my own US experience and a thesis I had written for my MA. I have found that I can use and reuse my various bits of work!

I made a point of employing women whenever I could, and was careful to work within union regulations. I joined the television union, the Association of Cinematograph and Television Technicians (ACTT), and became chair of the Freelance Shop. The fact that I was an employer as well as a technician was an anomaly which dogged many radical and left-wing filmmakers who wanted, or were forced, to work independently in the new corporate climate of the 1980s.

As time went on, our overheads grew and our turnover climbed to half a million pounds a year. I had to learn about budgeting, scheduling and forward projection. Running the company was taking up more and more of my energy and channelling it away from the work which I most enjoyed. I prefer to be judged on my creative work, not on how much money I can make.

In 1982 we were alone in the field, and for three years we were the only company regularly producing for the trade unions. But following the miners' strike of 1984, as the unions lost confidence and power, more of our commissions were for corporate videos. Although they allowed me to be more technically innovative and brought bigger budgets, I felt less at ease with them. What I cared about was how you could get across to people for good reasons rather than commercial ones. But many of my trade union sponsors were reluctant to commission anything but a plain, interview-based video in a media environment they perceived as inherently hostile. The only times they had access to mainstream television was when the unions were on strike and the leaders were forced into a defensive position.

I embarked on a part time MA at St Martin's College, partly to get some distance from the everyday production at Smith Bundy Video and partly to find some creativity. For my thesis I compared films for the labour movement in the 1930s with those I'd been so closely involved with in the 1980s. In both cases, the unions' suspicion of the medium and their lack of funds meant that their output was far outweighed by that of the companies whose employees they organise. The course allowed me to analyse the direction my own filmmaking was taking.

It had been a great chance for me at 22, but at 29 things were different. I had resisted doing corporate work for much too long. We began to make losses and I had to sack some longstanding employees who were understandably bitter. I wanted to hand over to someone else, but couldn't manage it. Eventually the company went bust.

In any case all I had wanted to do was direct, but it took two years and many disappointments before I managed to get established. I got an agent, put together a show reel, and continued to develop ideas. I broadened my contacts through organisations such as the First Film Foundation (a Yorkshire Television initiative which encourages first-time writers, producers and directors) the Directors' Guild and Women in Film. The First Film Foundation funded the development of a short play for Channel Four, but I was not allowed to direct as I lacked experience, particularly with actors. This was a recurring problem, so I enrolled at the National Film School on their National Short Course Training Programme and did several courses on working with actors. I also took acting classes on Saturdays.

One of the partners in Smith Bundy Video had earlier interested Michael Palin in a series based on an early twentieth-century comic novel. Channel Four Comedy Department had given a small development budget and I had adapted *Life with Eliza* into television scripts. After Smith Bundy, I set up a separate company and managed to get another development contract to make a pilot with Michael Palin. Unfortunately he then pulled out to do *American Friends* and we were left without a series.

At around that time I went with thirteen women producers on a two-week trip to the United States organised by the Media Exchange. It meant raising the £2,500 cost, and I got most of it from Wandsworth Council's business scheme. Since then I've worked with or for several of the women I met on the trip. In particular, Helen Greaves and Ruth Caleb, Head of BBC Drama Wales, who liked the *Eliza* idea which I then bought back from Channel Four. We cast John Sessions instead of Michael Palin, and I wrote and directed it as twelve 10-minute pieces. Helen produced the series for BBC2.

At the end of 1991 Helen took over as co-producer of *EastEnders*, which had become known as a training ground for new directors. Her co-producer was Leonard Lewis, who had taught me on the Directors' Guild course. They both knew my work and suggested I direct some episodes. In my first stint I did six. The series was running twice a week at that time and we rotated on a four-week schedule. I had been expecting it to be very hard. You must work at speed, using a multi-camera set up which was unfamiliar to me. It meant preparing a detailed camera script, directing from the gallery, and giving instructions to a vision mixer. But my camera supervisor was keen to try new things and I found the producers and the team extremely supportive. One of my episodes was about the death of Ethel's dog, Willy. I wanted lots of people in the market to have dogs, so that everywhere Ethel went she would be haunted by her loss. It meant extra expense, but they liked the idea and it worked.

I went on to do some episodes of *Brookside* – whose style and techniques are very different from *EastEnders* – then two plays by new writers for Carlton. That meant Beta location shooting on very tight budgets. My first *Brookside* episode involved a hot air balloon landing in the Close, and we got in a crane for the occasion. It was tricky to shoot so I storyboarded the whole thing, which rather surprised them. In these different ways, I managed to launch a directing career within mainstream television, although, because of my background, people still think of me as an outsider. The BBC can still feel like a bit of a club and you don't belong if you've gained your experience outside the big institutions. Despite my Smith Bundy years, at many an interview they only take into account the directing I've done since my first *EastEnders*.

I have not given up trying to produce more individual, quirky work, where I can do exactly what I want, rather than follow a pre-ordained format. I have written a number of scripts and documentaries specifically for grant funding, on the sort of topics that would not be considered by television. So far I have been supported by the Greater London Arts, the London Production Fund and the British Film Institute. This is the work I really value and that is personal to me, even though it is made on tiny budgets. Ironically, it is this work that often gets noticed and leads to mainstream directing jobs.

Since I started, there are many more women working in television, particularly as drama producers. But there are still not many women directors and very few in the technical grades like camera and sound.'

Reference

Baehr, H. and Spindler-Brown, A. (1987) 'Firing a broadside: a feminist intervention into mainstream TV' in H. Baehr and G. Dyer (eds) *Boxed In: Women and Television*, London: Pandora RKP

Part V: The changing face of television

17 Changing technologies

Changing technology: *changing consciousness*

Postmodern media from Marshall McCluhan to Jean Baudrillard

Those who are looking to work in the new century's screen media find themselves in uncharted territory. At the turn of the twenty-first century, we are watching the most dramatic changes in communications since the launch of the new mass media at the turn of the twentieth. A hundred years ago no one knew where those amazing new technologies – projected moving pictures and newspapers with photographs in them – would lead. Then, as now, everything seemed up for grabs in young media industries which had not yet become rigidified and had not yet developed formal skills, conventions and hierarchies. This, too, is a time for creativity and experiment.

In addition to the familiar four terrestrial channels, BBC1 and 2, ITV and Channel Four, hundreds more channels could become available through the digital compression of the broadcasting signal and transmission by fibre-optic cable. Already British cities are crisscrossed with a web of underground cables which can carry vast numbers of signals simultaneously. In this new wired world, cables relay satellite and terrestrial channels; they transmit channels created especially for the cable network – which may either be internationally based or as local as your immediate borough – and they introduce the new dimension of interactivity, offering services such as banking and home shopping.

New media based on computer technology hover around the borders of the medium we have hitherto defined as television. Digitisation and fibre-optic technology are paving the way to a convergence between the television, telecommunications and computer industries, so that it is unclear whether we are watching old technologies overlap or whether we are witnessing the birth of completely new types of media. 'When the world is wired nothing remains the same' (Taylor and Saarinen 1994). From the gory delights of games like *Mortal Kombat* to the more cerebral pleasures of library services on the Internet or CD-ROM, interactivity, accessibility and decentralisation make for a dream future.

But things are not quite that simple. Just as the cinema rapidly turned into an international business enterprise in the early years of the twentieth century, the dependence of the current changes on high-risk investment has meant that the basic technology, such as the ownership of satellites, of cable providers and of the equipment which will decode broadcast signals, is in the hands of very few entrepreneurs and is supranationally organised on rigid market lines. This has led to a narrowing of opportunity and of the types of programme that can be made for broadcast television. Those who would use the media creatively or for democratic communication are caught between countervailing forces.

The whirlwind of technological change has been paralleled by a positive avalanche of theory communicated through the rather old technology of print. For some years, the surest way to sell a cultural studies book was to make sure it had the word 'postmodern' in its title. Postmodern theory addresses itself to a world where old-fashioned certainties are no longer sure; where a sense of the forward progress of history has collapsed; and where meanings themselves are unstable. The vertiginous possibilities of computer-based technologies and the sense that everything is new and radically unpredictable seem to bear out the speculations of writers such as Jean Baudrillard (Baudrillard 1985).

In 1964 Marshall McLuhan celebrated the electronic revolution in his cult best seller, *Understanding Media* (McLuhan 1964). He argued that developments in technologies that are conveyors of ideas or tools for thinking amount to a change in consciousness itself. Today such developments have undoubtedly led to changing relations between television, or what should now be described as screen media, and their users.

The acceptance of developing screen technologies as a normal and automatic part of the way we conduct our domestic and business lives, has reorganised our mental experience of space and time, no less than the high-speed train and the aeroplane previously transformed our physical experience. Since the first communications satellite, Telstar, came into use in 1962, McLuhan's 'global village' has been a reality. Television is now able to transmit distant events instantaneously to our homes. *Sport Aid*, in 1986, created a series of satellite links for the first time. The Gulf War in 1991 was relayed to the world live from reporters in Baghdad for the US Atlanta-based Cable News Network as part of their 24-hour news coverage via satellite. Extensive air travel and mobile, lightweight television equipment have all played their part. The British viewer will, in recent years, have seen footage from programme makers and correspondents in innumerable parts of the world, including hitherto secret parts of China (Sue Lloyd Roberts reports for BBC News 1995) as well as daily observation of life in a distant Chinese town (*Beyond the Clouds*); the work of the police in Pakistan (*Karachi Kops*); television from across Africa (*African Summer*) and many other places previously merely glimpsed by the selective beam of television's observing eye. The immensity of the cultural, political and ethnic variations of the globe has become visible in a new way. At the same time the effects of industrialisation, commerce, travel and electronic and digital communications on the most remote parts of the world can be observed, reported, photographed and fed back via television in programmes which range from the outrageous Michael Moore on the Avon ladies who try to sell their products to the indigenous peoples in the Brazilian rain-forest (*Michael Moore's TV Nation*) to John Pilger's decade-long reporting for Central Television on the Indonesian government's repression in East Timor.

Our sense of time, of when things happened, has also been shaken up. The gap between 'now' and 'then' becomes confused and problematic when footage from the past is used and reused, often unidentified. Sometimes in factual and sometimes in fictional contexts the past is regularly juxtaposed with the present on our television sets. And yet a re-exploration of history, a re-examination of archive material and reconstructions of past events are making possible a much richer and more complex understanding of both personal and public histories.

While we expand our ability to record the historical and geographical worlds, those records have themselves become suspect because digital technology has severed the automatic link between the photographic image and reality. We can no longer assume that, if a scene was photographed, something was historically *there* at the time. Over the last thirty years or so, theorists have argued persuasively that the photographic image offers merely an *illusion* of reality. Manipulations at every stage of making a photograph or a film, including the filmmaker's own selectivity, have so influenced the way reality has been seen, that any representation of the real cannot be trusted (Winston 1995). Digital technology has made those theories appear frighteningly out of date, for the photographic media can no longer guarantee authenticity. An image may appear absolutely convincing, but may reproduce nothing that ever existed in the world. In Baudrillard's term, these are 'simulacra', copies of which there is no original, copies of themselves, a new sort of reality indistinguishable from representation.

The television image was always an illusion. Now its illusory quality is confirmed. 'Virtual' scenery, invisible to those in the studio, may now be electronically 'built' around the actors as a programme is recorded. BBC News has been broadcast from a 'virtual' studio since 1993. Reality has retreated.

Journalistic and academic writing about television and the new media has ranged from euphoric optimism to the deepest pessimism. Cultural optimism is at its most frenetic when it hails the 'ecstacy of communication' described by the high priest of postmodernism, Jean Baudrillard (Baudrillard 1985). It is a concept which can be rather too crudely applied to a multi-media, channel-zapping environment. Nicholas Negroponti, Director of the Media Lab at the Massachusetts Institute of Technology and founder of *Wired* magazine, welcomes a digital age in which a new generation will be 'released from the limitation of geographic proximity as the sole basis of friendship, collaboration, play and neighbourhood. Digital technology can be a natural force drawing people into greater world harmony' (Negroponti 1995).

Optimism can take a rather more sober form with the proposal that new technologies will facilitate a wider democratic participation, and bring access to power to ever wider groups of people. John Wyver (p. 160) speaks of the audience becoming 'co-creators rather than simply consumers'. Cultural pessimism, on the other hand, predicts a lowering of television standards and a world filled with illiterate children and media junkies. Critics speaking from a moral standpoint deplore the degrading effects of an increasingly undemanding television flow, laced with salacious and violent material. From an educational perspective, pessimists predict a decline in intellectual stimulus and community activity. In Neil Postman's words, these are 'technologies that undo their capacity to think' (Postman 1989).

So, are we heading for a television of abundance in the sense of a rich and varied choice, or will we get, in the words of the Bruce Springsteen song, '57 channels and nothing on'?

Below we will try to disentangle some of the many overlapping elements of the changes that are transforming the television of the twenty-first century, and the terms in which the debates about those changes have been framed. For television practitioners, the shape of future production and future employment will inevitably be within the context of these changes.

John Wyver: *producer of* The Net

L ooking to the future has provided exciting new opportunities for television producers in many different genres, from arts programmes to science and community-based programmes. Below producer John Wyver talks about how he explored new technologies for his two series of *The Net*, a magazine programme about computers and digital culture.

John Wyver

'W hen we made the first series of *The Net*, we were interested in the social and cultural implications of digital technologies and planned to complement the programmes with an extensive use of on-line services. That developed into the BBC Networking Club and eventually became an important part of our second series.

For that series, together with the design company Obsolete, we built an extensive World Wide Web site which, week by week, carried transcripts of the programme and additional material. For example, when we interviewed people for an item, we would spend 30 minutes or so talking to them, but, in television's incredibly wasteful way, we would only be able to use two minutes of that. So we put a transcript of the full interview on to the Web site for people who were interested in following it up. We also put a range of links from a particular item out into the Web where people could find out more information about the subject we were dealing with, and other general links for people who were interested in exploring what the Web could offer.

We developed a wide range of feedback mechanisms. We encouraged people to send us e-mail, and, when we could, we engaged in an e-mail dialogue with them. That meant that we got a very detailed sense of what at least part of the audience thought about the show, bearing in mind that only people who had Internet access could participate. People would send us thoughtful, extensive, sometimes quite rude but often very encouraging, critiques of the show.

We did Internet relay chat sessions after each programme, when a dozen of us would watch the programme and then go on to the Internet to 'talk' – actually that means to type – in an Internet relay chat (irc) channel about the programme. Usually sixty or seventy viewers logged on over the next couple of hours to tell us what they thought. We developed a mailing list so that people could get an automatic e-mail which told them about the response to the previous show, about what was coming on the next show and other stuff around the programme. We also experimented with a form of overlaying graphics using Ceefax on to the television screen. We produced a fact sheet, a video for sale about how to get connected to the Internet, and we finished each show with what we called the Netcetera – very fast frames with Web addresses and other information about the programme.

As the series developed, we responded to the way in which people were responding to us. I think that represented a real extension of the notion of accountability built into the BBC's charter and its ethos, which normally has more attention paid to its letter than to its spirit.

This has been the first time since I started working in television that I have had any sense of an audience watching. Normally when you make a programme, you might get one or two reviews, perhaps a handful of friends give you a polite version of what they really think, and you might get a dozen letters to the BBC, but there's little sense of an audience beyond a quantitative sense – of how many people seemingly watched it. Getting detailed individual responses is fantastically interesting and quite rare.

We were also part of a pilot experiment with the cable company Videotron. They have a crude but effective interactive system which involves running four cable channels in parallel. That meant that you could watch the show by itself or you could move to one of the other three channels which ran the show in a box, surrounded by changing graphics which gave much more detailed information. A viewer could move across the four channels seamlessly and get different graphics depending on the things they were interested in. In these different ways we were trying to exploit a range of new technologies which would extend the usefulness and the educational imperative of the programme. It was not a didactic, educational series in the traditional sense, but it attempted to stimulate interest in and understanding of digital technologies. It certainly led me to see how important the convergence of those technologies with traditional forms of broadcasting is going to be in the future.

I think that for a significant period, traditional forms of mass television will continue. There will always be large audiences for certain soaps, entertainment programmes, dramas, sporting events and music. But a lot of the other stuff is already beginning to fragment. With the cable and satellite channels already in place, we are seeing a move towards niche programming. I think that what will develop is a new form which will combine elements of broadcasting and Web publishing and also very important participatory forms, forms like those called MUDs or MOOs where you can communicate in real time with other people, or rather other identities, in a social space on the Internet.

There's a fundamental difference between the Internet and structures of broadcasting that have existed up until this point. Broadcasting, like other media in this century – newspapers, radio and films – has been built upon very limited distribution structures. There have only been a handful of broadcast channels, a handful of newspaper publishers, a handful of cinema chains; and those distribution structures have been the key to the forms of the media that have been offered to the public. The Internet, because of its non-hierarchical, web-like structure, doesn't operate with the idea of a central broadcaster or publisher disseminating material to an audience. It operates with all of the bits of the structure disseminating information to all the other bits, so it takes a horizontal form, rather than the vertical form in which a broad-caster traditionally speaks to an audience. If it is possible to harness that distributing structure and have the audience themselves contribute to the form that is developing, then you will start to change the structure of power that the media have worked with throughout the century. There is the potential to change how producers and others understand their relationship with their audience as the audience become co-creators rather than simply consumers.

Television is now much more open, and there are more ways for newcomers to start through independent production companies and cable and satellite systems. Many of the old definitions of television jobs have broken down. However, the structure is still not completely fluid. There are still certain skills that are needed. It remains essential for people who want to work in the medium to watch a lot of television, to think about what's good and what's bad about it, and to gain an understanding of the medium and how it works.

It is increasingly possible to present your own vision of the world to an audience through the Web, using video pieces that you make with your camcorder or with digital animations and so forth. You can genuinely find an international audience through this very egalitarian distribution structure. I think there is the potential for quite new ways of understanding media developing out of this kind of convergence. I don't quite know how it is going to happen, but I'm very interested in trying to contribute to it.'

From an interview given in August 1995.

Beyond television

Types of new technology

'The key to the future of television is to stop thinking about television as television', wrote Nicholas Negroponti (Negroponti 1995). New media technologies are intervening at all levels. They fall into several categories:

- *Those that provide new ways of delivering programmes into the home*, notably via cable and satellite dish, but also through a digital adaptation of the familiar telephone line, known as an Integrated Services Digital Network Line (ISDN). Interactive services, such as banking, shopping and telephony may be delivered along with the television programmes. Unlike the traditional forms of broadcasting, most of these new ways of delivering programmes involve some form of direct payment for the service.

- *Those used to enhance existing television programmes.* These include graphics and editing techniques, the use of computer technology to transform the images, and the creation of virtual spaces for the actors and presenters instead of conventional sets (*see* Titling, graphics and visual effects, p. 106 above.).

- *Those used for providing new types of source material.* Smaller electronic cameras are used for news gathering; concealed cameras can probe into secret places which have rarely been filmed before; home-recorded material is sent in by people who would not otherwise get to make programmes. Satellite telephones and transmitters make news and other forms of information instantly available from the most inaccessible parts of the world.

- *New formats which we recognise as similar to a television programmes, but which are new cultural forms in embryo*, including CD-ROM and the Internet. The convergence between computers and television is leading to multi-skilling and multimedia production.

- *A more interactive relationship with the audience* made possible by the convergence of computer and television technology and by utilising the Internet (*see* John Wyver, p. 250 above and Interactivity and multimedia, p. 257 below).

The digital revolution

The new television environment has been made possible by the processing, storage and transmission of information in digital forms. Digital technology can 'compress' information, so that it takes up much less space on the broadcasting spectrum, allowing potentially thousands of channels to be transmitted simultaneously. All UK broadcasters are moving to digital technology, which means an end to the 'spectrum scarcity' on which the duopoly of British broadcasting has been based.

The 1996 Broadcasting Act allowed for the setting up of six 'multiplex providers': agencies which can each carry at least three separate digital channels. This means that many more terrestrial channels are becoming available.

Digital technology is transforming the equipment used for filming and editing as well as broadcasting (*see* Digital recording, p. 53; Non-linear editing, p. 95). The digital mode breaks down the signal into discrete elements, rather like morse code breaks down letters into dots and dashes. This means that the image does not lose quality, however often it is broken down, copied and then reconstituted. It also means that any single one of the multitude of elements can be changed without affecting any of the others. Consequently, images and sound can be worked on in unprecedented ways – from cleaning up old films by invisibly removing the blemishes, to the creation of completely imaginary worlds out of existing material.

Satellite

Following an unsucccessful experiment in 1981, when the first satellite broadcasts were relayed along the few existing cables, Sky Channel in which Rupert Murdoch's News International holds a controlling share, was launched in February 1989 as a DBS (Direct Broadcasting by Satellite) service, picked up by individual satellite dishes. The signal was bounced off the Luxembourg-owned and operated Astra satellite. Its rival, BSB, British Satellite Broadcasting, which many had seen as the BBC of the stratosphere, launched in March 1990. Its franchise insisted on considerable amounts of original production and a higher quality signal. The two could not co-exist. Both were losing huge sums of money, so, in November 1990, they merged to form BSkyB. Because it was uplinked from the UK, the broadcaster came under the regulatory control of the Independent Television Commission.

Broadcasting from satellite crosses national boundaries, the signal is received across the 'footprint' of the satellite and can be relayed by cable networks. With digital compression the number of channels available on any given satellite is huge. It is organised in what Jeremy Tunstall describes as the 'packager' model of broadcasting, in which a single broadcaster gathers together a group of channels (Tunstall 1993), so that we now speak of 'channels' much as we used to speak of programmes.

Satellite channels do not provide a balanced mix of entertainment, education and information, structured throughout the day, as BBC1 and 2, ITV and Channel Four do; nor are they committed to broadcast nationwide. Some are not publicly available at all, but are booked for international businesses. The channels that British homes can receive from satellite may or may not be British based; may or may not be primarily directed at a British audience; may or may not be subject to British laws and regulations. Thus they include pornography channels and other forms of material, such as tele-evangelism, that would be filtered out by the British regulatory system. Channels tend to be more closely targeted – at a local area, at specific audiences, such as children or housewives at home in the afternoon, or at specific interest groups, such as sports fans or devotees of Hollywood movies. They include channels which are repeated at staggered hours, so that the viewer can pick them up at a time convenient to themselves. Transmitting the same movie on four or six channels with, say, a 15-minute delay on each, could produce Near Video On Demand (referred to in this age of acronyms as NVOD).

Satellite channels are all privately owned, mostly by American companies who put up the original launch money, which is then recouped through subscriptions, advertising, sponsorship and pay as you view. Many use a scrambled signal which may be decoded through a special decoder box, using a 'smart card' on payment of subscriptions. An increase in satellite reception will imply an increase in Pay TV.

(*See* Helen Swords, p. 139 and Rupert Rumney, p. 145 above on working for satellite channels.)

Cable

Cable has been used since the 1950s to relay the television signal to some subscribers. It had long been seen by Conservative politicians as the Trojan horse that might break the public service duopoly of the BBC and ITV networks, but for community campaigners it was an opportunity for genuinely local television (*see* Tony Dowmunt, p. 202).The first local cable television licences were granted in 1972 to five networks based in Swindon, Bristol, Wellingborough, Sheffield and Greenwich. They were modelled on the already existing US local cable stations, but attracted very few subscribers.

By the early 1980s, Information Technology was the buzz word. Television was thought of as only a part of a wide spectrum of new forms of communication, since fibre optic cable could also carry interactive services. Kenneth Baker, Minister for Information Technology, declared that 'laying down the cable network will be as important as laying down the railway network in Victorian England'. However, the government was determined that however revolutionary, the network should be laid down by private companies and used by private broadcasters 'without the present restrictions on programmes'. The BBC responded that cable on these terms would undermine public service broadcasting and would 'be socially divisive, sacrifice hard-won programme standards and coarsen a public taste which has been painstakingly developed by public service broadcasting' (Negrine 1985: 103).

Like all channels, cable channels must abide by the ITC's Programme Code, but they need not observe regulations regarding programme quality, imported programming, regional material and independent production. 'There are, in effect no regulatory directives on either the range or the sources of programme material' (Negrine 1994).

Eleven franchises were awarded in 1983, but the cabling of British cities and the take-up of the cable franchises only began to take off in the mid-1990s. It has proved easy to get a licence to run a channel, as fibre optic cable can contain thousands of channels, but a production company must broadcast its programmes through a cable provider, who ultimately selects what goes down the wire. It is still uncertain what shape the sector may take, but it is possible that a consortium of channels in collaboration with cable companies may emerge (Roger Wilson in discussion at National Film Theatre 1995). Many cable companies are American or Canadian owned. For example, the New York and New England Telephone Exchange have laid down the cables in Brighton.

Cable is proving to be cut-price television. When Janet Street-Porter launched *Live TV*, for Mirror Group Television, she claimed to be able to produce programming at £2,000 per hour in contrast to the usual £100,000 per hour for a documentary or £200,000 for a drama. Some producers at *Live TV* found themselves turning out up to six hours of material per day, as opposed to the three months or more that goes into the making of a single documentary for the BBC or Channel Four. Not many programme makers are going to make a living out of that. 'It's the new way', Rachel Purnell, Janet Street-Porter's Head of Programmes, told a British Film Institute conference. 'You're in the world of commerce and that really does make a difference' (*Changing Channels*, NFT, 19 May 1995). The same number of people who would previously make programmes now found themselves making whole 'channels'. As it turned out, Janet Street-Porter's energetic attempt to forge a new kind of television was soon pushed aside by Managing Director and ex-*Sun* Editor, Kelvin MacKenzie. He replaced it with a behind-the-screens soap opera based in the company's Canary Wharf offices, and such laddish offerings as *Topless Darts*.

New channels as often as not mean old material. Some, like UK Gold, run by the BBC and Thames Television, and SelecTV, run by the producers of many favourite comedy dramas and sitcoms, have been specifically launched to re-show their programmes. They give them a welcome second viewing and make money out of the extensive archives held by the television companies. Cable and satellite stations tend to fill the rest of their time with low-intensity, low-cost programming, usually studio-based celebrity chat shows, or actuality, local news and events. Although the Discovery Channel, the US cable channel, frequently co-produces, with the BBC and others, new channels tend to be wary of original programming, not least because of its cost, and much material is obtained free of charge.

But what about the hoped-for increase in public access to television production and in democratic participation? In the US, cable franchises are awarded by local bodies, unlike the national bodies that control cable in the UK. People have the *right* to airtime, under the First Amendment to the US Constitution which guarantees free speech. A developed network of local cable stations produce everything from evangelising religious programmes, home shopping and amateur dramatics, to political argument and propaganda (*see* Tony Dowmunt, p. 202). Under the conditions of totally open access, much of the output is boring and unwatchable by British standards. The selected items from US cable channels shown by Channel Four as *Manhattan Cable*, were way-out oddities rather than evidence of real democratic participation.

In Britain even 'access' programmes must go through the channel providers, who have the absolute right to select programmes. There are eighty-three providers operating cable franchises, but only twelve local areas where genuine local television takes place. Activists like Dave Rushton, Director of the Institute of Local Television, Edinburgh, argue that local cable could broadcast everything from news, sport, arts and music, to fairs and carnivals. It could give access to the local council and provide a forum where accountable people respond to complaints (Rushton 1995). The few examples include areas where the local council has collaborated in a cable franchise. The Milton Keynes Channel, started in March 1995, is run by the local authority together with further education establishments. It has broadcast a local election night and multimedia productions by local students. Cable 7 in Leicester is an open access channel on the American model. In their case the main shareholders are Canadians who are more prepared to experiment than many American owners.

At Edinburgh Television Trust, they aim to make programmes from a local perspective on global issues. There are not enough subscribers to satisfy the local broadcasters, so they have made links with a Berlin cable station company and even broadcast live down an ISDN line to Berlin's one million cabled homes.

Getting to make programmes for cable is not a lucrative business. Most companies employ less than fifty people, and none has the budget to commission programmes in the traditional sense. Those stations that are genuinely local are committed more to access for the general public, than to access for professionals. However, cable is only in its infancy. As it develops, more opportunities will almost certainly develop with it.

Interactivity and multimedia

The principle of interactivity is not as new as it may seem. Although it has taken time for broadcasters to move beyond a conception of a passive audience, as soon as more than one channel became available to viewers, they have been able to modify and, to a certain extent personalise, what they see. The following is an outline of the various levels of interactivity, all of which are intensifying in the new media climate:

Choice

The lowest level of interactivity is the decision when to switch on and off, followed by the ability to move between channels. With the coming of the remote control, zapping and channel surfing meant that whole new programmes could be constructed on the lines of 'Five minutes of the comedy, then let's flick back to see how the match is going' or 'the play has hit a boring patch, so what about the news?' Schedulers, if not programme makers, are acutely aware that slow-moving programmes or dull patches may lose them their audience, and short bursts of kaleidoscopic montage are a regular feature of most contemporary viewing.

When families are viewing together, the question of who will hold the remote reveals power and gender divisions within the household (Gray 1996). But more choice and the tendency to target specified groups rather than the audience as a whole began to change the nature of what had been a collective domestic experience into an individual relationship with the set. However, in the fully wired household with a set in every bedroom, the most important question remains whether the proliferation of channels will increase choice, or simply offer a bigger but less varied diet.

Time shift

The coming of the VCR has meant that programmes are no longer tied to their designated slots, and scheduling strategies are undermined as programmes are lifted from their original context. If two favourite programmes clash, the VCR owner may watch both. Commercials may be avoided by running through at speed. Some programmes, such as late-night films and educational material like BBC2's *The Learning Zone*, are now deliberately scheduled to be recorded and time shifted. However, the ability to bypass the schedules has given rise to new concerns about the 9 pm watershed, designed to help parents supervise their children's viewing. If a late-night movie containing frightening or upsetting material is recorded, there is no way to control the time at which it is viewed.

Teletext

Continuously updated text available on the television set, such as Ceefax and Oracle was first established in 1973. Viewers may seek out a variety of different types of written information, such as travel news, weather forecasts, news headlines, as and when they need them.

Education, publications and other networks

The Open University, launched in 1969 as a genuinely open learning institution, links television programmes with printed materials and personal tutoring with accreditation for those who enrol. The television programmes can be seen by all, and the contribution of the OU to adult education has been immense. In the field of media and cultural studies it has been at the forefront of new ideas.

All channels now complement their programmes with associated publications, and Channel Four's 'Talking Heads Club' also aims to give viewers an opportunity to get together for discussions and conferences. 'Interactivity', they claim, 'refers both to the technology that allows greater screen activity by viewers, and the implications for broadcasting, democracy and our sense of community.' With associated activities of this sort, the relationships generated by the box in the corner are not just between viewer and screen, but feed into the longstanding traditions of British adult education, and informal working-class self-education.

Feedback programmes

'Social Action' programmes have a mandate to link television broadcasting with charity fund-raising and other ways of involving people in specific target groups (*see* Helen Swords, p. 139 above). Phone-in programmes and talk-back programmes began in the 1980s as a form of audience comment on their television fare. Early in its life Channel Four aimed to increase 'active broadcasting'. It set up its 'Video Box': a booth set up with camera in place, so that any passer-by could walk in and record their comments. The calls were incorporated into programmes, such as *Comment* and *Right to Reply*. *Free for All* extended this interactivity with multiple telephone lines, video phones and 'ordinary people' sent off with Hi-8 video cameras to investigate topics as serious as the Ku Klux Klan in Wales. The genre of video diaries and 'ordinary people' shows has been based on the principles of access and interactivity.

Another form of interaction has been through the telephone helpline services set up when a particularly sensitive topic, such as AIDS or domestic violence, is dealt with, whether in a drama or a factual programme. Perhaps the most remarkable has been the ChildLine service, set up by Esther Rantzen in 1986 in association with her programme *Childwatch* – the first time that children were given the opportunity to call for help in confidence beyond the adults in immediate authority over them.

Interactive cable

The possibility of two-way communication is at the heart of the 'broadband communications' – the Information Superhighway – which cable makes possible. A set top box on the television will allow the subscriber to use the 'return path' to respond to the provider of the services. This is the transactional technology which allows home shopping and banking or video-on-demand, choosing a film from a library of titles to be transmitted on the cable. Westminster Cable together with BT have been running pilot schemes, and some cable households are offered interactive choices via handsets during the news, gameshows and sports programming. John Wyver describes his collaboration with the cable company Videotron for his programme, *The Net*, in which the cable channel made extra information available to viewers by transmitting simultaneously on several channels (p. 250). Andrew Curry, ex-*Channel Four News* and currently Manager of Interactive TV for Videotron, told a conference at the National Film Theatre, 'The desire is not choice, nor shopping, but connectedness ... Cable allows a direct discourse which bypasses public discourse and allows some authentic voice' (NFT 1995).

Interactive multimedia: CD-ROM

High-level interactivity, as in video games, can only be achieved with computer technology. Interactive CD-ROMs may include moving pictures as well as other media such as photographic stills and text. In an interactive drama the outcomes are predetermined, but there are several of them. Which one is made available to the viewer will depend on choices made as they move through the narrative. At certain points options are offered, based on moral or other choices: Should she kiss him or not? Should he go home early or stay out late? The story will continue according to the decision taken, much like a computer game.

A specialised division of labour has not yet evolved, and experimentation may be both creative and technical. Multimedia producers need to be able to do many of the tasks familiar from television, and several more too. Scripting, sound and video recording, designing, graphics and editing skills are all necessary to produce an interactive CD-ROM, together with computer skills. At Artec, a London-based multimedia consultancy and training agency, a group of four people have produced an interactive story distributed on CD-ROM for educating schoolchildren about AIDS.

The Internet

The computer-based, worldwide communications network known as the Internet establishes contact between widely dispersed individuals, many of them unknown to each other. Scanning the Net is a new leisure pursuit, an invaluable aid to research, and a way of gathering news information.

Those who criticise the centralising tendency of television information have embraced the Internet as a way of bypassing the filtering and shaping processes of the professionals and the institutions. Via the Net people can talk to each other, can put their own versions of events, can build up alternative networks of shared concerns (*see* John Wyver, p. 250 above).

A Dutch TV station VPRO advertises on the Internet for alternative news sources. Its television programme *W.E.B. World Receiver* tries to reach correspondents all over the world and invites them to make video reports. 'How can we judge the quality of the news on its own merits? Can we obtain a solid and reliable picture of world events when we depend on the regular media?' It compares the blanket coverage of US landings in Somalia with the partial coverage of Iraq and East Timor.

> Through the Internet small organisations and individuals obtain and spread information all over the world. In this television programme we want to use these same channels to obtain information. . . . the items are made by persons who are directly and locally confronted with these news facts. Our ultimate goal is to bring remarkable facts to the attention that otherwise remain unknown or misunderstood.
>
> (From a publicity leaflet, 1996)

The 'holy grail' sought for by multimedia is a technology that brings together television and computers, so that a normal computer may produce full-screen formation video, and video may be downloaded via the Internet.

Changing technology: *ownership and globalisation*

'Information will not be power, *meta*-information will be power', wrote historian John Gray, 'new technologies simply change the terms on which social and political conflicts are played out' (Hayward and Wollen 1993).

As the satellite and cable channels gain more prominence, ownership of UK television stations is becoming part of a global pattern. The BBC as well as commercial companies, such as Pearson, part of the Channel Five consortium, are developing international interests. Media moguls, of whom Rupert Murdoch is the most prominent, have seen in satellite technology a way of expanding their empires across national boundaries and of bypassing national restrictions. Murdoch owns newspapers and television channels in Australia, the Far East and the United States as well as broadcasting numerous transnational channels from the Astra and Star satellites. He gave up his Australian nationality to become an American citizen in order to circumvent restrictions on foreign ownership of American media. In the UK, Murdoch's companies own four national newspapers as well as a controlling share in BSkyB, and he has been campaigning for some years for greater access to UK broadcasting. This would mean a change in the regulations which limit the number of newspapers and television channels owned by any single organisation. Newspaper groups such as Murdoch's, which control more than 20 per cent of the market, are prohibited from owning more than 20 per cent of a television licence (regulations introduced in 1996). However, the move to digital broadcasting has brought new opportunities for international entrepreneurs including Murdoch, as existing terrestrial broadcasters lack the huge sums of money needed to invest in the new transmission and coding equipment required to launch the digital systems.

In his speech at the Edinburgh International Television Festival of 1989, which was a passionate argument for deregulation and the free market in the run-up to the 1990 Broadcasting Act, Rupert Murdoch told an audience of ambivalent British television practitioners that they need not be afraid of his power, since he controls the technology not the content. More channels mean greater diversity, he claimed, with wider choice for the audience and more space for producers to gain access to the airwaves. Nevertheless, there has been a tendency for a small number of international entrepreneurs to buy up 'intellectual product', the programmes, film libraries and picture libraries which, as software, can now be widely marketed using new technology.

The spectre of transnational media monopolies has led to fears on several levels. First there is the fear that deregulation could mean an avalanche of porn and other undesirable material. Sex and violence will always find an audience and the entrepreneurs are interested in profits not in content. Second there is the increasing cultural dominance of those Western nations where most programmes originate. American films and series can be made available to the rest of the world at a fraction of the cost of home-produced programmes, since they have already made their profit in the vast market which is the United States. Then there is the concern that the requirements of broadcasting across national boundaries will drive down the quality, leading to programmes that are bland and uninventive, sliding between cultures, offending no one and stimulating no ideas (*see* Rupert Rumney, p. 145). A strategy of Grundy Worldwide, the Australian programme maker that produces *Neighbours* and is now owned by Pearson, has been described as developing 'cheap and lucrative "template television", taking simple concepts for soap operas and games shows and "localising" them for broadcast in several countries' by featuring local languages and local characters (Horsman 1995).

Perhaps the most serious concern is that a concentration of ownership, especially between television and the press, reduces political choice. In Italy, media mogul Silvio Berlusconi swept to power as Prime Minister in 1994. His political party, Forza Italia, had been launched just before the election as a 'media confection' with virtually no on-the-ground representation, but it was backed by his four pop-entertainment television channels, which between them carried a 40 per cent share of the viewing audience (Hutton 1994).

The danger is that the new technology is bringing a concentration rather than a diversity of ownership and control, which national regulatory bodies may be powerless to restrain.

18 Television in the new century

T he television industry of the twenty-first century is likely be an unpredictable amalgam of current trends and attitudes, which will clearly not just disappear, and others which can scarcely be predicted. It will be both more global, via satellite and the transnational concentration of ownership, and more local, via cable and small-scale initiatives. It is likely to offer *more* of everything – more channels, more accompanying services – but that could also mean *less* diversity, as the commercial imperative drives out programmes that appeal to smaller or more selective audiences. It is likely to be more egalitarian – with a greater range of people having access to programme making – but also more divided, as 'pay as you view' means that the worse-off you are, the less choice you will have and the principle of universal provision is eroded. It is likely to be more difficult for new entrants to break into the shrinking areas of traditional drama and documentary making, while becoming easier to make one-off programmes or to get videos which have originated outside the broadcast companies on to the screen.

Definitions of 'quality', of 'responsibility to the audience' and of 'creativity', which have been referred to by so many of the practitioners who have contributed to this book, all need to be rethought within this changing climate. The free market model is aggressively on the ascendant, but changes in technology and structure have made it possible to reconsider what a broadcasting service could be like if it aims to open up access to stimulating political debate and to offer a balance of education and information together with a broad range of entertainment.

For those who are new to the industry, the 'tough, competitive world with no space for people who are not prepared to provide absolute commitment', described by Skillset, is likely to become even more fiercely competitive. Over the 1990s the ITV companies and the BBC all reduced the number of staff permanently employed. 'Rationalisation' and 'downsizing' took their toll as the terrestrial broadcasters saw their overall audience share reduce. The casualisation of existing labour forces and a pattern of freelance work on short-term contracts are likely to increase, while independent production companies operate on tighter margins and are often unable to plan further ahead than the next commission. Satellite and cable companies are expanding but employ tiny staffs and produce much lower-cost programming.

As in every other industry, the broadcasting trade unions which had great bargaining strength in the 1970s and controlled entry to many grades, have lost much of their power. This has opened up television to new entrants who would previously have been kept out, but the other side of the coin is that BECTU, which currently covers the television industry, is less able to protect its members against the vagaries of the job market.

Despite these upheavals, the content of British television is possibly richer and more diverse then ever before. Well-established genres, although inevitably uneven in quality, are flourishing. Meanwhile, new genres, many of them bringing access to the medium closer to ordinary people – video diaries, feedback programmes, the use of themes and seasons – are constantly evolving. Each of the terrestrial channels has maintained its distinctive character, allowing for a real exploration of popular taste on BBC1 and ITV, a great deal of innovation on BBC2, and a continued effort to address minority tastes as well as reaching to the further out realms of the possible on Channel Four (*see* Stuart Cosgrove p. 211 above). Links with the cinema industry, through *Film on Four* and *Screen Two*, have allowed the production of low-budget films that are free to address the issues of the day in a British context, rather than having to adapt to the requirement of distributors, who are usually American. From *My Beautiful Laundrette* in the early 1980s to *Trainspotting* in the 1990s, television has made a much-needed contribution to British cinema culture and opened up opportunities to younger filmmakers. There are outlets for video artists with tiny audiences, and massively popular drama series which reach 16 million or more. There are innovative consumer programmes, imaginative children's shows and the occasional plunge into tastelessness, with programmes like *The Word*, which saves public service broadcasting from a charge of worthiness. Not that everything is perfect – an overreliance on American programmes and a dangerous slide into sensationalism and intrusiveness have accompanied the explosion of trash TV in the 1990s, which sometimes seems obsessed with a package-holiday culture of sex and embarrassment. Production remains rather too London based, with only a gesture towards genuinely regional programming. Nevertheless, the diversity and richness of UK television still holds audiences in front of their sets, and continues to draw people into making programmes whatever the difficulties.

High-quality television, in all its diversity, will only be maintained within a visual culture in which critical viewing and tele-literacy go along with a love of the medium. Many people are aware of what might be lost if UK television rushes too far down the path of deregulation and an unprotected market. Never was it more important for involvement at every level – from active audience response to articulate campaigns on the part of television professionals. The broadening of the television output should not be allowed to lead to a narrowing of its range.

Technological optimism has too often overlooked the implications of the political and economic changes which have gone along with a changing technology. However, despite the uncertainty of the future, it seems safe to reiterate the view that producers John Wyver and Phil Redmond have both expressed in this book. This is an exciting time to be setting out on a television career. Just as watching television is rarely simply passive, working in television is never just a job.

References

Gray, A. (1996) 'Behind closed doors, video recorders in the home' in Helen Baehr and Ann Gray (eds) *Turning It On: a Reader in Women and Media*, London: Arnold

Horsman, M. (1995) 'Three lock horns in the battle of the TV titans', *Independent*, 8 May, London

Hutton, W. (1994) 'Moguls on the podium', *Guardian*, 30 March, London

Negrine, R. (1985) *Cable Television*, London: Croom Helm

Tunstall, J. (1993) *Television Producers*, London: Routledge

Winston, B. (1995) *Claiming the Real: The Documentary Film Revisited*, London: BFI

Key Texts

Baudrillard, J. (1985) 'The ecstacy of communication' in Hal Foster (ed.) *Postmodern Culture*, London: Pluto

Convergence: The Journal of Research into New Media Technologies. Biannual. Luton: University of Luton and John Libbey & Co.

Cubitt, S. (1990) *Timeshift: On Video Culture*, London: Comedia

Hayward, P. and Wollen, T. (eds) (1993) *Future Visions*, London, BFI

Inside Cable, Journal of Local Television and the Cable TV Industry. PO Box 5, Church Stretton, Shropshire SY6 6ZZ

Local TV International. Quarterly. PO Box 3456, Glasgow G73 4RU

McLuhan, M. (1964) *Understanding Media*, London: RKP

Morley, D. and Robins, K. (1995) *Spaces of Identity*, London: Routledge

Negrine, R. (1994) *Politics and the Mass Media in Britain*, London: Routledge

Negroponti, N. (1995) *Being Digital*, London: Hodder & Stoughton

Postman, N. (1989) *Amusing Ourselves to Death*, London: Methuen

Rushton, D. (1993) *Citizen Television: A Local Dimension to Public Service Broadcasting*, London: John Libbey

Rushton, D. (1995) *Local Television Reviewed*, Edinburgh: Insitute of Local Television

Taylor, M. and Saarinen, E. (1994) *Imagologies: Media Philosophy*, London: Routledge

Williams, R. (ed.) (1990) *Television: Technology and Cultural Form*, London, Routledge

Wilson, R. (1994) *Local Television: Finding a Voice*, Church Stretton: Dragonflair Publishing

Glossary

∙∙∙

ACTT Association of Cinematograph and Television Technicians. The trade union representing employees in film and television before amalgamation with the broadcast and theatre unions (see **BECTU**).

AFM Assistant Floor Manager. The junior person in the production crew who assists the stage/floor manager with such jobs as looking after the actors, checking the props and co-ordinating rehearsals and studio production (*see* Stage/floor manager under Work areas in the television industry, p. 28)

ambient noise The background sound inherent to a location such as traffic noise or air conditioning.

analytic editing Editing in which the sequence of images is constructed to follow an argument rather than a narrative.

animation A style of filming which creates movement from inanimate objects, whether they be sequences of drawings – as with a Disney film – plasticine puppets or merely moving diagrams. Usually achieved by exposing the film or videotape a few frames at a time and moving the drawings or models between exposures.

aperture Adjusting the aperture of a lens means enlarging or reducing the size of the hole at its centre formed by the surrounding iris, hence altering the exposure. The size is measured in f-stops. A large aperture (f-2) admits more light but reduces the depth of field; a small aperture (f-16) admits less light but gives a greatly increased depth of field. A lens may be 'opened up' or 'stopped down'.

appeals Short programmes which appeal for money on behalf of certain charities. Charity advertising and the conditions under which it is possible to appeal for money are strictly regulated under the ITC code and the BBC charter.

archive material Any film or other footage that is stored in a film archive for reuse. This may include material from earlier programmes incorporated into new ones (*see* Archive research, p. 166).

Astra The Luxembourg-based satellite operation which broadcasts the BSkyB channels and those of other European broadcasters.

Audience Appreciation Index (AI) This is a survey of viewers' opinions on the programmes they have seen, giving a range of appreciation ratings.

BARB (Broadcasters' Audience Research Board) A specialised research organisation which produces regular viewing figures in a variety of forms using several overlapping methods, including monitoring the switching on of television sets and conducting polls amongst the public.

barn doors Side flaps fitted to studio and portable lights, used to blank off part of a light source and control its spread and direction.

BECTU Broadcasting, Entertainment, Cinematograph and Theatre Union. The trade union representing employees in the film, television and theatre industries. (see **ACTT**).

Betacam Usually referred to as Beta, this is the standard videotape format. Broadcast quality is called SP.

blimp A substantial cover needed to muffle a noisy camera when shooting sound. An important breakthrough came when quieter cameras were developed in the 1960s.

blonde 2,000 watt lensless spotlight of the 'external reflector' type. So called because of the yellow colour of the head of the lamp.

boom A long pole with movable adjustments, from which a microphone can be suspended in a shockproof cradle. It may be a portable fishpole boom or it may be a large boom with adjustable extensions mounted on a movable base.

boom swinger The person who controls the boom so that the microphone is in the optimal position for each shot.

broadband communications The very large number of simultaneous interactive channels made possible by cable technology.

buzz track A recording of the ambient noise or the background atmosphere of a scene. Sometimes referred to as an 'atmosphere' track or simply 'atmos'.

camcorder An electronic camera which combines the camera and recorder functions. The term applies both to domestic and professional equipment.

cardioid microphone A microphone with a heart-shaped pick-up pattern.

character generator Equipment for generating lettering on the screen. Usually referred to by a specific brand name, such as a Chyron or an Aston.

Chyron see character generator. (*see* Rupert Rumney, p. 145, for a description of its use).

ciné-vérité Literally 'cinema-truth'. The use of the term has evolved and changed since it was first used by Jean Rouch to describe his documentary *Chronicle of a Summer* in 1960. It is usually used to describe 'fly-on-the-wall' style documentary shooting, using a hand-held camera and with very little interference from the filmmakers in the scenes they are filming (*see* Current documentary genres, p. 154).

clapper/loader The assistant on the camera crew whose job is to mark the shots with a clapper board and also to reload the camera magazines with film.

clapper board When shooting on film, the clapper board begins each take and identifies it on sound and in vision. The clap provides a point from which the image and the magnetic track can be matched together.

classic realist text A narrative constructed around a hierarchy of voices in which the voice of the real author is concealed, embedded within the text (*see* Critical narrative theories, p. 126).

colour temperature The warmth or coldness, redness or blueness, of any light source, measured on the Kelvin scale. The bluer daylight is at the 'hotter' end of the spectrum' (*see* Nick Hale, p. 73).

Community Action Programmes 'Community' or 'Social Action' programmes take up issues around health, crime, disability and similar topics and directly involve their viewers (*see* Helen Swords, p. 139).

compilation film A film that is constructed out of previously shot material.

consent form Anyone who may appear in a programme must give their written consent. They are usually asked to sign a 'consent form', which may consist of a sheet of paper with a standard form of words, to which they add their name and signature.

credits A television programme usually concludes with a caption that lists the names of the individuals who worked on or contributed to the programme. These are referred to as the 'credits'.

crew The group of technicians who work on a programme.

cross fade A transition from one shot to another in which the outgoing shot gradually disappears at the same time as the incoming shot gradually appears. Also called dissolve or mix.

cutting copy When using film, the editor must physically cut and join the film. This working print is known as the cutting copy. When it has been finalised the negative is cut to match it and a final print is produced.

cutting room The editing room. Usually used when working with film.

D3 or D5 Digital tape formats.

DBS Direct broadcasting by satellite, in which the television signal, bounced off the satellite, is received directly by individual satellite dishes.

Deco-doc Documentaries which use a wide range of techniques rather than observational filming.

decoder Many satellite channels use a scrambled signal which may be decoded through a special decoder box using a 'smart card' on payment of a subscription (*see* Beyond television, p. 253).

depth of field The distance from the camera within which subjects are in focus, or 'sharp'. Subjects closer to the camera or further away from the depth of field will appear out of focus (*see* **aperture** above).

diagesis The distinction between showing (mimesis) and telling (diagesis) points to the difference between the way a story may be conveyed in images, as in silent cinema, and the way a narrator *tells* the tale, most obviously in a novel written in the first person (*see* Analysis of the narrative form, p. 118).

diffuser Flame-proof 'spun' fibre-glass sheets fixed over a lamp, or some material such as tracing paper supported in a large frame, which diffuses the light, making it softer and reducing its intensity.

digital technology The digital mode breaks down the signal into discrete elements, rather like morse code. This means that the image does not lose quality, however, often it is broken down, copied and then reconstituted.

Direct cinema The term originates with the work of Robert Drew, Richard Leacock and the Maysles brothers in the US in the 1960s. Now sometimes used interchangeably with 'cine-vérité' to desribe 'fly-on-the-wall' style documentary shooting, using a hand-held camera and with very little interference from the filmmakers in the scenes they are filming (*see* Current documentary genres, p. 154).

dissolve A transition from one shot to another in which the outgoing shot gradually disappears at the same time as the incoming shot gradually appears. Also called cross fade or a mix.

dolly A mobile mounting for a camera. The camera is on a moveable crane-arm with considerable mobility in all directions. There is a seat for the camera operator who controls the height and camera platform direction using foot pedals. A motorised dolly may be controlled by an operator on the rear platform, or the dolly may be gently moved by a member of the camera crew known as a grip.

downlink The downward transmission from satellite to receivers.

dub The process of transferring a magnetic signal, whether sound or video, from one tape to another. The process of combining and balancing the sound-tracks, which is one of the last stages of editing, is known as the dubbing stage, or the dub.

DVE Digital Video Edit.

duopoly The system whereby two organisations have total control of their field. We speak of BBC and ITV controlling UK television as a duopoly until the coming of satellite and cable and the changes made by the 1990 Broadcasting Act.

EDL Editing decision list. The list of time code numbers which show the beginning and ends of each shot in an edited sequence. These can be typed into a computerised system which will automatically carry out the decisions.

edge numbers Printed numbers along the side of the frames on film. They are used to identify shots and to match print with negative.

effects
(a) *Visual effects* may be created in the laboratories for film, or for video through specialised video effects equipment. They include such devices as the image whirling round, folding over as if pages are turning, moving to a different part of the screen, etc. (*see* Visual fireworks, p. 106).
(b) *Special effects* is the description given to the dramatic reconstruction of events which must be carefully planned and carried out by trained experts, such as fires and explosions.
(c) *Sound effects* are the extra sounds which are added to the natural sounds of a scene. Often written as 'fx' (*see* Types of television sound, p. 80 and Sound editing, p. 103).

emulsion The light-sensitive chemical coating on film stock which records the image. Film stock manufacturers are constantly producing new emulsions with different speed and latitude. They are known by their stock numbers. Nick Hale refers to Kodak 7298 as a fast 16mm colour stock (*see* Nick Hale, p. 73; Cameras, film stock and formats p. 49).

ENG Electronic News Gathering (*see* News technologies, p. 186)

exposure The exposure of a shot depends on the amount of light that enters the lens. It is controlled by the aperture (*see* **aperture** above).

fade The fade-out is the gradual darkening of the shot until the image disappears, leaving a black screen. It is usually followed by a fade-in on the next shot. This is a very slow transition, usually to mark the end of a sequence.

fast stock A film stock with an emulsion that responds rapidly to the light that falls on it.

Fibre optic cable A form of cable made of fine glass filaments which can carry a very large number of interactive communications channels.

film noir A style developed in Hollywood in the 1940s for urban thriller and detective movies. They are characterised by a use of *chiaroscuro* lighting with deep shadows and night scenes; plots that involve flashbacks and complex doom-laden scenarios; and mysterious seductive women. *Double Indemnity* (Dir. Billy Wilder 1944) and *The Big Heat* (Dir. Fritz Lang 1953) are classic examples.

fine cut The final edited version of a programme. Also the title of a documentary strand.

fisheye lens An ultra wide-angle lens which gives a distorted, 'fisheye' effect.

fishpole boom A pole from which a microphone is suspended in a shock-proof cradle at one end, with the cable connector box at the other end. It is light enough to be carried by a sound recordist or sound assistant known as a boom swinger.

flood (light) A flood or wide beam is a broader spread of light, in contrast to a spot which is an intense, narrow-angled beam.

focus puller The member of the camera crew whose job is to follow focus on moving characters by changing the focus setting of the lens as a shot develops.

footage A way of referring to a quantity of filmed or taped material. For example, an editor may ask for some 'footage' of the Royal Family for inclusion in a film.

footprint (of a satellite) The area over which the signal from the satellite may be received.

footstep artist A performer who specialises in making an appropriate sound for many kinds of footstep.

frame
(a) Cine film is made up of a series of single frames, which are exposed one after the other at the rate of 25 per second. A video frame is made up of lines electronically scanned.

(b) The frame is also the border or limit of the shot. When we speak of 'framing', we are discussing what area of the scene to include within the frame (*see* Types of shot, p. 57).

franchise The right to broadcast within a given geographical area for a specific period of time, granted by the Independent Television Commission to a limited number of Independent Television companies (see Regulation, p. 14).

frequency response A microphone's frequency response is its sensitivity to a range of sound frequencies (*see* Microphone selection, p. 84).

fresnel lens A lens used in some light sources which enables the light spread to be adjusted from spot to flood (*see* Lighting, basic principles, p. 68).

f-stop The measurement of the size of a lens aperture. A large aperture (f-2) admits more light but reduces the depth of field, a small aperture (f-16) admits less light but gives a greatly increased depth of field. A lens may be 'opened up' or 'stopped down'.

gallery The studio control room where the studio director, vision mixer and the sound and video technicians watch the input from the studio cameras on a bank of monitors. They give instructions to those working on the studio floor using talkback systems.

game shows Programmes in which members of the public and celebrities take part in a competitive game in return for prizes.

gaze The word used to describe the intense way in which cinema is viewed. It is sometimes contrasted with a 'glance' at the television screen.

gels Coloured gelatine sheets which may be placed in front of the lights to create different intensities of reds, yellows and blues. They may also be used to alter the colour of the daylight coming in through the windows.

genre A way of referring to different types and styles of programmes, each of which has its own style, its own norms, its own grammar of programme making, its own history and culture (*see* Genres, schedules, ratings and the television flow p. 18).

grading The process whereby the shots in a programme made on film are matched for colour and quality by the film laboratories.

graphics Images created by drawing or lettering, rather than filming the real world.

grip The member of the camera crew whose job is to control the dolly, moving it along so gently that no jolt or movement will be visible in the shot.

gun mike A highly directional microphone (described as super-cardioid) designed to pick up sound within a very narrow angle of acceptance. Mounted on a long tube, they are described as 'gun mikes' or 'rifle mikes' because of their appearance. They can be used greater distances from the subject and may isolate the speech of an individual from that of the crowd.

HDTV High Definition Television. A high-quality digital system with a wide-screen picture.

hegemony The mixture of coercion and persuasion which those in power employ to ensure that their view carries the day.

Hi-8 Developed from a domestic camcorder, a Hi-8 camera is small and light and records on narrow videotape (*see* Cameras, film stock and formats, p. 49).

high band U-matic A semi-professional video format, of higher quality than U-matic.

high-key A scene lit in a high-key manner has a low contrast between the lights and shades, giving a bright and cheerful impression.

hot sky See **colour temperature**.

HMI A single, large, intense light source, balanced for daylight, with a high light-to-heat ratio.

independent company
(a) A company holding a franchise to broadcast as a member of the ITV network (*see* Figure 1, ITV Companies and services, p. 14). These companies make their own programmes, purchase ready-made programmes, and commission new programmes.
(b) A production company which makes programmes commissioned by the broadcasting organisations and other funders or investors.

Independent Television (ITV) The network of regionally based companies established by the 1956 Broadcasting Act whose programmes are funded by advertisments rather than by licence fee. The franchises are reviewed at regular intervals (*see* Figure 1, ITV Companies and services, p. 13).

Independent Television Authority (ITA) The regulatory authority which controlled the Independent Television Companies from 1955 to 1974 when it became the Independent Broadcasting Authority (IBA) because its remit was extended to include independent radio.

Independent Television Commission (ITC) The regulatory authority set up by the 1990 Broadcasting Act which came into being in 1991. The ITC licenses and regulates commercially funded television services in the UK.

Independent Television Network The arrangement by which the regionally based ITV companies share the single, national ITV channel. The Council of the Independent Television Association (ITVA), made up of representatives from each of the companies, works together with the Network Centre to decide on national schedules.

information technology (IT) A phrase to describe the whole range of communications technologies, of which television is only one.

infotainment Used to describe a mixture of information and entertainment – often used in a pejorative sense.

Integrated Services Digital Network (ISDN) A digital adaptor which increases the bandwidth of a telephone line.

intertextuality The interrelationship between different texts which is both part of the way that programmes are made – many programmes include references to other programmes and other media – and the way that viewers understand them, bringing their own memories of other programmes and other media.

ITO Industry Training Organisation (*see* Skillset and ft2, p. 217).

ITVA The Independent Television Association. The organisation which is made up of the ITV companies.

jump cut A cut from one shot to the same or a near identical shot. For example, if an unwanted phrase in an interview is eliminated and the camera has not changed position, the effect will be as if the subject has jumped within the frame.

key light The main light source which provides the 'key' to the scene's appearance. It defines the main shadows to be seen on the face (*see* Light sources, p. 69).

laboratories Usually referred to simply as the 'labs'. The companies who process and print cine film.

lavalier microphone A small microphone suspended by a lanyard around the neck of a speaker.

location co-ordinating The job of arranging transport, accommodation, parking, getting permission to film, and all those organisational tasks necessary to make location filming possible.

location filming Filming outside a studio, in the environment as it exists, whether in someone's home or on the streets, without specially built sets.

logging Listing the content of the shots, using the time code or other reference. This is an essential routine task, but Rupert Rumney speaks of its creative aspects (*see* Rupert Rumney: sports producer, p. 145).

low-key A scene lit in a low-key manner has a high contrast between the lights and shades, giving a sombre, dramatic feeling.

magazine Often referred to as a 'mag'. The detachable part of the camera into which the assistant loads the film ready for use. The spare magazines may be loaded with different speed stocks so that they will be available when needed (*see* Nick Hale: cinematographer, p. 73).

mise-en-scène Literally 'put into the scene', it is used to describe the characteristic 'look' of a film or programme, which is made up of everything in the frame, including set design, lighting, costume, etc. It does not include the specifically cinematic features such as length of shot or editing.

mix
(a) A transition from one shot to another in which the outgoing shot gradually disappears at the same time as the incoming shot gradually appears. Also called dissolve or a cross fade.
(b) The combination of several different sound sources. A sound 'mixer' will allow the operator to balance the input from several different microphones. In the studio gallery or control room, the audio control engineer (also known as the sound mixer or sound supervisor) selects and blends the various programme sound sources through an audio control console (also known as the board or mixer panel) (*see* Audio control, p. 89).

mm Pronounced 'mil'. The abbreviation for 'millimetre', used in referring to the width of film stocks. Most frequently used are 16mm, 35mm.

montage Although the word 'montage' can mean editing in general, it is most often used to describe a sequence which is built up through the juxtaposition and rhythm of images and sounds.

multimedia The coming together of a range of different media through digital technology. Producing CD-ROM entails video and computer skills.

multiplex providers Agencies that carry several separate digital channels. The 1996 Broadcasting Act made multiplexes available to the BBC, Channels Four and Five and the ITV companies, making a large number of terrestrial channels available for the first time.

neutral density filter (ND) Used on a camera lens to prevent overexposure, usually when working in strong sunlight.

niche A term from advertising which identifies a target group, which may be small but is highly specific. We now speak of 'niche programming'.

noise Used to mean unwanted background sound or visual interference on magnetic tape.

non-linear editing Editing in which the shots may be assembled and reassembled in any order. Both film and digital editing are non-linear.

non-sync With no synchronised sound. This is different from 'out of sync', which means that the sound is not synchronised correctly.

NVOD Near Video On Demand. This could be achieved by transmitting the same movie on four or six channels with, say, a 15-minute delay on each.

NVQ National Vocational Qualification. In Scotland it is known as a Scottish Vocational Qualification (SVQ). A work-based qualification to be established in all industries, setting the standards of competence necessary to be able to perform the task required (*see* Qualifications, p. 221).

observational filming The style of documentary filming which follows events rather than reconstructing them or using other filmic devices. It has similarities to direct cinema and *cine-vérité* (*see* Current documentary genres, p. 154).

off-line editing Video editing using a copy of the original tapes. The time code is 'burned in', so that each frame has a visible set of numbers. Off-line editing can be done on lower-cost equipment allowing more time for consideration and trying different versions.

on-line editing Video editing using the original tapes. It will follow the decisions made in the off-line edit, sometimes automatically programmed in using the time code, the specially generated digital code recorded on the tape which provides frame by frame identification.

Outside Broadcast (OB) A broadcast made from a mobile complex, which may include five or more cameras, editing and broadcasting facilities, or may be a single van. Used for sports, live theatre performances and other public events.

packager model The type of broadcasting typically employed by satellite and cable broadcasters in which the broadcaster 'packages' a group of themed channels, each with programming acquired in bulk.

PACT Producers' Alliance for Cinema and Television. The trade association which represents the interests of independent producers.

paper edit A written plan made in advance of editing using typed transcripts of the rushes. This is especially useful for video editing because it is a linear system and shots are less easily shuffled around during the editing itself.

parabolic reflector A metal or fibreglass dish about 3–4 feet in diameter. It increases the directionality of a microphone mounted at its centre.

pay TV A system by which the viewer pays a subscription, and in return receives certain television channels, either directly from satellite or via cable. Another system involves paying for specific programmes. The programmes are transmitted in an unviewable scrambled form, which the subscriber can access with the use of a decoder, in the form of a set top box and a 'smart card'.

pedestal The substantial mounting for a studio camera. It is on a wheeled base and has considerable mobility in all directions (*see* Figure 19, p. 70).

polar diagram A polar diagram shows the direction properties of a microphone, its pick-up pattern (*see* Figure 25, p. 87).

portapak Portable video camera and recorder designed for single person use.

post-production The work done on a programme after the filming stage has finished (*see* Post-production, p. 42).

pre-production The work done on a programme before the filming stage starts (*see* Pre-production, p. 38).

prime lens A lens with a fixed focal length, as opposed to a zoom, which has an adjustable focal length.

production period The filming stage of a programme (*see* The production period, p. 41).

pro-filmic event This is the scene which the camera will film.

promo Promotional material, such as a trailer for a forthcoming programme.

public service broadcasting The system under which UK television has evolved, in which certain obligations to the public are legally protected both from government interference and market forces. The principles were first enunciated by Sir John Reith, the first Director General of the BBC (*see* The growth of public service broadcasting, p. 9).

recce To recce a location is to check it out both for suitability of content and for practical considerations such as availability of parking.

redhead 800 watt lensless spotlight of the 'external reflector' type, so called because of the red colour of the head of the lamp.

Reithian The principles of public service in broadcasting first enunciated by Sir John Reith, the first Director General of the BBC (*see* The growth of public service broadcasting, p. 9).

representation To speak of the 'representation' of women, for example, is to speak of the way that they are shown on the screen – the sort of image of women presented to the audience. The representation of black people, of people with disabilities and other groups has also been a matter of concern.

rifle mike A highly directional microphone (described as super-cardioid) designed to pick up sound within a very narrow angle of acceptance. Mounted on a long tube, they are described as 'gun mikes' or 'rifle mikes' because of their appearance. They can be used greater distances from the subject and may isolate the speech of an individual from that of the crowd.

rolling credits The captions with the credit list at the end of a programme usually scroll up the screen, gradually revealing the names. This is also called a 'roller caption'.

rostrum camera A 'rostrum camera', either film or video, is set up facing an evenly lit surface on which drawings, still photographs or captions can be placed. It may run at various speeds, or may expose single frames one by one, so that a sequence of drawings may be filmed to achieve an animated effect.

rushes The rushes are all the material that has been shot during the production period, including bad takes and other unwanted material. The laboratories must rush to produce a quick print so that the director, producer and editor can view them the following day to check progress and to see if any re-shoots are needed. The rushes are the raw material for the editor.

satellite broadcasting Television broadcasting in which the programmes are beamed off one of the telecommunications satellites circling in space. Broadcasting from satellite is supranational; the signal is received across the 'footprint' of the satellite and can be relayed by cable networks. Satellite channels transcend national boundaries. Communications satellites are also used for news gathering and the transmission of material.

schedule The arrangement and sequencing of programmes during the day and over the weeks and months. 'Scheduling' is one of the most important activities of a television broadcaster (*see* Genres, schedules, ratings and the television flow, p. 18).

set The arrangement of scenery in a studio or location where filming will take place.

shooting ratio The ratio between the amount of material shot and that used in the programme. Observational filming tends to have a high shooting ratio, for example, as filming may go on for many days to produce a one-hour programme.

short end The end of a roll of film which is unused when the shoot is over. These may be returned and resold, often to students, at a reduced price.

shot A single shot runs from the point at which the camera is turned on to where it is turned off. The shots should be numbered in order of filming for the purposes of logging and retrieval during editing. When filming a drama, the same action may be repeated several times, in which case it is considered to be the same shot with several 'takes'.

show reel A compilation made by a filmmaker to demonstrate their work.

Skillset The industry training organisation (ITO) for the film, broadcasting and video industries. It is responsible for the design and implementation of National Vocational Qualifications and Scottish Vocational Qualifications (NVQs and SVQs).

slomo Slow-motion sequence.

slot Allocated space for a programme.

Social Action Units Units set up by TV companies to run appeals and involve the audience in community-based activities, such as fund-raising or linking with self-help organisations. They take up issues around health, crime, disability and similar topics and directly involve their viewers (*see* Helen Swords, p. 139).

sound effects The extra sounds which are added to the natural sounds of a scene. Often written as 'fx' (*see* Types of television sound, p. 80 and Sound editing, p. 103).

sparks The electricians who are responsible for the lights on a production. They take their instructions from the lighting cameraperson (cinematographer).

spectrum scarcity Until digital broadcasting became possible, only a limited number of wavelengths had been available for broadcasting. This is referred to as 'spectrum scarcity'.

spot (light) An intense, narrow-angled beam in contrast to a flood or wide beam, which is a broader spread of light. 'Spotting' is narrowing the beam of light.

spot effects Specific sound effects, such as a door slam, which are not 'laid' on the track but created 'live', often at the dubbing stage.

sprocket holes The holes which run down the side of cine film.

spun Flame-proof 'spun' is a fibre-glass sheet which may be fixed over a lamp to diffuse the light, making it softer and reducing its intensity.

Steadicam This mounting straps the camera supports to the body of the operator and incorporates a device which keeps the image steady (*see* Figure 18, p. 64).

Steenbeck A motorised editing table, known by its manufacturer's name. An essential part of a film cutting room's equipment.

stills Non-moving images. They may be photographs or still frames from a film or television programme.

sting A brief musical or visual insert or punctuation.

stock The word used for unshot film.

strap titles Lettering which runs across the bottom of the frame naming interviewees and participants.

stripping A form of scheduling which entails showing the same programme, or type of programme – sport, soap opera, chat show – at the same time every day, every week.

subscription channel A television channel that is available only to those who pay a subscription for it.

sungun A hand-held light which runs from belt batteries and can give an intense beam. Useful on location when other forms of lighting are impossible to set up (*see* Which lights?, p. 72).

super-cardioid A highly directional microphone (*see* Microphone selection, p. 84).

suture The surgical term for stitching up a wound. Used to describe the way a cut stitches up the gap that existed between the taking of two shots, making them appear continuous.

sync An abbreviation for 'synchronised sound': sound which is shot simultaneously with the picture and matches it exactly. 'Sync sound' is synchronised sound; 'non-sync' sound, or 'wild' sound, is sound which is shot separately from the visuals. If the sound matches accurately, it is described as being 'in sync'; if the match is not correct, it is described as 'out of sync'.

sychroniser A piece of cutting room equipment which enables film and magentic sound-track to be matched. Picture synchronisers, or 'pic syncs', usually come with a device which enables the user to watch the image (*see* Figure 29, p. 96).

tabloid By analogy with tabloid newspapers, 'tabloid television' is light, popular and entertainment based. The term is often used pejoratively of television news and factual programmes.

take A repetition of the action when filming a scene. Every time a shot is repeated it will have a 'take number' (e.g. 'Shot 6, take 5') for identification during editing.

talking heads The term used for interviews or other head and shoulder shots of people talking to camera.

telephoto A narrow-angle, long-focal length lens.

Telstar Low orbiting satellite which came into use by the BBC and other broadcasters in 1962.

time code A process which gives each frame of video its own digital identification. This is displayed on the screen as a series of numbers which usually show cassette number, hours, minutes, seconds and a frame counter. Time code allows computerised post-production equipment to locate a single frame and provides a reference system for running several video and audio machines in sync.

time shift The term used for recording programmes on a domestic VCR and viewing them at a time different from the one scheduled.

track
(a) A 'track' or a 'tracking shot' is any camera movement in which the camera is travelling along with the action.
(b) The shot takes its name from the 'tracks', similar to railway tracks, which are laid on the ground to take the wheels of the dolly on which the camera is mounted. The use of tracks ensures a very smooth movement.
(c) The sound of a programme is generally referred to as the 'sound-track', and the sound recordist will provide different types of sound, such as 'wild tracks' or 'buzz tracks'.
(d) In the preparation of the sound, separate 'tracks' are prepared, either on magnetic film stock or on tape, sychronised with the picture, each with a different type of sound. Thus there will be a dialogue track, an effects track and a music track. These are called 'dubbing tracks'.

track laying The editing process includes preparing the tracks and placing the sounds in the desired position (*see* Sound editing, p. 103).

transactional television Interactive television services via cable. These may include home shopping and banking as well as Video On Demand, which allows a viewer to choose a film from a library of titles.

trims The frames of film trimmed from the beginning and end of each shot during film editing. It is the assistant editor's job to file them carefully and find them when they are needed.

tungsten lamp Lamps with a tungsten filament used in film lighting.

U-Matic A form of semi-professional videotape.

uplink Sending a signal up to a satellite. It will then be 'downlinked', possibly in a different nation or territory.

VCR Video cassette recorder.

vérité Another word for observational filming which follows events rather than reconstructing them or using other filmic devices. It has similarities to direct cinema and **cine-vérité** (*see* Current documentary genres, p. 154).

VHS A type of videotape for domestic rather than professional use.

Video switching or **Vision mixing** When a programme is broadcast live or recorded 'as live', the input from cameras and other sources is edited instantaneously in the studio gallery or Outside Broadcast van by the director or a technician known as a 'vision mixer'.

voice-over (VO) A voice added to a scene which is not part of its natural sound. It may be the voice of a commentator or the voice of one of the participants.

VT Abbreviation for videotape, as in VT editor.

VU meter Volume Unit meter, which displays the intensity of the sound level measured in decibels and percentage of modulation. Used on recorders and audio mixers (*see* Figure 28, p. 95).

watershed The 9 pm 'watershed' is designed to help parents supervise their children's viewing and is observed by all terrestrial broadcasters. Programmes considered unsuitable for children may not be broadcast before that time.

white balance This means framing on a sheet of paper or some other white surface to 'tell' the camera what counts as white in these particular lighting conditions. Many cameras need to be rebalanced every time they are switched on.

wild shooting Shooting either picture or sound without synchronisation.

wild track Recorded sounds, usually on location, not made in synchronisation with the camera (*see* Types of television sound, p. 80).

wipe A device whereby the incoming shot and the outgoing shot are both at full intensity, but the incoming image chases the outgoing one off the screen. A wipe may use a variety of different shapes from folding venetian blinds to star bursts.

zoom lens A single lens with adjustable focal lengths. A zoom lens tends to be described by the ratio between its longest and shortest focal length, e.g. a 'one to ten' has a zoom ratio of ten. Similarly a 'ten by twenty-five' is a zoom whose minimum focal length is 25mm and longest multiplies that by ten, i.e. 250 mm.

Programme references

Absolutely Fabulous BBC 1992–6 (p. 117)
British sitcom satirising the fashion industry.

The Adventures of Robin Hood ATV for ITV 1959–60 (p. 115)
Adventure drama series.

African Summer BBC2 1995 (pp. 153, 248)
A season of dramas, documentaries and other programmes from and about Africa.

Agony Humphrey Barclay Productions for C4 1996 (p. 220)
Sitcom.

All the President's Men 1976 (p. 122)
US feature film.
Dir. Alan J. Pakula

American Friends 1991 (p. 241)
UK feature film.
Dir. Tristram Powell

Amos and Andy (US) 1951–3 (p. 219)
First American all-black sitcom. Withdrawn after protests from civil rights groups
because of its caricature portrayals of black people.

The Antiques Road Show BBC Bristol 1979– (pp. 137, 233)
A show which travels around the UK. Members of the public bring their antiques
to be valued.

Arena BBC2 1975– (p. 159)
Arts series.

The Ark BBC 1993 (p. 47)
Four-part series about London Zoo.
Prod./Dir./Camera Molly Dineen

Armchair Theatre ABC Television for ITV 1956–9; Thames Television for ITV
1970–4 (p. 114)
Series made up of one-off single plays.

Assignment BBC 1990– (p. 155)
Current affairs series dealing with overseas topics.

The Avengers ABC for ITV 1961–79 (p. 115)
Cult secret agent series, updated in the 1970s as *The New Avengers*.

Baby It's You Wall to Wall for C4, Discovery Networks and ITEL 1994 (p. 171)
Six part series on 'the natural history of the human baby'.
Dirs Leanne Klein and David Hickman

Back to Eden BBC Bristol 1992 (p. 234)
Dir. Deborah Collard for *10x10*

Barnaby Rudge BBC 1960 (p. 114)
Serial of the novel by Charles Dickens.

Barrymore LWT for ITV 1991– (p. 20)
Entertainment programme involving members of the audience. Hosted by comedian
  Michael Barrymore.

Beadle's About LWT for ITV 1986– (p. 138)
Entertainment programme in which Jeremy Beadle plays practical jokes on unsus-
  pecting members of the public.

Beirut to Bosnia BBC 1993 (p. 233)
Documentary series fronted by journalist Robert Fisk about the recent history of
  Islamic countries in the Middle East and Eastern Europe.

Best of Anne and Nick UK Living 1995–
Reruns of the BBC chat show hosted by Anne Diamond and Nick Owen.

Between the Lines BBC 1992–94 (p. 131)
Drama series centring on a police unit which investigates police malpractice.

Beyond the Clouds River Films for C4 1994 (pp. 48, 248)
Documentary series about life in a Chinese town.
Won the John Grierson award for 1994.

Bhaji on the Beach 1993 (p. 113)
UK feature film.
Dir. Gurinder Chada

The Big Breakfast Planet 24 for C4 1992– (pp. 138, 141–3)
Youth-oriented, breakfast-time entertainment programme.

The Big Flame BBC 1969 (pp. 131, 132)
Play in which the workers take over their workplace.
Scr. Jim Allen; Dir. Ken Loach; Prod. Tony Garnett

The Big Heat 1953 (p. 270)
US crime thriller of the *film noir* genre.
Dir. Fritz Lang

The Big Story 20:20 Television for Carlton UK for ITV 1993– (p. 105)
Current affairs series dealing with stories of immediate topical interest.

The Big Trip C4 1994 and 1996 (p. 48)
Travel programme shot on Hi-8 camcorders.

The Bill Thames Television for ITV 1984– (pp. 20, 115, 120)
Early evening police drama series.

Bill Posters is Innocent BBC Bristol 1989 (p. 234)
Dir. Stuart Greig for *10x10*

The Bionic Woman 1976– (p. 124)
US fantasy series around a woman with superhuman powers.

Birds as Prey Cicada Productions for C4 1990 (p. 74)
Documentary about hunters who shoot migrating pigeons. For the *Fragile Earth* strand.

Black and White BBC Bristol 1988 (p. 52)
Series in which two journalists, one black and one white, use concealed cameras to reveal racial prejudice.

Blazed APT/Maverick TV for Channel Four 1996 (pp. 52, 88)
Drama made on Hi-8 equipment, written and produced in collaboration with young people in Coventry.

Blind Date LWT for ITV 1985– (pp. 20, 91, 138)
Entertainment programme, hosted by Cilla Black, in which contestants select a partner with whom to go on a 'blind date' holiday.

Bloody Bosnia C4 1993 (pp. 21, 93, 153)
A season of programmes which show the consequences of the war in Bosnia and place it in a wider context.

Blue Arts Council of Great Britain for C4 1993 (pp. 102–3)
Director Derek Jarman explores the implications of his failing eyesight and his impending death from AIDS.

Blue Juice 1995 (p. 234)
UK feature film about surfing in Cornwall.
Dir. Peter Salmi

Blues and Twos Zenith North for Carlton ITV 1993– (p. 152)
Documentary series about the emergency services.

Boys from the Blackstuff BBC Pebble Mill, Birmingham 1982 (pp. 78, 113)
Five-part drama series about low pay and unemployment.

Breakfast with Frost BBC1 1993– (p. 180)
Television personality David Frost interviews politicians.

Brideshead Revisited Granada for ITV 1981 (p. 114)
Eleven-part drama series adapted from the novel by Evelyn Waugh.

Brief Encounter 1945 (p. 223)
Classic British feature film about a short affair.
Dir. David Lean

Brief Encounters C4 and BBC 1994– (p. 234)
Eleven-minute films by new directors.

British Sounds Kestrel Films for LWT 1969 (p. 128)
Avant-garde political film, arguing for revolution in 1960s Britain, by the celebrated French director, Jean-Luc Godard. Commissioned by LWT but not shown.

Brookside Mersey Television for C4 1982– (pp. 6, 60–1, 78, 116, 120, 213, 222, 223, 224, 242)
Soap opera about the inhabitants of a close in the suburbs of Liverpool.

Cagney and Lacey 1981–8 (p. 115)
US series about two women police officers in New York.

Calendar Yorkshire Television 1969– (p. 164)
Local news magazine programme.

The Camomile Lawn Zed Productions for C4 1992 (p. 47, 114)
Four-part drama series based on novel by Mary Wesley, set during the Second World War.

Can I ask you a personal question? – The 'Man Alive' story BBC2 1993 (pp. 151, 168)
An account of *Man Alive*, the BBC series about personal problems and private lives.

Capital City Euston Films for Thames for ITV 1989–90 (p. 128)
Series about high-flyers in the City of London money markets.

Cardiac Arrest Island World for BBC 1995– (pp. 124, 131)
Flip but deadly serious hospital drama series.

Casablanca 1942 (p. 223)
Classic Warner Brothers wartime movie.
Dir. Michael Curtiz

Casualty BBC1 1986– (pp. 47, 115, 120, 121, 234)
Hospital drama series.

Cathy Come Home BBC 1966 (pp. 68, 126, 131, 194)
A moving and realistic play about homelessness. For the *Wednesday Play* series.
Scr. Jeremy Sandford; Dir. Ken Loach; Prod. Tony Garnett

Channel Four News C4 1982– (pp. 180, 183, 184, 186)
Early evening in-depth coverage of current news stories

Chef! BBC1 1993–6 (p. 220)
Six-part comedy series in a hotel kitchen.

Children in Need BBC 1980– (p. 137)
Annual charity event.

Childwatch BBC1 1986 (p. 259)
Programme hosted by Esther Rantzen centring on the safety and protection of children.

Chinatown 1974 (p. 122)
US feature thriller.
Dir. Roman Polanski

Chronicle of a Summer (*Chronique d'un été*) 1960 (p. 267)
French *cinéma vérité* documentary film.
Dirs Jean Rouch and Edgar Morin

Citizen Kane 1941 (p. 58)
Classic US feature about the downfall of a newspaper magnate.
Dir. Orson Welles

Civilization BBC 1969 (p. 160)
Series in which critic and arts policy maker, Sir Kenneth Clark, examines Western
    art in the context of the ideas and values of Western civilisation.

Clarissa BBC 1991 (p. 114)
Three-part costume drama based on the novel by Samuel Richardson.

The Clothes Show BBC 1986– (p. 138)
Magazine programme on the fashion industry.

Colluden BBC 1991 (p. 75)
A documentary following a year in the life of a Poplar primary school.
Dir./Camera Dianne Tammes

A Complaint of Rape BBC Bristol 1982 (p. 155)
One of the fly-on-the-wall documentary series *Police*. It caused a public outcry and
    led the police to improve their procedures in dealing with possible rape victims.
Dir. Roger Graef

Confessions BBC1 1995– (p. 138)
Entertainment programme in which Simon Mayo extracts confessions from a studio
    audience.

The Conversation 1974 (p. 79)
US feature film in which a sound engineer uses his skills to unravel a mystery.
Dir. Francis Ford Coppola

The Cook Report Central Television for ITV 1987– (pp. 47, 152, 163)
Current affairs series fronted by investigator Roger Cook.

Coronation Street Granada for ITV 1960– (pp. 3, 20, 21, 115–16, 151, 213, 219, 220)
Soap opera based in a working-class street near Manchester.

Correspondent BBC2 1995– (p. 157)
Foreign affairs, magazine style programme.

The Cosby Show 1984–92 (p. 219)
US sitcom around Bill Cosby and his family.

Cracker Granada for ITV 1993– (pp. 101, 125)
Drama series based around the work of a psychologist who helps the police but has
    problems keeping his own life together.

Crimewatch UK BBC 1984– (pp. 19, 152, 158)
Programme in which members of the public are invited to help the police solve
    certain crimes.

Crossroads ATV for ITV 1964–88 (p. 220)
Soap opera based in the Crossroads Motel.

Cutting Edge C4 1990– (pp. 21, 91, 151, 162)
Strand for observational documentaries with strong narratives.

Cybill CBS (US) shown on C4 1996– (p. 213)
Comedy about a 40-something small-time actress starring Cybill Shepherd.

Dad's Army BBC 1968–77 (p. 117)
British sitcom poking gentle fun at the Home Guard during the Second World War.
Prod. David Croft

Dallas Lorrimer Productions (US) shown by BBC 1978–91 (p. 15)
US soap opera on the lives of the oil-rich Ewing family.

The Darling Buds of May YTV for ITV 1991–3 (p. 113)
Comedy drama series of rural life in the 1950s. Based on the novels of H. E. Bates.

Days of Hope BBC 1975 (p. 128, 131)
The struggles of a group of left-wing activists from the First World War to the
    General Strike of 1926.
Dir. Ken Loach

The Dazzling Image C4 1990 (p. 130)
Strand for the work of avant-garde filmmakers.

Deadline Real Life for C4 1995 (p. 164)
Six-part series about the YTV news magazine *Calendar*.

Decision Granada for ITV 1976 (pp. 155, 175)
Three observational documentaries about how large organisations reach decisions.
    They included British Steel, the British Communist Party and a local Council.
Dir. Roger Graef

Def II BBC2 1988–92 (pp. 21, 106)
Strand of youth programming.

Desmond's Humphrey Barclay Productions for C4 1989–94 (p. 219)
Situation comedy based in a barber's shop in Peckham.

Die Kinder BBC 1990 (p. 130)
Six-part thriller centring on a woman whose children are abducted.
Scr. Paula Milne

The Dirty War POW TV for C4 1993 (pp. 163–4)
Documentary in the *Critical Eye* strand.
Tessa Shaw and Christine Ward-Pearce

Disappearing World Granada for ITV 1970– (pp. 151, 157)
Strand for ethnographic documentaries.

Dispatches C4 1987– (pp. 19, 21, 156, 180, 240)
Current affairs strand.

Dixon of Dock Green BBC 1955–76 (p. 115)
Police series featuring Jack Warner as P.C. Dixon.

Double Indemnity 1944 (p. 270)
US *film noir*, nominated for several major Academy Awards.
Dir. Billy Wilder

Drifters New Era Films 1929 (p. 151)
Silent documentary about the lives of North Sea herring fishermen.
Dir. John Grierson

Drop the Dead Donkey Hat Trick for C4 1990– (pp. 117, 120)
Sitcom based in a television newsroom.

Dr Who BBC 1963–96 (p. 115)
Fantasy series for children about a time traveller.

The Dying Rooms Lauderdale Productions for C4 1995 (p. 212)
Documentary on the scandal of Chinese orphanages that allow children to die.

Dyke TV C4 1995 (p. 213)
Four slots for lesbian programming.

EastEnders BBC1 1985– (pp. 21, 116, 121, 242)
Soap opera based in the East End of London.

Emergency Ward 10 ATV for ITV 1957–67 (p. 115)
Hospital drama series.

Equinox C4 1986–
Strand for programmes on science and technology.

The Essential Guide Diverse Productions for C4 1993 (pp. 93, 166)
A three-part history of the Bosnian conflict using newsreels, cartoons and visual
effects. For the *Bloody Bosnia* season.

Eurotrash C4 1993– (p. 5)
Late-night youth programme with a European aspect.

Face to Face BBC 1958–60 (pp. 65, 168)
A series of intimate interviews with well-known individuals conducted by John
Freeman. The format was revived by Jeremy Isaacs in 1989 as part of *The Late Show*.

Fall of the Romanov Dynasty 1927 (p. 92)
Compilation film made from archive footage.
Dir. Esfir Shub (USSR)

Family BBC1 May 1994
Four-part drama on a family living on a Dublin housing estate.
Scr. Roddy Doyle; Dir. Michael Winterbottom

The Family BBC 1974 (pp. 151, 174)
Fly-on-the-wall documentary which follows the fortunes of the Wilkins family in Reading.
Dir. Franc Roddam; Prod. Paul Watson

Film on Four C4 1982– (pp. 46, 113, 263)
The strand for longer dramas, usually co-produced, designed for cinema exhibition as well as television.

The Final Cut BBC1 1995 (p. 119)
Four-part political drama, sequel to *House of Cards* and *To Play the King*.

First Take Anglia Television for ITV 1993– (p. 237)
Slot for short films by new directors.

The Fishing Party BBC 1986 (p. 74)
Documentary for the *Forty Minutes* strand, following a group of friends who work in the City while they are on a Scottish fishing trip. It portrays their opinions as well as their activities.
Dir. Paul Watson

Forty Minutes BBC2 1981–92 (p. 151)
Documentary strand for films of 40 minutes in length.

The Fosters LWT for ITV 1976–7 (p. 219)
Sitcom featuring a black family from South London.

Four Weddings and a Funeral 1994
Successful UK comedy feature film, partly financed by C4.
Dir. Mike Newell

Fourteen Up Granada for ITV 1971 (p. 165)
The second in a long-running documentary project. *Seven Up* filmed a collection of seven-year-olds from very different backgrounds. The participants have been revisited every seven years.

Fragile Earth C4 1982–
Documentary strand that deals with ecological issues.

Free for All Filmit Productions for C4 1994 (p. 258)
Topical 'access' magazine programme in which members of the public undertake investigations.

Frontline C4 1993– (p. 157)
Current affairs strand for personal reports.

Funky Black Shorts BBC2 1994 (p. 114)
Short dramas centring on the black and Asian experience.

Funny Bones 1995 (p. 234)
US/UK feature film.
Dir. Peter Chelsom

The Gamekeeper BBC Scotland 1995 (p. 234)
Six programmes on a year in the life of a gamekeeper.
Dir. Stuart Greig

The Gentle Touch LWT for ITV 1980–4 (p. 115)
Drama series about a woman CID officer in London.

Ghosts in the Machine Illuminations for C4 1986 (pp. 160, 161)
Six programmes showing experimental video work from around the world.
Prod. John Wyver

The Girlie Show C4 1996– (p. 213)
'A magazine series aimed at women who enjoy behaving badly'.

Gladiators LWT for ITV 1992– (pp. 48, 53)
Athletes compete in fantasy scenarios.

Good Morning with Anne and Nick BBC 1992–6 (p. 5)
Morning chat show with Anne Diamond and Nick Owen.

Grange Hill BBC 1978– (pp. 6, 222, 223)
Children's drama set in a comprehensive school.

Grown Ups BBC 1980 (p. 119)
Drama in the *Playhouse* strand.
Dir. Mike Leigh

Hazell Thames Television for ITV 1978–9 (p. 67)
Private eye drama series.

Hear My Song 1991 (p. 234)
UK feature film produced by Film Four International.
Dir. Peter Chelsom

Hearts of Gold BBC 1989– (p. 138)
Esther Rantzen invites viewers to nominate members of the public who deserve
  acclaim.

Hello Do You Hear Us? Central Television for C4 1990 (p. 151)
Documentary series for C4's *Soviet Spring* season.
Dir. Juris Podnieks

Help! Thames Television for ITV 1979–91 (p. 138)
Community action series.

Hill Street Blues MTM shown on ITV then C4 1981–7 (p. 115)
US cops drama shot in a hyper-realist style.

Hollyoaks Mersey Television for C4 1995– (pp. 220, 224–5)
Slick young people's soap opera set in Chester.
Scr./Prod. Phil Redmond

Hollywood Men September Films for Carlton for ITV 1996 (p. 175)
Sequel to *Hollywood Women* and *Hollywood Kids*. Four documentaries on the
  attention-seeking activities of aspirant male stars and bodybuilders in tinseltown.

Homeland Central Independent Television for C4 1991 (p. 174)
Director Juris Ponieks' passionate documentary about his native Latvia.

The House BBC2 1996 (p. 174)
Six-part fly-on-the-wall documentary behind the scenes at the Royal Opera House,
  Covent Garden.

House of Cards BBC 1990 (p. 119)
Four-part political thriller from the novel by Michael Dobbs.

Housing Problems British Commercial Gas Association 1935 (p. 58)
Classic British documentary which first contained interviews with working-class
  people.
Dirs Edgar Anstey and Arthur Elton; Interviews by Ruby Grierson

The Human Jungle Wall to Wall for C4 1996 (p. 172)
Documentary series on the psychology of living in cities.
Prod./Co-Dir. Leanne Klein

100 Women Scottish TV for ITV 1994 (pp. 79, 165)
Series in which different groups of 100 women discuss topical issues of interest to women. Chaired by Sheena McDodonald.

In the Beginning Wall to Wall for C4, Discovery Networks and ITEL 1994 (p. 171)
First programme in the series, *Baby It's You* for which director Leanne Klein was awarded an Emmy in 1995.

In the Company of Men BBC2 1995 (p. 154)
Three fly-on-the wall documentary programmes following a company of Welsh Guards.
Prod./Dir./Cam. Molly Dineen

In Two Minds BBC 1967 (p. 131)
Drama in the *Wednesday Play* series about mental illness, drawing on the work of psychoanalyst R. D. Laing.
Scr. David Mercer; Dir. Ken Loach; Prod. Tony Garnett

Inspector Morse Zenith for Central Television for ITV 1987–93 (p. 113)
Detective drama. BAFTA best drama in 1993; John Thaw won BAFTA best actor in 1989.

Interrotron Stories BBC2 1995 (pp. 68, 166)
US series in which dramatic reconstructions and unusually filmed interviews take a new look at certain crimes.
Dir. Errol Morris

Intimate Stranger LWT 1974
Thirteen episode drama series.
Prod. Richard Bates

Jancis Robinson's Wine Course BBC1 1995 (p. 77)
Ten-part series on wines from around the world.

Jeanne Dielman, 23 Quai du Commerce, 1080 Bruxelles 1975 (p. 59)
Belgian feature film by the celebrated avant-garde filmmaker.
Dir. Chantal Akerman

The Jewel in the Crown Granada for ITV 1984 (p. 114)
Much-praised fourteen-part drama series based in India at the end of the British Raj.

Jonathan Dimbleby LWT for ITV 1995– (p. 180)
Discussion programme in front of a live audience.

Just Like Coronation Street Reality Productions for C4 1984 (p. 51)
Two documentaries about changes to a community in Oldham.

Karachi Kops FK Films for C4 1994 (p. 248)
Five-part fly-on-the-wall documentary series about the police in the Pakistani city.

Karaoke BBC/C4 1996 (pp. 5, 220)
The first of two drama series – the second is *Cold Lazarus* – which centres on the relationship between the writer and his text. Both were written by the celebrated television playwright, Dennis Potter, while he was dying of cancer. It was co-produced, in an unprecedented collaboration, by the BBC and C4 as part of Potter's dying wish.

Kavanagh QC Central/Carlton for ITV 1995– (p. 115)
Drama series featuring a barrister from a working-class background.

The Kennedys Thames Television for ITV 1992 (p. 169)
Four-part series using archive material and interviews on the history of the foremost
    American political family.
Series Prod. Phillip Whitehead; Prod. Roger Bolton

K: Kenneth Clark 1903–1983 Illuminations for BBC2 1993 (p. 161)
A critical profile of the influential broadcaster and cultural administrator.
Prod. John Wyver

Kes 1969 (p. 131)
UK feature film about a boy who trains a kestrel.
Dir. Ken Loach

Kilroy BBC 1987– (pp. 34, 79, 138)
Studio discussion series involving the audience, presented by Robert Kilroy Silk.

Knee High Amy Hardie Productions for C4 1994 (p. 58)
The world from the point of view of a toddler. Part of the *Look Who's Talking*
    season which gave children the space to express their views.

LA Law NBC (US) 1986– (p. 115)
US series on life in a Los Angeles law firm.
Prod. Steven Bochco

Late Night Line-Up BBC 2 1966–72 (p. 202)
Late-night arts discussion programme.

The Late Show BBC2 1989–95 (pp. 159, 160, 211)
Late-night arts magazine.

The Leader, His Driver and the Driver's Wife Lafayette Films for C4 1991 (p. 47)
On Eugene Terreblanche, leader of the AWB, the South African white separatist
    party. Made in director Nick Broomfield's characteristic style in which Broomfield
    appears as a blundering filmmaker, never quite catching up with his subject.

The Learning Zone BBC2 (pp. 19, 226, 258)
Night-time educational programmes, designed to be recorded for later viewing.

Lessons of Darkness BBC and Canal Plus (France) 1992 (pp. 161–2)
Visual contemplations of the oil fires in Kuwait caused by the Gulf War.
Dir. Werner Hertzog

The Life and Adventures of Nicholas Nickleby C4 1982 (p. 115)
Charles Dickens' classic novel adapted for the stage by David Edgar. The theatre
    production was filmed on stage for the television series.

Life on Earth BBC Bristol 1979–80 (p. 233)
One of the many natural history and wildlife series presented by David Attenborough.

Life with Eliza BBC Wales for BBC2 1992 (pp. 241, 242)
Twelve light-hearted pieces based on the nineteenth-century stories. With John
    Sessions.
Dir. Beryl Richards

Live Aid BBC 1985 (p. 138)
Live pop concert broadcast simultaneously from Wembley Stadium in London and
    JFK Stadium in Philadelphia, US, to raise money for the famine-stricken lands of
    Africa.

The Liver Birds BBC 1969–79 (p. 219)
Sitcom about young women sharing a flat in Liverpool. Revived in 1996.

Lockerbie Granada for ITV 1990 (p. 158)
Drama documentary about the 1988 disaster in which an airliner crashed on the small Scottish town.

London BFI 1994 (p. 59)
Feature-length film in which a voice-over narrator tells of journeys around London while the images look at the lesser-known parts of the city in a fresh way.
Dir. Patrick Keiller

London Programme LWT for ITV 1975–
Regional current affairs magazine.

London's Burning LWT for ITV 1988– (p. 115)
Drama series on a London fire brigade.

Love, Love, Love BBC Bristol 1994 (p. 235)
Short film in the *10x10* series.
Dir. Nick Quinn

The Magic Roundabout BBC 1970 C4 1993– (pp. 107, 120)
Puppet animation series for very young children.

Making Out BBC 1989–91 (p. 78)
Drama series based on the lives of six women working in a Manchester electronics factory.
Scr. Debbie Horsfield

Making the Grade BBC 1988 (p. 74)
Documentary about young musicians.
Dir. Michael Houldey

Man Alive BBC2 1965–81 (pp. 65, 151, 168, 176)
Series which explored social and personal problems.
Eds Desmond Wilcox and Bill Morton

Man with a Movie Camera (*Chelovek s kinoapparatom*) 1929 (p. 49)
Russian film exploiting modern techniques of camerawork and film editing.
Dir. Dziga Vertov

The Manageress Zed Productions for C4 1989–90 (p. 131)
Drama series. A woman manages a football team.

Manhattan Cable C4 (p. 256)
Extracts from the US access channel.

Max Headroom Lakeside for C4 1987 and 1989 (pp. 106, 128)
One-off play and then an entertainment series featuring a computer-generated character.

The Media Show Wall to Wall for C4 1987–93 (pp. 159, 170, 171, 240)
Magazine series on aspects of the media.

Michael Moore's TV Nation BBC2 1994–5 (pp. 248–9)
Investigations done in a jokey, personal style by American presenter Michael Moore.

Middlemarch BBC 1994 (p. 114)
Six-part costume drama based on the novel by George Eliot.

The Midnight Hour BBC2 1994 (pp. 34, 180)
Late-night discussion between politicians and journalists which reviews the parliamentary day.

Mighty Morphin' Power Rangers Saban Entertainment for Fox (US) shown on ITV 1994– (pp. 4, 14)
Controversial US children's series featuring teenagers who metamorphose into fighting monsters.

Miss Marple BBC 1984–92 (p. 120)
Detective drama series featuring the elderly spinster detective created by Agatha Christie.

Monitor BBC 1958–67 (p. 159)
Arts magazine programme.

Morning in the Streets BBC 1959 (pp. 102, 151)
Impressionistic documentary.
Dir. Denis Mitchell

My Beautiful Laundrette 1985 (p. 263)
Feature film made for the *Film on Four* strand.
Dir. Stephen Frears

Naked News: The Anchor C4 1995 (p. 190)
Documentary on presenters on US television. Part of the *Naked News* series.

The National Lottery Live BBC1 1994– (p. 137)
Razzmatazz around each week's winning lottery numbers.

The Nation's Health BBC 1978 (p. 131)
Drama series about the shortcomings of the National Health Service.
Scr. G. F. Newman; Dir. Les Blair.

Natural Born Killers 1994 (p. 49)
Notoriously violent film about Bonnie and Clyde style serial killers, scripted by Quentin Tarantino.
Dir. Oliver Stone (US)

Neighbours Grundy Worldwide shown on BBC 1985– (pp. 5, 121, 215, 261)
Cosy Australian soap.

The Net Illuminations for BBC Education 1995 (pp. 250–2, 259)
Series on new media technologies.
Series ed. John Wyver

Network Seven LWT for C4 1987–9 (pp. 46, 106)
Youth magazine slot.

News at Ten ITN for ITV 1967– (pp. 20, 103, 180, 190)
Prime-time half-hour long news.

Newsnight BBC2 1980– (pp. 167, 180, 183, 194–200)
Late-evening news magazine and discussion programme.

Newsround (originally *John Craven's Newsround*) BBC 1975– (p. 180)
News presented for children.

The Nick C4 1994 (pp. 154, 233)
A documentary record of five months in a Leeds police station.
Dir. Paul Berriff

Night Mail GPO Film Unit 1936 (p. 151)
Classic British documentary which uses music by Benjamin Britten, poetry by W. H. Auden and reconstructed scenes to celebrate the railway postal service.
Dirs Harry Watt and Basil Wright

Nine O'Clock News BBC1 1971– (p. 180)
The BBC's main news bulletin.

999 BBC Bristol 1992– (pp. 19, 158)
'Reality television' series, mixing drama and documentary, actors and those involved in real-life emergency incidents.

No Fixed Abode Granada for ITV 1992 (p. 52)
A series, originally for the current affairs strand *World in Action*, in which reporter Adam Holloway poses as a homeless person, recording his experiences using a hidden camera.

Northern Exposure CBS shown on C4 1992– (pp. 79, 87)
US drama series based in a town in Alaska, full of idiosyncratic characters.

NYPD Blue ABC (US) shown on C4 1994– (p. 115)
Gritty US cops drama produced by Steven Bochco.

Omnibus BBC 1967– (p. 159)
BBC arts strand which took over from *Monitor*.

On the Record BBC1 1989 (p. 180)
Comment and interviews on Westminster politics. Noted for its title sequence which turns the Houses of Parliament into a predatory crocodile.

Only Fools and Horses BBC 1981–96 (p. 117)
London-based situation comedy centring on the misfortunes of two 'independent traders' of dubious merchandise.

Open Door BBC 1973–83 (p. 202)
Open access programme which gave a voice largely to campaigning groups. Produced by the Community Programmes Unit.

Open Space BBC 1983– (p. 202)
The programme which replaced *Open Door*. It makes programmes together with individual members of the public, rather than organised groups.

Our Friends in the North BBC2 1996 (p. 78)
Epic political drama, following the fortunes of four friends from Newcastle over thirty years.

Panorama BBC1 1953; relaunched 1955– (pp. 3, 5, 19, 163)
The BBC's main current affairs programme.

The Passing 1991 shown on BBC2 1993 (p. 162)
Video artist Bill Viola offers an impression of birth, death and the fluidity of life between them.

People to People C4 1983–9 (p. 203)
Documentary series linking people's lives to current events.

People's Century BBC 1995– (p. 92)
Twenty-six part archive and interview series which aimed to show the twentieth century from the point of view of ordinary people worldwide.

The Poisoner's Handbook 1995 (p. 113)
Feature film made for the *Film on Four* strand.
Dir. Benjamin Ross

Police BBC Bristol 1982 (p. 155)
Fly-on-the-wall series which followed Thames Valley Police.
Dir. Roger Graef

The Politician's Wife C4 1995 (pp. 130–1)
Drama which takes the topical theme of male politicians cheating on their wives.
  This politician's wife turns the tables.
Scr. Paula Milne

Pop Goes the Easel BBC 1962 (p. 159)
Film about young 'pop' artists made for the *Monitor* arts series.
Dir. Ken Russell

Pork Pie Humphrey Barclay/Essential Productions for C4 1995 (p. 220)
Sitcom in six episodes, a follow-up to *Desmonds*.

Posh Frocks and New Trousers Barrass and Co. for Thames for ITV 1989–90 (p. 140)
Fashion magazine programme.

Pot Night C4 1994 (p. 230)
Themed evening with programmes on the subject of cannabis.

Pride and Prejudice BBC 1967 (p. 114)
Pride and Prejudice BBC 1995 (pp. 47, 114, 121)
Two of the many adaptations of Jane Austen's classic novel as costume drama series.

Priest 1994 (pp. 113, 119)
Feature film made for the BBC's *Screen Two* series.
Dir. Antonia Bird

Primary Time-Life Broadcasting 1960 (pp. 60, 154)
Possibly the first direct cinema film. It follows John F. Kennedy and Hubert
  Humphrey in their competition for the Democratic nomination as Presidential
  candidate.
Dir. D. A. Pennebaker; Prod. Robert Drew

Prime Suspect Granada for ITV 1991–6 (pp. 131, 234)
Police drama series following the work of a top woman detective.
Scr. Lynda La Plante

The Prisoner ATV for ITV 1967–8 (p. 115)
Cult drama series starring and directed by Patrick McGoohan.

Public Eye BBC 1989– (p. 155)
Social affairs strand.

Question Time BBC1 1979– (pp. 165, 180)
A studio audience poses topical questions to politicians and public figures.

Rear Window (US) 1954 (pp. 69, 123)
Classic thriller in which a wheelchair-bound photographer and his girlfriend observe
  and solve a murder.
Dir. Alfred Hitchcock

The Red Light Zone C4 1995 (p. 212)
Late-night programming space given over to programmes dealing with sexuality,
  prostitution and sexy women.

Right to Reply C4 1982– (pp. 7, 174, 258)
In which programme makers respond (or refuse to respond) to viewers' critiques.

Rising Damp YTV for ITV 1974–8 (p. 219)
Sitcom around characters in a rooming house.

Roseanne ATV (US) shown on C4 1988– (p. 213)
Zany family sitcom starring Roseanne Barr.

Rumpole of the Bailey Thames Television 1978–9; 1983; 1987–8; 1991–2 (p. 115)
Comedy drama series featuring a bumbling but effective barrister.

Sarajevo: Street Under Siege BBC2 1993–4 (p. 18)
A nightly two- to three-minute report from a single street in Sarajevo while it was under siege from Bosnian Serb forces.

The 'Savage' Strikes Back C4 1991 (p. 173)
Documentary strand looking at reactions of tribal peoples to the encroaching modern world.

Screen Two BBC2 1984– (pp. 46, 113, 263)
The BBC's slot for filmed dramas which also get cinema exhibition.

The Secret BBC Bristol 1994 (p. 235)
Short film for the *10x10* slot. On a man with obsessive-compulsive disorder.
Dir. Clare Kilner won Royal Television Society Award for the best student film.

Secret History C4 1991– (pp. 158, 232)
Strand of documentaries which take another look at certain moments in recent history.
Won 1992 RTS award for best documentary series.

A Sense of Guilt BBC 1990 (p. 114)
Seven-part drama series of interwoven emotional relationships.

Seven Up Granada for ITV 1964 (p. 165)
The first in a long-running documentary project. *Seven Up* brought together a group of seven-year-olds from very different backgrounds. The group have been revisited every seven years.

Shallow Grave 1994 (p. 113)
Highly successful feature film part-funded by C4.
Dir. Danny Boyle

The Shock of the New BBC 1980 (p. 160)
Robert Hughes presents an eight-part series on a century of change in modern art.

The Shooting Gallery C4 1995 (pp. 212, 237)
A showcase for short films and new directors in the form of an all-night cinema club.

Short and Curlies C4 1989–94 (pp. 114, 216, 234, 237)
Eleven-minute films by new directors, commissioned in collaboration with British Screen (replaced by *Brief Encounters*).

Short Stories C4 (pp. 230, 232)
A strand for documentaries made by new directors.

The Singing Detective BBC 1986 (pp. 113, 119)
Dennis Potter's celebrated series in which a writer in hospital with a serious skin disease, finds his fiction intervening in his life.

Sister Wendy's Odyssey BBC2 1992 (p. 18)
Nun and art critic, Sister Wendy Beckett, makes engaging, perceptive and often totally unexpected comments on celebrated paintings and sculpture around Britain and Europe. Followed up by a series of two-minute items on single works of art.

Six O'Clock News BBC1 1984– (p. 180)
BBC's early evening news bulletin.

Sixth Continent BBC Bristol 1993 (p. 234)
A contemplation of Romney Marsh for the *10x10* slot.
Co-sponsored by South-East Arts. Dir. Tom Connolly

Small Objects of Desire BBC Bristol 1990–3 (pp. 19, 171, 233)
A series exploring everyday objects.

Songs of Praise BBC 1961– (p. 138)
A Sunday service from congregations around the country.

South Bank Show LWT for ITV 1978– (pp, 159, 160)
ITV's main arts strand, produced and presented by Melvyn Bragg.

Soviet Spring C4 1990 (p. 153)
A season of programmes of various types looking at changes in the last years of the
Soviet Union.

Space between Words BBC/KCET TV (US) 1971 (p. 151)
Five documentary programmes on the breakdown of relations in various situations,
including an industrial dispute, the United Nations and a family.
Dir. Roger Graef

The Spin BBC2 1995 (p. 191)
John Sweeney presents a series about pressures on journalists.

Sport Aid: The Race against Time BBC 1986 (p. 248)
International fund-raising event, following up the work of the 1985 Live Aid concert.

Stars in their Eyes Granada for ITV 1990– (p. 108)
Entertainment programme in which members of the public imitate the stars.

The State of the Art Illuminations for C4 1987 (pp. 78, 160–1)
Series on contemporary art, using ideas and images for the 1980s.
Scr. Sandy Nairne; Prod/Dir. Geoff Dunlop; Series Prod. John Wyver

Steptoe and Son BBC 1962–5; 1970–4 (p. 117)
British sitcom about the misfortunes of father and son rag-and-bone men by
acclaimed comedy writers Ray Galton and Alan Simpson.

Sunday Night at the London Palladium ATV for ITV 1955–67; 1973–4 (p. 20)
Live entertainment from the popular London theatre.

The Sweeney Euston Films for Thames TV for ITV 1974–8 (p. 115)
Tough cops drama series. Noted for its scenes of violence unprecedented on British
television.

Sylvania Waters BBC/ABC (Aus) 1993 (p. 175)
Twelve-part observational series following a comfortably-off family in an Australian
suburb.

Tactical TV APT Film and Television for C4 1993 (pp. 204, 205)
One of the series *Channels of Resistance* which dealt with local initiatives in television around the world.

Takeover TV C4 1995 (p. 203)
Access programme which goes for the outrageous rather than the worthy.

Taking Liberties BBC 1989– (p. 155)
Programme which monitors the abuse of civil liberties.

Tango of Slaves C4 1994 (p. 157)
Israeli director Ilan Ziv looks at the relationship between photography and memories.
He accompanies his father back to Warsaw to look for traces of Jewish life in
the years of the Ghetto.

Telethon 88 Thames Television for ITV 1988 (p. 139)
Annual charity and fund-raising television jamboree.

The Television Dante C4 1987 and 1990 (p. 170)
The first eight cantos of Dante's *Inferno* presented in a rich visual style by director Peter Greenaway.

10x10 BBC Bristol 1984– (pp. 18, 46, 216, 233–5, 237)
Ten minute films on original topics commissioned from first-time directors.

Terminus British Transport Films 1961 (p. 73)
A day in the life of Waterloo station. An early film by director John Schlesinger.

That's Life BBC 1973–95 (p. 138)
Highly popular studio-based programme which investigates consumer complaints and other problems. Hosted by Esther Rantzen.

The Thin Blue Line C4 1989 (p. 68)
Documentary which painstakingly reconstructs a crime from the different viewpoints of several witnesses.
Dir. Errol Morris

This Morning Granada for ITV 1988– (p. 20)
Daytime magazine series.

This Week Associated-Rediffusion 1956–68; Thames TV 1956–92 (pp. 75, 155, 157, 169, 177)
Reporter-led investigative current affairs series.

Three Days of the Condor 1975 (p. 122)
US New York based spy thriller.
Dir. Sydney Pollack

Till Death Us Do Part BBC 1965– (p. 117)
Sitcom featuring the character of Alf Garnett, a model for all kinds of prejudice. Remade in US with the now familiar 'Archie Bunker'.

The Time ... The Place ... Thames/Anglia for ITV 1987– (pp. 138, 140, 180)
Studio audience participation discussion programme.

Titicut Follies US 1967 (p. 176)
First film of celebrated American documentarist Frederick Wiseman which takes a merciless look at the conditions in an institution for the mentally ill.

Tolstoy Remembered by His Daughter BBC 1970 (p. 169)
An archive and interview reminiscence programme for the longrunning *Yesterday's Witness* series.
Dir. Michael Rabiger

Tonight BBC 1957–65 (p. 152)
Current affairs magazine programme with a light touch.

The Tonight Show (US) NBC 1954– (p. 83)
Celebrity chat show.

Topless Darts Live TV 1995– (p. 256)

Touch of Evil 1958 (p. 59)
US thriller (feature film).
Dir. Orson Welles (US)

Town Hall BBC 1992 (pp. 47, 152)
Eight-part documentary following the problems of the local council in the London Borough of Lewisham.
Dir./Cam. Charles Stewart

Tracking Down Maggie C4 1994 (p. 47)
Director Nick Broomfield tries and fails to catch up with Margaret Thatcher.

The Trainer Wars Big Star in a Wee Picture Productions for C4 1991 (pp. 211–12)
The Third World implications of First World style culture.
Dir. Stuart Cosgrove

Trainspotting 1996 (pp. 122, 128, 263)
UK feature film on drugs and comic despair amongst Scottish youth. Wholly funded
  by C4.
Dir. Danny Boyle

Treacle C4 1988 (p. 234)
First-time director Peter Chelsom's film for C4's *Short and Curlies*, the slot for new
  directors.

True Stories C4 1987 (p. 157)
Strand for longer, more in-depth documentaries.

Twenty-eight Up Granada for ITV 1985 (p. 165)
The fourth in a long-running documentary project. *Seven Up* brought together a
  group of seven-year-olds from very different backgrounds. The group have been
  revisited every seven years.

Under the Sun BBC 1989– (p. 171)
Ethnographic documentary strand, dealing with societies 'at the edge of rapid change'.

Undercover Britain C4 1994– (pp. 52, 153, 158, 233)
Investigative documentary strand, using covert filming.

Undercurrents Production company: Small World (pp. 203, 206)
Reports of campaigns and grassroots activism distributed on video.

The Underworld BBC1 1994 (p. 68)
Six documentaries about the British gangs of the 1940s and 1950s.

The Unforgiving C4 1993 (p. 157)
Documentary in the *True Stories* strand, part of the *Bloody Bosnia* season.
Dir. Clive Gordon

The Unknown Famine Thames Television for ITV 1972 (p. 177)
Jonathan Dimbleby's report on the famine in Northern Ethiopia for the current affairs
  programme *This Week*.

The Unknown War Thames Television for ITV 1988 (pp. 164, 169)
The history of the Korean War.
Prod. Phillip Whitehead

Up the Junction BBC 1965 (p. 126)
Play about young people in South London filmed in a realist style that was shocking
  in its time. For the *Wednesday Play* series.
Dir. Ken Loach; Prod. Tony Garnett

Video Diaries BBC2 Community Programmes Unit 1990– (pp. 52, 202)
Diary-style programmes, each filmed by a member of the public and completed under
  their own editorial control.

Video Nation BBC2 Community Programmes Unit 1994– (pp. 18, 202)
Video notes on selected topics by members of the public from a wide variety of
  backgrounds. *Video Nation Shorts* are nightly two-minute reflections by viewers
  on their own lives and other topics.

Vino Expresso Royal College of Art for BBC Bristol 1989 (p. 234)
For the *10x10* series.
Dirs Peter Salmi and Carl Prechezener

Visions of Heaven and Hell Barraclough Cary for C4 1994 (p. 172)
Three one-hour programmes about the future.
Prods/Dirs Mark Harrison and Leanne Klein

Wallace and Gromit BBC 1995 (pp. 48, 107)
Plasticine puppet animation
Dir./Animator Nick Park won an Oscar in 1996 for *A Close Shave.*

War Cries C4 1995 (p. 157)
Six-part documentary series in which the director chooses a topic with which they
are personally involved.

The War Room BBC 2 1993 (p. 154)
Direct cinema observation of Bill Clinton's Presidential election campaign by the
team that made *Primary* in 1960.

Ways of Seeing BBC 1972 (p. 160)
Four-part series on art and how we understand it. Presented by the critic and writer
John Berger.

We Are All Neighbours Granada for ITV 1993 (p. 157)
On a village outside Sarajevo as it collapses into war. Part of a three-part series on
war produced by Granada's ethnographic programme, *Disappearing World.*
Dir. Debbie Christie

The Wednesday Play BBC 1964–70 (pp. 114, 126, 131, 132–3)
Series of single plays.

Weekend World LWT for ITV 1972–88 (p. 167)
Weekly current affairs programme concentrating on politics and politicians.

Who Bombed Birmingham? Granada for ITV 1990 (pp. 152, 158)
Drama documentary arguing the innocence of the six men convicted of bombing
two Birmingham pubs in 1974 on behalf of the IRA.

Wingnut and the Sprog Maverick Television for C4 1994 (p. 158)
Drama made in collaboration with young people in the North of Belfast.

Without Walls C4 1990– (p. 159)
C4's weekly hour given over to the arts and popular culture.

The Word Planet 24 for C4 1990–5 (pp. 14, 16, 138, 140, 263)
Late-night youth-oriented entertainment programme, notorious for its obsession with
the tasteless and disgusting.

The World at War Thames Television for ITV 1973 (p. 157)
Twenty-six part series using archive footage and interviews to retell the story of the
Second World War.

World in Action Granada for ITV 1963– (pp. 19, 52, 77–8, 152, 155, 156, 163, 180)
Long running current affairs programme.

Yes, Minister BBC 1980–2; 1984–8 (p. 117)
Satirical British sitcom about the perils and intricacies of government, reputedly
Margaret Thatcher's favourite television programme. Became *Yes, Prime Minister*
in 1984.

Yesterday's Witness BBC 1969–80 (pp. 157, 169)
Oral history series in which witnesses tell of public events in which they have taken part.
Exec. Prod. Stephen Peet (1969–80)

The Young Ones BBC 1982–4 (p. 16)
Surreal cult 'sitcom' about a student household.

Z-Cars BBC broadcast live 1962–5: pre-recorded 1966–78 (pp. 115, 126)
Liverpool-based police series with a more realistic aspect than previous police dramas.

Index

···

Please note: page references for programmes are to be found in the *Programme references* list, pp. 282–301.